Joachim Wentzel

An Imperative to Adjust?

Skill Formation in England and Germany

VS RESEARCH

Bibliographic information published by the Deutsche Nationalbibliothek
The Deutsche Nationalbibliothek lists this publication in the Deutsche Nationalbibliografie;
detailed bibliographic data are available in the Internet at http://dnb.d-nb.de.

Dissertation am Europäischen Hochschulinstitut, Florenz, 2009

1st Edition 2011

All rights reserved
© VS Verlag für Sozialwissenschaften | Springer Fachmedien Wiesbaden GmbH 2011

Editorial Office: Dorothee Koch | Anette Villnow

VS Verlag für Sozialwissenschaften is a brand of Springer Fachmedien.
Springer Fachmedien is part of Springer Science+Business Media.
www.vs-verlag.de

No part of this publication may be reproduced, stored in a retrieval system
or transmitted, in any form or by any means, electronic, mechanical, photo-
copying, recording, or otherwise, without the prior written permission of the
copyright holder.

Registered and/or industrial names, trade names, trade descriptions etc. cited in this publication
are part of the law for trade-mark protection and may not be used free in any form or by any
means even if this is not specifically marked.

Cover design: KünkelLopka Medienentwicklung, Heidelberg
Printed on acid-free paper
Printed in Germany

ISBN 978-3-531-18063-2

Joachim Wentzel

An Imperative to Adjust?

VS RESEARCH

Abstract

This study examines educational systems and the changes observed within them alongside changes in the wider political economy. The research was conducted through comparative case studies of England and Germany, two countries that in the varieties of capitalism (VoC) literature exemplify two very different types of economic coordination (thereby, this study follows a "most different research design"). Expanding upon the VoC approach, this book analyses not only vocational education and training but also school education and higher education, since these two areas contribute decisively to national skill formation. The point of departure is the puzzling observation that the current reforms of the educational systems in both countries depart from the paths predicted by the VoC approach. The study thus argues against institutional path-dependency in the two countries and in favour of an ideational approach based on discursive institutionalism.

The theoretical chapter (second chapter) opens this study with a discussion of discursive institutionalism, policy diffusion, and conceptual mechanisms of institutional change. It also provides a framework that accounts for path-deviant discourses and reforms. This is followed by a description of the three educational areas in both countries and an outline of the paths that the systems should have taken if they had evolved path-dependently. Thereby, this chapter serves as a reference point against which recent developments are assessed (fourth chapter). Next, the visions and aims of the governments are identified through a textual discourse analysis of various British government White Papers that formulate policies on skill formation. The same procedure is applied for relevant policy papers in Germany (fifth chapter).

Finally, the transformation of visions into concrete policy measures is analysed by focusing on three important reform measures in each country (sixth chapter). On the basis of the policy cycle stages these measures are traced back to their original intentions, which are then compared with the implemented initiatives. This procedure sheds light on how reforms match and potentially alter the existing institutional design, how ideas drive educational reforms, and how they resist, "bend", or even vanish once they are implemented through concrete policy initiatives.

Contents

Abstract		5
1	Research outline	11
1.1	Preliminary considerations	11
1.2	Varieties of capitalism	11
1.3	Recent developments in education policy	12
1.4	Reasons for change	16
1.5	Procedure and basic clarifications	17
1.6	Research design and structure of the book	19
2	Theoretical framework	23
2.1	Introductory remarks	23
2.2	The origins of discursive institutionalism	25
2.3	Discursive institutionalism	28
2.4	Sequences of institutional change	34
2.5	Drivers of institutional change: the policy diffusion literature	37
2.6	Discourse and ideas	48
2.7	How do institutions change? Five mechanisms.	49
2.8	Conclusion	52
3	Case selection: Why comparing England and Germany?	55
3.1	1st set: The 'varieties of capitalism' and institutional complementarities	55
3.2	2nd set: Education systems	58
4	Education systems in England and Germany	61
4.1	School education	62
4.2	Vocational education and training	73
4.3	Higher education	96
4.4	Conclusion	112
5	Governmental paper analysis	115
5.1	Textual discourse analysis	115
5.2	Analysis of governmental papers in England	119
5.3	Analysis of governmental papers in Germany	158
5.4	Comparison	177
5.5	Critique of argumentation	207
6	Educational reforms: process tracing and evaluation	217
6.1	Policy reforms in England – three cases and their selection	219
6.2	Policy reforms in Germany – three cases and their selection	262
7	Conclusion	295
8	Bibliography	303

Acknowledgements

This book appeared originally as my doctoral dissertation, which I defended in December 2009 at the European University Institute in Florence, Italy. I would like to thank my supervisor, Prof. Martin Kohli, as well as the entire defence board, which consisted of Prof. Adrienne Héritier, Prof. Vivien Ann Schmidt and Prof. Ewart Keep, for their comments and recommendations.

My deepest gratitude goes out to my parents Dorothea and Gerhard Wentzel, who always supported me both morally and materially, and to my wife Annett Wunder, for whom I am literally not capable of finding the appropriate words of thanks. It is to them that this book is dedicated.

1 Research outline

1.1 Preliminary considerations

"Lifelong learning," a "knowledge-based society," a "new culture of learning," the generation of skills in order to "maintain international competitiveness," or "PISA"[1] – all of these terms show the paramount importance that is currently given to one particular policy field, namely educational policy. As a result, educational systems are currently in flux; being changed, adapted, and reformed in many different countries. England and Germany do not, therefore, constitute an exception in this regard. As an initial glance at the English and German agendas for educational policy in the last decade shows, a plethora of reforms have taken place. As we will see, these reforms resemble each other in many regards. Given similar discourses, this might hardly be surprising. However, contemplating these developments from a theoretical perspective reveals the central research puzzle of this study. According to theoretical considerations, we should expect fundamentally different reforms to be implemented in fundamentally different institutional structures. The political economy literature on the varieties of capitalism (VoC) highlights these expectations. So, how can we account for this puzzling situation of similar reforms in different institutional settings?

1.2 Varieties of capitalism

The VoC literature offers us a preliminary theoretical approach to political economy, and thereby provides a possible perspective on expected developments in educational policies. This approach describes stable patterns of complementary institutions (Hall and Soskice, 2001). The mix of institutions leads to distinct regimes that differ in how they coordinate and link these institutions together. VoC distinguishes between two types of political economies, both of which are considered to have comparative institutional

---

[1] Abbreviation for "Programme for International Student Assessment". This study is coordinated by the OECD.

advantages. Germany is a kind of prototype for the coordinated market economies (CME), while England is affiliated with the liberal market economies (LME). Both prototypes are characterised by high degrees of stability, as both LMEs and CMEs ensure positive feedback and high returns through institutional complimentary, with every little cog in the wheel meshing. Education systems - perceived as being a constitutive component of each political economy - are also considered and categorised by the VoC-related literature (Estevez-Abe, Iversen and Soskice, 2001). In general, works in the VoC tradition draw a distinction between political economies that embark on a specific skill approach and those that concentrate on the generation of general skills (Iversen, 2005). The German CME is an example of the former group, whereas the English LME is supposed to emphasise general skills. This output-statement about education systems is drawn from evidence on how vocational education and training (VET) is organised in both families of political economies. Vocational education and training in the form of apprenticeships, so these authors argue, is likely to generate industry-specific skills, as it is conducted as a cooperative venture between industry (employer associations and unions) and the state. The authors thus mainly refer to the German type of dual apprenticeship. Broadly speaking, they contend, for instance, that England is mainly aligned with a general skills approach because vocational education is not as closely coupled with business and industry as is the case in Germany (such as school-based or college-based education; compare with Estevez-Abe, Iversen and Soskice, 2001). However, drawing this relatively sharp distinction based on the existence of vocational education institutions neither takes into account the increasing importance of school, college, and university-based vocational education nor can it account for some of the recent developments in both countries. Therefore, I claim that in order to appreciate the issue fully, and in order to draw conclusions about the respective education systems, one has to take into consideration these systems in their entirety. I further contend that school education and higher education decisively contribute to the skill traits of a political economy. Therefore, these two areas will be included in this study. Moreover, one needs to elaborate on the discourses in education policies in order to detect reform-drivers for developments that are unexpected from a theoretical point of view.

1.3 Recent developments in education policy

As political economies change so do education systems. According to the above mentioned literature we would assume that political economies change not only incrementally but also within a frame of considerations about "institutional

1.3 Recent developments in education policy

comparative advantages". In other words, we would expect change to occur in a highly deterministic way with respect to the specificity of skill output patterns. These educational institutions are themselves in flux. We can observe two interesting trends. Firstly, it is becoming increasingly obvious that vocational education and training-institutions (in contrast to school and higher education) do not alone allow for a comprehensive understanding of a country's strategies, as school education, and in particular higher education, are progressively more involved in the generation of vocational education (as is suggested by the literature). A first glance at some empirical evidence shows that the German dual apprenticeship system has tried to become more 'general' in order to ameliorate accusations of being too inflexible to cover new emerging occupations (Deissinger, 2004).

Table 1: Recent developments in school education in Germany and England

School Education	Germany	England
Reforms and Discourses	• reducing the school length for higher secondary education • discussion about reducing the 3 track school system to 2 tracks • discussion about how to revalue Hauptschule • OECD PISA-study	• "Education Maintenance Allowance" (to stay on after compulsory schooling) • Tomlinson Group on 14-19 reforms; more choice in compulsory schooling • Diplomas - modularisation in compulsory schooling • Curriculum 2000 for modularised A-levels • more choice and flexibility in 14-16 period

In England, by contrast, we observe that political considerations have led to a concerted effort to promote apprenticeships, which by and large are shaped in the vein of traditionally German apprenticeships. An increasing focus has been given to college-based programmes (e.g. the so-called foundation degrees), which are decisively shaped by employers (to meet their skill demand), and to increasing the options available for pupils (from the age of 14 on) to pursue more occupationally tailored courses according to their interests.

Admittedly, these institutional changes do not tell us much about how successful they have been. Only if we are able to make a statement about how many students such programmes attract and how they are demanded and accepted by business and industry can we draw conclusions of the kind drawn by Estevez-Abe et al. (Estevez-Abe, Iversen and Soskice, 2001). Yet, these new educational initiatives, on the institutional side at least, raise questions about validity of the distinction between specific and general skill patterns. Secondly, and again referring to institutional developments, we cannot detect a coherent approach towards a concentration on general or specific skills. What we see is a great variety of policy measures that are arguably not confined to policies in special vocational education and training-institutions but which reach into school education and higher education as well, where vocational education is increasingly also conducted. The most important reforms in this sector are outlined in tables 1.1 to 1.3.

Table 2: Recent developments in vocational education & training in Germany and England

Vocational Education & Training	Germany	England
Reforms and Discourses	• apprenticeships provide an insufficient number of openings • *Lernfeldkonzept* - more modules and move away from 'mono occupation'- approach • full-time vocational school leavers may be awarded and examined by the chambers	• various apprenticeship types to tighten connection with business and to tackle specific skill shortages • problem of low reputation, lower degree of standardisation, low participation rates

What we observe in both countries is a large variety of educational reforms in all areas. Forecasting the next section of this chapter, and again recognizing that these reforms have not yet been evaluated, we see that the diversity of changes is

1.3 Recent developments in education policy

not as different as one might assume: Germany is attempting to shorten school periods, while England's are short already. England is introducing more individual choice for pupils in the last two compulsory school years, a clear deviation from its comprehensive approach to schooling. Germany comes from the opposite direction and is discussing reforms that reduce the three-track school system to two tracks, while trying to link pupils from lower secondary schools as early as possible with the labour market, as England does. In vocational education and training we even see slight converging developments, as England is embarking heavily on a German-style apprenticeship programme, whereas Germany is trying to gradually open up its strict occupation based vocational education and training-approach. Higher education is broadly characterised by the gradual introduction of market mechanisms in both countries. Yet in this area the German system is undergoing a transformation process that to a large extent will lead it to resemble the English system (the introduction of tuition fees, bachelor and master degrees, clearer university stratification). How can we understand why countries embark on policies that seem, at first glance, to run contrary to what we would expect from a theoretical point of view? Being more descriptive, why does England, for instance, make concerted efforts to implement and promote its apprenticeship programmes, when the theoretical assumption is that the generation of specific skills does not underpin England's competitiveness? Why does Germany, for example, want to change a school approach that for decades was conducive to the vocational education and training-system and to Germany's success in generating specific skills?

Table 3: Recent developments in higher education in Germany and England

Higher Education	Germany	England
Reforms and Discourses	<ul><li>tuition fees</li><li>Bologna process</li><li>"Initiative of excellence" which leads to an increased competition among universities</li><li>funding will become dependent on assessment</li><li>facilitating access</li></ul>	<ul><li>tuition fees while facilitating access</li><li>strengthening the university-business nexus</li><li>"foundation degrees" - strengthening vocational education elements in higher education</li><li>expanding the system to hit 50 per-cent target</li></ul>

1.4 Reasons for change

I suggest here that the answer to these questions lies in the significance of ideas and the common beliefs which political actors adopt and according to which they shape policies. Structural changes in the environment of education systems have a sustainable impact on education systems themselves. As we will see later on, however, the structural challenges to both political economies are not fundamentally different, such as a shift to a more services-oriented economy, the great loss of jobs for unskilled workers, and austerity in welfare policies for which education policy becomes ever more crucial. Furthermore, I assume that policy solutions to perceived problems can not be directly derived from structural changes but are filtered and channelled by dominant ideas and perceptions. Thus, a response in one country can vary substantially from the response of another country even though the challenge is the same. I suggest that the concept of "path-dependency" is not appropriate for understanding some of the major changes taken place in the two educational systems. My belief is that in situations of change and reform it is ideas and common beliefs that explain the puzzling varieties of reforms undertaken in both countries, as they are the guidelines by which reforms are conducted. Amongst these guidelines are the common beliefs that we are living in a knowledge-based society, that citizens have to be up-skilled as much as possible, that higher educational institutions should produce either a valuable work-force or excellence in research, that competition among education institutions leads to better results, and the idea that educational periods should be as short as possible.

Although the concept of the so-called knowledge-based society is rather fuzzy, it serves as an example of how the study is conducted. Works by Stehr (Stehr, 2005) or Brown, Green and Lauder (Brown, Green and Lauder, 2001) have shown different aspects that underpin the importance of knowledge for contemporary societies. They show that knowledge and innovation are the main trajectories by which economic progress in western political economies has been attained; how knowledge has increasingly become an important factor for social stratification; that knowledge has become an ever more important production factor; and that earning returns to skilled people have risen in the last few decades. The "knowledge-based society" is one of the key notions used in governmental papers (White Papers, preambles, speeches, government declarations) to justify particular policy initiatives in the area of education.

Restating the theoretical idea of this book, I propose that in times of change political economies fundamentally change at the institutional level, with common beliefs and convictions serving as guiding ideas and principles for these

changes.(Blyth, 2002; Schmidt, 2008). However – and this has to be emphasised – only a policy evaluation, i.e. an assessment of the policy outcomes, can enable us to draw conclusions with respect to three issues:
1. Are common education patterns visible, such as (e.g.) a general and/or specific skill pattern?
2. How deeply embedded are education systems in political economies? Are they really a complementary component or are they characterised by a logic and existence of their own that is stronger than the political economy literature suggests?
3. At what stage are ideas adopted to the institutional setup of a political economy and how are ideas "translated" into it? Where is the point at which international or European ideas become domestically tailored? Can "ideas" profoundly alter the institutional structure of a political economy at all?

Thus, putting it very broadly, the research question that this book intends to answer is:

> What drives change in educational policies?

1.5 Procedure and basic clarifications

In order to answer this question, this study will analyse reforms and developments in educational policies in England and Germany. It shall not concentrate on pedagogical concepts or a comparison of a detailed curriculum. Rather it shall elaborate upon how educational systems change in reality and compare this to what we would expect from the theoretical literature. In other words, the book focuses on the programmatic setup of the educational systems and examines them from a macro-perspective as to how they form a component of a national political economy. That is not to say that questions about educational content do not matter at all for this work. As, for instance, Estevez-Abe et al. (Estevez-Abe, Iversen and Soskice, 2001) and Culpepper (Culpepper, 2007) show, statements about skill specificity are general statements about the content of educational programmes. Yet, this evidence is not derived by analyzing the curriculum of particular schemes in detail. Rather it is gained by examining (vocational) education (and training) and its importance in terms of participation rates and recognition actors who harness these educational institutions. Thus, this book adopts a perspective that tries to understand education's importance for the whole national political economy. It is exactly this perspective that is adopted in this book.

The programmatic and institutional setup of the English and the German educational systems will be analysed in three different areas: school education, vocational education and training, and higher education. Thus, this study will include, alongside school education and higher education, two educational areas that are not usually acknowledged in the political economy literature.

The research encompasses the last decade by starting with the 1997 election victory of New Labour, headed by Tony Blair, in Great Britain. The mantra "education, education, education" – according to Blair's own words his three top priorities as prime minister – led to more accelerated efforts to change and reform the educational system in England (see historical chapters; Blair, 1996). Only one year later the Social Democratic Party of Germany, with Gerhard Schröder as its leader, replaced the Christian Democrats as the strongest party in Parliament and thus appointed the government.

As a starting point, the theoretical framework of this book can be introduced with the following preliminary assumption: I contend that both countries embarked on policies that are not explainable by the concept of "path-dependency". Yet, it is also not merely mutual approximation or "policy mirroring", i.e. that policies from one country are directly applied in another. Interestingly enough, we observe common "perceived" challenges in both countries and, therefore, common patterns of arguing on an abstract level. England and Germany perceive themselves situated in a globalised world, competing internationally in open markets within knowledge-driven societies. Such a situation requires the skills of the whole population be adapted and upgraded and that the pool of qualified employees be increased. This creates an environment in which education is increasingly perceived as the main lever for social participation.

We might speak about similar ideas, beliefs and convictions that propel educational change. Assuming that it is ideas that decisively impact educational reforms, we might ask whether this then leads automatically to similar outcomes. Putting it in other words and from another perspective, how and at what point during a policy cycle are ideas, beliefs and convictions "translated" into a national context? Leaving aside the issue of similar outcomes, we might still expect deviations from the path we would predict the system to pursue if it was to act path-dependently. Consequently, the research will be based on the following assumption:

> Reforms in educational systems are driven by ideas, common beliefs and convictions which lead to non-path-dependent outcomes.

The research design and research structure with which this assumption shall be scrutinised is described in the following section.

1.6 Research design and structure of the book

The study will be conducted by means of a case-study with a "most different research design" (George and Bennett, 2004; Gerring, 2006). The provisional evidence outlined in this chapter indicates that England and Germany have similar discourses and reform initiatives that would suggest a degree of similarity between both countries in the field of educational policy. This is surprising given that England and Germany are commonly considered as being two very different political economies with differing educational systems.

Thus, we might ask, what commonality has led these two different countries to conduct similar discourses and to pursue policies that are far less diverse than one might suspect? As noted above, the main contention of this book says that ideas and common beliefs are the explanatory factor that drives this development. The aim of this study is to explain and describe how ideas impact on educational policies and how these policies are transferred, translated, and understood in the given institutional frame.[2]

To this end, the paths along which educational reforms are expected to occur will be outlined. This is followed by an analysis of governmental papers on educational policies in order to detect the driving discourses and basic assumptions on which educational considerations are based. As a third empirical step, an in-depth case study of three reforms per country (one reform for each educational area, i.e. school education, vocational education and training, and higher education) will elucidate how these discourses impact on the given reform initiatives and how and to what extent they deviate from the expected paths.

Consequently, the structure of the book will be as follows: First of all the theoretical background of this study will be outlined. The starting point is the varieties of capitalism literature. Of course, this literature is not designed to be static, but it is nonetheless rather inflexible in its ability to account for institutional change. At this point the concept of path dependency will be introduced drawing on the VoC literature. Political economies are expected to change and develop along a path that guarantees high returns (Pierson, 2000). However, what is needed, given the context of recent developments in educational policy, are theoretical approaches that contend that change beyond a path is possible, even while still being institutionally based. "Discursive institutionalism" will supply tools and concepts that render path-deviating developments understandable. A great deal of attention is devoted to ideas and

---

[2] On the translation of ideas see Gorges, 2001, 141. Gerring distinguishes between descriptive inferences (which ask *what* and *how*) and causal inferences (which ask *why*) in Gerring, 2004, 349. Bennett and Elman distinguish three different purposes of typologies: descriptive, classificatory, and explanatory. The primary purpose of this study is descriptive (Bennett and Elman, 2006, 466).

discourses and how they can possibly alter institutional setups (for instance Schmidt, 2008; Rueschemeyer, 2006; Campbell, 2002).

The third chapter will begin by explaining and justifying the choice of England and Germany as the two cases to be studied in this work. Based on the theoretical literature a "most different research design" is to be deployed. It will provide an understanding for the diversity of the political economies in general and for the distinctiveness of the educational system in partiular. The following historical account provides a theoretical and systematic description of the English and the German educational systems. This empirical part is based on secondary literature. The main purpose of this chapter is to generate, for both systems, ideal-type paths (subdivided into the three sub-areas) on which one might expect educational systems to evolve if they were path dependent. This will serve as a background against which the empirical evidences of the following chapters will be assessed.

The primary source-based empirical work will start in chapter four with a Critical Discourse Analysis of English and German governmental papers. If we assume that ideas, beliefs and convictions have a considerable impact on education policy, then the discourses in the papers will reveal which ideas are relevant, which considerations drive educational reforms, and what the expectations are for educational systems in a national institutional architecture. Moreover, this analysis serves as a basis for selection of those reforms on which the following chapter will focus.

Returning to the supposition that we will encounter similar ideas to which political actors refer when they speak about reforms, we are still lacking a clear picture of how these ideas are to be translated into concrete policy initiatives.

Hence, the fifth chapter serves as an examination of concrete policy reforms. The intention is to analyse one reform per educational area (school education, vocational education and training, higher education) by tracing the reform processes, thus examining three reforms per country. The selection of reforms is dependent on the preceding analysis of the papers. The reforms must be chosen according to the following criteria: First, the reforms must have passed an entire policy cycle. Proposed initiatives that have not yet been implemented will not be taken into account, as these initiatives do not allow for an evaluation. Secondly, the reforms must play a significant role in and have importance for the educational discourse of a country. This will be revealed by the analysis of the papers and thus will also reflect the perception of political actors. Thirdly, the reforms as derived from the analysis of the papers are those that are able to potentially alter the institutional setup, as outlined in chapter three. The expectations associated with these reforms will be assessed against what might be expected according to the theoretical literature. If there is a considerable

1.6 Research design and structure of the book 21

difference between these, this relevant reform will qualify as one worthy of elaboration. As a result, this chapter will shed light on two crucial issues for this book with respect to the research hypothesis: on the one hand, we will be able to draw a conclusion as to if a particular reform has departed from an expected path; and on the other hand, we will see whether and how ideas are translated into reforms and what impact ideas have on potential developments outside the 'dependant' path.

The final chapter will compare the evidence from both countries. The theoretical analysis will contribute to the political economy literature on educational systems. It will explicitly integrate school education and higher education. It will argue against too strong of generalisations, such as with the dichotomy between general and specific skills. Lastly, it will attempt to contribute to the larger literature on political economy and social policy, both which still lack an in-depth and comprehensive appreciation of educational systems.

2 Theoretical framework

2.1 Introductory remarks

When contemplating the above mentioned empirical examples against the background of the varieties of capitalism literature, we observe a puzzling mismatch between reality and theory. On one side, is it not the case, according to this strand of literature, that institutional change is bound to occur within a particular political economy-logic, classified as either liberal market economies or coordinated market economies? On the other side, is not the empirical evidence counter to what we would expect to find if we were to follow the theory? At least three different questions arise that need to be answered if we hope to shed light upon what appears at this point to be a puzzle:

4. Firstly, we need to know *what prompts* change in educational policy. We might suspect other driving forces to reform exist than those suggested by varieties of capitalism scholars. Therefore, we need a theoretical framework that offers explanations for institutional change which go beyond those (rather functionalistic) explanatory patterns offered by adherents to the varieties of capitalism approach (Blyth, 2003, 219). I suggest that the discursive institutionalism and the policy diffusion literatures can account for the unexpected changes in educational policies. In other words, one might say that it is the diffusion of ideas and policies among political economies that explains some of the recent changes in the area under examination.

5. Secondly, *how* do institutions change? The mechanisms used by Streeck and Thelen in the volume "Beyond Continuity" (2005) will provide us with tools that describe institutional developments.[3] Moreover, we can draw inferences from their analysis as to the "degree" of institutional inertia and the extent to which institutions can change profoundly or merely change incrementally (see section 2.7).

6. Thirdly, evaluating a reform initiative detached from the institutional surrounding and without taking into account the sustainability and extent with which reforms are implemented runs the risk of arriving at unfounded and

---

[3] The mechanisms that describe how institutions change are displacement, layering, drift, conversion and exhaustion.

misleading analysis. Therefore, we need to ask to *what extent* the intended reforms have actually occurred and have, thereby, led to an altered overall institutional design in the relevant area. Tracing the reform processes will provide evidence in this respect. We might imagine that at a given point during the implementation of a reform initiative path-dependant tendencies become so strong as to "bend" initiatives in an unexpected and unintended way. Therefore, tracing these processes will reveal the power of diffused ideas and policies.

The varieties of capitalism literature is unlikely to assist in our understanding of why and how institutions have changed, as it relies on a strong notion of institutional complementarity, which allows for only a restricted range of options for institutional change. Hence, we need other tools to account for these developments. For this purpose, two sets of literatures will be used, one to examine the *what prompts* and one to the *how* of institutional change. The latter question on *what extent* will be answered in a later section by means of the tools provided by Streeck and Thelen (2005; section 2.7).

The former question of *what prompts* institutional change leads us to three strands of theoretical literature that should be integrated together so as to provide a coherent theoretical framework for this research: discursive institutionalism, ideational institutionalism and policy diffusion. Even though both ideational institutionalism and policy diffusion deal with diffusion processes, processes which are "contagious" according Lee and Strange (2006, 886), interestingly these two literature strands have rarely been linked together. The intention of applying these two strands of literature in this research is rather similar: both theories assist us in grasping mechanisms of institutional change that are not ultimately determined by national institutional settings. Thus, the diffusion of ideas and policies may eventually lead to profound institutional change which the "new institutionalisms" could not have anticipated (Blyth, 2002; Schmidt, 2008).[4]

Yet, it is necessary to create a coherent and comprehensive theoretical framework that consistently combines both strands. It is among the critiques of the varieties of capitalism and the "new institutionalisms" that there is a need to find a "theoretical container". I contend that "discursive institutionalism" is the appropriate approach for this task. It highlights the influence of discourse during periods of institutional change and thereby embraces "ideas" in the broadest sense of the term. Vivien Schmidt, as the principal scholar of this approach,

---

[4]Both authors criticise historical and rational institutionalism. They use this critique as a starting point from which they depart for establishing their theories. Schmidt's criticism refers also to sociological institutionalism, which together with historical and rational institutionalism falls under what is now referred to as "new institutionalism".

understands "discourse" as a concept with two main traits. Firstly, she identifies ideas as the substantial content of discourses. Discourses are the means by which ideas are dispersed. She perceives ideas at three different levels of generality, namely as policies, programmes and philosophies (Schmidt, 2008). The second complementary trait is the interactive component of discourses, which emphasises the way in which ideas are debated and discussed. Consequently, this approach stresses the importance of discourse as a platform and starting point from which policy initiatives depart.

One might argue that grasping ideas as broadly as Schmidt does is neither conducive to a differentiated and elaborated understanding of "discursive processes" nor serves as a theory which succeeds in reducing complexity. However, this approach is highly seductive, as it puts ideas (in terms of philosophies) and policies (as in policies and programmes) under one roof for the purpose of remedying the stasis that exists among the "new institutionalism" theories when it comes to accounting for institutional change. [5] Moreover, this approach contributes to the critique of the varieties of capitalism literature, which is a main reference point against which this book argues. Hence, it is the combination of discursive institutionalism's ability to contribute to the critique of the varieties of capitalism and "new institutionalisms" and the opportunities this approach offers for explaining institutional change beyond the already known patterns of these theories that renders discursive institutionalism as the theoretical underpinning of this book.

The next paragraph turns to the criticism of the three "new institutionalisms" and the varieties of capitalism literature and the issues discursive institutionalism is brought in to overcome (see section 2.2). The subsequent paragraph will shed light on this theoretical underpinning (see section 2.3). Thereafter, we turn to a model that helps us understand how ideas are used in different sequences of institutional change (see section 2.4). The elaboration of the theoretical framework is concluded by taking a closer look at how ideas appear at a less abstract level by referring to the literature on policy diffusion (see section 2.5).

2.2 The origins of discursive institutionalism

The origins of discursive institutionalism There are three reasons why discursive institutionalism is an appropriate theoretical underpinning for this research. Firstly, it emphasises the significance of institutions in this work. Secondly, its

---

[5] See further below for both an in-depth elaboration on this issue and for remarks on the complementarity of both approaches (see section 2.6).

critiques of varieties of capitalism and historical institutionalism are strong and it provides this research with needed explanatory tools for institutional change that go beyond those provided by the other approaches. Thirdly, discursive institutionalism offers a method to combine the impact of ideas with policy diffusion arguments. These strands will be needed to account for "unexpected changes" in England and Germany – "unexpected" because the above mentioned theories cannot account for them (Blyth, 2002; Campbell, 2002; Schmidt, 2008). The origins of discursive institutionalism stem from its critique of the three "new institutionalisms". It does so in at least three major ways. First of all, discursive institutionalism argues against an overly strict application of any of the other three theories. According to the three theories that are subsumed under the heading of "new institutionalism," institutional change and even more importantly institutional resistance and maintenance, are due either to path-dependent constraints (historical institutionalism), to rational calculations of actors in a given institutional environment (rational institutionalism), or to the following of norm-appropriate rules (sociological institutionalism; compare with Schmidt, 2008, 314). The three approaches are not easily reconciled and possess different logics. Discursive institutionalism, by contrast, intends to allow the three institutional theories to prove their impact on institutional developments (Schmidt, 2005, 2).

Secondly, discursive institutionalism is an attempt to take ideas and discourse seriously. Schmidt criticises especially historical institutionalism and rational institutionalism for referring to ideas only when their initial tool kit falls short of providing a theoretical explanation and fails to describe stasis and change (Blyth, 2002, 20 ff.; Schmidt, 2006b; Schmidt, 2008).[6]

This leads automatically to the third point of criticism, which is also the most profound. This is the lack of a method to account for transformative institutional change beyond the logics of the three above-named theories and varieties of capitalism. By seeking to balance agency and structure and by emphasising discourses and ideas (as discourses' substantive content), discursive institutionalism is less rigid and thus more able to consider different meanings and structural contexts in which actors operate during periods of institutional change.

Yet we need to be careful in handling this approach and its accusations that rational choice institutionalism is economically deterministic, historical institutionalism is historically deterministic, and sociological institutionalism is

---

[6] Blyth contends that these two theories take ideas seriously. He claims that proponents of these theories use "ideas as 'fillers' or auxiliary hypotheses to solve pre-existing problems within their respective research programs" and thereby violate – to some extent – their own theoretical logics (Blyth, 2002, 17).

culturally deterministic. Such accusations can be easily applied to discursive institutionalism itself, namely that it is ideationally deterministic or even relativistic (Schmidt, 2008, 304). In order to eschew this "determinism-trap" we must not neglect the fact that an analysis of policy reforms can be misleading if – for example – path-dependent constraints that might hinder a reform from being fully and entirely implemented are neglected. Therefore, the research design of this book, though claiming that drivers of institutional change go beyond the varieties of capitalism and historical institutionalism tool kit, includes an evaluation of the reforms in order to elucidate whether and how "ideas" take hold. Thereby, this study gives varieties of capitalism (and historical institutionalism) the opportunity to be proven correct.

Criticism of varieties of capitalism is mainly put forward implicitly as a critique of historical institutionalism, one of the three theories which are pooled under the heading of "new institutionalism". Indeed, varieties of capitalism can be conceived as a parsimonious typology directly derived from historical institutionalism. One might understand varieties of capitalism as a way to underpin historical institutionalism in that it provides two ideal-typical examples of how forms of political economy persist. This is where "institutional inertia" applies. The notion of institutional complementarity, which renders a transformative change of one institution in a political economy almost impossible, is close to what is known in historical institutionalism as path-dependency. Thus, it comes as no real surprise that evolutionary and incremental change – processes used in the historical institutionalism literature – are applied in the varieties of capitalism literature as well (Hall and Thelen, 2006; Schmidt, 2006a, 16). The implication of this is that, on the one hand, varieties of capitalism and historical institutionalism face similar issues in explaining change and, on the other, that critiques made on the basis of the approaches' shared concepts are valid for both. Objections raised against the ability of historical institutionalism to account for transformative institutional change are easily applicable to varieties of capitalism as well.

The most serious criticism of varieties of capitalism relates to its inability to account for "path-breaking" institutional change, much like the criticism levelled against historical institutionalism. The reasons for this incapacity lie in varieties of capitalism's overly-functionalistic and static view paired with an over-emphasis on coordination and complementarity in political economies. Combined, this disallows institutional changes beyond path-dependent and hence procedures that supposedly provide positive feedbacks. "Real transformation of the system as a whole" (Schmidt, 2006a, 15 f.) becomes nearly impossible. Varieties of capitalism and historical institutionalism champion path dependency as an explanatory logic (compare with Schmidt, 2006b, 36). Yet we are facing developments in educational policies that have the potential to escape their current paths. The purpose of this chapter is to create a theoretical framework that attempts to overcome the above discussed shortcomings.

2.3 Discursive institutionalism

The main reason for choosing discursive institutionalism as a theoretical starting point for this analysis is its ability to account for institutional change. Yet, what exactly is it that renders this approach more appropriate than others? The theories outlined above, against which discursive institutionalism argues, share an inclination to offer mono-causal mechanisms for explaining institutional maintenance and development. According to the three so-called "new institutionalisms" these are path-dependent and institutional complementarity-constraints for action, rational calculations of actors, or norm-conformative behaviour. Elaborating on discourses and ideas as their substantive content, however, allows for various potential explanations of institutional change to emerge, as we will see further below. Indeed, as a brief glance over a few empirical examples in the educational area shows, institutional change does not appear to be explainable by any one single theory. What is it that makes discursive institutionalism more flexible? Of crucial importance is its understanding of "discourse". Schmidt distinguishes between two components of discourses, one that emphasises *ideas* as the substantial content of discourses and one that elucidates the *interactive processes* by which ideas impact policies.

2.3.1 Ideational component of discourses

On the ideational aspect, ideas are conceptualised at three levels of generality (compare with Schmidt, 2008, 306): policies, programmes, and philosophies. This distinction refers heavily to the distinction made by Peter A. Hall in his 1993 article (Hall, 1993). Policies encompass specific policy solutions put forward by politicians (Schmidt, 2008, 307). One might talk about the quotidian adaptation of instrumental settings of policies, a first-order change process (Hall, 1993, 281). "Ideas" as in policies are underpinned by "ideas" as in programmes, the second level on the generality scale. Programmes reflect the underlying philosophy and are derived by analysing the status quo, defining the problems and issues to be considered, and providing solutions (norms, methods and instruments) by which concrete policy initiatives are ultimately developed. Thus, programmes act as a form of hub between policies and philosophies. Alterations in programmes are called second-order changes (Hall, 1993, 281 f.). Ideas as "public philosophies" sit at the most abstract level of generality. These are the most profound and subtle ideas. By the same token, however, they are also the least salient ones. These philosophies, values and principles show up clearly in policies and programmes; yet, the philosophies remain, relative to the two other types of ideas, in the background. The concept of "public philosophies" matches what Hall names paradigms; hence changes on this most abstract level are classified as third-order change (Hall, 1993, 283 ff.). Consequently, policies and programmes are more easily detectable, as they are discussed and debated whereas philosophies remain more hidden. Hence, we see that it is its definition of ideas that makes it feasible to use discursive institutionalism in order to embrace ideas (corresponding with the ideational literature) and policies and programmes (associated with the policy diffusion literature).

Discursive institutionalism classifies these three *levels* of ideas into two *types* of ideas: namely cognitive and normative. Ideas of a cognitive character describe situations and issues and attempt to specify a cause and effect relationship in order to understand how things work (Campbell and Pedersen, 2007, 93; Rueschemeyer, 2006, 228). Thereby, they provide maps and guidelines for political action in terms of objectives, purposes and the means by which the objectives are to be attained, not to mention cognitive ideas' ability to determine and define the social problems that public action seeks to tackle in the first place. A strong cognitive discourse is one that succeeds in convincing the public that the proposed reforms are necessary. Thus, the "real truthfulness" of the argumentation is secondary to the convincing power of the ideas (Schmidt, 2005, 7).

Normative ideas, by contrast, attempt to justify change by reference to their appropriateness, with an appeal to values, attitudes and identities (Schmidt, 2006a, 19). Hence, this aspect refers to a normative legitimisation of the discourse by posing the questions "'what is good or bad about what is' in light of 'what one ought to do'" (Schmidt, 2008, 306; see also Schmidt, 2005, 7; Campbell and Pedersen, 2007, 93; Rueschemeyer, 2006, 228).

2.3.2 Interactive component of discourses

However, discourses do not merely consist of ideas as their substantive content. Discourses also comprise the "interactive processes by which ideas are conveyed" (Schmidt, 2008, 305). Hence, the emphasis on structure by the "new institutionalism" literature is complemented with the agency aspect of discursive institutionalism (Schmidt, 2008, 305). Discursive institutionalism as conceived by Schmidt distinguishes between coordinative discourses and communicative discourses. The former is particularly salient in – as Schmidt calls it – compound political economies, mostly those with proportional election systems. Coordinative discourse refers to the coordination needed in order to incorporate the wide range of actors (such as coalition partners, social partners and relevant administrative units) that are needed for consensus building in the policy making process. By contrast, so called "simple polities", such as England, emphasise communicative discourses. Due to the concentration of power in the government in most majoritarian electoral systems, finding consensus among various public stakeholders is not a primary concern. However, communicating ideas (policies and programmes as the most visible components of ideas) to the general public in order to obtain broad acceptance of a given political action is vitally important, especially if the political actor hopes to win future elections. Moreover, discursive institutionalism attempts to account both for transformative and unexpected (Schmidt, 2008, 314, 316) institutional change on the one hand and agency on the other – two aspects that are neglected by the varieties of capitalism and historical institutionalism literature. Therefore, discursive institutionalism seeks to overcome the structure versus agency divide. "Background ideational abilities" and "foreground discursive abilities" are the concepts by which Schmidt aspires to offer another component for a theory of institutional change that balances structure and agency (Schmidt, 2008, 314 ff.). Once again, her point of departure is the critique of "new institutionalism". She criticises the three theories for their constrained understanding of institutions, which the theories perceive as given and which constitute the structures (historical institutionalism) and the context in which actors pursue their preferences or norms (rational institutionalism and sociological institutionalism; compare with Blyth, 2002, 18 ff.; Schmidt, 2008, 314). Hence, these institutions are conceived of as being an external constraint on the actors. All three "new institutionalism" theories possess a great deal of explanatory power in providing explanations for institutional maintenance and perpetuation in terms of what is "expected". Unexpected developments, however, presuppose actors whose abilities are beyond the explanatory factors offered by the "new institutionalism". Schmidt's concept of "background ideational abilities" comes closest to the perspective of the three institutionalist theories in that it serves as a structure that constrains actors' actions. By contrast, however, institutions are not perceived of as being only external to actors but also internalised by them. Hence, institutions do not only provide structure but serve also "as constructs created and changed by actors" (Schmidt, 2008, 314). Therefore, Schmidt assigns to actors a second ability, which she calls "foreground discursive abilities". By this she means a

2.3 Discursive institutionalism

"logic of communication, which enables agents to think, speak, and act outside their institutions even as they are inside them" (Schmidt, 2008, 314).

Through this "logic of communication", in combination with the actors' ideational background abilities, Schmidt attempts to render the "unexpected" aspects of institutional change more expectable. Discourse, understood as an interactive process, matters here. Institutions may confine actors but at the same time institutions are subject to being changed by actors, who may either directly alter them or use them differently than originally intended (Schmidt, 2008, 316). Consequently, actors are not necessarily and inevitably equipped with a linear logic that allows them to act only in a rationally calculated, path-dependent or norm-appropriate rule-following manner. Instead actors' abilities consist of at least two traits: the day-to-day generation and maintenance of communication about institutions that they incorporate and perpetuate, and the communication about institutions conducted as if they were outside of them. It is the interaction between these two abilities that accounts for the adoption of "ideas" – as it is grasped by Schmidt – that are not explainable by either of the mechanisms offered by "new institutionalisms".

Thereby, Schmidt places prime importance on what actors think and say about change, because it is here that putative "critical junctures" (historical institutionalism) and their drivers can be discovered and made more accessible to our understanding. Only the ability to reconsider institutions from a "bird's eye view" – even while at the same time confined by them – allows for the observation of what exists beyond the known institutions, in other words, to allow consideration of the policies, polities and politics of other political economies. Without the interaction of these two abilities, policy diffusion would have no starting point for the processes that eventually lead to what we know as policy diffusion among countries. Thus, not only theoretically but also practically for the accomplishment of the analysis of the research, this consideration is of prime importance because it allows for an elaboration of the factors that impact institutional change beyond those offered by the varieties of capitalism and historical institutionalism literature. This is reflected in the research design, which puts great efforts into tracing processes and debates that might ultimately lead to institutional change.

2.3.3 Putting the pieces together: how to apprehend the nature of ideas

"Ideational institutionalism" (Hay, 2001), "constructivist institutionalism" (Hay, 2006), or the similar term as used by Vivien Schmidt and Campbell and

Pedersen (2001) are approaches that all turn to similar issues. Consequently, much of the work of these authors refer to Schmidt, and vice versa. John Campbell offers a visual representation of how these concepts relate to each other (see Table 4).

Table 4: Ideational matrix taken from Campbell 2004, 94.

	Concepts and Theories in the Foreground of the Debate	Underlying Assumptions in the Background of the Debate
Cognitive (outcome oriented)	*Programmes*	*Paradigms*
Normative (non-outcome oriented)	*Frames*	*Public Sentiments*

This useful 2x2 matrix provides an attempt to classify different types of ideas and their effects on policy-making. We can easily observe some similarities to the abovementioned article by Hall and the work by Vivien Schmidt. The quadrants will be outlined in the coming paragraphs. This grid is based on two conceptual distinctions, namely ideas residing in the background of public discourses versus those that are used ostensibly; and secondly between cognitive and normative ideas. Campbell combines these four concepts into his 2x2 matrix. He identifies four types of ideas and thereby describes what influence these ideas exert on policies: paradigms, public sentiments, programs, and frames.

Paradigms sit in the background of a debate and thus constitute the underlying assumptions of actors. At the same time they are cognitive in nature, hence they constrain the debate by identifying problems and the appropriate solutions to them. Paradigms limit the range of possible alternatives and thereby elucidate the ideational assumptions on which elites conduct their debates.

Public sentiments also reside in the background of a debate, and are therefore not explicitly spoken. Yet, in contrast to paradigms, they denote the normative side of the coin. This means that ideas as public sentiments normatively constrain the range of policy options according to perceptions of their legitimacy. Whereas paradigms consider the viability and feasibility of programmes, public sentiments refer to the normative assessment of programmes, if they are perceived as "good" or "bad" programmes in reference to the ideational assumptions of the public.

Whereas public sentiments sit in the background, **frames** are outspoken normative ideas. Hence, this notion refers to what Vivien Schmidt has called communicative discourses, when elites attempt to communicate and thereby legitimise political action. Frames act as symbols and concepts that politicians use in order to embed their policy decisions. Thus, in contrast to public sentiments, frames are used consciously and intentionally for legitimising political action.

Programmes are a combination of frames and paradigms in that they are communicated in the foreground (like frames) and are cognitive in nature (like paradigms). Again, this is an act of communication, in the terms of Schmidt. In this case, however, ideas as in programmes are above all used by political actors as prescriptions and guidelines for concrete political actions (policies). Grasped in this way, programmes denote a route of political action that actors pursue.

Yet, paradigms, public sentiments, frames and programmes do not sit at the same level. The first two refer to underlying assumptions in the background of debates and are the basis in which frames and programmes are nested (Campbell, 2004, 100). It goes without saying that frames and programmes are ostensible and salient in public debates; paradigms and public sentiments, however, are far more difficult to detect because of their background character. Uncovering these two types of ideas is a major task the empirical analysis of this book faces.

These four concepts are useful for the analysis of the empirical data in this research not only because they offer a means to understand how ideas affect policy-making but, moreover, because they help us to comprehend how ideas are shaped and how they can be classified by means of the two conceptual distinctions made above. In other words, the grid depicts four different definitions of ideas by describing their effects.[7] Thus, this is a necessary step in order to anticipate and address the criticism that ideas are too vaguely, broadly, and arbitrarily defined. We can see that this grid embraces the concepts as sketched by Schmidt and Hall. First of all, it appears that the distinction between two types of ideas – namely cognitive and normative ones – is rarely contested (Rueschemeyer, 2006; Campbell, 2004, 90 ff.; Schmidt, 2008). Also the horizontal distinction between "concepts and theories in the foreground of the debate" and "underlying assumptions in the background of the debate" is – by and large – similar to what Schmidt understands as "foreground discursive abilities" and "background ideational abilities" (Schmidt, 2008).[8] Moreover, the different types of ideas as conceptualised by Hall and Schmidt can be easily incorporated into Campbell's grid. Hall's notions of "instruments setting" (which refers back to first-order change) and "policy instruments" (changes which result

---

[7] One needs to be cautious, however, not to define ideas in terms of their functions. That would assume a causal relation between an idea and its functions that might not exist.
[8] However, Schmidt puts an even greater emphasis on agency, as she is also interested and concerned with how single actors "work" and perceive the world around them.

in second-order change) are comparable to programmes in Campbell's and Schmidt's work, and, if they are normatively justified, are comparable even to "frames" (Hall, 1993). Paradigms, as used by Hall, and public sentiments, as used by Schmidt, refer to the background column of Campbell's grid.

So what is this description good for? The grid shows us how ideas operate and have an impact on politics and policies. Naturally, the quadrants do not exert an impact separately from one another. They are highly linked, as Campbell himself notes by stressing that the foreground items (programmes and frames) rest on the underlying assumptions (paradigms and public sentiments). Thus, this grid offers an ideational framework in which policies evolve. Yet, it does not indicate when and in what chronological order ideas unfold and lead to outcomes. Blyth's temporal sequence model of ideas elucidates how ideas are used at different points in time (Blyth, 2002). Three of his five sequences might be of use for this research and they are thus presented in the coming paragraphs. For the empirical analysis we need to keep in mind that the ideational framework sketched above provides a detailed understanding of how ideas operate – cognitive or normative, in the foreground or the background – at every point in the following model.

2.4 Sequences of institutional change

The "ideational turn" in comparative political economy has challenged all three "new institutionalisms", including historical institutionalism which shares crucial concepts and mechanisms with varieties of capitalism. For Mark Blyth, one of the main proponents of ideational institutionalism, it is in particular the critique of the stasis of historical and rational institutionalism that he uses as a point of depature (Blyth, 2002, 17 ff.). To review, this stasis is the inability of historical and rational institutionalism to account for profound institutional change (compare with Gorges, 2001). "Taking ideas seriously" is one of the most significant appeals of the ideational institutionalism literature. Authors in this intellectual tradition contend that both rational and historical institutionalists make use of "ideas" when their explanatory patterns fail to account for transformative institutional change. As Blyth states, historical institutionalists use "ideas" merely as auxiliary arguments; yet, these "auxiliary devices" do not match the logic of their theoretical framework (Blyth, 2002, 20 ff.).

The diffusion of ideas and the diffusion of policies are associated with different levels of abstraction: whereas the latter accounts for concrete policy adoptions, diffusion of ideas describes a higher level of abstraction. However, adopting similar ideas does not necessarily and inevitably lead to the same

2.4 Sequences of institutional change

policies. An ideational approach embedded in an institutional tradition can account for differences in policies due to institutional configurations despite common ideas. Moreover, it can show how ideas have been shaped by policies in different institutional settings. Yet, as Blyth shows in his book "Great Transformations: Economic Ideas and Institutional Change in the Twentieth Century" (2002), prevailing ideas at a given time may be conducive to the pursuance of similar policy approaches among various countries. Discursive institutionalism shares with ideational institutionalism the emphasis on significance of ideas and, moreover, complements it by highlighting the importance of the interactive component of discourses, an aspect which in the ideational literature is not as elaborated (compare with Schmidt, 2006b, 16). Thus, discursive institutionalism complements ideational institutionalism with a theory of interaction.

Returning to the definition of discourses by Schmidt, we have so far addressed the contentual and interactive component of discourses. Mark Blyth answers the question of *when* ideas are used in situations of institutional change. Blyth establishes a theory of institutional change that emphasises particular time sequences and the function that ideas adopt at each respective instance, as well as the functions which are assigned them. He formulates five hypotheses about ideas for five different points in time (Blyth, 2002, 34 ff.). He thereby provides a framework that attempts to show how ideas impact different points in time during periods of institutional change. In other words, he disaggregates reform processes into five sequences. The theory turns into an elucidation of how ideas are used differently in particular sequences.

Sequencing and contemplating sequences of institutional reform serves the purpose of tracing when ideas might be tailored to a specific national context; of noting how a single idea is used in different instances; and, in addition, of answering the crucial theoretical question: namely if and how ideas succeed in destabilising and delegitimising existing institutions. Three of Blyth's five hypotheses will be adapted to fit the purpose of this research.

Reducing uncertainty

So far *uncertainty* has been an important theme in this chapter. Uncertainty implies a situation in which political action becomes imperative but the choice over the appropriate course of action in unclear. In an instance of uncertainty, in periods of crisis or in times when reforms are inevitable, ideas lead to a reduction of complexity and thereby can stabilise and channel actors' actions and decisions. Ideas provide – both in the foreground and in the background – a preselection mechanism which assists political actors in choosing the option they perceive as being most appropriate. These cognitive and normative constraints that ideas exert on actors confine the range of solutions that actors consider, allow for frames which legitimise policy proposals, and thereby reduce uncertainty (Campbell, 1998).

To briefly illustrate this aspect in educational policies, one might state that crises or at least reform necessities in educational policies are often accompanied and underpinned by a general belief in the power of markets. Hence, non-market based options would be de-selected in favour of market based ones, thus possible alternatives are discarded and at the same time uncertainty is reduced.[9]

"Weapons" in order to de-legitimise existing institutions

Institutional change not only refers to finding and implementing the right political action. As an intermediary step, ideas serve as a means for revealing malfunctions in existing institutions. Thereby, ideas de-legitimise these institutions. In other words, ideas destabilise recent institutions with the purpose of replacing these "condemned" institutional buildings with new constructions. Again a brief glance ahead at the empirical evidence of this book exemplifies the possible "weapon-character" of ideas: the idea of a European higher education area has served to de-legitimise the traditional German certificate structure at universities, which awarded mainly Magister and Diploma degrees. The main argument launched against these degrees was that they do not meet the appeal to make higher education degrees more comparable across Europe, let alone the appeal to shorten study periods.

Ideas as institutional blueprints

The third sequence to be outlined here turns to institution building. Ideas, as argued by Blyth (2002, 40 f.), act as institutional blueprints for new institutions. Referring to the example mentioned in the previous paragraph, one might say that the idea of a European higher education area and the Bologna process which

---

[9]Along these ideational lines, collective action and coalition-building becomes viable and feasible. This aspect reflects the second hypothesis that Blyth puts forward. I will not further elaborate on this hypothesis or on the fifth hypothesis ("following institutional construction, ideas make institutional stability possible", see Blyth, 2002, 41 f.), as the significance of the sequence model for this research lies particularly in showing how ideas serve to overcome uncertainty and their role in destabilising and re-establishing new institutions.

gave form to this idea provide Germany with a blueprint that facilitates new institutional building. In a slightly later stage these ideas contribute to institutional stability, up to the moment at which these institutions are again contested and confronted with destabilising ideas in instances of uncertainty.

Whether normative or cognitive, situated in the foreground or in the background of debates, the sequence model has illustrated how ideas exert an impact at different periods of time in a reform process. Thereby they occupy various functions and purposes. Now that we have an ideational grid with which to classify ideas, and a sequence model with which to spot specific sequences of institutional alteration processes, we still need an idea of how ideas are driven. In the following section we will gain an abstract impression of the potential driving forces behind ideas.

2.5 Drivers of institutional change: the policy diffusion literature

To re-iterate the central puzzle, the objective of this research is to understand why countries embark on policies that seem to run contrary to what we would expect from a theoretical point of view. The claim of this book is that ideas can account for these unexpected developments. Discursive institutionalism paves the way to theoretically account for these ideas. Diffusion theories go a step further in describing the mechanisms and forms through which ideas diffuse and why and how political economies follow suit and adopt them.

The origins of the policy diffusion literature cannot be traced back to criticism of the "new institutionalism" theories as clearly as was the case with discursive and ideational institutionalism. Indeed, the starting points of historical institutionalism and the varieties of capitalism literature in particular, on the one hand, and the policy diffusion literature, on the other, are at opposing poles. The conceptual interests of both strands are very different: whereas historical institutionalism attempts to show the restrictions, stickiness and inertia of existing institutions for future decisions, the policy diffusion literature seeks to present a "general analysis of global policy integration" (Simmons, Dobbin and Garrett, 2008). Nonetheless, this literature strand will be incorporated into the theoretical framework and serves a certain purpose: it illuminates what considerations and incentives may prompt political actors to contemplate diffusing policies, through which we can attain an abstract impression of the potential drivers of ideas and the mechanisms through which these ideas diffuse.

However, we have to be cautious not to be too rigid when trying to grasp policy diffusion: though internationally spread policies are nationally adopted, national institutions might nevertheless substantively influence these policies.

Institutionalist scholars might state that this would prove institutionalist analysis right. Yes and no. Yes, it proves this strand of literature right as it shows the impact institutions might have on the policy implementation process; but no, it does not necessarily confirm this literature with respect to the range of considerations and debates that fuelled the ultimate decision. Hence, these policies may be the result neither of rational considerations nor of institutional constraints, or of considerations which stress institutional complementarity, but instead a decision whose driving factors are beyond those reasons stressed by varieties of capitalism and historical institutionalism. One crucial assumption of most diffusion theories is that governments – once they face pressures to reform in a given policy area – compare domestic policies with the policies of other political economies. This evidence can accompany, guide and even drive national political actions. Diffusion is defined as processes in which

> "prior adoption of a trait or practice in a population alters the probability of adoption for remaining non-adopters" (Strang in Simmons and Elkins, 2004, 172).

Thus, the main statement of the policy diffusion literature is that policy choices of national political economies are interdependent (Braun and Gilardi, 2006, 304) and cannot be regarded separately from decisions taken in other political economies. The independence of national policy decisions serves as the null hypothesis of this literature (Simmons, Dobbin and Garrett, 2006, 787).

The following paragraphs will discuss various mechanisms by which policy diffusion and the underpinning drivers for adopting diffusing policies can be explained. The depiction is mainly based on the literature of Simmons, Dobbin and Garrett, but will be complemented by additional scholars. Though the mechanisms as outlined by these authors mainly describe phenomena in economic and financial policies, we can make use of them in their abstract form and apply them to educational policy.

With reference to Simmons, Dobbin and Garrett (2007) we can identify four distinct approaches for explaining policy diffusion across countries, namely: 1. constructivism and the emphasis on epistemic communities, 2. learning from own and peer groups' experiences, 3. diffusion of policies due to competing countries, and 4. coercion which stresses the existence of a dominant actor. The following paragraphs will be focused mainly on the first two theories.[10]

---

[10] The diffusion mechanism called *coercion* will be not be used in this study. Coercion means that policies are imposed by powerful organisations or countries (Braun and Gilardi, 2006, 309). One might question if this is a diffusion mechanism in the first place, since it does not stress horizontal interdependencies but hierarchical pressures. Yet, apart from coercion in terms of military power one might also think about soft pressures. On example is conditionality, i.e. when certain requirements are set in order to receive aid or loans (Simmons, Dobbin and Garrett, 2007, 455). Policy leadership

2.5 Drivers of institutional change: the policy diffusion literature

However, "diffusion through competition" will also be outlined. As will be shown, this theory raises some major issues and will ultimately be discarded in this research.

Each of the diffusion approaches is subdivided into three analytical levels. To begin with, each approach is underpinned by specific assumptions about how actors behave within a policy diffusion process. Secondly, forms and causes of diffusion need to be separated. Thirdly, a distinction between different diffusion mechanisms is needed. Mechanisms refer to the mode and manner of how policy diffusion impacts institutions. It is through the analysis of these mechanisms that the diffusion approaches gain their particular characteristics, even more so given that some diffusion forms associated with different theories show striking similarities.

2.5.1 Constructivism

Constructivists trace changes in policies to changes in ideas. The crucial source of ideas are discourses (Simmons, Dobbin and Garrett, 2007, 450). Yet – and this is in contrast to "diffusion through learning" – actors possess only bounded rationality. That is to say, actors lack the capacity to fully estimate the costs and benefits of policy options. Thus, and again different from "diffusion through learning", policy choices are less based on solid evidence of the expected output and outcome of a given initiative. According to constructivist diffusion theory choices are more often based on fads, common international norms and on the conviction in the appropriateness of a given initiative.

Braun and Gilardi refer to *common norms* that facilitate the diffusion of policies (2006, 310). The reference is not to a particular culture in one country or of a specific peer group.[11] Rather it is about the prevailing common norms that dominate recent discourses on a supranational level.[12] Braun and Gilardi take

---

in another option example (Simmons, Dobbin and Garrett, 2007, 456): a country opts for one kind of policy and due to its power, dependant countries pursue the policy leader. Both concepts do not apply in the area of educational policy. In higher education and in particular in research there is the inclination to perceive the USA as the reference model. However, the reactions of countries to this "peer country" are not coercive in character. Another example is the implementation of the Bologna process in Germany. The "expectation to comply" should not be equated with "coercion", as a form of "compulsion to comply". Developments in this area are instead best grasped with concepts already outlined in the section above about constructivist explanations for policy diffusion. The same applies to "hegemonic ideas" as a Gramscian way of accounting for prevailing policies.

[11] On this issue see further below the diffusion mechanism called "learning from cultural reference groups".

[12] Here we can see the difference between the literature on policy diffusion and that concerned with "ideational diffusion": the former adopts a bottom-up perspective and thereby attempts to trace

two steps in one by claiming that common norms that lead to common perceptions about policies eventually lead to common policies. However, the institutional-based ideational literature (e.g. Blyth, and to some extent also varieties of capitalism) shows that common ideas and norms do not necessarily lead to common policies. Nevertheless common ideas and norms may be conducive to the diffusion of specific policies. Therefore, this form of diffusion is important for the analysis of the English and German educational systems. An example makes this application to the area of education even more clear. Braun and Gilardi note that:

> "Common norms provide actors with similar views on which courses of action are appropriate and which are not, and therefore lead them to basically think in the same way" (2006, 10).

A supposition thus might be that higher education policy reforms in Germany are led by this mechanism, as the trend to introduce market mechanisms into higher education is reflected both by the common norm of the superiority of the market (compare with Simmons, Dobbin and Garrett, 2008) and by the tendency of countries to apply market mechanisms in higher education. Consequently, it is hardly surprising that England (and the USA) serve as the main reference point for most European initiatives in this area.

Taken-for-grantedness as a transmitter of policy diffusion is likely to be a complementary explanation for the German higher education reforms. This diffusion type reflects the diffusion of policies because they have become "accepted as the normal or even the obvious thing to do in given contexts" (Braun and Gilardi, 2006, 311). This quotation also elucidates the difference from "common norms": "common norms" provide a definition of the context, whereas "taken-for-grantedness" refers to the feasibility of the course of action which the context requires. Early school enrolment and shorter schooling periods come into mind as reforms and practises which are by and large uncontested and do not seem to be further evaluated. Possible and feasible alternatives are discarded in favour of a putatively better and more effective solution, a solution with a taken-for-granted superiority over other alternatives.

If we are to pose the original constructivist question, we need to ask how policies become socially accepted. Answering this question not only provides us with the "key to understanding why they diffuse" (Simmons, Dobbin and Garrett, 2007, 452), but allows us to identify two different mechanisms by which policy

---

political action back to what are called internationally valid "common norms"; the latter, by contrast, asks about the spread and the influence of ideas and is unprejudiced and unbiased with respect to the divergence or convergence of concrete policy initiatives.

2.5 Drivers of institutional change: the policy diffusion literature

approaches become socially accepted: one by following a leading country, the other by so-called "epistemic communities" (e.g. expert groups; see coming section on learning) which spread their knowledge and thereby influence what are considered to be the recent policy fads (see various examples for that in Simmons, Dobbin and Garrett, 2007, 451 f.).

Both mechanisms pose the risk that policies will be adopted without careful considerations of potential drawbacks or alternative options. Moreover, we might assume these mechanisms tend to emerge in situations of transition, change or pressure due to malfunctions in existing institutions. In times of uncertainty and changing norms actors are more likely to be susceptible to influences by leading successful countries or epistemic communities (Blyth, 2002, 34 ff.; Simmons, Dobbin and Garrett, 2007, 454).

"Following the leader", as the first mechanism can be called, consists of two constructivist arguments. In the first place it can describe the emulation of policies based mainly on the conviction that the success of a country abroad needs to be and can be domestically adopted. Careful in-depth deliberation about the usefulness of mimicking a specific scheme plays a minor role in this process. Secondly, and this preceeds the first point, successful experiences abroad must be perceived as successes in the first place. Again, the domestic context and environment tend to be disregarded. The context, however, is decisive, as a failure at home may only be perceived as such in reference to a success abroad.

In education policy in England and Germany we would expect this mechanism to have a potential impact in at least two areas. First, the German dual apprenticeship scheme is perceived in England as the ideal prototype for generating work-related skills. Therefore England – so the hypothesis goes – attempts to follow suit. The in-depth analysis will reveal if this is possible given the very different educational cultures and – as the varieties of capitalism literature tells us – fundamentally different institutional designs in which the dual apprenticeship scheme must be incorporated. The Bologna process and the introduction of stratifying measures into the German higher education system may be an example of influences running in the opposite direction.

On epistemic communities, Haas is among the most prominent scholars to analyse these communities, which he defines as a:

> "network of professionals with recognised expertise and competence in a particular domain and an authoritative claim to policy-relevant knowledge within that domain or issue-area." (Haas, 1992, 3)

Epistemic communities are characterised by four features: firstly, they share normative and principled beliefs which guide the actions of the community members; secondly, they refer to common cause-and-effect-relationships which predetermine their choices for policy solutions to given problems; thirdly, they share a similar criteria for weighing and acknowledging relevant information; and fourthly, they share a common policy enterprise (see Haas, 1992, 3; King, 2005, 98). Hence, epistemic communities may provide blueprints, road-maps (King, 2005, 99; Blyth, 2001) or "theories of action and corresponding models of behavior" (Simmons, Dobbin and Garrett, 2007, 452) which can be of critical importance in times of crises and uncertainty.[13] Thereby, the epistemic communities do not only become more influential actors, but simultaneously the ideas and beliefs which the communities incorporate and disseminate become more politically salient solutions. Through epistemic communities ideas circulate from societies to one or more countries and their respective governments. Thus, epistemic communities may contribute to and influence the likelihood of convergent state behaviour and international policy coordination (Haas, 1992, 4). This aspect must be kept in mind in particular when turning to the Bologna process, the Copenhagen process, and the PISA study: all these processes provide opportunities to share information about educational policies and they all impact educational policy decision-making.

Regarding epistemic communities, we would predict that "networks of professionals with recognised expertise and competence" (Haas, 1992, 3) influence national policy making. The OECD and EU are potential epistemic communities; PISA, the Bologna process and the Copenhagen process are potential levers whereby policies may diffuse. If we were to believe the constructivist argument for diffusion, we would predict converging tendencies in educational ideas and policies due to political actors which emulate the policies promoted by leading countries or by epistemic communities.

2.5.2 Learning

The basis for *learning* as a diffusion mechanism is a change in ideas in a similar way as in the constructivist argument; learning, however, stresses the rational and observational considerations of political actors who decide on the basis of evidences to either adopt a diffused policy initiative or not (Simmons, Dobbin and Garrett, 2007, 450, 460 ff.). Hence, ideas and beliefs are changing because new evidences about one's own or others' experiences alter them. Rational learners are supposed to promote this process by means of cost-benefit analyses of different options. Simmons et al. stress how this point contrasts to the constructivist diffusion theory in saying that:

---

[13] As Haas points out, in situations of uncertainty due to shocks or crises, epistemic communities can potentially contribute to overcoming institutional inertia (see Haas, 1992, 14).

2.5 Drivers of institutional change: the policy diffusion literature

"Learning does not occur when policy makers simply adapt to the policy shifts of others, but only when their beliefs about cause and effect change." (Simmons, Dobbin and Garrett, 2007, 460)

Learning from success is one of three items Simmons and Elkins subsume under the heading of "new information" as a reason for a country to adopt policies from the international environment (Simmons and Elkins, 2004, 174 ff.). Here the driving force for policy diffusion is information, i.e. information about policy practises elsewhere which provide incentives for domestic policy decisions. Learning from success is the most obvious form of information that might lead political economies to reconsider their policy choices and practises.

Again, educational policies provide an affirming example for the significance of this mechanism. The OECD PISA-study selected the high-performers and the low-achievers in a scholastic performance test of 15-year-old schoolchildren. According to this theory one might predict the study's findings to have exerted massive pressure on German politics to improve Germany's ranking in this test, after unexpectedly low achievement was found in the target group. Nevertheless, Germany may also be considered as a transmitter of best practises. England, for instance, regards the German dual apprenticeship system as a benchmark towards which English vocational education and training policy should be oriented. Yet, within this question there lies another issue that is beyond the issue of information: is "best practise" an objectively or subjectively generated conviction and what or who "decides" whether a given policy is a benchmark for others? The analysis of the national discourses will help us to shed light on this issue.

Learning through communication, by contrast, refers to diffusion processes related to the exchange of information among crucial actors and epistemic communities which are networked and connected to each other (Simmons and Elkins, 2004, 175; Campbell, 2002, 30; Simmons, Dobbin and Garrett, 2006, 795). The EU, the OECD, and in education policy also the German Federal Republic provide these kind of networks.[14] Hence, we suspect diffusion processes to occur when actors use international platforms to exchange experiences regarding policies, from agenda setting through to implementation and evaluation.

The third form that is subsumed by Simmons and Elkins under the heading of "new information" is *learning from cultural reference groups* (2004, 175 f.). When change is unavoidable and there is uncertainty about the right course of action to adopt, cultural similarities with countries in which reforms have already

---

[14] Since education policy in Germany is under the ambit of the federal states there are various boards and committees which try to coordinate initiatives and ensure common standards.

taken place might offer and preselect possible alternatives. Moreover, these cultural similarities might be used to back the choice in the national discourse.

As promising as it might sound, this mechanism is – by and large – inappropriate for our purposes. If we understand "cultural reference" in the context of an educational-cultural reference we would not expect this mechanism to have any impact given that England and Germany are at opposite poles regarding education policies, as the oncoming chapter will point out.

We can distinguish three mechanisms by which "diffusion through learning" can be grasped: social knowledge as a host for policies, Bayesian learning and channelled learning (Simmons, Dobbin and Garrett, 2007, 460 f.).

Social knowledge refers to diffusion of policies on the basis of shared knowledge among elites of what is appropriate and effective. As such, this notion is almost tantamount to the influence of epistemic communities as described in the section on constructivism.

Bayesian learning, which is derived from economics, describes a procedure by which evidence and data are added to prior data in order to project policy initiatives into the future. Bayesian learning describes the prototype of rationally considering information, assessing it, recognising cost and benefits of initiatives and taking into account all possible options.

Hall's influential article in 1993 provides a good example for channelled learning. This procedure elucidates how political actors use cognitive shortcuts in order to announce and justify policy decisions. In doing so they tend to highlight the successful performers and underrate under-performers. Hence, it is a shortcut because political actors are inclined to pre-select from all available information (by which they reduce uncertainty, see section 2.4).

If learning as a diffusion mechanism is to be confirmed we would expect to encounter actors whose beliefs have changed due to new emerging evidence and who therefore carefully compile information, rationally consider this information and ultimately apply this knowledge in order to change policies. According to this strand of thought, governments perceive policies in other countries as a "natural experiment" from which they can derive conclusions (Simmons, Dobbin and Garrett, 2007, 461). This is not to say that the compilation and evaluation of information is unbiased. It might be tempting to collect all available information on successful policies. This is "channelled" learning. Moreover "learning" requires actors collect and consider information in order to identify success stories and which political economies are recognised as cultural reference groups, according to which they can render less complicated the choice of which policies to adopt.

If information collection – as the main mechanism of learning – was to be channelled by the success of other countries, we would anticipate the English

2.5 Drivers of institutional change: the policy diffusion literature

higher education system to provide a model for Germany and the German vocational education and training system to serve as an example for English initiatives in this area, whereas the development of school education is not entirely predictable, as both countries seem – at first glance – to learn particular aspects from each other.

2.5.3 Competition

Diffusion through *competition* is different from the constructivist diffusion theory and the learning diffusion theory as it is focused on utility maximising behaviour. Thus, enhancing the competitive advantage vis-à-vis competitors is the core impetus. Policy changes are, therefore, not caused by changes of ideas – as is the case in the two other diffusion theories – but are traced to shifts in (external) incentives (Simmons, Dobbin and Garrett, 2007, 463).

In contrast to coercive measures, diffusion through competition describes a vertical power relation (see footnote); competition occurs between competitors on approximately the same level. The basic underlying assumption is that governments are well-informed about their competitors' policies. In vying for competitive advantages, governments attempt to outperform (this embraces also the so-called "race to the bottom") their competitors with respect to the attractiveness of their own political economies for investors.

There are two potential mechanisms of utility maximising behaviour which governments pursue, one which assures material payoffs and one which provides reputational payoffs. *Material payoffs* occur if a country increases its attractiveness, e.g. by reducing taxes for companies. This constitutes an externality to which the environment of the country might feel obliged to react. In this material competition, another country that feels affected by this measure might adopt a similar policy in order to remain attractive as well (Simmons and Elkins, 2004; Simmons, Dobbin and Garrett, 2008). Hence, we observe a situation of competitive interdependence (Braun and Gilardi, 2006, 308); policy decisions in one country have effects on policy decisions in another country. Yet material payoffs can also be derived from cooperative interdependence (Braun and Gilardi, 2006, 308). In this case, countries choose to cooperate with each other in order to increase their payoffs.

Reputational payoffs, by contrast, occur if particular policies and practises reflect common sense or "a normative consensus" (Simmons and Elkins, 2004, 173). In other words, practises that reflect the prevailing global norms and ideas may create negative externalities for non-compliers, not directly in terms of financial costs and benefits but in terms of reputational benefits for those who join in the common sense ideas and practises and reputational costs for those who do not. Braun and Gilardi call this *symbolic imitation*, which refers to political action that proves a government's commitment to common sense on the international level (2006, 311 f.). The aim is to engage in political, economic or cultural activities that are perceived as appropriate and are therefore legitimising. Braun and Gilardi state, that:

> "symbolic imitation as a diffusion mechanism does not alter beliefs on the effectiveness of policies; rather, it rewards behaviour that conforms to socially valued models, thus altering the relative size of the payoffs associated with policy alternatives" (2006, 312).

Yet we face serious problems in using "diffusion through competition" in this theoretical context.

1. The underlying assumption of the competition theory is that shifts in incentives lead to changes in policies. Based on utility maximising behaviour, rational actors attempt to increase the competitiveness of their political economies. So far, this assumption is in perfect alignment with the basic assumption of the VoC literature. Now, however, it becomes more challenging. Whereas the VoC approach suggests that political economies would concentrate their endeavours on initiatives which provide and stress the specific institutional complementarity of a political economy, "diffusion through competition" scholars would argue that political economies try to outperform competitors within the same policy area, attracted by the prospective of direct short-term effects (e.g. tax policy; Simmons and Elkins, 2004). Hence, on the basis of utility maximising behaviour, two different arguments can work: One which tries to stress the peculiarity of a political economy and one which eventually leads to converging developments. Thus, applying utility maximising behaviour within different theoretical contexts may lead to astonishingly different inferences. Utility maximising behaviour – as the basic assumption on which this diffusion theory rests – can lead to various outputs which the "diffusion through competition" theory can only partly account for.

2. As outlined, the initiatives by which a political economy attempts to outperform its competitors are mainly those with short-term effects (Simmons and Elkins, 2004). Education policy, however, is characterised by long time horizons. In the same vein we might further argue that policy initiatives which may ultimately serve the maximisation of utilities are based on gathering and considering information; in short, on learning in the first place.

3. Another reason for challenging this theory lies in the general theoretical argument of this book: If ideas and common beliefs account for policy changes, one expects "diffusion through competition" to be embraced in the theoretical

2.5 Drivers of institutional change: the policy diffusion literature

framework as outlined so far. Utility maximising behaviour as the main motive for political action is channelled through common norms, through the conviction that action is necessary, and through what is perceived as a success or as useful information. One might assume that the attempt to adopt the German dual apprenticeship scheme in England is triggered by utility maximising behaviour; yet in terms of applicability one would instead predict that England would pursue another path if it was to maximise its utility given the institutional difficulties England might face in implementing a dual system (see the coming chapters). In short, "diffusion through competition" will be regarded as a diffusion argument that can be accounted for be constructivist theory and learning theory.

Even though "diffusion through competition" is integrated into the first two theories, utility maximising behaviour cannot be entirely disregarded, as a casual glance at governmental discourses suggests that it has great argumentative influence on these discourses. Yet, regarding diffusion mechanisms, the assumption is that policy changes based on utility maximising behaviour can be grasped as constructivist or learning mechanisms.

The constructivist theory and the "diffusion through learning" theory share one crucial similarity that is of paramount importance for this book: Both theories rest on the assertion that changes in policies are caused by changes in ideas (Simmons, Dobbin and Garrett, 2007, 463). Therefore both theories provide mechanisms of policy diffusion which can account for the spread of ideas. In doing so, they offer an ideational challenge to endogenous explanations of change and the concept of path-dependency. Putting it another way, these theories can elucidate potential converging tendencies. "Diffusion through competition", by contrast, is used as a means in the argumentation presented in educational discourses.

Having sketched the main mechanisms of the policy diffusion literature, the next section will go a step further and outline the core of this theoretical framework. The concepts, mechanisms and tools used so far facilitate our understanding of institutional change but remain theoretically isolated from one another. The coming paragraphs attempt to theoretically link the three approaches by highlighting the significance of ideas and discourse in each of the approaches.

2.6 Discourse and ideas

Before turning to the mechanisms that assist us in describing how institutions change, the connecting factors and interfaces of all three approaches need to be stressed one last time. Crucially important for this endeavour are the concepts of ideas and discourses because these two notions will help to unite the three literature strands in order to obtain one coherent theoretical framework. The significance of both notions for discursive institutionalism has already been highlighted. Now we need to link them to the policy diffusion literature and the ideational literature. Therefore, in the following we will subsume the understanding of ideas and discourses in the policy diffusion and the ideational literature under the definition of ideas and discourses offered by discursive institutionalism.

2.6.1 Ideas

The definition of "ideas" in discursive institutionalism is rather broad. Referring to Schmidt's "level of generality", ideas range from concrete policies to abstract background philosophies which underpin and accompany current discourses (Schmidt, 2008, 306). The question arises as to whether the understanding of "policy" as in the policy diffusion literature and "ideas" as in the ideational literature fit under the roof of the discursive institutionalist framework? The literature on the diffusion of liberalism by Simmons, Dobbin and Garrett (2008) affirms this supposition. These scholars attempt to prove the worldwide spread of economic and political liberalism (Simmons, Dobbin and Garrett, 2008, 2). For their analysis they make use of the entire range of "ideas": liberalism, grasped as a philosophy, is being broken down into indicators such as marketisation and democratisation, which one can understand as the more applicable version of the philosophy, maybe even as programmes. These indicators are detected by scrutinising policy change in single countries, hence by analysing change in terms of programmes and policies. The same observation is valid for "ideas" as in the ideational literature. "Ideas" in this strand of the literature are not grasped merely as "philosophies" but easily occupy the whole range Schmidt assigns to "ideas", particularly if they are traced and linked with their concrete applications (Rueschemeyer, 2006; Blyth, 2002; Gorges, 2001; Lynggaard, 2007; Legro, 2000; Howorth, 2004). Hence, it is noticeable that neither the policy diffusion literature nor the ideational literature operate with clear cut concepts that are comfortably subsumable under discursive institutionalism though the naming implies so.

2.6.2 *Discourse*

"Discourse" is another concept which is used by both strands and which we seek to subsume under the definition of "discourse" in discursive institutionalism. Both discursive institutionalism and ideational institutionalism highlight the importance of discourse, especially in order to trace how ideas are ultimately implemented in the institutional setting of a political economy. It is used in a similar way in both strands, namely as the carrier and "transmitter" of ideas. Thereby it is possible to make statements about the effects of ideas and about how ideas change and are adapted both horizontally and vertically once they are contested in a national discourse.

In the policy diffusion literature, however, the notion of discourse is by and large absent. Yet, the elaboration of "discourse" in the work of Schmidt can assist us here. She conceives of discourse not only as the carrier of ideas but also "the interactive process by which ideas are conveyed" (Schmidt, 2008, 309). Furthermore, she distinguishes the interactive component into communicative and coordinative discourses, hence into processes in which policy decisions are deliberated and decided upon (coordinative discourse), and those in which they are discussed and communicated to the public (communicative discourse). If we now assume that the receiver of a diffused policy adopts the policy voluntarily (except for coercive policy diffusion processes), then we might suspect that these initiatives are deliberated and debated in a coordinated and communicated manner which greatly resembles what discursive institutionalism calls "discourses". Though not explicitly mentioned in the relevant literature, discourses are the platform on which ideas (hence also policies) are transmitted. Therefore, mechanisms of policy diffusion are triggered, channelled and ultimately applied by means of discourses in which policy options are carefully considered.

To sum up, discursive institutionalism, with its emphasis on ideas and discourses, is able to theoretically embrace the policy diffusion and ideational literature, and it thereby serves as the theoretical framework for this research.

2.7 How do institutions change? Five mechanisms

So far we have paved the way for ideas and discourses to have an influence on institutional change. Moreover, different usages of ideas in specific sequences have been pointed out as important. This has been followed by an elaboration on forms of policy diffusion and diffusion mechanisms which explain how diffused policies impact institutions. In other words, the diffusion mechanisms connect diffused policies with institutions, but they do not identify the "point of impact" on current institutions. Streeck and Thelen provide descriptive patterns of institutional change through which we can understand the different patterns of how institutions evolve once they are exposed to these "point of impact". In other words, how does the new or amended institution relate to the one which is being superseded? Is one institution entirely displaced by a new one? Or is a new one installed while the already existing institution is phased out? Do both perhaps exist coequally? Streeck and Thelen provide five tools with which institutional change can be traced: displacement, layering, drift, conversion and exhaustion (see Streeck and Thelen, 2005, 18 ff.). These tools will be presented in the following few paragraphs.

2.7.1 Displacement

The first mode of institutional change that the two authors present is called displacement. This mechanism describes the substitution of one arrangement with a new one. Hence, vulnerable, defective or unfeasible institutional configurations are "discredited or pushed to the side in favour of new institutions and associated behavioural logics" (Streeck and Thelen, 2005, 20). An example for this mode is the rather sudden implementation of bachelor and master degrees in – by now – most German states, which displaced Magister and Diploma degrees.

2.7.2 Layering

The second mode of institutional change is layering. It denotes a less abrupt form of change than displacement. Instead, layering describes a process in which one institution is introduced either alongside or on top of existing arrangements. Though usually slower and more incremental, layering might lead to quite a profound change of institutions, especially if several small steps of layering ultimately contribute to one overarching reform. Of course, on the one hand, one of the crucial questions is the intensity and stress with which "layered" policies are introduced; on the other hand, it is crucial to understand the incentives actors have in using this new policy (or scheme). The case of the English foundation degrees, introduced alongside the traditional degrees in higher education, exemplifies this mode of change.

2.7.3 Drift

As opposed to displacement and layering, drift is not an intentional way of changing an institution, if it is about institutional change at all in the truest sense of the concept. Above all, drift accounts for a changing environment which ultimately alters the initial purpose of an arrangement. Streeck and Thelen say: "the world surrounding an institution evolves in ways that alter its scope, meaning, and function" (2005, 25). The German school education serves as an example for drift as a mode of change that reflects the environment rather than the institution itself: the three-track approach was for decades considered to preselect those who would pursue an academic path and those who would tend to embark on an occupational career, with a slight distinction in level between the second and the third track (*Hauptschule*, lower secondary education). Nowadays, however, the third track has in most states evolved into a low-ability trap with a disproportionally high share of pupils from migrant backgrounds, while the de-facto minimum school degree required by most employers for starting an apprenticeship is the middle track. Thus, we see that stability in an institution can lead to problems if it fails to adapt to changing social conditions; thereby the institutions might take on unintended functions that were not initially anticipated by policy makers.

2.7.4 Conversion

Conversion describes a mode of change by which institutions are "redirected to new goals, functions, or purposes" (Streeck and Thelen, 2005, 26). Again, this mode is not about institutional change per se, but about recalibrating institutions. Both the English and the German higher education systems serve as good examples for what conversion signifies: during the 1970s both higher education systems were opened and universities declared their intention to become mass universities. Even today this decision continues to have a large impact on both higher education settings as both struggle to reconcile excellence in teaching and research, on the one hand, with the provision of appropriate infrastructure to allow more young people to study, on the other.[15]

---

[15] Growing student numbers are politically welcomed in both countries.

2.7.5 Exhaustion

The fifth mode of institutional change is called exhaustion (Streeck and Thelen, 2005, 29). It describes institutional breakdown rather than change. A prominent example for the gradual breakdown of a whole scheme is the so called "traditional apprenticeship scheme" in England, which had vanished almost entirely by the beginning of the 1980s. This has a significant impact on vocational education and training policy in England to this day, as the analysis will clearly show.

2.8 Conclusion

This theoretical framework draws on three strands of literature, with discursive institutionalism serving as the "theoretical container" that embraces the framework. This theory puts "discourse" at the centre of its analysis. Thus, it is "discourse" which theoretically allows "unexpected" institutional change to occur. Discourses consist of two traits: firstly, they deal with ideas as their substantive content; and secondly, they represent interactive processes by which these ideas are conveyed. Ideas exist at three levels (policies, programmes and philosophies) within which scholars distinguish two types of ideas (cognitive and normative). The interactive process can be understood in terms of coordinative and communicative discourses. Structure and action are reconciled by introducing the interacting concepts of "background ideational abilities" and "foreground discursive abilities". In the process of institutional change ideas have varying impacts and are used differently at specific points in time (uncertainty, destabilising "weapons", blueprints). Drivers of ideas can have different characters: ideas which emphasis common and prevailing norms and values, those which have a competitive direction of influence, and those which draw on learning experiences.

Yet, before concluding this chapter on the theoretical framework, we need to again return to the starting point of these considerations: we must exercise caution not to disregard varieties of capitalism and historical institutionalism altogether, as this might prove equally misleading. To exemplify this point, imagine a policy discourse of a path-breaking character. Imagine further that this path-breaking policy is implemented. Does this process already allow us to discard the main notions of varieties of capitalism and historical institutionalism, such as path-dependency? Let us take this example even further and think of a convincingly conducted coordinate and communicative discourse on which the decision is based; a thoroughly and neatly implemented policy; and yet the

2.8 Conclusion

initiative does not succeed in attaining the significance and importance politicians initially assigned to it, with the system which it was expected to replace still prevailing.[16] Could this scenario not be described by varieties of capitalism and historical institutionalism? Therefore, we need to be carefully not to finish the analysis too early. Instead we need to trace the processes (a procedure which is commonly used in comparative case studies) in order to tie ideas to political action on the one hand, and to evaluate the reform on the other (Schmidt, 2008, 308). This procedure is necessary because it might be possible that "institutional stickiness" or "institutional inertia" caused by path-dependency hinders an initiative from evolving and thereby prevents a reform measure from succeeding. Hence, varieties of capitalism and historical institutionalism arguments represent both a kind of null hypothesis against which political action will be evaluated and arguments which are nevertheless easily incorporated into this theoretical framework.

---

[16]In educational policy one might think of a scheme that fails to attract pupils or students in the originally expected manner.

3 Case selection: Why comparing England and Germany?

Choosing countries for an in-depth case study always runs the risk of being arbitrary. The following section will provide a scientific justification for the choice, taking the research design of this book into account. The cases selected were Germany and England[17], which meets a "most different research design". The choice is based on two typology sets upon which this chapter will elaborate. The first set shows how different institutions of a political economy interact with each other, how together they build an 'institutional regime' of which education systems are a constitutive part, and how this institutional interaction defines each particular political economy. Consequently, education systems have different designs, mainly due to the environment in which they are located. This typology will perceive education systems in a rather superficial manner. The second set of approaches will take a closer look at the differences between the English and the German educational systems and the concepts whereby these differences become salient and tangible.

3.1 1st set: The 'varieties of capitalism' and institutional complementarities

Since the aim of this research is to show how education systems develop and change while also being embedded in a broader institutional setting, this first typology block refers to the 'varieties of capitalism' (VoC)-literature in terms of its most prominent contribution by Hall and Soskice (2001). This literature represents the most recent and significant attempt to explain how different spheres and institutions of political economies are interlinked and how this coupling and coordination among these institutions characterises each political economy. The VoC-literature is rooted in a parsimonious distinction between Liberal Market Economies (LME) and Coordinated Market Economies (CME). Even though both types vary fundamentally in the way in which they are

---

[17]The concentration of this book is on England and not the UK, as the Scottish education system is rather different from the rest of the UK's system(s) and thus renders generalisations about a UK-wide education system almost impossible.

institutionally designed, they have – in an ideal typical manner – one crucial feature in common. LMEs and CMEs are characterised by institutional coherence, in that their diverse institutions fit, support and reinforce one another. In a competitive environment, institutional coherence (the appropriate term that is used in this context is 'complementary institutions') is conducive to economic competitiveness. Thus, the fewer institutions that fit with each other, the less this political economy will able to compete. According to the VoC approach, Germany and the UK (thus England) are considered as the 'prototype' of CMEs in the German case and LMEs in the case of England. The approach attributes a high degree of institutional coherence to these two countries (Hall and Soskice, 2001; Campbell, 2006). They are ideal examples of political economies that are based on complementary institutions, a claim that was decisively argued by Hall and Soskice in their famous contribution "An Introduction to Varieties of Capitalism" and which was later confirmed in a paper by Hall and Gingerich, among others (2004; for a critical assessment of this argument see Campbell and Pedersen, 2007 and Kenworthy, 2006). What distinguishes CMEs from LMEs is basically the way coordination and interaction takes place among institutions and the kind and shape of institutions both types rely upon.

In the literature LMEs are characterised by flexible labour markets, poorly developed vocational training systems, weak welfare states including limited unemployment benefits and low employment protection standards, strong competition among firms in the absence of strong corporatist structures, and financial markets that provide rather easy and fast short-term capital to firms. In addition, the relatively easy provision of capital, the flexible labour market and the focus on general skills render radical product innovations more likely in LMEs than in CMEs (Hall and Soskice, 2001, 27-33). England is seen as an LME as these features characterise – among other countries – the English political economy.

The production regime of CMEs, in contrast, is basically concentrated on production methods and products that result from the use of sector and firm specific skills. The reliance on corporatist structures provides for a more highly developed vocational training systems; more cooperation among firms, particularly among those in the same sector; and a more generous welfare state with a greater focus on employment protection than in LMEs. Finance providers also differ as they prefer to offer long-term capital commitments, whereas access to financial means in LMEs is more dependent on current profitability (Hall and Soskice, 2001, 21-27, 32). According to the literature, Germany is a CME.

Thus, Germany and England are – in terms of the VoC approach – two political economies that are fundamentally different in how they are structured. Following a most 'different research design', it therefore makes sense to opt for

3.1 1st set: The 'varieties of capitalism' and institutional complementarities 57

these two countries. Both types constitute an 'institution-regime' in which business has to adapt its strategies and endeavours. Education, which in the VoC-literature is mostly confined to vocational education (so e.g. Estevez-Abe, Iversen and Soskice, 2001), is a constitutive part of this 'institution-regime'. 'Varieties of capitalism' has been a very influential attempt to tackle concerns about globalisation and its converging tendencies, which some fear will eventually lead to a 'race to the bottom'. In showing that political economies not only differ fundamentally but that this fundamental difference is a key to economic success, the VoC-approach attacks the 'globalisation-mania'.

Interestingly, inferences can be drawn from this typology for the educational systems. An elaboration on a particular interconnection between two institutions – which are of crucial significance for this book – will highlight these interconnections in more detail, especially that between education systems and labour markets. Maurice, Sellier et al. (1986) provide what is arguably the most prominent work on a theoretical classification of this link. They distinguish between countries with a vocational space and those with an organisational space. Countries, such as Germany, that cluster around the first group are characterised by labour markets in which demand and supply is segmented according to occupations generated by the vocational education and training system. Thus, the labour market is an image of the training market with its concentration on occupations. Therefore, there is a close correlation between skill generation and labour market structure. In contrast, organisational spaces, like in the English case, possess a looser coupling and a recruitment practise that is far more dependent on the structure of the firm or company. More recent works speaks of internal labour markets (ILM systems) as opposed to occupational labour markets (OLM systems; see Marsden, 1999; Müller and Shavit, 1998; Brzinsky-Fay, 2006, 3 f.). Assuming that the demand for particular skills on the labour market reflects the economic emphasis of political economies, this typology can assist our understanding of successes and failures of educational reforms. Supposedly, the mechanism works differently in both countries, as England and Germany are viewed as the opposing poles with respect to this link (compare Brzinsky-Fay, 2006, 3).

Germany and England are supposed to have different political economies. 'Different' refers to both the way single institutions look and operate, and the way they coordinate their operations with each other. A closer glance at the link between education systems and labour markets seems to confirm the difference between the two countries. Differences in interaction, however, do not reveal the actual design of education systems. The next typology set will take a closer look specifically at the educational systems.

3.2 2nd set: Education systems

The second typology block is concerned more directly with the details of the educational systems. Here again, as will become clear below, the 'most different' research approach can be applied, as Germany and England are mostly affiliated with different types. Examining recent discussions about education reveals that 'education' can begin right after birth (childcare, crèches and kindergartens) and virtually never stops throughout the remainder of an individual's life (keyword: life long learning). Yet, this study limits itself to a narrower understanding of the term. 'Education' or 'education systems' in this book thus refers to school education, vocational education and training, and tertiary education. In order to justify the choice of countries, the following description will reference some of the evidence used in later chapters.

Allmendinger (1989) offers an extremely useful and enlightening typology for bettering our understanding of education systems. She distinguishes between different types of educational systems along two dimensions: standardisation and stratification. By standardisation, Allmendinger refers to the degree national education systems meet the same standards throughout the country. Relevant variables for operationalising this dimension are curricula, teachers' training, school budgets, and the uniformity of school-examinations.

Surprisingly, Germany's educational system is highly standardised, despite its federal character. The German Länder are responsible for school and tertiary education. There exists, however, a coordinating organ (joint meeting of the states' ministers of education, Kultusministerkonferenz) that is responsible for the orchestration of German education policies among the Länder. This coordination is particularly important and valuable with regard to the countrywide acceptance of school, university, and professional training-certificates. In addition, the standardisation of the German educational system is revealed by the similar training of teachers and reasonably comparable expenditures of the Länder for schools, universities and vocational establishments.

In this respect we see one of the few similarities between the two countries, as the English school system is highly standardised as well, basically due to its centralised structure. As regards university degrees, there is technically a standardisation of degrees in England. Practically, however, degrees vary according to the university from which they are awarded.[18]

Stratification, by contrast, refers to two aspects. First, whether the education system is characterised by "tracking" and, second, to the proportion of a cohort

---

[18]This indicates a form of stratification as we will see further below.

that attends the maximum number of school years offered by the system (Allmendinger, 1989, 233). In addition to being standardised, the German education system is characterised by a high degree of stratification. Already at the age of ten (this applies to most of the Länder) pupils are selected according to their aptitudes and placed in one of the three school tracks. Permeability from one level to the other is quantitatively rare, especially upgrading movements. Institutional stratification in the British school system is, by contrast, far lower then in Germany. From age 5 to age 16 pupils attend comprehensive school and it is only afterwards that the British school system stratifies between those who follow another two years of school in order to attain the A-level, which allows for entry to higher education; those taking on vocational education; and those leaving the education system entirely.

As regards German tertiary education, the picture changes quite profoundly. German students who qualify for a tertiary education can attain university degrees that are – by and large – accepted equally all over Germany regardless of the universities from which they come. In the British tertiary education system, however, students are selected by universities (according to school marks and financial backgrounds), which ultimately leads to degrees from some universities having a higher reputation than degrees from other universities. The term "Oxbridge" stands as a synonym for this phenomenon and marks a significantly higher degree of stratification in England (though not called so by Allmendinger; one might refer to this as a non-formally institutionalised stratification), as opportunities in the labour market vary with regard to the universities from which students come.

The vocational education and training systems in Britain and Germany vary as well, in particular regarding their standardisation and job specificity (Steinmann, 1999). In Germany the importance of the dual apprenticeship scheme cannot be overstated, as the whole field of vocational education and training revolves around this scheme. Consequently, this main pillar leads to a remarkably high degree of standardisation, not only with respect to qualifications but also regarding the educational pathways which lead to these qualifications. The main qualificational outputs are occupations, which decisively structure the training and labour market. Here we see reasons why the 'vocational principle' is deeply anchored in the German society (Hellwig, 2005; Deissinger, 2004, 77 ff.). Vocational specificity is high because the demand for a particular occupation is not transferable to another occupation, as each occupation is characterised by highly specific occupational skills and aptitudes.

England, by contrast, has no independent vocational training subsystem (Deissinger, 2002, 32). The English vocational education and training system is integrated into the general education system. The so-called National

Qualifications Framework clearly reflects this integrated approach (Steedman, 2005, 6 f.). As Deissinger puts it, the framework "is clearly a hotchpotch of disjointed approaches", which leads to a vocational education and training system that is confusing, fragmented, and – despite its output-oriented qualification system – undoubtedly less standardised than the German system (Deissinger, 2002, 32; Ertl, 2002, 64). Moreover, the English vocational education and training system relies less on employer commitment, is more strongly oriented towards school-based vocational education and training, and has – and this aspect is particularly different from Germany – a stigma and reputation problem. It is often considered as the "low-ability ghetto" (Steedman, 2005, 17), as the more-talented largely enter academic educational pathways. In Germany, however, the link with employers is strong, as is employers' commitment, and having passed an apprenticeship is a well-respected educational qualification.[19]

Summing up, the English and the German educational systems are typically considered to be fundamentally different in all three areas under consideration: school education, vocational education and training, and tertiary education. Yet, I contend that educational reforms in both countries resemble one another to a large degree. That, however, neither automatically implies that the institutional origins are alike as well, nor that their effects (output and outcome) are the same. In order to understand the background against which reforms have taken place, we need to have an idea of the basic shape and structure of these systems, one which goes beyond the above-mentioned theoretical classifications. This description will be done in the next chapter.

---

[19] The aspect of 'employer commitment' is further elaborated upon in the country-specific section by using Steedman's typology of supply-led and demand-led apprenticeship systems (Steedman, 2005).

4 Education systems in England and Germany

In order to consider how educational systems change we need to investigate whether, in the first instance, the systems have indeed changed. This chapter thus serves as a 'calibration device', a reference point against which changes will be estimated. In other, more theoretical, words, this chapter will trace the path to which we would expect systems' developments to adhere if they evolved "path-dependently". Hence, the main characteristics of the three areas under consideration, namely school education, vocational education and training, and tertiary education, will be outlined for both countries. The following chapters are structured according to these areas, thereby allowing us to compare the differences and similarities between these areas in our chosen countries.

Two preliminary remarks are necessary before getting started with outlining the educational system in Germany. Firstly, until the reunification in 1990 the Western and Eastern parts of Germany had fundamentally different educational systems. This applies to all three areas under consideration: school education, vocational education and training, and higher education. Since 1990, however, the Eastern part has – apart from a few minor differences in some of the states – adopted the Western system. Thus, for the sake of simplicity, when referring to periods before 1990 the historical outline will concentrate on the Western German educational system because reforms and discourses since 1990 basically stem from and are based on the Western German approach.

Secondly, one important consideration when attempting to understand German education policy is the federal structure of the state. The educational system is one of the policy areas most affected by federalism because the Länder possess a great deal of independence in this sector. Despite this independence in matters of education, there exist coordination boards that are successfully engaged in coordinating and – on a voluntary basis – harmonising qualifications and awards, as well as occasionally proposing education policy initiatives. Thus, it is not necessary to paint a 'collage' consisting of 16 small pictures in order to portray the basic structure of the German educational system. It suffices to describe one basic structure from which states deviate – by and large – only marginally. The English system does not present these kinds of challenges because education in all three areas is centrally organised.

4.1 School education

As has already been mentioned in the case selection chapter, "stratification" appears to be an appropriate tool for highlighting the major differences in school education of both countries. Allmendinger defines stratification as the "proportion of a cohort that attains the maximum number of school years provided by the educational system, coupled with the degree of differentiation within given educational levels (tracking)" (Allmendinger, 1989, 233).

4.1.1 England

4.1.1.1 Brief historical review of the English school system

The abolishment of the Tripartite System in 1976 was a decisive point for school education in England. This System, established in 1944 by the Butler Education Act, divided secondary school into Grammar School, Technical Schools, and Modern Schools (the so-called tripartite system). The Grammar Schools hosted the academically most talented pupils (around 25 percent), Technical Schools provided for mechanical and scientific subjects (around 5 percent) and the Modern Schools accounted for the vast majority of pupils. After primary education pupils took an exam, to so-called "11-plus", which selected which specific school-track a student would follow. This exam was criticised for being heavily socio-economically biased and discriminatory towards children from working class families.

As this critique coincided with the poor educational performances of Modern Schools, the idea of introducing of a comprehensive system gained more currency.[20] This system, implemented throughout the UK in 1976, marked the end of the tripartite system. Yet the comprehensive system did not entirely prevail, as grammar schools have survived in many areas in England until today (Wiborg, 2009, 9). With a compulsory schooling age of 16, this system has to date remained unaltered in its core. However, beginning with the Conservative government under Margaret Thatcher from 1979, we do see tendencies towards the inclusion of more choice and diversification into the system.

Of critical importance for understanding current English school education policy is the provisions of the Education Reform Act, passed in 1988. The main idea of this reform was to create a school-market in which parents and pupils are

---

[20]Ideal typically, comprehensive education is characterised by non-selective schools, mixed ability classes, late subject specialisation and measures to equalise resources between schools (Green, Preston and Janmaat, 2006, 138).

able to compare the performance of different schools. Basically, the act consisted of five items (Machin and Vignoles, 2006, 1 ff.): The National Curriculum 1. withdrew individual school's freedom to set up their own curricula and syllabuses and instead established a compulsory set of subjects and contents. On the basis of this nationwide harmonised set (subdivided into five key stages), nationally managed assessments 2. are carried out which provide for the creation of league tables of schools 3. allowing for comparisons between different schools. Parents and pupils can make use of these tables because the "catchment area" principle was slightly relaxed, so that 4. parents were able to choose the best school for their children. Additionally, schools have a financial incentive to perform as well as possible because 5. the funding of schools was made dependent on school enrolment numbers.

4.1.1.2 Basic structure of the English school system

The five measures implemented by the Education Reform Act in 1988 are still applied today. The structure of the English school system is thus quite simple: compulsory school started at the age of five and ended at the age of 16. Constructed in the form of a comprehensive school, pupils remained together for the duration of these eleven years before they chose either to attend a sixth form college (the academic pathway leading to the GCE A-level or an equivalent degree) or to pursue a vocational or vocational education pathway. In principle this structure still holds today.

The combination of publicly available test score information ('league tables') which reveals pupils' performances (assessed by means of the National Curriculum) in combination with making schools' funding dependant on enrolment figures has ultimately led to the emergence of a 'school market'. The Education Reform Act was a big step towards a marketisation of school education (Machin and Vignoles, 2006, 1 ff.). Yet, as people are only allowed to enrol their youngsters in schools in their district (so-called 'catchment area'), parents from wealthy backgrounds have moved to particular areas in order to attain the best possible school education for their offspring (The Guardian, 2007b), which has exacerbated the gap between schools with good performances and those with more mediocre scores. The reform meant centralisation and devolution at the same time: the national curriculum is regulated centrally and is therefore binding for all schools, but simultaneously schools have gained more autonomy as they act as competitors in the 'school market' (Machin and Vignoles, 2006, 8).

School enrolment begins at the age of five. Compulsory schooling in England is separated into five so-called 'key stages'. There are national assessment tests after each key stage. Up until the age of 16 (end of key stage 4) English pupils remain together, leading schooling to have a minimum duration of eleven years.

The end of compulsory secondary schooling is marked by the General Certificate of Secondary Education (GCSE). Though the English school system is based on a comprehensive education, the last two years of compulsory schooling (key stage 4 between the ages of 14 and 16) have been made less comprehensive as more optional elements, such as vocational oriented subjects culminating in a General National Vocational Qualification (GNVQ), have been introduced. This illustrates a continuing tendency for the use of selection, streaming and setting, which has been persistent despite the formally comprehensive system (Wiborg, 2009, 11). This system has been increasingly watered down by "promoting a greater diversity of school types" (Wiborg, 2009, 11). Around 50 percent of teenagers continue school education after general secondary school (Sharp, 2002, 2 f.). These students finish the two extra years of schooling with the General Certificate of Education Advanced-level (the so-called A-level).

Equivalent to the (former) GNVQ in the 14-16 phase, there are also Vocational Certificates of Education at the higher secondary level (also called vocational A-levels). These qualifications are available in different subjects that mostly involve studies about a particular industry or business sector. In 2000 they replaced the Advanced GNVQ and have, since 2004, gradually been substituted by 'applied GCE'. Hence, currently both academic and vocational qualifications in the 16-18 period are labelled GCE.[21]

All examinations are centrally organised (all students sit the same exams nationwide). The qualifications are awarded by external awarding and assessment bodies which are regulated and supervised by the Qualifications and Curriculum Authority (QCA), a non-departmental public body (see Hatcher, 2006). This examination procedure allows for the creation of school rankings that compare schools' performances.

State schools are mainly tax-financed. Private schools (somewhat perplexingly called public schools), by contrast, are generally not subsidised by the state. Therefore, private school fees tend to be rather high and thus private schools are accessible only to pupils from wealthy backgrounds. These private

---

[21] Qualifications have been constantly changed, either substantially or just relabelled. For an overview over VET reforms in the last decades see Wright and Oancea, 2005; for changes of qualifications in particular Clark, Conlon and Galindo-Rueda, 2005, 84.

4.1 School education

schools play an important role, particularly when it comes to the sixth form, as almost 20 percent of all British sixth form pupils attend them (Sharp, 2002).[22]

4.1.1.3 Changes and developments in the English school system

By and large the school education system with respect to key stages 1 to 3 has been rather stable. From age of 14 onwards, however, the English education system has been under constant re-construction. The most recent blueprint was presented by the 'Working Group on 14-19 Reform' (called the Tomlinson report after the group's chairman) in 2004 (DfES, 2004a). Its suggestions, the corresponding governmental White Paper, and the subsequent reforms clearly reflect the main issues of English school education. These are: the share of pupils progressing in education after compulsory schooling is too low in comparison to other developed countries; young people are not well prepared for work as they often lack 'Key Skills' ('Skills for Life') such as IT-skills or communication-skills; many vocational qualifications do not meet the needs of learners and employers regarding their content and therefore the value of qualifications is unclear; and the qualification system is confusing and fragmented.

The "Curriculum 2000" reform launched in 2000 seeks to introduce modularisation and choice into the higher secondary education schooling curriculum. This reform will be further analysed in the relevant reform chapter (see chapter 6.1.1).

However, the durability of Curriculum 2000 proved to be rather short. The latest discussions in educational policy revolve around "diplomas". Initially, "diplomas" were the core suggestion of the Tomlinson Group in 2004 to create a unified diploma framework and system for all 14-19 year olds, one which comprises all types of educational and vocational training qualifications. This would have also meant a gradual phasing out of the traditional qualifications such as GCSEs and A-levels. The diploma framework would have been divided into four levels and was supposed to provide more clarity. The idea of this overarching framework, however, has not yet been put into practise. Prestigious qualifications, such as GCSEs and GCE A-levels, would have had to have been dissolved but for political reasons there has been hesitation to do this. The White Paper "14-19 Education and Skills" issued in 2005 rejected the proposal of an overarching diploma system (DfES, 2005a). Instead the Government decided to retain A-levels and GCSE and to reform just the vocational component of school education, basically through substituting the 'applied GCE' with a new

---

[22] One might speak about a de-facto instead of formal stratification.

qualification called the 'diploma' as from 2008. Thus, the 'diploma framework' has been abandoned.

Beginning with diplomas in five employment-related areas, by 2013 further diplomas will be constructed in 14 areas. A diploma will be offered alongside GCSE and GCE A-levels and is a mix of vocational and academic education. Students will also be required to gain work experience. These diplomas have been developed by the DfES and industry representatives. They are, therefore, meant to be "employer-led diplomas".

'Education Maintenance Allowance' (EMA) is another major policy initiative intended to enhance participation in post-compulsory education. EMA is a weekly payment to young people (aged 16-19) from low-income families. It is an incentive for this group not to drop out of education immediately after compulsory schooling. The first evidence confirms that so far this initiative has, to at least a small degree, been successful (Machin and Vignoles, 2006, 13 f.).

One of the latest discussions in educational issues revolves around the question of whether compulsory schooling should be prolonged from 16 to 18. Former Prime Minister Gordon Brown just recently launched this proposal (BBC, 2007; The Guardian, 2007a). In so doing, Brown wanted to ensure that all pupils continue either education or training in order to prevent young people from leaving education without appropriate qualifications and workplace skills. Around 267,000 16 and 17 year olds are currently not in any form of post-compulsory school education, while the number of job-vacancies for low-skilled people continues to shrink (see for instance Crouch, Finegold and Sako, 1999).

4.1.1.4 Main features of English school education

The most prominent feature of the English school education system is its comprehensive institutional approach from 5-16, with a low degree of stratification. In comparison to Germany this feature remains prevalent, even though English "comprehensive education is incomplete and differentiated", mainly due to the survival of grammar schools and means of streaming and setting (Wiborg, 2009, 2, 10). Another peculiarity of the English education system is its various attempts to ensure "parity of esteem" between academic and vocational education. Interestingly enough, and as the above outlined examples show, most initiatives are focused on attempts to "upgrade" vocational education; academic oriented school education, for example A-levels, are excluded from these considerations, as the discussion about the diploma framework has shown. Hence, we encounter a situation where the very attempt to provide a "levelled playing field" among both strands of education leads to its own undermining. Moreover, reforms are given only short periods to establish themselves and to have an impact.

As a consequence, despite numerous attempts to upgrade vocational-oriented school qualifications, academic-oriented A-levels are still regarded as the main and most renowned route; vocational-oriented school education by contrast lacks acceptance, e.g. when it comes to admission to institutions of higher education. Thus, stratification in England is less an issue of formal differentiation of different school forms, as it is in Germany, and instead arises mainly in an informal way: academic oriented school education is the calibration device around which all initiatives (mainly those focussed on vocational education) are estimated and assessed. It is this condition that led Tomlinson to speak of the academically oriented A-levels as the "gold standard" of English school education (2003, 202).

4.1.2 Germany

4.1.2.1 Brief historical review of the German school system

After the Second World War, Germany fell back on the traditional three-track educational system that had existed in the Weimar Republic: after 4 years of primary schooling pupils were selected according to their talents to follow a lower, middle, or higher secondary track. This selection procedure, occurring on the threshold from primary to secondary schooling, still prevails today, albeit in different forms according to the regulations of the federal states. Soon after the war the need to cooperate and coordinate school education became all too apparent as the Länder started to drift apart, threatening the right of free movement provided for in the constitution (Art. 11, Abs.1 GG) because of different types of degree patterns, issues with the mutual recognition of these degrees and different school forms. These developments led to the establishment of the "Standing Conference of the Ministers of Education and Cultural Affairs of the Länder in the Federal Republic" (Kultusministerkonferenz, KMK) in 1948, which decided to harmonise core aspects of school education among the Länder in order to guarantee common standards.

The Grand Coalition of Willi Brand (1969-1972) succeeded in amending the Basic Law by introducing the principle of joint cooperation between the Länder and the federal level regarding education planning. As a consequence, a second higher board was founded, a joint commission of the Länder and the federal level (Bund-Länder-Kommission für Bildungsplanung und Forschungsförderung (BLK)). However, the idea of a common education plan failed due to disagreements between the states. The "joint decision trap", reinforced by sometimes very sharp ideological divisions (like the discussion about comprehensive schools)[23] is one of the peculiarities in the German educational landscape which has characterised all reform initiatives in the German education sector since 1946. Therefore, change is mostly confined to the regional level. However, despite all the incremental and regional changes, the comparability of degrees and certificates was and is by and large guaranteed by the Standing Conference of the Ministers of Education.

However, the school education system has not changed in a vacuum. The secondary school on the intermediate level (Realschule) has become the quasi standard school qualification – in the first 20 years after the war this was clearly the lower track, at this time also called the "people school" (Volksschule), nowadays known as the Hauptschule.

These developments have led to a situation in which in terms of options in school education there are three tracks (or even four track system if we consider the so-called "comprehensive schools" as a fourth track) but where in reality the school system in big cities and university cities tends to become a de facto two track system: an academic pathway in the higher secondary schools leading to the university entrance qualification and a lower secondary track, focussing more on practical skills and preparing students for vocational education after schooling (Führ and Furck, 1998, 257).

4.1.2.2 Basic structure of the German school system

School education in Germany is under the ambit of the federal states. The most influential and prominent feature of the German school system is its three-track approach in all the Länder, e.g. the division of secondary school pupils into different schools according to their skills/degrees.

Compulsory schooling starts with primary school at the age of six and lasts 4 years. Overall, compulsory schooling lasts a minimum of 9 years. It is at the transition from primary to secondary education where the three-track-system begins: pupils are recommended to pursue either lower secondary schools (Hauptschule), intermediate secondary schools (Realschule), or upper secondary schools (Gymnasien), which pupils finish with the university entrance degree (Abitur). The lower secondary schools last 5 years (9 years of school education in total) and the intermediate secondary schools last 6 years (10 years of school education in total). Regarding the upper secondary schools the picture is slightly

---

[23] In contrast to Britain, "comprehensive schools" in Germany means that all three tracks are combined under one roof. Yet, there is no single track as in Britain.

more diverse. West Germany had traditionally had 9 years of post-primary school education (13 years in total) for the Abitur. Since unification, some Eastern German states such as Saxony and Thuringia have followed a 12 year strategy, which has been incrementally adopted by nearly all other states with the exception of Brandenburg and Rhineland-Palatinate (this so-called G8 reform is further analysed below). Moving between the tracks in either direction, upgrading and downgrading, is theoretically possible. Practically, however, bottom-up moves are extremely rare, whereas up-down transitions are far more common. Being in a lower track makes it very difficult to upgrade as the tracks proceed at different teaching speeds.

There are generally no final examinations for the lower and the intermediate secondary school. This is different for the upper secondary school, where the Abitur is awarded after final written and oral examinations. Broadly, two approaches exist among the Länder in how these final examinations and their assessment are organised: a few Länder allow schools themselves to set-up the examinations but most of the states organise these examinations centrally on the basis of a coherent syllabus. Regardless, assessments of the examinations are done by the school teachers. Hence, there is no coherent examination procedure in Germany.

"Schooling time" (in terms of school days) is one of the few issues which exhibits remarkably diversity between the Länder. In Western Germany the school day has generally been a half day whereas in the German Democratic Republic full-time schooling was standard. Currently there is a clear trend towards all-day schooling (KMK, 2008).

The majority of schools in Germany are public.[24] Private schools play a minor role in the German school system; an equivalent to the large significance of the English public schools is therefore not existent.

4.1.2.3 Changes and developments in the German school system

The first result of the so-called PISA study conducted by the OECD caused shockwaves and brought school education back on the agenda nationwide.[25] This study revealed a lack of literacy and numeracy of German pupils in comparison to other OECD countries. In addition, the study revealed discrimination against pupils with particular social origins (migrant families, deprived households, and low educational background) and a tendency of the German school education system to perpetuate these disparities (Bildungsberichterstattung, 2006, 49).

---

[24] As opposed to England, public schools in Germany signify non-private schools.
[25] PISA stands for Programme for International Student Assessment.

Concerns about the quality of school education are compounded by organisational issues, in particular the length of schooling in the higher secondary track that leads to the Abitur. Providing better education in a shorter period has thus become a common theme in recent debates on school education in Germany. However, within the Länder we can observe some reforms may gradually spread over the country. Two examples which illustrate this policy adoption process are the increasing significance of full-time schools and the shortening of higher secondary schooling.

In 2001, 94.6 percent of schools were organised as half day schools. By 2005, 15.2 percent of all pupils opted for full-time schooling offers (KMK, 2007, 7 ff.). Thus, the situation with regard to time spent at school is gradually changing, with full day schools becoming much more prominent. This trend is confirmed by an increasing number of pupils entering these schools (KMK, 2007, 11). The purpose is twofold: firstly, it serves to keep pupils in school for a longer period of the day, thereby ensuring that they do their homework and increasing their overall school performance; and, secondly, full day schools allow both parents to pursue regular jobs. In this respect, half day schools represent a heritage from the times when the entire family life revolved around the male breadwinner. As figures show, there is a clear trend in all Länder towards full-time schooling, though at a modest level (KMK, 2007, 7). There is a small east-west imbalance discernable, as Saxony and Thuringia are clearly in the lead in terms of share of full-time schools.

Another reform that is spreading all over Germany and which is omnipresent in the educational discourse is the Abitur after 12 years. This reform will be further analysed in the relevant reform chapter (see chapter 6.2.1). A further initiative to decrease the completing age of school education is to enrol school beginners at an earlier age. In comparison to England, where 100 percent of all 6 year olds are already in school, the share in Germany is rather modest at around 50 percent. Yet, there is a trend towards earlier school enrolment (Bildungsberichterstattung, 2006, 45).

A further debate seen in the discourse revolves around the Hauptschule (lower secondary school). This school type has become the 'low-ability ghetto' of the German educational system (Steedman, 2005, 17): one fourth of all pupils in the 9th class are in a Hauptschule and the share is steadily decreasing. Furthermore, most of the pupils are children from migrant families (they account for up to 80 percent) and/or from socially deprived backgrounds (Bildungsberichterstattung, 2006). As the educational level of children in Germany is highly dependant on the parents' educational and socio-economic background (Baumert, Stanat and Watermann, 2006, 95 ff.), there is a self-perpetuating mechanism with few chances of escape.[26]

4.1.2.4 Main features of German school education

The main feature of German school education is its three-track design. If we understand 'stratification' as a "degree of differentiation within given educational levels" (Allmendinger, 1989, 233), we can clearly ascertain that Germany has a high degree of stratification with respect to school education. Already at the age of nine or ten children are divided into different educational tracks.

Apart from this three-track design, the "time-dimension" also characterises German school education, namely the comparatively late school enrolment ages and the comparatively longer lasting higher secondary education. Both traits have recently been a matter of debate. Another characteristic is the traditional absence of any vocational orientation in school education. This task was left to the dual apprenticeship system. Today, due to a declining number of apprenticeship openings, an increasing number of school leavers are forced to directly enter the labour market. This aspect has made the issue of vocational education in general school education more important and has, therefore, led to a change of thinking.

---

[26] This has recently been criticised by the United Nations Special Rapporteur on the right to education, Vernor Muñoz who explicitly emphasised the "high co-relation between social/migrant background of students and educational achievement" and thereby urged Germany (the Länder governments) to reconsider the three-track system. This correlation is all too obvious in Hauptschulen (Muñoz, 2007, 2). The early selection procedure, made already at the age of 9 or 10, has a huge impact on the future opportunities of pupils (Allmendinger, 1989, 235; Müller and Shavit, 1998, 6 f.). The early separation of pupils into the different tracks leads to a highly stratified picture, the maximum and minimum number of schooling years can vary by as many as four years. Klaus Hurrelmann, scientist and recently in charge of the so-called Shell youth study in Germany, said in an open letter to all ministers of education that leavers from the Hauptschule have virtually no chance on the training market and are extremely confined on the labour market (Der Spiegel, 2006b). This development is exacerbated by the fact that training places in the trade branch are incrementally vanishing and new branches like the service sector or IT-sector require skills and aptitudes that pupils from lower secondary schools can rarely meet. Already in some fields every third apprentices is a high secondary school leaver whereas intermediate secondary school leavers dominate the training market (Der Spiegel, 2006a). Thus, paradoxically the German school system, which was originally intended to provide educational programmes for pupils with different skills and aptitudes, has at the lower end increasingly been recognised as a system that restrains and confines children's development based on the type of school they attend. Hurrelmann suggest a reversal of these mechanisms, as a child's potentials is not the focus of consideration; it is the track (and thus the institutional design of school education) which pre-determines a child's potentials and opportunities (Hurrelmann in: Der Spiegel, 2006a).

4.1.3 Comparing both school systems

As to the major differences between both systems, and thus to the basic principles which underpin them, the German separation of the educational process into three tracks versus the English comprehensive schooling approach seem to be diametrically opposed; and in fact they are. The philosophy behind both approaches is completely different: the purpose of the German three-track system is to respond to the different levels of pupils and to prepare them selectively for post-school working life. The English approach revolves around an integrated schooling system in which pupils with different aptitudes learn from each other and where the least-talented profit from more-talented classmates. Yet, this perspective needs to be readjusted: the share of English pupils attaining a privately financed education is considerably higher than in Germany (around 40 percent in England as opposed to not even 6 percent in Germany)[27], which weakens the comprehensive system through the persistence of highly selective grammar schools.

Thus the possession of a comprehensive school system is not tantamount to having an entirely un-stratified system. Taking into consideration the greater chance of grammar school students being admitted to a well-known university we might well speak of stratification in English school education. Another major difference is the way school education pathways are organised. England offers many options for the 14 to 19 year olds regarding the subjects they want to follow. Moreover, the English school system increasingly allows for modularisation, e.g. the accumulation of different qualifications at different times, which then leads to eligibility for final examinations. The German school curricula are stricter and offer fewer options. This difference continues in vocational education and training, as will be made clear in the next section.

Some recent developments, however, illustrate interesting movements in both countries. Earlier school enrolment ages and shorter higher secondary pathways in Germany are an indicator of a decrease in the school leaving age, closer towards that which is found in England. As the dual apprenticeship system in Germany is not able to meet the demand for places anymore, vocational education to provide pupils with some basic tools to support their search in the training or labour markets has increasingly become an issue in school education.

In England, attempts to include vocational education in school education have been numerous and, to a certain extent, confusing. What has driven this development was both the lack of options for pupils in the comprehensive school

---

[27]According to Eurydice 'government-dependent private' schools refers to schools which are not public/state-run but receive more than 50 percent of their financing from the public authorities; see http://www.eurydice.org/ressources/eurydice/pdf_images/052ENXX010B07x0101f.pdf.

system on the one hand and on the other, the lack of agreed upon vocational education patterns for all post-compulsory school leavers, which could have offset some of the main deficiencies of school education. In Germany, by contrast, fewer schooling years were compensated and complemented by the dual apprenticeship system, particularly by means of vocational schools.

As vocational education has gained significance, though a huge share of school leavers still enter the labour market directly, British politicians (such as Brown) have considered extending compulsory schooling. England has thus, since the decline in significance of work-based training, steadily emphasised formal vocational schooling to a greater degree(Grubb, 2004, 50) – something which is now visible to some extent in Germany as well.

4.2 Vocational education and training

In a classical liberal vein "education" is perceived of as a good the purpose of which is not to only increase future chances on the labour market or to guarantee higher wages. Instead, "education" is seen as a consumption good, an end in itself, a good that serves the creation of a self-conscious, reflecting, democratic and valuable citizen as a part of a society (Foreman-Peck, 2004, 72; Crouch, Finegold and Sako, 1999; Bailey, 2003).

Vocational education is different. It is concerned with the investment in human capital, with the preparation for the labour market, and with matching education-offers with businesses' demands. As such, it is a means to an end. School education and higher education are – broadly speaking – determined by two actors: the pupil or student on the one hand, and the school or the higher education institution on the other. In vocational education, by contrast, employers are also crucial because they are the immediate users of this kind of education. It is for this reason that employer impact on vocational education is a particular trait of this educational area and a critically important factor with respect to training and trainees' chances regarding the transition from school/education to work.

Four concepts will help us shed light on the crucial differences between England and Germany regarding vocational education. Firstly, both systems are commonly associated with entirely different approaches. A distinction can be drawn between a competence-based, output-oriented approach in England and the German approach, which follows the vocational principle of a more input- and curriculum-oriented basis (Hellwig, 2005, 2; Ertl, 2002, 57). Interestingly, this typology not only helps delineates the main differences between both systems but simultaneously assists us in understanding major reform initiatives in both countries.

Secondly, the distinction between a competence-based approach as opposed to a vocation-based approach matches to a great extent the typology developed by Maurice, Sellier et al. (1986; see chapter 3). Based on case studies of France and Germany, they tried to understand how labour markets in political economies are structured and how labour-market outcomes are linked with educational qualifications and skills. As we will see, we can swap England for France in our analysis and thereby attain a useful distinction between both systems.

Thirdly, Steedman's (2005) distinction between vocational systems that are demand-led and those that are supply-led refers exactly the above mentioned issue, namely how and to what extent employers are involved in the provision of vocational education.

Fourthly, standardisation is another factor that highlights some of the differences. Standardisation refers to three aspects: the standardisation of certificates; the standardisation of education pathways that lead to certificates; and the certificates' reputation and acknowledgement in society and business (Smithers, 2002, 4 f.). We are able to talk about an independent vocational education subsystem only if vocational education is linked to the requirements of the labour market, businesses and employers. Otherwise it is nothing more than school education, specialised for the provision of particular, work-relevant skills.

4.2.1 England

4.2.1.1 Brief historical review of the English vocational education and training system

Even though England traditionally had a strong employer-led apprenticeship scheme, its significance declined dramatically in terms of participation through the 1980s and 1990s. By 1990, only around one percent of all employees in England were engaged in an apprenticeship (Grubb, 2004, 8; Bessy, 2002). The decline (compare with Gospel, 1995) in significance of the traditional apprenticeship scheme had several causes: firstly, apprenticeships were mainly to be found in traditional manufacturing sectors. With the industrial sector declining and the services sector gaining in importance, traditional apprenticeships were losing their significance because no equivalents were introduced in the services sector. Secondly, apprenticeships in England were regulated by the social partners. The growing dissatisfaction of employers with

4.2 Vocational education and training

the scheme (in terms of cost and skills) and the increasing devaluation of the unions, which reached its climax in the beginning of the 1980s under the Thatcher government, weakened the social partnership basis of the apprenticeship scheme. A third reason for the steady decline of apprenticeships was caused by the concentration of the English economy on the short-term profitability of stock market capitalism, which led to a situation in which employers were less willing to invest in apprentices. (Grubb, 2004, 7).[28]

Fourthly, high unemployment rates among the youth and the lack of an appropriate training schemes led to the introduction of the Youth Training Scheme (YTS; Grubb, 2004, 7). This state-driven scheme was supposed to provide skills and competences in order to increase the trainability and employability of those youngsters who had not succeeded in finding a training place or job. The scheme had, however, a major flipside: during the decline in significance of the traditional apprenticeships, the YTS was closely associated with apprenticeships and actors applied a similar language to the scheme (Gospel, 1995). As low school-achievers were the main target group of this scheme, this led it to garner a poor reputation, one which spread to the apprenticeship scheme and caused an even greater loss in status, alongside with complaints about the apprenticeships' training durations of up to five years and poor degrees of standardisation and transferability.[29]

As England was increasingly considered to lack well educated and skilled workers (Ryan and Unwin, 2001, 99), the Modern Apprenticeship Scheme introduced by the Conservative Government represented a major attempt to revalue work-based vocational education and training. It was piloted in 1994 and rolled out in 1995. It aimed to offer more skills on the intermediate level, as this scheme was offered at NVQ level 3, whereas the YTS sat at level 2 (in 1989 renamed to Youth Training).[30] The 1997 introduction of the Foundation Modern

---

[28]This is one of the core observations that lead "varieties of capitalism" scholars to the contention that political economies structurally differ in their approach to skill formation (Estevez-Abe, Iversen and Soskice, 2001; Iversen and Soskice, 2001; Hall and Soskice, 2001; Steedman, 2005).

[29]The poor reputation of YTS stems from the fact that many young people did not achieve any qualification and were made redundant as soon as the training period ended (Fuller and Unwin, 2003a). At the same time, most of the major problems persisted: youth unemployment rates remained high and the concentration on the least-talented young people led the (perceived) lack of intermediate practical skills to persist.

[30]Of decisive importance for understanding the English vocational education and training-area is the National Qualification Framework (NQF), initially introduced in 1986 by the Qualification and Curriculum Authority (QCA). The framework was a major effort to standardise and streamline the qualification system and to allow for greater permeability among different education pathways by means of a qualification credits transfer system. The framework covers all learning modes in secondary schooling, further education, vocational education and training, and higher education. It is subdivided into skill levels. Thus, the QCA accredits qualifications by associating them with the

Apprenticeship Scheme at level 2 mostly replaced the Youth Training Scheme.

However, vocational education in England has an image-problem, not only recently but at least since the period after the Second World War. Neglecting the causal roots of this issue, part of the problem stems from the clear distinction between vocational and academic education and from the fact that vocational education has been seen as being for those who have fallen off the academic ladder. "Parity of esteem" has thus become one of the most important guidelines for recalibrating the vocational education sector. Another main problem has been the diversity of awards and qualifications. This led the Conservative Government in 1986 to introduce the National Council of Vocational Qualifications to set up National Vocational Qualifications within a comprehensive framework in order to tackle confusion and incomparability in this area. These qualifications serve as certifications for people's skills; however, they neither indicate the way these skills were acquired nor do they help in the transition from school to work (Smithers, 2002). Moreover, training has become an almost entirely state-driven endeavour with employers playing only a minor role.

4.2.1.2 Basic structure of vocational education and training in England

Apprenticeships English Modern Apprenticeships are characterised by a framework that combines on-the-job and off-the-job skills and qualifications. They comprise on-the-job skills in the shape of National Vocational Qualifications (NVQs); off-the-job qualifications such as technical certificates; and Key Skills qualifications such as working in teams, problem solving, communication and using new technology. NVQs are vocational on-the-job certificates based on standards set by industry. Individuals can attain eligibility for these NVQs in various ways; through an apprenticeship, on-the-work experiences, colleges, or through acquired work experiences. Thus, people with particular aptitudes may attain these official qualifications without having gone through a formal vocational education pathway.

Key Skills (including literacy and numeracy), also called Skills for Life, are supposed to be of use in most occupations and comprise six subjects, such as communication, information communication technology, and improving own learning and performance. They are a constitutive component of the Modern Apprenticeship framework.

Technical certificates such as BTECs or OCR Nationals are work-related off-the-job qualifications available in different subjects. They are usually studied

---

relevant NQF-levels. Qualifications on similar levels are pooled in order to render them comparable.

at colleges (sometimes also in schools) and underpin practical on-the-job experiences with theoretical knowledge. Suggested by the National Skill Task Force in 2001 and put into force shortly thereafter, the reason for the introduction of a theoretical component by means of a technical certificate was due to dissatisfaction with both the lack of theoretical understanding of the apprentices and the extremely diverse on-the-job training outcomes (compare with Steedman, 2001, 78).

Initially the Modern Apprenticeship scheme was divided into two streams: Advanced Apprenticeships (formerly Advanced Modern Apprenticeship, before that Modern Apprenticeships) leading to a National Vocational Qualification (NVQ) on level 3 and Apprenticeships (formerly Foundation Modern Apprenticeships, before that National Traineeships) aiming at NVQ level 2. These are the core schemes on which this work will focus. These types are aimed at 16 to 24 year-olds. In 2004 this scheme was broadened to include Young Apprenticeships (for 14 to 16 year-olds) and Pre-Apprenticeships (also called "E2e", Entry to Employment; for those who have potential but are not yet ready to enter an apprenticeship). Furthermore, the 25 year age limit for Apprenticeships was withdrawn.

The Department for Education and Skills (DfES) suggests that the Apprenticeship programme takes at least one year and the Advanced Apprenticeship two years. The exact shape of the individually-tailored training plan should acknowledge the skills and attained experiences of the apprentices and is dependent on the apprenticeship as such and employers' discretion in particular. Above all, the training plan stipulates the balance of work and study for the apprentices and time releases for off-the-job training with learning providers. Yet, there is no statutory entitlement to off-the-job training and education. Even the training duration is not legally set and thus needs to be determined within the training plan. Consequently, the training duration is dependant on the apprenticeship programme and sector, the employers' discretion, and the aptitudes of the trainee.

Apprentices can be directly contracted by an employer or with a training provider. In the first case it is the responsibility of the employer to remunerate the apprentices. Apprentices in the Modern Apprenticeship programme without an "employed" status (compare with Fuller, Beck and Unwin, 2005, 301) are contracted with training providers that pay them a training allowance (in 2005 around £40 to £50 per week). It does not come as a surprise that students of the lower level Apprenticeships are less likely to hold an "employed" status than students of Advanced Apprenticeships (Fuller, Beck and Unwin, 2005, 301).[31]

---

[31]Thereby, we understand why authors consider MAs as a training and labour market programme and as such as a successor of the Youth Training Scheme rather than an attempt to revive the traditional

As a consequence, most of the apprentices are channelled through the Learning and Skill Councils (LSCs)[32] to a "training provider" such as employers and private companies, but also to further education colleges, Group Training Associations, Local Authorities, and non-profit providers. (Steedman, 2001, 79).[33] Initially established in 14 prototype sectors, there are currently around 180 Modern Apprenticeship frameworks in over 80 industry sectors.[34]

The traditional English apprenticeships in the past were demand-led (Fuller and Unwin, 2003a, 9). Today, however, we see a system in which training places are offered mostly because training providers approach employers and ask for openings. Thus, employer (self-) commitment is low, a fact that indicates England's classification as belong to the supply-led apprenticeship group (compare with Steedman, 2005, 7; for further elaboration on this aspect see the concluding part of this section). Figures from 2001 prove the low employer commitment in England, as only 5 percent of all trainees in the Modern Apprenticeship programme are trained directly by an employer (Ryan and Unwin, 2001, 105).

Hence, the supply of apprenticeship openings might not necessarily correlate with the demand by employers for qualified staff, as employers only occasionally directly demand apprentices. This mismatch is likely to become even bigger due to the financing procedures and incentives of the state for private training providers. Both the relevant governmental department and private training providers are keen to engage as many apprentices as possible with the providers because every additional apprentice is conducive to attaining government targets and to providing additional funding for the providers (Steedman, 2001, 80). As a consequence, there is a risk that training might be biased towards low-cost provision, which does not necessarily correspond to local needs (Ryan and Unwin, 2001, 107). Here again we find an indication of a lack of standardisation in terms of pathways. As Deissinger (2002, 32) puts it, there are

> "no clear institutional stipulations, legal regulations on training, and that the various training providers act more or less autonomously, competing against one another in a variety of ways on the open training market and forging links with other players."

The formal input of industry into the structure of Modern Apprenticeships is

---

apprenticeship scheme (Deissinger, 2002, 32; Ryan and Unwin, 2001).
[32]Formerly this was the Training and Enterprise Councils (TECs).
[33]Providers are usually private training companies, but they might also be Further Education colleges, voluntary sector organisations, Chambers of Commerce or employer 'Group Training Associations'.
[34]Learning and Skill Council, http://www.apprenticeships.org.uk/.

4.2 Vocational education and training

managed by the Sector Skill Councils (SSC), which have replaced the National Training Organisation (NTO). The purpose of these Councils is to establish links with employers in industry sectors and persuade them to collaborate with the programmes (Misko, 2006, 13). The SSC is an employer-led, state-sponsored and state-licensed organisation which represents employers' interests regarding work-related skill issues. Thus, there is a significant impact and representation of employers in setting up the MA scheme. One of their main tasks is to ensure a smooth fit between the skills of the employees and those skills demanded by business and industry. Hence, as summed up on the public Modern Apprenticeship information site by the Learning and Skill Council, "Apprenticeships are designed by business for business."[35] SSCs develop and maintain national occupational standards to meet industry needs and demands.

The managing and financing of apprenticeships is rather complex, since various actors and organisations are involved. As we have already seen, most of the apprentices are channelled through the Learning and Skill Councils (LSCs) to training providers.[36] The funding works in the following way: the relevant governmental department funds the regional LSC units which then distribute the money to the training providers. Off-the-job training and assessment is wholly funded by the LSC, hence by the state. LSCs contract with local learning providers which manage and organise training and assessment services for employers.[37]

School-based pathways The institution-based vocational education pathway is highly fragmented, complex and in a constant state of flux. This, however, does not apply to the intra-sectoral structure of vocational education, since particular vocational education programmes are not perceived as hierarchically ordered as the y are in Germany, where the dual apprenticeship is clearly still the most influential and prestigious programme for this age- group when it comes to vocational education and training. School-based educational pathways have gradually become more prominent. "Full-time vocational education achieves a ratio of 25 percent in England among the 16 and 17 year olds and is thus coming from mere 15 percent in the mid 1980ies" (Machin and Vignoles, 2006, 10).

---

[35]Learning and Skill Council, http://www.apprenticeships.org.uk/lscapprenticeships/Templates/Employers/BaseTemplates/.
[36]Learning and Skill Council, http://www.apprenticeships.org.uk/lscapprenticeships/Templates/Employers/BaseTemplates/.
[37]The local learning provider can advise the employer on all kinds of administrative and training related issues, such as supervision at work, wages, time given to learning and study, quality assurance for their training and Health and Safety in the workplace, and/or arranging the training plan. The so-called 'Train to Gain' programme of the English Government also attempts to create links with employers and to convince them of the advantages of training young people; compare with site, http://www.traintogain.gov.uk/.

Generally institution-based vocational education and training for post-16 year-olds is provided in further education or sixth form colleges. The range of offerings in these institutions is huge and more varied than in Germany (Misko, 2006, 26). These college-based vocational pathways are often a preparation for further education, including for higher education, or are a chance for catch-up training in order to obtain labour market relevant qualifications and skills for those who left school without being trained or employable.

The equivalent to NVQs in on-the-job training are General National Vocational Qualifications (GNVQ) for off-the-job classroom-based vocational qualifications. GNVQs are available in schools and colleges alongside GCSEs or A-levels and are related to occupational areas in general rather than particular job-specific skills. GNVQs were introduced in 1992 and were expected to bridge the traditional academic pathway (A-level) and the work-based pathway leading to NVQs (Steinmann, 1999, 38). As with NVQs, GNVQs pursue an output-oriented approach, i.e. the achievement of a particular outcome (skills and aptitudes) is important, rather than the pursuit of a particular syllabus or learning programme.

As with NVQs, GNVQs are based on a modular concept of units, i.e. each qualification consists of mandatory, optional, and additional units. The units can be separately assessed and accumulated in order to gain the whole GNVQ. These GNVQs are now gradually being replaced by vocational General Certificates of Secondary Education (Vocational GCSEs), which can be obtained from the age of 14 onwards. This marks a small but interesting deviation from the comprehensive school approach until the age of 16 in England. However, also the post-compulsory school pathway leading to the GCE A-level, a pathway with a traditionally academic-dominated curriculum, has been opened to more vocational education contents. Here vocational AS- and A- levels have been introduced to bridge the academic and the vocational pathways. These programmes exemplify the attempts to attain 'parity of esteem' between vocational and academic education through revaluing vocational education in relation to the academic route (Grubb, 2004, 13; Fuller, Beck and Unwin, 2005, 86 ff.).

4.2.1.3 Changes and developments in vocational education and training in England

Apprenticeships in England have been in constant flux. These developments will be the subject of the reform chapter further below. Up to 2005, 17 so-called 'City Academies' were established in England. What makes these City Academies (also called Skills Academies) unique is their dual-status of being regular state schools, on the one hand, while simultaneously on the other hand being sponsored by business, or faith or voluntary non-profit organisations. The sponsors are not only involved in the financing but also in developing the curriculum, in the organisation of the Academies and in the professional development of the teachers and trainers. The Labour Government plans to increase this number to 200 in 2010 (Labour Party, 2005, 3). Their post 16 curricula are focused on sector-specific education, such as textile or automotive industries.

Criticism of the concept of City Academies has been manifold. The teacher's union NASUWT fears that business interests will become too involved in education issues. This deviates from the principle of public responsibility for education (BBC, 2006a; BBC, 2006b). Furthermore, City Academies would lack democratic accountability. Since they are treated like charitable organisations they are not obliged to fully disclose their financial structures even though they are mainly funded by tax-payers. Members from Labour – the initiator of these academies – are also critical. The Ex-Labour leader Neil Kinnock denounced Academies as distorting the choice of preferred education, since Academies are allowed to choose their pupils and not the parents to choose the schools (BBC, 2006a). Furthermore, he also criticises the influence of sponsors on the shape of the Academies, including on the curricula and in the training of teachers.

4.2.1.4   Main features of the English vocational education and training system

The English vocational education area is highly contested and extremely complex. Attempts to give this system more structure and to fill the vacuum caused by the decline of traditional apprenticeships have led, paradoxically, to an ever more complex and incomprehensible vocational education area. Neither have the whole framework and qualification system (e.g. the GNVQs or NVQs are hardly known by employers and students; Machin and Vignoles, 2006, 12) been understood by employers, teachers, students, and their parents (Machin and Vignoles, 2006, 10), nor has the economic value of these qualifications become clear.

As a consequence, the economic return to these programmes is low and vocational qualifications still have a considerably lower labour market value than their academic equivalents (Machin and Vignoles, 2006, 12).[38] Part of the problem is that less able students in particular choose the vocational route, which

---

[38]Interestingly, this observation is not valid for older vocational qualifications, such as the HNC/HND, which lead to a substantial wage premium (Machin and Vignoles, 2006, 13).

leads these qualifications to have a bad reputation from the perspective of the employers. Since many new jobs are created in the services sector and many are located in the low-wage sector, for most jobs it is sufficient to simply obtain on-the-job training. On the other end, people often use vocational education qualifications as "entrance gates" to tertiary education.

Initiatives in the English vocational education and training area were introduced with mainly two goals in mind: firstly to structure the area and simultaneously make the vocational route more prominent, also through increasing further options; and secondly to upgrade vocational education in comparison to the academic pathway ('parity of esteem'), also through introducing mixed-forms such as, for example, vocational A-levels or vocational GCSEs. Yet, despite huge efforts English vocational education and training is still a second best option and the academic path through GCE A-levels to tertiary education remains the most prominent and also the most prestigious option.

The biggest problems were summarised by the 'Modern Apprenticeship Advisory Committee' (MAAC) in 2001: "critical weaknesses identified included: declining participation by young people; low completion rates, with only about a third of all apprentices completing their frameworks; and weaknesses in training, assessment and data collection. Many young people and employers were still unaware of exactly what an apprenticeship involved" (MAAC, 2001). As we will see later on, most of these problems still persist.

4.2.2 Germany

4.2.2.1 Brief historical review of the German vocational education and training system

Following discussions and reading articles about vocational education and training in Germany leads to the impression that the German vocational education and training system is synonymous with the dual apprenticeship system. And indeed the dual system, as a combination of on-the-job and off-the-job education and training, has been the dominant scheme in this area for decades. Tracing its roots back to the Middle Ages, the apprenticeship system survived the national-socialistic regime and became from 1945 onwards the main pillar of vocational education and training. Nevertheless, it was not until the 1970s that they were perceived as an integral part of the German education system. This was due to the fact that apprenticeships were attributed to the economic sphere, as most of the vocational education took place on-the-job. This attitude changed during the period of economic decline in the 1970s, triggered by

4.2 Vocational education and training

the Oil Crisis, when the supply of apprenticeships could not match the increase in demand. Consequently, school-based training places were established and expanded.

Although the system has been subject to many reforms over the years, changes remained inherent within the system. One problem was the vast array of occupations that had been taught through the dual system. The reduction from 900 occupations in 1945 to 606 in 1971 and eventually to 342 in 2006[39] was accomplished by the amalgamation of occupations into occupational fields. The idea was to promote a modular structure with more general vocational education modules in the beginning and specialisation modules thereafter. Though this idea lost influence in the 1980s, it regained significance from the middle of the 1990s, with businesses demanding more flexibility among vocations due to the rapid technological developments.

4.2.2.2 Vocational Education and Training in Germany

The dual apprenticeship system
As mentioned in the section about English school education, Tomlinson referred to the GCE A-level as the 'gold standard' (Tomlinson, 2003, 202). Applying this notion to the German vocational education and training-system, the dual apprenticeship system is clearly the 'gold standard' and most of the other vocational education 'currencies' revolve around this standard.

The 'dualism' of the German apprenticeship system refers to the two learning sites of an apprenticeship: the training provider (an employer) where trainees become acquainted on-the-job with the work of an occupational field; and the part-time vocational school.[40] In the school site the knowledge of the practical site is underpinned with theoretical knowledge about work processes. Also general knowledge such as, for example, mathematics, German, English, or sports, is part of the school curriculum.

Chambers of Industry and Commerce play a crucial role in the whole apprenticeship procedure. They register trainees, hold examinations, certify the appropriate aptitude of trainers and advise companies on training issues (Deissinger, 2004, 79). The combination of the on-the-job certificate approved

---

[39] Compare with Misko, 2006, 20; Federal Institute for Vocational Education and Training, http://www2.bibb.de/tools/aab/aabberufeliste.php.; Federal Institute for Vocational Education and Training, http://www.bibb.de/de/wlk26560.htm.
[40] The term 'Dualism', however, might be misleading to the extent that it indicates that both sites are of equal value. In fact, the on-the-job component accounts for around two-thirds, and the off-the-job component for only one-third, of the whole apprenticeship (Frommberger and Reinisch, 2002, 80).

by the Chambers with the part-time vocational school certificate leads to a recognised occupation, the heart of Germany's 'vocationalism' approach (Hellwig, 2005, 2).[41]

The cooperation of the various entities which are involved in the system (federal states for vocational schools, the federal level, unions and employer organisations) is coordinated by the 'Federal Institute for Vocational Education and Training' (Bundesinstitut für Berufsbildung, BIBB; Ertl, 2002, 55). As with school education the responsibility for ensuring nationwide standards of the vocational school component lies with the joint meeting of the states' ministers of education (Kultusministerkonferenz, KMK). The employer concludes the "articles of apprenticeship" (Ausbildungsvertrag) with the apprentice and remunerates the apprentice.

In terms of participation and completion rates the dual apprenticeship system is clearly a model of success (see Deissinger 2004, 82): The completion rate in 2005 was at 85.3 percent.[42] Around 50 percent of all people under 22 years old have finished an apprenticeship. This is an interesting figure, as it stands in sharp contrast to the English completion rates of Modern Apprenticeships (completion rates in England are around 53 percent; Learning and Council, 2007, table 7). Even though the number of openings have been declining since the beginning of the '90s, as of 2004 the system still provides around 43 percent of school leavers with a vocational education (Baethge, 2007, 44; BMBF, 2006, 3, 20). This share includes 14 percent of students with a higher secondary school education, which would also allow for university entrance.

Full-time vocational school programmes and the transition system
First of all, we need to sharply distinguish between two broad types of school-based vocational education programmes. On the one hand, there are programmes offering courses for occupations which the dual system does not cover. This applies mainly to the traditionally women-dominated occupations in the health and care sector. Normally these school-based programmes are to be accompanied by internships as a substitute for the on-the-job component of the dual system.

On the other hand, however, there are programmes in the so-called transition system, which is mainly for those people who have not been successful

---

[41]The duality of learning sites has, moreover, led to an odd situation: whereas the on-the-job component was regulated on the federal level (since 1969 by law) and run by the social partners through self-administration, the vocational school component, being affiliated to school education, was under the ambit of the Länder. Consequently, an apprentice has two legal statuses: s/he has a civil law claim as an employee, and a public law claim as a pupil. As will be clear later on, this "duality of claims" is a major difference between the school-based vocational education and the putative emulation of the English modern apprenticeship scheme.
[42]Federal Statistical Office Germany, http://www.destatis.de/basis/d/biwiku/beruftab10.php.

4.2 Vocational education and training

in finding an apprenticeship opening. The significance of these programmes is increasing.[43] As a trend, with the decline in apprenticeship openings in the dual system, full-time vocational schools have risen in importance as they (partly) offset and ameliorate a number of the deficiencies at the 'first threshold'. Practically speaking, one of the main functions of these full-time vocational school programmes is the 'parking function', i.e. providing young people intermediate courses until they are able to start an apprenticeship. This applies in particular to two subtypes of school-based vocational education and training, namely the vocational foundation year (Berufsgrundbildungsjahr) and the vocational preparation year (Berufsvorbereitungsjahr).

Both programmes are normally pursued by students who have not found a vocational education opportunity on the 'first training market'. The vocational preparation year is designed as a programme that is supposed to increase the 'trainability' of the student and is meant to facilitate the search for an apprenticeship opening. The vocational foundation year is also aimed at unlucky training-seekers, and not just the more talented ones. This year – given that it is accepted in a particular occupational field by the chambers and given that an employer is willing to recruit a graduate from this programme – may be accredited as the first year of a regular dual apprenticeship.

The vocational foundation year, vocational preparation courses, and ordinary vocational schools clearly illustrate the dependence of the German vocational education and training system on the dual apprenticeship-"gold standard". The first two programmes provide courses for students who are not yet ready to take up an apprenticeship. These courses clearly aim to integrate their students into the regular first training market.

4.2.2.3 Reforms in the German vocational education and training system

Various measures have been undertaken to strengthen the dual system. Broadly speaking there are two main challenges to which the dual apprenticeship system is exposed: recruitment problems on the one hand (mainly due to a lack of apprenticeship openings and a putative lack of 'trainability') and problems with its design as such on the other. Since the first aspect will be further analysed in more detail in the reform chapter, the second issue shall be stressed here.

---

[43]Even though in 2003 only 700,000 out of 2.7 million students attending non-academic vocational courses were enrolled in a full-time vocational school (Deissinger and Hellwig, 2004, 161), the significance of this alternative to a dual apprenticeship has gradually become more important. The number of full-time vocational school students increased dramatically between 1993 and 2001 from 363,351 to 541,676 (Deissinger, 2004, 82).

What was once considered as the largest advantage of the apprenticeship system, namely its application of 'vocationalism' as its underpinning principle, has increasingly turned out to be a hindrance, particularly in new occupational areas. The concentration on entire occupations, rather than on separate and accumulated (on a modular basis) competencies, causes a constant need and pressure to adapt to new economic environments and occupational circumstances. This adaptation process is regulated by the Federal Institute for Vocational Education and Training in collaboration with the social partners.

Apart from the fact that flexible and spontaneous new-orientations and developments are difficult to implement,[44] the focus on 'vocationalism' does not allow for interfaces between different occupations or for an easy re-arrangement of knowledge from different occupations. Moreover, in recent years there has been an employer demand for more broadly-based training and for a greater concentration on sequential processes rather than on the subject-separated lessons of vocational schools (Steedman, 2005, 20). One answer was the introduction of the so-called 'Lernfeldkonzept', allowing for a more process-oriented mode of teaching in vocational schools. However, wholesale reorganisations of entire training and work systems to shift the focus to processes rather than mere occupation based actions are difficult to attain in a system such as the German one (Misko, 2006, 15).

Furthermore, putting the focus on the achievement of a particular occupation which – in theory – prepares the pupil for lifelong employability in this occupation is hardly reconcilable with the seemingly omnipresent discussion about lifelong learning and the idea that sustainable employability is attainable only through constant lifelong further training. Indeed, as research shows, despite the good initial vocational education, further vocational education in Germany is relatively underdeveloped in comparison to England and other European countries (Misko, 2006).

Moreover, the federal government has undertaken initiatives in order to encourage employers to recruit more trainees. After the legislative proposal for a 'training levy'[45] failed in the second chamber, the government has since followed a strategy to promote, support, and increase employers' voluntary engagement.

The so-called 'Training Pact' (Ausbildungspakt) between the federal government and business and industry associations in 2004 most clearly reflects these kinds of efforts.[46] Business and industry agreed to provide 25,000 additional long-term internships per year as well as 30,000 additional new

---

[44]See Federal Ministry of Education and Research, http://www.bmbf.de/de/1644.php.
[45]Ausbildungsplatzabgabe; a contribution payable by those employers who are capable but not willing to engage in the dual system
[46]Federal Ministry of Education and Research, http://www.bmbf.de/pub/ausbildungspakt_2004.pdf.

4.2 Vocational education and training

apprenticeship openings. Even though these targets are not binding, the sword of Damocles in the form of a training levy exerts some soft pressure on business and industry to adhere to the agreement. The 'Training Pact' is supposed to stimulate and trigger a collective effort to solve the severest training market problems. The Pact was planned to run for three years but has since been prolonged to run until 2010. However, it has become clear that effects of the Pact, given there are any direct effects, are minimal.

The situation on the training market improved slightly in 2005/06. By September 2006 576,000 new apprenticeship-contracts were concluded, 26,500 more then in the previous year (Engelbrech and Ebner, 2006). Though the increase nearly matches the stipulations of the 'Training Pact' it is not clear whether this development was caused by the Pact or by the gradual economic recovery of Germany after some years of cyclical downturn. However, experts still speak of a lack of around 160,000 training places (Engelbrech and Ebner, 2006, 2). Still only approximately 23 percent of all firms and companies in Germany are engaged in the dual system. Simultaneously, more and more school leavers directly enter the labour market without any vocational education and/or training (the number of people in this group tripled between 1992 and 2005 from 23,300 to 82,600)[47] and demand for full-time vocational schools is increasing. Apart from this initiative which suspended the training levy, awareness-raising campaigns, often in form of advertisements, have been launched in order to reinforce the significance of the dual apprenticeship scheme and to convince employers of the importance and benefits of recruiting apprentices. In order to support employers, training place developers (Ausbildungsplatzentwickler) have been introduced as well as the so-called 'STARegio' programme, which focuses on regions where the supply-demand relationship is particularly unfavourable (Deissinger and Hellwig, 2004, 165; Deissinger, 2004, 88).[48]

Alternatives to the dual apprenticeship scheme have also been considered. Consequently, the state has become increasingly engaged in the vocational training area. This engagement is seen as a way to bypass the huge dependence of the dual apprenticeship scheme on the overall economic situation in Germany in general and from the economic situations of single branches in particular. Since the amendment of the Vocational Training Act of 2005 it has become possible for graduates of full-time vocational schools to get access to the chambers examinations and thus to attain a certified vocational qualification, which was previously reserved only for the dual system.[49] Thus, the link to employers as training providers in the dual scheme has been loosened (yet still

---
[47] Federal Institute for Vocational Education and Training, www.bibb.de/dokumente/pdf/Ab1104.pdf.
[48] See also Federal Institute for Vocational Education and Training, www.bibb.de/redaktion/staregio/.
[49] This reform will be further analysed in the reform chapter.

strong) and the competition for a training opening on the first training market has slightly eased.

As the principle of 'vocationalism' is quasi sacrosanct in Germany, efforts to provide alternatives have been incremental and cumbersome. The pursuance of the 'vocational principle' in German training and labour policy leads to stable occupational patterns in both the training and labour markets. This stability is conducive to transparency for employers, employees, and trainees. Transferability is, at least in theory, easy, as 'occupations' understood as certified qualifications are the major units that structure demand and supply on the labour market. This stability, however, comes at a price: namely inflexibility, which becomes even more glaring when considered in comparison to the English practice. Establishing new occupations, like i.e. in the IT trade, might absorb too much time and thereby lack the ability to respond to economic changes in general and the demand for specific occupational profiles in particular, as even the Federal Ministry of Education and Research has noted.[50]

The 'modularisation' of vocational education and training is considered as the way out of the above discussed dilemma. Although there are different ways to 'modularise' vocational education and training (Ertl, 2002, 57 ff.; Deissinger, 2004, 91 f.), 'modularisation' commonly refers to the introduction of vocational education and training building blocks rather than entire occupation frameworks. 'Modularisation' serves the following purposes: firstly, it facilitates the quick adaptation to changing work environments; secondly, it fosters a greater individualisation of vocational education and training pathways and hence takes into account personal potentials, aptitudes, and already attained experiences; and thirdly it allows for a greater portability of qualifications between different vocational education and training pathways (Deissinger and Hellwig, 2004, 167). Steps in this direction have so far been modest and cautious. Given, however, the difficulties in decision making due to the involvement of numerous actors, and given the still deep belief in the dual apprenticeship system and the 'vocational principle', the steps taken towards 'modularisation' are nevertheless remarkable. There are ongoing attempts to break up the concept of 'mono occupations' and to instead pool occupations that have related training schemes (Deissinger, 2004, 90; Misko, 2006, 21).

Consequently, in a few occupational areas (IT trade, office and communication clerk) key qualifications are being taught that are at a latter stage of the apprenticeship complemented with compulsory elective courses (Deissinger, 2004, 90). Thereby, apprenticeships become more adaptive and individualised while apprentices still attain the occupational degree (Deissinger,

---

[50] Federal Ministry of Education and Research, http://www.bmbf.de/de/1644.php.

2004, 91). In order to provide for transparency in an emerging system in which modules play a greater role, the Federal Ministry of Education and Research announced in its Vocational Training Report its intention to introduce a uniform certification and qualification framework throughout Germany (Deissinger and Hellwig, 2004, 167). This has not yet been put into practice. Hence, the route towards 'modularisation' has also been propelled by the attempt to increase the portability of qualifications across German borders and to facilitate the opportunity for trainees to undergo part of their vocational education and training abroad (Deissinger and Hellwig, 2004, 168).[51]

4.2.2.4 Main features of the German vocational education and training system

The German vocational education and training system revolves around the dual apprenticeship scheme. The imbalance of supply and demand on the training and labour market and a rapidly changing occupational environment, however, have prompted the government to take considerations and actions that go beyond two of its main characteristics: its strict confinement to clearly defined single-occupations (in the literature also called the German "concept of vocation", see Ertl, 2002, 57), and its reliance on employers for the conduct of the on-the-job component of the dual system. The cautious introduction of modular elements is not tantamount to a total deviation from 'vocationalism', yet it indicates attempts to combine the German "concept of vocation" with a few competence- and modular-based elements.

Meanwhile, we are also witnessing efforts to uphold the system 'as we know it'. As Deissinger (2004, 78) puts it, the "reliable participation of firms is one of the key requirements for the successful working of vocational training." This participation is gradually diminishing as more and more employers hesitate to take on trainees, justified mainly with reference to the high expenditures for training. Consequently, only about 23 percent of German firms and companies have been engaged in the dual apprenticeship scheme in recent years.

The state has tried to offset this shortage through a greater involvement in the training process. Moreover, as a consequence of the shortage of training places the school-based vocational education and training sector is expanding, pathways for further education have become more numerous, and cooperation with external training providers has been intensified, without, however, deviating

---

[51]As to the internationalisation of VET, it will be interesting to observe the influence of the discussion about a 'European Qualifications Framework', as agreed upon in the Copenhagen declaration of 2002, on the German dual apprenticeship scheme. This issue will be elaborated upon further later in this research. As a first reference see Meyer, 2006.

from the basic concept of occupations. 'Vocationalism' and the participation of employers in the training process remain the cornerstones of the German vocational education and training. Recent developments, however, show that two cornerstones do not seem to suffice to maintain the German vocational education and training area in these times. Therefore they have been complemented in recent years by at least two further cornerstones, namely the modularisation (and a more competence-orientation) of vocational education and training schemes and the increasing significance of state involvement in vocational training.

4.2.3 Comparing both vocational education and training systems

We can ascertain from the above discussion that the English and German vocational education and training systems have some major differences. Crucial for understanding these differences in the vocational education and training systems is the distinction between the occupational-orientation in Germany versus the English competence-based output-orientation.

The typology developed by Maurice, Sellier and Silvestre, in which the German structure ranks as a "qualificational space" and the French as an "organisational space," helps us in understanding also the differences between Germany and England (Maurice, Sellier and Silvestre, 1986). In a qualificational space vocational education is of great significance for labour mobility, as attained qualifications, as in "occupations", are the main criteria for recruiting and promoting employees. The concentration on occupations as "qualificational regimes" (Steinmann, 1999) comes along with standardisation and vocational specificity (Maurice, Sellier and Silvestre, 1986; Müller and Shavit, 1998, 4). The demand and supply on the labour market revolve around occupations, which provide indications as to how the labour market is arranged and segmented. These labour markets, called occupational labour markets (OLM) – as is the German one – are less dependent on internal business structures than internal labour markets (ILM). In OLM it is the certified occupational qualification that counts (Brzinsky-Fay, 2006, 3f.).[52]

In an organisational mobility space – such as the English one – the link between vocational education and occupational opportunities is looser. What counts here, in particular, is work-based knowledge and on-the-job experiences.

---

[52]Fascinatingly, directly related to the chapter about the country-choice for this research, the particular structure of the transformation from school/vocational education to work seem to allow for inferences to entire political economies (and vice versa), as specific features of this transition tend to be more likely in political economies with a focus on specific modes of coordination and cooperation than in others (Hannan, Raffe and Smyth, 1996; Estevez-Abe, Iversen and Soskice, 2001).

Furthermore, the specific organisational recruitment and promotion structure of firms and companies is extremely relevant (Müller and Shavit, 1998, 4; Allmendinger, 1989, 249).

The distinction mentioned earlier between vocational-based and competence-based vocational education systems is the logical further development of the Maurice et al. typology, with a greater focus on the generation of vocational education. An apprenticeship in Germany leads to an officially recognised vocational degree, certified by the Chambers and the state.[53] It is not competences or skills that are the major outcome of the German dual apprenticeship system but vocations (Berufe) which people attain and which allow them to work as a recognised clerk or craftsman.[54] It is exactly this mechanism, based on the "concept of the vocation" (Ertl, 2002, 57), which is the core of the German "vocational principle" (Hellwig, 2005, 2). This has major implications for the structure of the labour market: employees with certified occupations are those which are in demand. At this point we see the deeper meaning of the notion of "qualificational mobility space" as coined by Maurice et al.: firstly, there is a clear link between the vocational qualification and its usability on the labour market (Müller and Shavit, 1998, 4). The certified occupation is the crucial information for employers who intend to recruit staff. Of course personal competences and work experiences play a role as well, but a secondary role to the qualification.

The concentration on the occupation (vocation) as the decisive information is possible because, secondly, the degree of standardisation in the vocational area in Germany is high, not just in terms of qualifications but also in terms of pathways and curricula that every trainee has to pass through (Hellwig, 2005, 2).[55]

Thirdly, binding professional standards ensure the transferability of qualifications to a labour market that is highly occupationally structured. Moreover, certified occupations account for the classification of the wage system and for affiliations and eligibility in the German social security system. As we witness in Germany, a high degree of occupational specificity and occupational segmentation of the labour market induces societal stratification, as the occupation to a large extent determines status and identity (Ertl, 2002, 57). Although the academic route is reserved for high achievers at school, which

---

[53]Recently, there are around 350 certified occupations in Germany, such as Doctor's Assistant, Banker, Dispensing Optician or Oven Builder, subdivided into seven business and industry sectors.
[54]These are so-called 'apprenticeship occupations' (Ausbildungsberufe). Only those who have finished an apprenticeship are allowed to call themselves as belonging to a particular occupation.
[55]The legal frameworks for the apprenticeships in Germany comprise regulations for duration, remuneration, balance between on-the-job and off-the-job education, and length of working days.

consequently leads to an accumulation of low school achievers in vocational education and training, the dual apprenticeship and the students who pass it enjoy a good standing. This is reflected by comparably high participation and completions figures on the one hand and relatively high degrees of employer commitment to the dual apprenticeship scheme on the other hand, especially as compared to England.[56] Thus, it comes as no real surprise that the occupation is the main and most important information about a person in the German world of vocational education and employment.

England, by contrast, follows a different strategy, one that is competence-based and output-oriented. Again, referring to the concept of standardisation, two aspects have to be mentioned in the English case: first of all, there is no coherent standardised pathway that leads to a qualification/occupation; secondly, however, the qualifications themselves are standardised through the National Qualification Framework (NQF). Thus, there is an area of tension in English vocational education and training between heterogeneous educational requirements and a homogeneous qualification approach (Deissinger, 2002, 32 f.). The coupling between vocational education and training and the labour market is loose, not least because of the low employer commitment. Here firm internal labour market structures prevail because of the low degree of work-related training in the educational system.

The standardisation of qualifications by means of the NQF, however, results in a confusing situation. As Deissinger says:

> "The national qualifications framework is clearly a hotchpotch of disjointed approaches, despite the fact that its stated purpose is to integrate and to promote transfer between different education and training paths and to create (formal) equality among qualifications on the same level." (Deissinger, 2002, 32; in the same vein Ertl, 2002, 64)

This quotation indicates that 'standardisation' not only refers to the nationwide similarity of each particular qualification. Moreover, 'standardisation' is understood as means for transparency, putting qualifications in a parsimonious recognition-framework that allows for easy comparisons and a comprehensive overview. The English National Qualifications Framework seems too complex in this regard.

The rather opaque qualification scene in England (Modern Apprenticeships

---

[56]The real dividing line in Germany is not between those pursuing the academic and those pursuing the vocational route (as the literature suggests for England; that is what the notion 'parity of esteem' stands for), but between those who have an acknowledged training after compulsory schooling and those who do not. This is the case because the transition to employment in an occupational system is mostly based on the condition of having accomplished an apprenticeship.

can be considered as a first attempt to pool different qualifications into one framework) nonetheless has a major advantage: its modularisation and output orientation. A qualification, as for example a National Vocational Qualification (NVQ), in a particular occupational field consists of different modules that can be learnt and assessed separately. The accumulation of these modules ultimately leads to a qualification in a specific occupational field which can easily be complemented with other qualifications. The way these qualifications were attained plays a subordinated role: whether the person obtains the knowledge and aptitudes in ordinary schools, further education colleges, or in the parents' business, is not of relevance. This approach is strictly output-oriented because only the output is stipulated, not the route to its attainment.

As a consequence, individualised vocational education paths are possible to an extent which they are not in Germany. In Germany standardisation comes at the price of inflexibility because individualised paths are not possible, trainees with good aptitudes and experiences still have to pass through an official educational path in order to be eligible for the chamber exams.

Therefore the English approach is fundamentally different from the German "vocationalism" in which the passing of a collectively fixed training and learning plan is a constitutive component of the occupational degree. English Modern Apprenticeships represent exactly the attempt to give the accumulation of qualifications a common framework. Thus, the equivalent for the English way of modularisation, competence-basis and output-orientation is for the German vocational education and training area the focus on occupations with fixed frameworks and its learning and training pathway orientation.

The concept of standardisation highlights yet another crucial feature which distinguishes the two systems: no matter whether we find standardisation in terms of qualifications or standardisation of pathways which lead to these qualifications, this still does not reveal the usability of these qualifications on the labour market. Therefore, qualifications need to be acknowledged in a recognised framework in order to make different sets and accumulations of qualifications comparable. Consequently, when we talk about standardisation of educational measures we have to consider three aspects: firstly, whether there are common educational pathways; secondly, the way in which the output of qualifications is structured; and thirdly – and this aspect has not yet been taken explicitly into account – how qualifications are embedded in a commonly accepted and recognised 'acknowledgement grid' that allows people to classify them according to their significance and value.

One decisive aspect in this respect is the involvement of employers. This reveals another particular feature of English Modern Apprenticeships that stands in stark contrast to the Germany system. Steedman provides a typology in arguing that differences in system structures can be understood as a function of how systems rely on employer commitment (Steedman, 2005, 5 ff.). She distinguishes between systems that are demand-led and those which are supply-led. According to this typology, demand-led apprenticeships are characterised by high employer commitment. Training places are a function of employers' supply, thus employer demand apprentices. As a consequence the training market is determined by the willingness of employers to provide training places. Germany is an example of this pattern. The situation in England is different. In the past the English traditional apprenticeships were demand-led as well (Fuller and Unwin, 2003a, 9). Today, however, we see a system in which training places are offered mostly because training providers approach employers and ask for openings. Thus, employer (self-) commitment is low, a fact that indicates England belongs to the supply-led apprenticeship group (Steedman, 2005, 7).

In the sections above another sharp distinction between both systems became clear: the German dual apprenticeship scheme was and still is a unique educational path, a path of its own which is not integrated into but is instead separated from full-time education. In order to increase the inducement for putative trainees as much as possible, England, by contrast, allowed the apprenticeship system to be integrated into the full-time education structures and, thereby, allow for a greater permeability between different paths (ensuring entrance qualifications for tertiary education, yet with all the drawbacks this might have for the supply-demand relationship; Steedman, 2005, 6 f.)[57]

Yet, in comparison to Germany, Modern Apprenticeships have thus far not become that popular. Furthermore, and again in contrast to Germany, England lacks a stable vocational education pattern that delineates the sector and has not yet developed an independent vocational training subsystem (Deissinger, 2002, 32). With reference to Tomlinson, who says that the English A-level is perceived as the educational "gold standard", England lacks such a standard in vocational education, one which Germany clearly has in its dual apprenticeship system (Tomlinson, 2003, 202).

The starting point of both countries' vocational education and training systems is very different. In the literature both the English and the German vocational education and training systems are often used to create typologies – serving as opposite poles. The German 'vocational principle' and England's output-orientation seem to be irreconcilable. Yet, the miserable situation in the training and labour market in both countries has led to considerations which have been unheard of in the older traditions of the systems: the recent English Modern

---

[57] The indicator 'separation/integration of apprenticeships into full-time education structures' together with the indicator of 'employer commitment' further underpins Steedman's typology (Steedman, 2005, 5 ff.; Deissinger, 2002).

4.2 Vocational education and training

Apprenticeship scheme and its combination of on-the-job, off-the-job, and general skills training resembles the German apprenticeship scheme. It is as obvious attempt in English educational policy to pursue a 'vocationalisation' approach – thus following a principle around which the German vocational education and training system has traditionally revolved (Deissinger, 2002, 32).

The main difference in this respect has been the high employer commitment. Though stronger than in England, the need to install more school-based vocational education and training in Germany reflects the fact that employer commitment is shrinking. Since commitment is declining and the demand for work-based vocational education and training outnumbers the supply, the German government is attempting to increase school-based vocational education and training offers, thus rendering the system less dependent on cooperation with employers. Consequently, Germany is suffering from a supply problem for apprenticeships whereas England is suffering also from a demand problem, as the Modern Apprenticeship scheme has massive problems attracting good-calibre students, which leads to large reputational issues. In terms of Steedman's typology, both vocational education and training systems are attempting to maintain/increase employer commitment and build demand-led apprenticeship systems (Steedman, 2005, 5 ff.). Nevertheless, both have to offset the decrease/insufficiently quick increase in employer commitment with school-based vocational education and training. As a consequence, one notices similar problems in both countries concerning the role and the contribution of employers to vocational education and training.

In another aspect both systems were also originally distinct, namely in the degree of state-involvement. The German apprenticeship scheme is managed mainly by the social partners; state involvement is rare. In England, by comparison, state involvement is ubiquitous as school-based vocational programmes and Modern Apprenticeships are basically state-run. Some scholars (Deissinger, 2002, 31; Ertl, 2002, 171) see in the English approach to vocational training an essential feature of the Thatcher government, namely that "Modern Apprenticeships are co-financed by the public sector, making them a 'State initiative for revitalising the training system'".

What we witness in Germany, however, is in its basic approach not so fundamentally different. The crisis in the dual apprenticeship system was not solved outside the public sector by the social partners (a training levy would have brought a financial incentive for employers to engage apprentices) but has been tackled from inside, in particular through the extension of non-work-based options.

Summing up, both systems are changing and try (in the case of England) or feel forced (in the German case) to deviate from their traditional paths. That is not to say that both systems have become alike; they still show remarkable differences. However, as Deissinger and Hellwig put it from a German perspective: "the nature of the reform debate shows parallels to reforms in Anglophone countries" (Deissinger and Hellwig, 2004, 160). Moreover, the reform steps undertaken seem to indicate a development on two levels: we either see a move of one system in a direction that was traditionally associated with the other system, or a move towards each other as they adopt various features from one another, which simultaneously leads to internal diversification at the national level. This does not tell us anything, however, about how these reforms respond to other institutions in a given political economy and whether they are successful in achieving the desired aims. This will be the subject of a detailed policy evaluation at a later stage of this book.

4.3 Higher education

Innovative research systems and well-working teaching structures are not only very prestigious; they also generate highly skilled individuals. As the government papers will show later, having abundant highly skilled labour is considered to be conducive to a high skill economy with low unemployment rates, and to an economy which can successfully compete on international markets and thereby produce greater wealth for all, including the lower educated people. Liefner et al. put it in the following words:

> "A society's economic competitiveness is dependent on the performance of its higher education institutions." (Liefner, Schätzl and Schröder, 2004, 23)

Therefore, and this is a great similarity between England and Germany, both countries actively and extensively consider and engage in this area; and this is also why in both countries the higher education systems have been the subject of many reforms and changes.

Yet, the distinction offered by the political economy literature between general and specific skills – the former supposedly prevailing in England and the latter in Germany – does not appear to be appropriate for understanding developments in higher education. However, the concepts of stratification (Allmendinger, 1989, 233) and marketisation are applicable (Hartwig, 2004) as a means to detect differences and developments in the two higher education systems. Both concepts seem to be somehow two sides of the same coin: the stratification among higher education institutions (the term "Oxbridge" exemplifying this characteristic) in England coincides with market measures introduced in part to cope with the differences in demand for study-places due to the imbalance in esteem. In Germany, by contrast, clear "beacon-universities" do not so far exist, and market elements have been slow in coming. The concluding section will shed light on these issues in further detail.

4.3.1 England

4.3.1.1 Brief historical review of the English higher education system

Higher education is considered to be the most prestigious educational path in most countries, as it is in England and Germany. The 'real value' of higher education, or even more precisely of academic and scientific-oriented higher education, can be revealed by comparing it with vocational education and vocational-based higher education.

In Germany vocational education in the form of dual apprenticeships is highly regarded, as is higher education. In England, however, higher education far more prestigious relative to vocational education and is clearly the path most school leavers want to pursue. This is due to the tradition of English higher education.

Immediately after the Second World War English government reports commented on the need to expand higher education (Pratt, 1992, 31). Expansion, however, was conducted mainly via the same methods as in the pre-war period, namely by expanding technical colleges rather than the prestigious universities. The expansion of economically relevant higher education was considered to be necessary, however, universities were reluctant to offer these studies and they retained exclusive degree-awarding power. Even though initiatives were undertaken (introduction of colleges of advanced technologies that awarded a Diploma in Technology, which was not a degree only in name) the need to expand remained up through 1960 when the government commissioned Lord Robbins to review the higher education system in England. The report was published in 1963 and took the position that higher education should be available to all those who are qualified (Pratt, 1992, 33). Though this is the liberal approach to higher education that still today dominates, Robbins championed expansion from a clearly stratified perspective in which traditional universities could preserve their top position in terms of reputation and quality. Yet in the aftermath of this report several prestigious universities were founded, including Stirling, Essex, Sussex and Warwick.

Nevertheless, the higher education area was and remained divided into universities on the one hand and technical colleges (later labelled 'polytechnics')

on the other. This structure is commonly called the "binary system" (see i.e. Pratt, 1992, 31). These colleges and polytechnics were not only different in terms of the courses they offered (vocational education instead of academic and theoretical studies); they differed also in the way they were governed (part of the public sector and thus under the ambit of local education authorities). Universities, by contrast, were "exclusive, selective, and autonomous" and concentrated on mainly the arts and humanities (Pratt, 1992, 31). In terms of extension, colleges and polytechnics were a success, nearly trebling their number of students from 100,000 at the end of the 1960s to around 280,000 at the end of the 1980s. At the same time extension rates among universities within the same period were comparably modest yet still remarkable: from 211,000 to 380,000 (Pratt, 1992, 34).

The Further and Higher Education Act in 1992 not only changed the funding structure of higher education, as each country in the UK was given its own funding council, but more importantly undertook the "unification" of the "binary system", hence the transformation of polytechnics into universities (among other things they gained degree-awarding powers). This marks one of the latest decisive structural changes from an elite university system to mass universities (Pratt, 1992, 42). Interestingly enough, though not formally regulated, the distinction between different esteems of universities in the English higher education area remains: research-intensive institutions with high reputations in academic teaching on the one hand and vocational-oriented former-polytechnics on the other. Thus, there is still a kind of stratification in England, even if on an informal level, with "Oxbridge" et al. still being the beacon-universities that students attempt to enter.

The Dearing report marks another influential review document for higher education in England (Dearing, 1997). Issued in 1997, this report decisively paves the way for what was later to be known as foundation degrees. Striving for the target of a 45 percent participation rate by young people in higher education, the Dearing Committee argued in favour of further expanding the sub-degree level. As the name, however, implies, the initiative by the government does lead to a degree, namely foundation degree. Moreover, the Dearing report advocates levying tuition fees, which were introduced soon afterwards in 1998, even though New Labour had consistently opposed tuition fees in the pre-election campaign (Tomlinson, 2005, 155).

4.3.1.2 Structure of the English higher education system

The higher education system in England is subdivided mainly into universities, higher education colleges, and a very small number of private colleges that account for only around 0.3-0.5 percent of all higher education students and which are therefore negligible in this analysis. With the reforms of 1992 polytechnics were converted into universities. Thus under the label 'university' we encounter many different programmes, ranging from purely academic subjects to clearly vocational education-oriented programmes. In general the central government in London is responsible for legislation on higher education.[58] Three levels are responsible for the governance of higher education: the Department for Innovation, Universities and Skills (DIUS) (until 2007 the Department for Education and Skills, DfES), the Higher Education Funding Council for England (HEFCE), and the higher education institutions themselves. The DIUS decides upon the main guidelines for higher education (e.g. how to allocate funding, introduction of tuition fees) and the global expenditures. There are, however, many issues which the department is not allowed to be involved in: the direct allocation of funding to single universities; the academic programmes of universities; recruitment and other personal decisions including salaries; and the admission of students.

In general, the higher education entrance qualification is the A-level. Yet A-levels can be bypassed, for instance by people who finished an apprenticeship and want to attain a foundation degree. As higher education institutions are autonomous bodies, each institution determines its own admission criteria. The admission procedure is competitive. The Quality Assurance Agency has developed a qualification framework for higher education in England, starting with the certificate level (Certificates of Higher Education), then the intermediate level (e.g. Diplomas of Higher Education and foundation degrees), the honours level (bachelors), the masters level (masters and other postgraduate certificates), and the doctoral level (doctorates) (compare with Clark, 2006, 22). The most important threshold is the one between the intermediate and honours level, as the bachelor degree (the lowest degree at the honours level) is the traditional undergraduate degree.

Degrees are awarded by individual institutions. Degrees attained at institutions with no degree-awarding power have to be validated either by

---

[58]Scotland is presently able to regulate this sector autonomously (general taxation and allocations of public spending for the four countries remain in the ambit of the UK government) whereas Wales and Northern Ireland possess fewer independent competencies in this area. The reforms in 1992 led to the division of the UK-wide funding councils into three councils, i.e. since then Scotland and Wales fund their higher education system separately from England and Northern Ireland.

external bodies or through co-operation with a degree-awarding higher education institution, as is done with foundation degrees.

In the 19th century higher education was by and large a private endeavour. However, over the course of the 20th century higher education institutions became dependant on the state, in particular with respect to their revenues, and they are therefore considered to be public. Yet, higher education institutions are legally independent, autonomous, self-governing bodies and hence able to independent decide many significant issues, for instance regarding their admission policy, the teaching-research nexus and tuition fees.

Funding is administered by the Higher Education Funding Council for England (HEFCE). It distributes the financial resources that it receives from the British government to each single institute. Higher education institutions are given a block grant which consists of two components, a fund for teaching and a fund for research. The fund for teaching takes into account – apart from some basic maintenance allocations – the number of students enrolled in an institution and the tuition fees raised by the institutions. Since its introduction in 1986 the research assessment exercise (RAE) has been the measure for calculating the funding for research. Since then, funding to universities is to a large extent co-determined by their academic performance (Clark, 2006, 45).

Research infrastructure In the UK (hence also in England) research activities are carried out in four different sectors: the business enterprise sector, the higher education sector, the government sector, and the private non-profit sector. In 2004 the first sector alone spent almost two-thirds (65.7 percent) of the Gross Domestic Expenditure on Research and Development. Higher education institutions account for 21.4 percent and Government expenditure for 9.7 percent (Clark, 2006).

As opposed to HEFCE-funding, direct governmental expenditure on research is even more selective and is granted by the Research Councils (of which there are eight). Funds by the Research Councils are awarded to specific researchers or groups of researchers who apply with a detailed research proposal. Thus, the dual support system in England consists of block grants allocated by the HEFCE in order to maintain and develop research infrastructure and of special grants by the Research Councils for particular programmes and projects.

A trend shows that there is an ongoing specialisation between those institutions which focus their endeavours on teaching and those which maintain a larger research infrastructure (Clark, 2006, 38).

Meanwhile, there is a third stream of funding intended to promote the transfer of knowledge. This stream was initially championed by the Lambert Review, which was commissioned by the government to explore new ways of business-university collaboration. To date 22 Centres for Knowledge Exchange

4.3 Higher education

(CKEs) have been established with funding by the HEFCE. These Centres are found in universities and provide "shared services for business and community partners".[59]

4.3.1.3 Reforms in the English higher education system

The concept of "expansion" dominates the higher education scene. The introduction of tuition fees was seen as an additional way to increase revenues. Initially introduced and capped at £1,000 in 1998, tuition fees for full-time home undergraduates, to be paid by students or their parents, were soon raised to £3,000 by 2006. The threshold of £3,000 is being fully exploited by nearly all higher education institutions. Tuition fees for overseas students are normally considerably higher. Coincidentally, public funding per student has fallen (Clark, 2006, 60). Various initiatives have been implemented to tackle the propensity to gradually phase-out student from lower income households, including maintenance grants of up to £2,700 for this group of students and an Office for Fair Access (OFFA) whose mission is to ameliorate the worst effects of tuition fees.

The introduction of foundation degrees (see reform chapter) was primarily intended to increase higher education participation rates. For Germany, the Bologna process poses a great number of problems. The situation in England is fundamentally different. The framework of three consecutive cycles of higher education qualifications (bachelor, master, PhD) is basically modelled on the English (UK) system.

4.3.1.4 Main features of the English HE system

Again referring to the notion of the "gold standard", in English higher education this is clearly associated with honours degrees. Attempts to alter the qualification structure have spared the honours degrees, as will be discussed in depth in the reform chapter. Thus, all qualifications are measured against these honour degrees. However, stratification exists also in another context: the reputation of a university that a graduate comes from still determines to a large extent the value of a degree on the labour market. As a rule of thumb, the former polytechnics have not yet been able to penetrate into the phalanx of the traditional universities with respect to this "esteem-competition". The end of the so-called "binary-

---

[59]Compare with: http://www.hefce.ac.uk/reachout/heif/centres/.

system" between polytechnics and universities further propelled the expansion of higher education. Marketisation plays a bigger role in England than it does for Germany: the Research Assessment Exercise and the competition for students, especially among the teaching-intensive higher education institutions, exemplify this aspect.

Presently, higher education in England is not only in demand because of its teaching and research standards and performances, or because of the government's intention to achieve a 50 percent youth participation rate in higher education by 2010 (Machin and Vignoles, 2006, 15). Moreover, it is because England lacks an accepted and well-regarded vocational education route that higher education is seen as even more attractive.

4.3.2 Germany

4.3.2.1 Brief historical review of the German higher education system

Similar to school education, since the foundation of the German Federal Republic higher education has been under the ambit of the Länder. Furthermore, again analogous to school education, higher education was not reformed and reshaped entirely after the Second World War but was modelled after the system used during the Weimar Republic (Führ and Furck, 1998, 413 ff.). This development was driven by the conviction that the system as such was worth maintaining. In reaction to their ideological subordination between 1933 and 1945, higher education institutions were constitutionally guaranteed freedom in research and teaching.

Furthermore, higher education regulations ensured high degrees of autonomy expressed through self-administration. In the 1950s the baby boom-age cohort of the early 1930s arrived in higher education institutions. The increased demand for higher education (although at the beginning of the 1950s the share of any one age-group with a university entrance qualification was only around 5 percent) led to an expansion of higher education institutions all over Western Germany. The foundation of the science council (Wissenschaftsrat) in 1957 was of prime importance for the extension and planning of higher education (Führ and Furck, 1998, 415). This common advisory board of the Bund and the Länder, with the cooperation of scientists and researchers, decisively promoted the expansion, leading to a doubling of teaching capacity by the end of the 1960s.

Since the end of the 1960s another trend has been to integrate engineering schools and higher technical schools into the higher education sector as universities of applied science (Fachhochschulen). Today, universities of applied science teach theoretical skills and their application in the occupational world, whereas universities are concentrated on a theoretical and abstract comprehension of subjects.

The German higher education system has been challenged in many ways. The number of students doubled between 1970 and 1990; between 1980 and 2000 the number increased from 1.36 million to 1.8 million just in the West-Länder (Hartwig, 2004), whereas the available resources remained by and large the same (Küpper, 2002, 5). In Germany we observe the peculiar situation of a massive student expansion, on the one hand, with all the facility and resource problems this causes, while, on the other, Germany's overall participation rates in higher education are, according to the OECD, moderate in comparison to other European countries (36.6 percent and thus well below the OECD average of 54 percent, OECD, 2007, 280). This situation has created a growing demand for higher education from both school leavers and employers.

In 2006 the so-called federalism reform led to an amendment of the Basic Law that had huge impacts on higher education. First, however, it makes sense to review the situation before the implementation of this, the biggest constitutional amendment in the history of the German Grundgesetz. Initially in 1949, responsibilities for education (school education and higher education) were exclusively conferred on the Länder. The expansion of education along with an increase in costs for education led to the involvement of the Bund in higher education by means of two legal instruments, the constitutionally guaranteed financial support for the creation and expansion of higher education facilities (Art. 91a and 91b GG) and the German Framework Act in Higher Education (Hochschulrahmengesetz). The aim of the Framework Act was to maintain homogeneity among the states in some core areas. This act regulated the tasks of universities, access to universities, and the organisation and administration of universities. Within this already very detailed framework the Länder operated and regulated higher education through even further and more detailed legal provisions (Hüfner, 2003, 149).

4.3.2.2 Structure of the German HE system

Two types of higher education institutions can be found on the German higher education landscape: universities and, since the 1970s, universities of applied science (Fachhochschulen).[60] Generally speaking, universities offer the

---

[60] Beside these two main types there are two other higher education institutions which should be mentioned. Berufsakademien are found only in seven Länder, however, they play an important role in

traditional academic portfolio of subjects, from the humanities and social sciences to medicine and the sciences. The Fachhochschulen are normally concentrated on one or a few subjects (colleges of art and music, technical colleges or ecclesiastical colleges) and provide more practical and occupation-relevant knowledge than do universities.

The range of subjects and the differences in degrees are, however, not the only differences between these two institutions; they also have different legal statuses and rights (Hüfner, 2003, 147). For students this means that they cannot embark on a PhD solely at a university of applied science, as these institutions have no doctoral-degree awarding power. This power remains exclusively with regular universities.

As a rule of thumb, the prerequisite for being admitted to universities is the general higher education entrance qualification, hence the Abitur (higher secondary school degree).[61] Access to some subjects (and not to universities as in England) is restricted and regulated by means of a numerus clauses, e.g. for subjects like medicine or architecture where applicants need to have attained a certain grade point average at their school-leaving qualification or a waiting period in order to be allowed to start the studies.

The higher education system in Germany was for a long time characterised by an absence of fees. This has recently changed. As a way to increase revenues and to restrict the number of so-called long-term students, and in order to reduce the overall duration of study, most of the Länder have introduced tuition fees. Until recently, students could attain three different types of degrees at universities: the "Diplom" degree; the "Magister" degree; and state examinations. The latter type of degree is available only in few subjects, such as law, medical science and teaching. Here it is not the university that conducts the examinations but the state, i.e. the relevant ministries of the Länder. The reason for the special treatment of these subjects lies in their high public relevance and interests, which thus requires standardisation and impartiality. In universities of applied science students obtain a "Diplom" degree with the addition FH (Fachhoschschule;

---

particular in Baden-Württemberg from where this form spread into the six other Länder. Students in these Berufsakademien pursue occupation-integrated studies, i.e. they are engaged with an employer by whom they get paid and they work in the firm in order to get acquainted with the routines of the company. In addition they visit the Berufsakademie, where they receive teaching comparable to Fachhochschulen. As such the occupation-integrated study works like the dual apprenticeship on a more elaborate level. Secondly, there are a limited number of private universities, though these are (so far) of small significance to the overall German higher education scene (Hüfner, 2003, 153).

[61] Admission to universities of applied science is already possible after 12 years of schooling which is the so-called Fachhochschulreife (after 12 ascending years of schooling). Earlier admission to universities of applied science is also possible with the higher education entrance qualification restricted to a specified field of study (Fachgebundene Hochschulreife).

4.3 Higher education

university of applied science). Since the declaration of European ministers of education in 1999, the so-called Bologna process, bachelor and master degrees were introduced and have since become increasingly important and had a tremendous impact on the German higher education system. At first this two-track system was introduced in a trial format, but since 2002 it has been applied across the country.[62]

The higher education landscape of Germany is determined by the federal structure of the state. The federalism reform of 2006, which altered the competencies assigned to the Bund and Länder, had a significant impact on the governance of higher education. This amendment law reflects perfectly the conflict over competences between the Bund and the Länder. The responsibility for the organisation and administration of higher education institutions was given back to the Länder. Along with a strengthening of the professoriate in the university boards, intermediate examinations and pre-diplomas, bachelor and master degrees, and the Juniorprofessur-ship were introduced. Most prominently, the federal states are now allowed to levy study fees, though this is due not only to the 2006 reforms but also to a ruling by the Federal Constitutional Court.

Thus, Germany has seen a paradigm shift through the introduction of fees for public universities (although these are still relatively modest), and an increasing number of Länder are making use of these. Higher education was one of the most hotly debated issues in advance of the federalism reform. The first part of the reforms, which included the provisions on higher education, came into effect in 2006. However, higher education was only one of the topics that were a subject of the huge bargaining process over competences, a process which resulted in a remarkably increase in competences of the Länder. The competences of the federal level are now confined to access to and the qualifications of higher education. Therefore, the Bologna process is relatively easy to implement on this level. In addition, the Bund is still co-responsible for co-financing devices and facilities in cooperation with the relevant Land. In other words, the Bund has a 'right to pay'. Previously, common standards among qualifications had been guaranteed by the Framework Act in Higher Education (Hochschulrahmengesetz). However, since the federalism reform the Länder are in principle allowed to derogate from this Act. In this way, the German higher education system is both decentralised and centralised at the same time: decentralised regarding the nationwide situation, centralised with respect to each single Land. Yet, interestingly enough, these developments coincide with the

---

[62] At a first glance one might contend that the German qualifications system at universities is also two-tracked, with "Diplom" and "Magister" degrees. The main difference, however, exists in the fact that these degrees can be obtained independently from each other, whereas a master degree is the successive degree of a bachelor degree.

federal initiative to establish the so-called "initiative of excellence", which will be a subject of the reform chapter.

As a rule of thumb, the financing of the German higher education system is entirely borne by the Länder. Since the federalism reform the federal government no longer contributes to the expansion and construction of higher education institutions. The federal level directly contributes only to the area of science and research. Moreover, and despite federal financial support, research at higher education institutions has become increasingly dependent on third party funding (Hartwig, 2004, 5 f.), either from research supporting organisations (like the German Research Foundation) or from the economy. It is likely that tuition fees will become a very important revenue pillar for financing higher education in Germany, as they are in England, where fees account for nearly 18 percent of universities' income. However, thus far higher education is almost entirely financed by the public authorities.

Is it important to elaborate on research policy to understand higher education policy and reforms? It is, because traditionally teaching and research at German universities form a unity that is supposed to be mutually reinforcing, e.g. students profit from the research activities of higher education institutions and researchers profit from new innovative and inspiring students. This traditional bond has been increasingly weakened: bachelor degrees being non-research intensive degree. They thus represent a deviation from the policy of generating purely academic higher education degrees, as with the "Magister" and the "Diplom". Simultaneously, research in extra-university institutions has become increasingly important.

Research in Germany is performed in three sectors, by higher education institutions, private non-profit and non-education institutions, and industry and business. Most research at higher education institutions is carried out at universities; Fachhochschulen contribute only a small part. This university research includes most of the publicly financed R&D activities. Mainly large-scale projects that are difficult to integrate into the university framework are undertaken by private non-profit institutions.

The most prominent and famous private non-profit and non-education institutions in this sector are the Max Plank Gesellschaft (MPG), the Fraunhofer Gesellschaft (FhG), the Helmholtz Zentren (HGF), and the Wissenschaftsgemeinschaft Gottfried Wilhelm Leibniz (formerly BLE, Blaue Liste-Einrichtungen). Researchers in these institutions are often Professors at universities as well. Thus we can see a personal link between higher education and these research institutions. Broadly speaking, all these institutions are jointly financed by the Bund and the Länder.

Highly selective funding for excellent projects is carried out by the

Deustche Forschungsgesellschaft (DFG). In general, the German research system is highly decentralised and, to an extent, complex and even confusing. One contributing factor to this complicated picture is the federal structure in which the Bund has confined competencies in research and even so more in teaching issues. However, even at the federal level competencies are dispersed. Apart from the Federal Ministry for Education and Research (BMBF) the Federal Ministry of Economics and Technology also contributes to research efforts. That is why one has sharply to distinguish between research and teaching activities, which is quite a challenging task in the environment of a university where research and teaching activities easily intermingle. Another major complicating factor is the variety of intermediate bodies. The DFG, Science council (both are main actors for the initiative of excellence), and the BLK are only the most influential bodies to be listed here.

4.3.2.3 Reforms in the German higher education system

The Initiative for Excellence is supposed to promote higher education in general, but in fact it promotes research in and with universities above all. From 2006 to 2011 this programme is to be given €1,9 billion, of which the federal government will contribute 75 percent and the Länder 25 percent, as agreed upon in the Bund-Länder Commission for Educational Planning and Research Promotion (BLK) in 2005 (see further analysis in the reform chapter).

In terms of degrees, the co-called Bologna process marks a radical change for the German higher education landscape. Germany has committed itself to implementing these changes for the sake of an integrated European higher education area and comparability of higher education degrees. In Germany these changes are also driven by the hope that these will shorten the average study periods, which are being perceived as lasting too long in comparison to other OECD-countries. Most federal states plan to gradually phase out the old degrees (Magister, Diplom) and to completely substitute them with bachelor and master degrees by 2010. State exams, as used in medicine, law and teacher training are not being treated coherently: whereas future teachers are increasingly awarded the new degrees, future lawyers and medical practitioners still have to sit state exams.

The introduction of tuition fees for public universities marked the end of a (nearly) tuition fee-free higher education area. The federal framework legislation for higher education disallowed tuition fees. Half a dozen Länder sued the federal level for the introduction of fees and in 2005 the Federal Constitutional Court opened up the option for Länder to levy tuition fees. Up until now only half of the Länder have made use of this ruling in one form or another.[63] The following trend is visible: Länder in Eastern Germany and in those Länder in the West with governmental participation by the social democrats do not levy tuition fees (exceptions being Bremen for students who live outside Bremen and Saxony for students who attain a second degree). Among those Länder which already levy a tuition fee, the students who are most likely to be obliged to pay are those who study longer than the standard period of study. Thus, one initial purpose of the fees was to provide long-term students an incentive to quickly complete their studies. Now, however, tuition fees tend to be increasingly applied both countrywide and to all students.

Traditionally, line-item budgets have been the standard in higher education, i.e. every single cost of a higher institution has to be assessed before the budgeting period and the whole budget has to be negotiated between representatives of the institution and the relevant Länder ministries, which must subsequently be approved by the Länder parliament. Recently however, instead of applying this type of cameralistic accounting, higher education institutions have been given a lump-sum budget ("global budget"). The usage of this global budget is by and large left to the institutions' own devices. Thus, higher education institutions nowadays have the possibility of assigning expenditures more flexibly and, therefore, of gaining more competences. However, payroll costs are normally still borne by the Länder, as they are the employers of the civil servants employed at higher education institutions (professors, administrative staff, etc.).

On the selection of students, each university is legally bound to offer a place for a first degree to applicants with a higher education entrance qualification. Thus, selection is only carried out if the number of applicants countrywide exceeds the number of places available. The task of distributing these places according to objective criteria, like school finishing degrees or waiting periods (Wartesemester), is carried out by the central clearing house for places in degree programmes (Zentralstelle für die Vergabe von Studienplätzen, ZVS). This characteristic feature of the German higher education system is now being increasingly challenged from different sides, facilitated by the federalism reform that conferred broader competences to the Länder in higher education issues. The

---

[63]In fact, the regulations for tuition fees in the Länder are extremely diverse. Some raise no tuition fees at all and charge just a very moderate semester contribution, which is hardly more than a semester ticket for public transportation and a small administrative fee. Tuition fees are different from these contributions, firstly because they are considerably higher and are not earmarked. In some Länder the first course of studies is free of charge but for each successive course tuition fees are levied. In a few other Länder students are charged from their first university course onwards. Not only do the regulations vary; the amount of tuition fees also varies considerably, from zero in i.e. Berlin or Saxony up to €900 for a second course of study in Baden-Württemberg.

new master degree (introduced with the Bologna process) is commonly compared to the old Diplom-degree. Yet, in terms of access there is now a big difference: whereas the Diplom is an entire study of its own, the master is a supplement on top of a bachelor degree. Thus, master degrees are not first degrees, which allows universities to select the students for their master programmes.

Secondly, the Initiative for Excellence will increase the pressure to apply selection criteria. At first glance this might sound surprising, as the initiative is oriented towards research and not teaching. But as figures from the university in Karlsruhe (one of the nine awarded universities so far) show, the "beacon-effect" has lead to an increase in applicants by around 27 percent within only one year (Die Zeit, 2008e).

4.3.2.4   Main features of the German HE system

The fact that higher education has increasingly become a major device for climbing the social ladder and that more and more career entry points require higher education qualifications has led to two important developments. Firstly, there is an identity and legitimacy crisis as universities struggle to match their academic orientation with an increasing demand to prepare students directly for the labour market. Secondly, as universities have to a large extent taken on the function of a 'training company' that allows students to directly enter the labour market, universities play an increasing role in social and labour market policies. As a consequence, higher education has lost the degree of independence that it had gained by the beginning of the 1970s. Higher education policy has become one of the focal points of regulatory policy. Stratification and marketisation traditionally played a minor role; yet the above mentioned reform initiatives point to the increasing use of selection and market mechanisms.

4.3.3   Comparing both higher education systems

In my consideration, the concepts of stratification and marketisation reveal some major differences between the English and the German systems. Allmendinger defines and deconstructs stratification into two aspects: the proportion of a cohort that attains the maximum number of school years; and the degree of differentiation within given educational levels (Allmendinger, 1989, 233). The first indicator does not apply here, but the second aspect is of relevance. If we compare the English and the German higher education systems we observe the following: whereas the German higher education system was characterised by a strikingly low degree of stratification (striking, because students came from a highly stratified school system), the English higher education landscape always exhibited large graduations in prestige, reputation, and future chances for students. The notion of "Oxbridge" captures like no other term the difference in esteem for different higher education institutions. The second side of the same coin is selection. Here again we find a difference between England and Germany: English universities are allowed to select the applicants according to school degrees. In Germany, however, it is not about being accepted to a particular university but to a particular subject. Yet, even this selection procedure applies to only a few subjects. Thus, there is no selection of students on the part of universities.

Traditionally the German higher education system has been highly unstratified: there are neither "beacon" universities that are the equivalent of "Oxbridge" in England and differences between universities revolve around different subjects or persons (like professors), not around single institutions. Nor is there stratification caused by selection procedures. As a rule of thumb everybody is allowed to study anywhere s/he desires. Academic standards in higher education institutions – taking into account the difference between universities and universities of applied science – are by and large equal across institutions. Similar degrees in specific subjects are validated equally and educational standards are similar as well. Moreover, the higher education system is by and large deprived of market mechanisms. Something akin to market-like mechanisms exist neither in the relation between students and universities, nor between universities in relation to public authorities.

However, the above sketched developments indicate that these characteristics may be changing. The Initiative for Excellence is one such development. Though mainly concentrated on research rather than teaching, the initiative attempts to create "beacon universities" that receive extra-funding. This is a remarkable deviation from the approach that has been pursued to date, in that it moves away from the traditional egalitarian approach to higher education institutions.

The concern of falling behind in the international science world was the driving reason behind the Initiative for Excellence and fundamental reconsiderations about the traditional unity of teaching and research and the usage of research resources in particular. The Bologna process can be understood in this vein, as disconnecting teaching and research functions by allowing the option of following a rather clear-cut non-academic vocational education that leads a bachelor degree.

Therefore, the Initiative for Excellence and the Bologna process should be

4.3 Higher education

considered in close relation to each other, as both represent a development that has the potential to alter German higher education profoundly: more vocationalism through the introduction of bachelor degrees, which ultimately leads to an increased decoupling of teaching and research. This process coincides with a weakening of the egalitarian approach among universities.

One essential component of Allmendinger's definition of stratification is the degree of differentiation within given educational levels (Allmendinger, 1989, 233). If we consider higher education as one such education level, we observe a great degree of stratification in England, both between degrees and between higher education institutions. Honours degrees are well regarded, whereas it remains to be seen if foundation degrees, though being degrees, will be appreciated as a "real" degree or as a mere "sub-honours" degree.

The place of study also plays a very important role in how a degree is later valued, for instance on the labour market. Even though most of the higher education institutions with degree-awarding powers are universities, there is still a huge difference in esteem between the old universities (Oxford and Cambridge), the "redbrick universities" (i.e. Essex and Warwick), and the new universities, which are mainly the former polytechnics. Moreover, there are financial incentives to further separate research from teaching, with the evolution of pure teaching institutions, mainly those with a vocational background, versus research intensive institutions, mostly those with high-profile students.

The purposes of marketisation in higher education are manifold (Jongbloed, 2003, 113 f.): strengthening student choice, improving quality and variety of the services in the sector, increasing efficiency, enhancing cost-awareness for students and institutions, making donation dependent on performance, etc. Thus, marketisation is meant to address the adjustment challenges higher education institutions are exposed to with the shift from an industry-based society to a knowledge-based society, a shift which renders higher education a key issue as it is a key contributor to the increased competitiveness of the overall political economy (Liefner, Schätzl and Schröder, 2004, 23).

Various measures and stipulations are used to introduce "marketisation" in higher education, of which many are to be found in England but not (not yet, or to a lesser extent) in Germany (Küpper, 2002; Hartwig, 2004): students compete for university places at their preferred university; higher education institutions compete in a market for revenue and scientific reputation; higher education institutions in particular and countries in general are in an international competition for renowned "higher education institution- and research-places" (compare with Jongbloed, 2003). Thus, the introduction of market mechanisms in higher education is another dimension that traditionally distinguishes between the higher education systems of Germany and England.

In Germany, we do currently see some modest steps towards the inclusion of market mechanisms in the system: the Initiative for Excellence promotes competition between universities; students for master degrees can be selected; and lump-sum budgets make universities more accountable for their own affairs.

Moreover, these market mechanisms indicate not only increased competition between the actors in the system; additionally, they profoundly alter the governance structure in the area of higher education, especially the relationship between the state and higher education institutions. Therefore marketisation is inseparably linked with the modification of governance structures. One critical point is the financing of higher education institutions because the way in which revenues are distributed (warranted) to the institutions allows for innovative steering mechanisms, as we will see later on. Apart from the "market" between the distributors of funding and higher education institutions, there is also increasingly a market between institutions and students: tuition fees, selection procedures and access restrictions are the most prominent of the possible regulations on this market, all of which are currently used in England.

Beginning with the higher education admission procedure, students compete for places at particular universities. Published university rankings and traditional university reputations guide students in their choice and lead to fierce competition for the best places. Yet, there is not only a competition among students for university places but also a competition between universities for students. What sounds like a contradiction is actually the consequence of the funding policy for higher education institutions: those universities that specialise in teaching rather than research are keen to accept as many students as possible because funding is dependant on student numbers. This procedure is likely to further increase the 'esteem-gap' between the traditional universities and the new ones. The research assessment exercise marks the entry of marketisation elements in the area of research as well.

Hence, the English higher education system is a stratified one, one in which market mechanisms are applied broadly and determine the governance structure in the field of higher education. Thereby, England serves as a template that Germany is currently seeking to model itself upon.

4.4 Conclusion

So far this research has examined theoretical works and empirical evidence that reveal how the systems were traditionally shaped, how they have evolved over time, how England and Germany differed in this development, and how they are

4.4 Conclusion

classified by the theoretical literature. The following chapter will turn to an analysis of governmental papers on educational policy issues. Hence and thereby referring to the research puzzle, why is this procedure needed for this study? The main traits and characteristics that have been discovered in the previous chapter are the following:

1) School education in England is characterised by a long compulsory schooling period up to the age of 16 with fewer degrees of stratification. Thereafter, choices become greater and the system gets more stratified. Germany, by contrast, is distinguished by an early selection procedure that leads to a high degree of stratification already at the age of 10 (in most Länder).

2) The German vocational education and training system is highly standardised and an occupational orientation prevails in vocational education and training as well as in the labour market. The English situation is sketchier both in terms of standardisation and in terms of acknowledgement. Yet, its qualification-orientation offers a greater degree of flexibility. Employer involvement is considerably lower whereas direct state involvement is much higher than in Germany, which leads to the distinction of a supply-led system in England and a demand-led (with respect to dual apprenticeships) system in Germany. Moreover, we observe a huge difference between England and Germany regarding the degree of esteem that each has for vocational education and training.

3) In contrast to school education, the English higher education system shows a great degree of stratification, whereas the German one does not. In terms of marketisation we observe clear signals that market mechanisms have been introduced in England, whereas in Germany these have traditionally played almost no role at all.

The political economy literature (VoC), by contrast, does not make an attempt to classify educational systems according to different institutional characteristics. What this set of literature does instead is to provide an estimate of which sort of skills are rewarded by different political economies. It concludes that – among others – the German (CME) and the English (LME) political economies rely on different types of skills, the former on specialised skills and the latter on general skills (Estevez-Abe, Iversen and Soskice, 2001). Criticism of this parsimonious categorisation has been expressed from several different perspectives. For instance, some claim that it overestimates the importance of school education in LMEs while simultaneously underestimating the increasing importance of any kind of post-compulsory education. Others claim that it underestimates higher education and lacks of a method by which to categorise it, e.g. as either an area which is affiliated to general skills or to specific skills. Yet, it provides an interesting distinction, as it is not focused on educational systems in particular, but derives its evidence from contemplating political economies broadly.

Hence, what we would theoretically expect are educational reforms which fulfil both of the following requirements:

Firstly, that educational reforms move along the paths and characteristics sketched above; and secondly, that educational reforms are aligned with the skill profiles that receive high rewards in the respective political economy.

Taking into account the above sketched empirical evidence, however, leaves us with the uneasy impression that these two requirements might not be met. The analysis of governmental papers will facilitate our understanding of how educational reforms are justified and what drivers are considered to propel educational reforms.

There are several reasons for choosing governmental papers as the source for this part of the empirical work. Firstly, these papers show the expectations, estimations, and functions that the governments associates with educational policy. Thereby we are able to distinguish among several sub-discourses in the broad educational discourse and to discover the prevailing sub-discourse(s). This also involves taking the governments at their word, which is a prerequisite for assessing the reforms against their initial objectives. Secondly, we shall see the main drivers for educational reforms. This will enable us to answer the question of whether governments' decisions on reforms – at least rhetorically and to be proven by the reform analyses later on – are underpinned by the considerations presented above, i.e. if they cling to a path and/or stress their comparative advantages.

Thirdly, most policy initiatives in both countries are launched by the government (by the executive authority) and not by the parliaments (legislative). Therefore, from an ideational and rhetorical perspective governmental papers provide us with a comprehensive understanding of what drives educational reforms on one side and, on the other, with a contextual frame in which the reforms are embedded. The analysis of selected reforms will be conducted by tracing the reform processes. This procedure will shed light on the question of how these discourses are translated into policies and if we are able to draw any conclusions on whether the systems are deviating from the paths as outlined in this chapter, if the systems are converging towards each other, if one is coming to resemble the other, or if we see parallel developments or even increasing differences.

5 Governmental paper analysis

5.1 Textual discourse analysis

Ideas, ideology, and common beliefs that may guide a policy decision-making process are embodied in discourses. Thus, working out the underpinning beliefs and attributes of actors, or – applied to this topic – the driving ideas behind educational policies, involves the analysis of discourses. Yet, though discourses may be the right place to detect ideas and attributes of actors does not mean discourses are confined to specific sources. In fact, every human action involves communication and thereby entails a discourse. Consequently, there is a huge and influential tradition of closely linking discourse theory with social theory, as seen in the works of Foucault, Mouffe, Laclau, etc. In this strand of thought, discourse is understood as a system of social relations and practices (Howarth, Norval and Stavrakakis, 2000, 4).

Starting from this very broad and comprehensive definition, the concept as applied in this research is more limited in scope. My working definition of "discourse analysis" is based on an understanding of the subject that is concentrated on "the close study of language in use" (Taylor, 2001, 15). Yet, the technique used in this book is not confined to linguistic analysis alone. It is rather a discourse analysis that contemplates texts, documents, speeches etc. in their social context. Therefore discourse analysis is conceived of "critically" in that it scrutinises the usage of discourses in particular contexts, their embeddedness in social life and tackles questions such as, for instance, to what extent rhetoric corresponds to social reality. Hence, in this book we are talking about "Critical Discourse Analysis" (CDA), which is the terminus technicus in the social sciences. The intended use of discourse analysis is critical in the sense that "language is involved [...] in ideology" (Fairclough, 2001, 229). Thus, elaborating on the use of language by means of a critical discourse analysis (thereinafter CDA) is a useful tool for researching social change (Fairclough, 2001, 229). Consequently, the CDA "toolbox" contains less theory-oriented tool and instead makes use of more practical and applied tools in the broad area of discourse analysis (Stavrakakis, 2004, 163).

CDA asks about the changes that have taken place regarding forms of interaction, where interaction is understood as an act of communication.[64] A discourse is a mediating factor in the event of policy reforms (Schmidt, 2005, 6). Materials such as governmental documents and the speeches of political actors accompany the policy-making processes and are indispensable components of policy reforms. For this research the analysis of the language/discourse used in official documents is of critical importance in at least two senses: on the one hand, discourses transport actors' attitudes, ideas, and beliefs about policy issues. These imply the formulation, identification, and definition of problems as well as what constitute feasible and viable solutions. On the other hand, discourses precede policy-making processes and thus precede institutional change. It is the interface of both aspects that is at the core of this book. Actors' attributes and ideas must be differentiated and broken down all the way down to the level at which they serve as implicit guidelines to policy action. The idea of a "knowledge-based society", for instance, is almost omnipresent in Western political economies. One of the pivotal question this research attempts to answer is: "Do similar ideas lead to similar outcomes?" In other words, how does the notion of "knowledge-based society" affect – for instance – school policy? The manner in which language and semiosis figure in ongoing social processes (such as 'technologisation' or 'globalisation') provides extremely useful instruments for understanding changes in policies (Fairclough, 2001, 232). The medium of language that will be scrutinised in this book are official documents (such as White Papers), thus written language. Therefore, the most viable choice from the range of possible methodological options is what Fairclough has called "textually oriented discourse analysis" (Fairclough, 2003, 3). Fairclough's CDA framework, which he exemplarily applied in the analysis of a 1998 Green Paper on welfare reforms published by the British Government, will be used in this research (Fairclough, 2001, 229 ff.).

Fairclough's framework is divided into five stages. The first stage serves as a description of the discursive environment in which the text is embedded, as well as he social problem that the discourse addresses. The second stage shows the position of the text in the political order. The third stage is the core of the CDA, the in-depth textual, linguistic analysis (to be further described below). The fourth stage deals with "hitherto unrealised possibilities for change in the way social life is currently organised" (Fairclough, 2001, 236). This stage examines existing gaps and contradictions in discourses, as well as in sub-discourses that are embedded in a broader discourse. The fifth stage is a reflective stage that looks back on the entire analysis and attempts to identify the

---

[64]For a useful distinction between coordinative discourses (communications among those persons directly involved in a policy discourse, e.g. for the purpose of coalition building) and communicative discourses (communications to the general public) see Vivian Schmidt, 2005, 10 f.

5.1 Textual discourse analysis

researchers' own position within the analytical process (Fairclough, 2001, 236). However, one point needs special emphasis. Namely, that the textual discourse analysis is not an end in itself, as the intention of this book is not to describe and discern power relations or to contribute to the creation of social theory in the vein of Foucault, Mouffe, etc. Instead, this "textual oriented discourse analysis" is used as a clear-cut tool kit, which is both interwoven in the research design of this book and, on the basis of the theoretical framework, is focused on detecting the drivers of institutional change (compare with Fairclough, 2003, 2). The one and only purpose of this analysis is to discern the argumentation structure of policy initiatives with the aim to extract ideological guidelines that might be conducive to institutional change.

In order to accomplish this task, Fairclough's framework needs to be modified and adapted for the purpose of this book. This will be done in three steps, which are described below.

First step
In this book, the first and the second stages of Fairclough's framework are combined. Firstly, I will delineate the different contexts in which the examined documents were written. Different contexts impact the form that official documents take. A governmental paper in an pre-election period might be different from one written right after an election; a document might also be a response to a report by a specific working group or task force that was commissioned to examine a particular issue; or a paper could be a direct reaction to a specific problem that is perceived by the public to be of special significance. Furthermore, the documents will be placed in a policy context in order to understand the cognitive process through which specific issues become prevalent.

With reference to the theoretical framework, we acknowledge that institutions and ideas not only accompany and confine political action; they also determine and modify what we perceive and define as being a problem in the first place. Moreover, ideas might be able to "ideationally" impact considerations of other additional or different problems and their solutions. It suffices at this point to state that "problems" have to be treated with care, as they might only exist as socially created constructs, based only on the recent prevailing perceptions of the public and of political actors (Fairclough, 2001 calls this aspect "obstacles to the social problem", 236 f.). This leads to the question of when in the policy-making process – based on a policy cycle – the document is issued. In other words, what role does the document play in a specific policy making process and how and to which degree is it conducive to the policy outcome.

Second step
Fairclough's third stage shall be redefined and relabelled as a "structure and proposals" section. It is here that the structure of the document will be outlined. This will be followed by a sketch of the main policy suggestions and initiatives the document entails.

Third step
In contrast to Fairclough's framework, the third section contains not only the in-depth textual and linguistic analysis but will instead integrate this aspect into an analysis and deconstruction of the underlying argument on which the policy initiatives and proposals of the papers are based. These arguments are essential in that they are normatively and ideationally loaded and thus reflect the intentions and expectations associated with the initiatives in question. This section, called "analysing the argument", digs down to the basis of the argument in order to reveal actors' ideas, visions, aims and attributes. The aim is to produce a dense line of reasoning that begins with the abstract views and shows how these eventually lead to policy proposals. The causal gap between ideas and outcomes will remain and will not be resolved until the selected reform is analysed.

The concluding section (see chapter 5.4), which follows the analyses of the papers, serves three purposes. Firstly, the main ideas accompanying educational policy reforms will be pointed out. This challenging task will pull together the different notions found in the papers. Ideas will be clustered according to the groups (e.g. ideas pursing economic, social, or purely educational goals) in which they belong. Furthermore, these ideas will be ascribed to different levels of abstraction, with the highest level including notions such as "knowledge-based society" or "globalisation", which then eventually lead to concrete instructions regarding the ideas' application to reality. Secondly, by using academic literature this part is also devoted to a critical evaluation of the main arguments on which the policy proposals are based. Thus, this part largely resembles the fifth stage in Fairclough's framework, since the development of the lines of argumentation in the papers will be scrutinised as well. Thirdly, this part will conduct some preliminary work on the tracing of educational reform processes. For this purpose the three policy reforms per country (on which the "process tracing" of this research is concentrated) will be connected to the relevant ideas at their various levels of abstraction in order to facilitate their evaluation in the upcoming chapter.

5.2 Analysis of governmental papers in England

Traditionally, Green Papers and White Papers form a logical unit published by one or more departments and which thus reflect the government's opinions about the issues being addresses within the papers.[65] Both types of papers are intended to be devices for communicating with the citizens about future plans and initiatives.[66] In the English context, a Green Paper precedes a White Paper in that it opens up political discussions and discourses about relevant topics through a consultative process. These papers are focused more on assessing the status quo, discovering the problems and envisioning possible solutions. Mostly, however, they are formulated in an imprecise, rather broad visionary way, through which the government presents its future societal and policy objectives. Green Papers are also consultation document through which the government asks for comments from those groups that are putatively affected by a proposed policy.

White Papers, on the contrary, are in most cases immediately followed by legislation. Though they are formally of a non-binding character, they often anticipate upcoming policy reforms. The short introductions to these papers, which refer to the relevant preceding Green Paper, are followed by a precise description of how social issues might be solved – not only in abstract terms, as in their Green counterpart, but in terms of concrete remedies and initiatives. Recently, however, fewer Green Papers have been published in the field of educational policy than White Papers. Instead, Green Papers have been widely substituted by Consultation documents, Task Force Reviews and Working Group Reports, and in a few cases even by White Papers.

By and large, however, White Papers comprehensively reflect the perceptions, attributes and ideas of political actors, as these papers are still the pivotal preliminary documents for governmental actions. This is the main reason why this research concentrates on White Papers: because they represent the appropriate starting point for the empirical analysis. Since White Papers in most cases refer to a preceding paper, report or review, I will implicitly interweave these into the analyses of the White Papers, i.e. not as thoroughly as the actual analyses yet sufficient enough to understand how the policy-making process evolved.

Nonetheless, despite having argued in favour of White Papers as opposed to

---

[65] See http://www.dfes.gov.uk/publications/keydocuments2.shtml for a definition of Green Papers and White Papers by the Department for Children, Schools and Families (DCSF).
[66] Both are communication discourses that communicate governmental plans to the public. However, both types of paper do not assume the shape of a dialogue communication but are instead more of a one-sided notification by the Government (Fairclough, 2001). In the terms of Vivien Schmidt we can call this "communicative discourse" (Schmidt, 2005, 13).

Green Papers I will begin the analysis with a Green Paper. Elaborating on this Green Paper, however, constitutes an exception. It will be analysed because it was the first governmental paper directly relevant to this research that was issued by New Labour after the party gained power in 1997 following 18 years of Conservative governments. Moreover, the paper marks the first official government statement on educational issues and on how New Labour intended to address the Conservative legacy in educational issues. The analysis of this Green Paper will be followed by an analysis of White Papers in chronological order; making the Green Paper the exception which proves the rule.

5.2.1 Green Paper "The Learning Age: a renaissance for a new Britain" (DfEE, 1997b)

Context of the paper
According to the adapted three step-approach, we need to first portray the social and political context and the social problem as outlined in the paper. The Green Paper (DfEE, 1997b) was published in the same year as New Labour won the general elections and took over power from the Conservatives. Under the mantra "education, education, education" the paper embodies many of the general ideas and visions developed by New Labour, ideas which ultimately led to more concrete policy plans in the White Paper "Learning to Succeed: a new framework for post-16 learning" (DfEE, 1999). Therefore, both papers form a logical unit (Coffield, 2000).

The Conservative Government left office having altered the education system through many substantial reforms, beginning with the Education Reform Act of 1988 (Pierson, 1998, 131; Tomlinson, 2001, 263; Smithers, 2001, 1; Whitty, 2005, 4). Decisive steps towards a commodified education market were taken during the period of conservative rule[67], including league tables and increased independent financial responsibility for each educational institution. Simultaneously, central control over the curricula (in fact, the "national curriculum") and local education authorities was increased, as were assessments and inspections of institutional performance (Tomlinson, 2001, 263; Tomlinson, 2003, 196; Whitty, 2005, 2 f.; McLean, 1988, 200 f.).

Surprisingly, these policies were by and large maintained and continued by New Labour. This continuity applies also to the fact that the English educational

---

[67]Van Thiel and Pollitt summarise the Conservatives' market-oriented approach to public management reform with the following words: "[...] if possible move all parts of public services into the private sector; if that is not possible, introduce some kind of market-type mechanisms and competition within public services" (van Thiel and Pollitt, 2007, 61).

system remains under constant construction to the present day (Tomlinson, 2001, 262 ff.; Newman, 2002, 77 ff. to public service reforms). Smithers describes the situation as follows:

> "What is remarkable about all the apparent change is how little it differed at root from the policies of the previous Conservative administrations. Many of the education reforms which the Conservatives had introduced from 1988 onwards, and which were bitterly attacked by the Labour opposition of the time, now became the backbone of the Blair programme." (Smithers, 2001, 1)

The Green Paper and the corresponding White Paper (DfEE, 1999) directly addressed the most contested area of education for the 14-19 age-group, in other words – as post-16 is obviously included in this time span – to post-compulsory education others than higher education. Both papers make references to some overarching basic assumptions and perceptions about the economic and social world. Hence, they highlight increasing international competition, the need to be competitive in this changing environment, and the critical significance of learning and skills for the required adaptation process. Additionally, they stress the importance of a culture of learning, which underpins the endeavour to build a cohesive integrated society. Thus, an economically utilitarian approach to education is complemented with social goals.[68]

As the title already indicates, then Secretary of State for Education and Employment, David Blunkett used the Green Paper to proclaim the "Learning Age". A definition of what "Learning Age" actually means is missing. Instead the impression conveyed is that it is an unquestioned and unquestionable fact of the current era. This is highlighted by the following sentence from the Green Paper: "In our hearts we know we have no choice but to prepare for this new age [...]" (DfEE, 1997c, 1).

Though based on the Green Paper, the White Paper published two years later and entitled "Learning to Succeed: a new framework for post-16 learning" slightly changes the "Learning Age" notion and instead talks about the "knowledge and information economy" (3). In this context we also encounter another central keyword(s), which is constantly used in the papers to describe the changing environment, namely competition/competitive/competitiveness. Perceived changes in the economy and accelerated international competition are considered to be causing tremendous changes to all sections of society. It is against this backdrop that inferences to knowledge accumulation, and hence to

---

[68] For Smithers this marks a derivation from the previous government, as New Labour emphasised the "twin goals" of educational policies and not just a single economic goal (Smithers, 2001, 3; in the same vein Tomlinson, 2003, 195)

the education system, are drawn. This requires that the state address the changes through appropriate political measures. Learning and knowledge accumulation are assigned crucial roles in this process. Foreshadowing the corresponding paper of 1999, we observe a guiding vision that serves to orient policies designed to address the above process. Under the heading "Our Vision for the new Millenium", the White Paper published in 1999 says:

> "Our vision is to build a new culture of learning which will underpin national competitiveness and personal prosperity, encourage creativity and innovation and help build a cohesive society." (DfEE, 1999, 6)

First 1999 White Paper goes even further in arguing that an environment has to be built which nurtures a "love for learning", as it is learning that allows individuals to explore and discover their own talents and potentials; encourages independence and a healthy and active life within strengthened families; and which also lead to a "greater appreciation of art, music, poetry and literature, and develop our potential as rounded human beings"(3). Consequently, a culture of lifelong learning has to be created. In short, taking into account the above portrayed expectations that are ascribed to education policy on the abstract discursive level, one understands why Tony Blair's mantra "education, education, education" attained such central importance for New Labour (Blair, 1996).

Structure and Proposals
The main suggestions of this Green Paper are the following:
- establishing Learning and Skill Councils to replace Training and Enterprise Councils;
- creating a "University for Industry" (Ufi) in order to widen access to further, higher and adult education;
- expand further and higher education by providing an extra 500,000 young people by 2002;
- individual learning accounts and "smart cards" recording young people's learning progress;
- increasing cooperation with employers and trade unions to develop appropriate learning programmes;
- building a qualificational system which embraces vocational academic qualifications.

5.2 Analysis of governmental papers in England

Analysing the Argument
This paper is, even more so than the following papers, characterised by the urge to adapt to recent challenges as quickly as possible. Moreover, the desire to improve upon the policies of the previous government is all too apparent in this paper. According to the paper, policies must be aligned with the following principles, which are a sort of "working sub-aims", in order to fulfil the overarching vision (see DfEE, 1999, 6). These principles as outlined in the Green Paper (and later referred to in the White Paper of 1999 (DfEE, 1999, 6)) are:
- investing in learning to benefit everyone;
- lifting barriers to learning;
- putting people first;
- sharing responsibility with employers, employees and the community;
- achieving world class standards and value for money;
- and working together as the key to success.

Whilst these principles guide the main vision (the "culture of learning"), there is another set of principles, mentioned on the same page, with which policies of change should be aligned (6). These are:
- change should promote excellence and participation;
- employers should have a substantial stake in shaping post-16 education and training;
- systems must be learner driven and responsive to the needs of individuals, businesses and their communities;
- equal access to education, training and skills opportunities should be a priority, with equal opportunity in the mainstream of provision;
- people should have access to support in the form of good advice and guidance and, where appropriate, financial help;
- and accountability, efficiency and probity should be promoted at every level.

We are able to see here how a vision (learning age, information and knowledge economy) has been broken down into more concrete guidelines, though not yet directly applicable ones which could provide a detailed manual for policy action. Imagine a triangle diagram with the visions on the top; principles and major guidelines would sit on the second floor. The third layer would specify the guidelines for a particular policy field and the fourth would be devoted to concrete policy proposals. Third and fourth floor issues are dealt with in the White Paper based on the proposals of its Green predecessor, which is mainly about the first and second floor's issues.

5.2.2 White Paper "Excellence in schools" (DfEE, 1997a)

Context of the paper
The White Paper "Excellence in schools" (DfEE, 1997a) was almost the first White Paper published by the New Labour government. The fact that David Blunkett, the Secretary of State, was in charge of this White Paper shows the importance ascribed to education and skills and thereby reflects the mantra "education, education, education", proclaimed by Blair in the pre-election campaign as the top 'three' priorities for a New Labour government. Despite the fact that education policy was one of the most contested policy fields in the pre-election period, New Labour retained the main architecture and principles introduced by the preceding government. Following another rhetorical mantra, namely "standards, not structures" (5, 12; Walford, 2005, 4), the government continued to adhere to, for instance, the policy of choice and diversity at the secondary level, regular testing of pupils and published school league tables. New Labour's main educational action points for their first five years in office were announced to be the following (compare with Labour Party, 1997):
- cut class sizes to 30 or under for 5, 6 and 7 year-olds;
- nursery places for all four year-olds;
- attack low standards in schools;
- widen access to computer technology;
- lifelong learning through a new University for Industry;
- increased spending on education as the cost of unemployment falls.

New Labour stated in its 1997 manifesto that "Education has been the Tories' biggest failure. It is Labour's number one priority" (Labour Party, 1997). This statement was followed by a small paragraph about the critical importance of education for the future of the nation, highlighting that "It is an economic necessity for the nation" (Labour Party, 1997). New Labour underpinned their rhetoric by announcing their intention to increase spending on education immediately upon entry into power.

Structure and Proposals
Interestingly enough, the White Paper by and large excludes making accusations against the Conservatives and instead directly underlines – rhetorically – the deep significance of education policy for the New Labour government. It begins with a foreword by the Secretary of State of the Department for Education and Employment (DfEE) in which he emphasises the crucial importance of education for New Labour, children and the economy. This is followed by six chapters, with each addressing a particular area, such as "Standards and accountability" or

"Modernising the comprehensive principle". The main proposals are, among others:
- setting up "Education Action Zones", in order to concentrate action on places where performances are worst;
- introducing a "Standards Task Force" and a "Standards and Efficiency Unit" at the DfEE;
- more transparent annual league tables of schools' performances;
- devolution of monitoring functions back to Local Education Authorities (LEA) which are to be assessed by Ofsted (education inspection body);
- new threefold framework of schools (aided, community, foundation);
- the creation of specialised schools;
- the increased role of parents in education;[69]
- "accelerated learning" for the most-talented.

Analysing the Argument
On page five of the White Paper we learn that the overall approach to educational policy will be underpinned by six principles:
1. education will be a the heart of government;
2. policies will be designed to benefit the many, not just the few;
3. the focus will be on standards, not structures;
4. intervention will be in inverse proportion to success;
5. there will be zero tolerance of underperformance;
6. government will work in partnership with all those committed to raising standards.

At first glance the emphasis on standards, rather than structures, is striking. After having experienced a plethora of reforms in education polices under the Conservative government, New Labour's intention was to retain the institutional architecture of that field and to focus efforts on the performances and standards that the system generates. It will become apparent later on in this empirical chapter that New Labour deviated from this principle and that the government did in fact introduce various new schemes.

In the first chapter of this White Paper, in which the above mentioned principles are explained in further detail, the government presents its main vision of an English education system. The goal is to attain a society in which everyone is well-educated and life-long learning becomes the norm, with the ultimate objective being to meet the "twin goals" of economic prosperity and social

---

[69] According to Wright and Oancea this is the first time that a White Paper contains an entire chapter on the role of parents in school education (Oancea and Wright, 2006, 26).

cohesion. The "twin goals" of economic and social aims referenced throughout the White Paper.

Yet, having a first glance at the first few pages of the paper, one is struck by fact that the economic aspect of the "twin goals" is given particular importance. In his foreword Blunkett stresses the imperative of "investing in human capital in the age of knowledge", which involves that "we will have to unlock the potential of every young person" in order to "compete in the global economy" (3). The close relationship between economic goals and educational policies is again highlighted in the sentence: "Priority is indeed being given to education, to employability and to investment for the future" (4). The two quotations exhibit the use of a few dominant keywords: human capital, age of knowledge as a reference to what is called a knowledge (-based) society, competitiveness, global economy, investment and employability.

"Education, education, education" – the dictums of New Labour that indicated its first 'three' priorities – in combination with the above referenced quotations reveals the hope and aspirations associated with education policy: education as a universal remedy to fight economic and social disadvantage, to ensure international competitiveness, to survive in a globalised age of knowledge, and to foster employability. Consequently, education is not just a policy field among many others that New Labour intended to turn upside down; it was perceived of as the main lever to attain social and economic goals. Thereby, a utilitarian approach to education becomes tremendously apparent. Even though we will see that subsequent White Papers also refer to this "twin aim", we can already state that the traditional purpose of education – to educate young citizens on how to become members of a democratic society and provide them a tool through which to attain self-actualisation and self-fulfilment – disappears almost entirely in this approach (Crouch, Finegold and Sako, 1999, 5). Thus, the discourse about educational targets and about education as an end in itself is subordinated to a discourse on social cohesion and social inclusion and an economic discourse about a knowledge society and international competitiveness.

However, is there a more subtle hierarchy of discourses between these two latter discourses? Put differently, is there a dominant discourse fuelling the educational discourse with ideas and guidelines along which educational policy is to be aligned? It might be fruitful to attempt to answer this question by considering it from the perspective of the paper's proposals. Going back to the beginning of this White Paper we might be able to trace the policy proposals backwards and thereby make inferences about their underpinning ideas (the proposals are listed in this section under b) Structures and Proposals, marked with hyphens).

5.2 Analysis of governmental papers in England

Keeping in mind the idea of "standards, not structures" we are able to subsume initiatives under the broader aim of raising standards. Social goals, as opposed to economic ones, play at best a minor role despite that this set of goals is one of the twin-sibling of the "twin goals". Moreover, we encounter a logic that is defining for the English argumentation: pursuing economic goals is tantamount to pursuing social goals, because what serves the economy provides also for the creation of jobs. This logic is based on the assumption that being unemployed is one of the major reasons for social exclusion.

5.2.3 White Paper "Learning to Succeed: a new framework for post-16 learning" (DfEE, 1999)

Context of the paper
The second White Paper (DfEE, 1999) on educational issues released by New Labour directly refers to the Green Paper "The Learning Age: a renaissance for a new Britain", issued in 1997. This White Paper turns to the most contested area of the English education system, namely the post-compulsory schooling period aside from higher education. New Labour immediately began with a very ambitious paper with regard to its vision and its detailed policy proposals. As we will see later on, the proposals put forward in this paper entail some very profound reform initiatives. As distinct from the school education paper these proposals stress the necessity to reform the post-16 area structurally. The notion of reforming "standards, not structures", as formulated in the previous White Paper about school education, does not apply here. The proposals illustrate New Labour's tendency to assume more central control over education and training policy; the actual delivery of education and training, however, remains a local issue. The notion and vision of "lifelong learning" is of prime importance for this paper.

Structure and Proposals
The foreword by the Secretary of State for Education and Employment David Blunkett is followed by an Executive summary that contains small summaries of the subsequent nine chapters in which specific policy initiatives are described in more detail. The first chapter outlines New Labour's "vision for the new millennium". In the second chapter this vision is contrasted to the status quo, from which conclusions are drawn as to what needs to be done. Chapters three to eight outline the concrete proposals of the DfEE that are intended to improve the status quo and move towards their vision. Chapter nine maps the timetable for implementing the proposals, chapter ten turns to the consultation document and

Appendix one to three address some special issues. The main proposals of this paper are the following:

- the foundation of a central Learning and Skills Council for England (LSC), which assumes responsibilities from the de-centrally organised Training and Enterprise Councils (TEC), as well as taking over the funding of colleges from the Further Education Funding Council for England and the advising tasks from the National Advisory Council for Education and Training Targets (NACETT);
- comprehensive support and advice services for 13-19 year olds throughout the system;
- establishing ConneXions (counselling, advice and careers service for young people), which encourages young people to stay on in education and training after compulsory schooling;
- learning Gateway for 16 and 17 year olds who need extra support in career and learning issues; measures tackling truancy in schools and exclusion from schools.

Analysing the Argument
The paper proposes a clearly formulated aim, namely the pursuit of a vision that is defined as a:

> "new culture of learning which will underpin national competitiveness and personal prosperity, encourage creativity and innovation and help build a cohesive society." (6)

Lifelong learning is at the core of this new learning culture, a culture that "must nurture a love for learning" (3). Like the preceding Green Paper, the White Paper makes a case for reforming education and training in order to cope with the challenges exerted by the "transition from the industries and services of the past, to the knowledge and information economy of the future" (3). The race between England and its competitors to quickly adapt to the changing environment was seen as requiring a new approach to skills for the altered labour market structures. This approach must enable people and businesses to succeed. The vision of a new learning culture is underpinned by six very broadly defined principles, such as "investing in learning to benefit everyone", "putting people first", or "working together as the key to success" (compare with "Structures and Proposals" of Green Paper "The Learning Age: a renaissance for a new Britain" (DfEE, 1997b)). The main inferences drawn from these principles are the concentration of control and supervision in the hands of the government

5.2 Analysis of governmental papers in England 129

supported by partnerships between all relevant actors under the roof of the new LSC. The commitment to the vision and its underpinning principles is supplemented by National Learning Targets that allow for the assessment of the strategy (14). It is the firmness with which New Labour assumes the responsibilities for post-16 education and training and the conviction that these issues must be dealt with at a central political level which marks the main difference between successive initiatives.[70]

After having shown the overarching vision, the paper goes on to criticise the status quo by delineating the deficiencies that hinder England on the route to accomplishing this vision. Weaknesses of the current system are – as shown on pages 16 and 17 – low staying on rates after compulsory schooling; too many low-skilled people who find themselves in a vicious circle of deprivation and disadvantage; difficulties in dealing appropriately with people with special needs; poor levels of basic skills amongst adults; employers' difficulties with skill shortages; poor support and advice for young people; and too general, 'one-size-fits-all' educational programmes that do not allow for tailored teaching of students with different talents. Pages 18 and 19 outline the policy actions that have already begun and those that are planned. This part is introduced with the sub-headline "tackling social exclusion and increasing access and participation". Examining these policies provides a clear indication of what the government understands as "social exclusion" and, respectively, "social inclusion". An economic understanding of these terms prevails, i.e. the conviction that education and training facilitate labour market access and that it is the inability to enter the labour market which is tantamount to social exclusion. Yet, just a few pages before this section, in chapter one, which deals with the "vision for the new millennium", social exclusion/inclusion is defined in terms of information, which has become the pivotal determinant for being included or excluded:

> "Society will continue to be divided between the information rich and the information poor." (13)

This is one example that demonstrates the ineluctable importance of tracing back the reform processes, as concepts are easily diluted, changed or even excluded all together when they are applied in a concrete policy context. Yet, the paper makes it clear that social inclusion is not a one-way street and cannot be achieved by policy measures alone. Individuals are assigned a pivotal role as well in the "new culture of learning and aspiration" (13). The state provides "equality of opportunity" and the individuals are required to take the opportunities that are

---

[70]This aspect is closely related to administrative issues, which will be dealt with in the concluding section.

offered. The Welfare to Work programme (14) shows once more the understanding of social inclusion in its economic sense, the government's utilitarian approach to education, and the clear message to the people to increase their employability.

"New partnerships" are also of crucial importance for realising the vision. The government, individuals, employers, providers and communities are members of this partnership. The links between these groups, however, are not of a similar character. Whereas the government interacts with individuals and communities in a coercive manner, the relationship with employers is based more on voluntary cooperation (64 ff.). The involvement and engagement of employers in England is one of the central themes in post-16 education and training and will be discussed later in this book (Coffield, 2000, 241).

The lifelong learning approach, as outlined in the paper, displays two inconsistencies, one in breadth and one in time. The foreword speaks of the overarching significance of lifelong learning as both a contribution to the future of the economy and as something that is conducive to creating an integrated society. The latter aspect is, however, by and large omitted when it comes to the detailed policy initiatives. What emerges instead is a utilitarian approach that measures learning only in terms of its economic purposes (Coffield, 2000, 239).

The second issue relates to an inconsistency in time. A "conventional" approach to education considers only education for children and teenagers. A lifelong learning approach complements the "conventional" one by including also adults as learners, regardless of age. In the paper one entire chapter is devoted to this issue. Two institutions assume central significance for the pursuit of the adult education component of lifelong learning: the LSC and the University for Industry (UfI) (57), both of which were not established as of the publication of the paper. Since its establishment, the LSC has been charged with coordinating and managerial functions such as ensuring employers' involvement. Specific reference to the whole group of potential receivers of learning is missing. The UfI was actually intended to be a provider of education for adults. By offering part-time programmes it was especially geared towards those who were already employed. Anticipating later developments, it has to be said that the UfI was never implemented.[71] Thus, we see that the rhetoric about lifelong learning is not really backed up with concrete initiatives.

---

[71] The term Ufi, however, still exists but in a different context. It is the agency which runs the distance learning platform www.learndirect.co.uk.

5.2.4 White Paper "Schools – Achieving success" (DfES, 2001)

Context of the paper
The White Paper "Schools – Achieving success" (DfES, 2001), published in 2001, was the first educational White Paper after New Labour's re-election in the same year. This time also saw the restructuring of the departments. From this legislative period onwards the department for educational policies was labelled "Department for Education and Skills" (DfES). Thus, "education" was given an entire department of its own; its predecessor, the "Department for Education and Employment" (DfEE) was split after the elections into the DfES and the "Department for Work and Pensions". Estelle Morris, a former teacher, became Secretary of the DfES.

The subject of the 2001 paper was school education, i.e. education for those aged 5-16.[72] The main focus of the paper is, however, on secondary schooling, thus key stages 3 and 4.[73] Labour initiatives in education so far had been mainly concentrated on further education, thus the period after compulsory schooling. The "School Standards and Framework Act", however, did have some important implications for schools. Two points in particular need to be mentioned here: firstly, the National Curriculum was relaxed to allow for more flexibility in Key Stage 4. Secondly, and more indirectly for the quotidian work of schools, the Local Education Authorities (LEA) were adjusted to a new school and further education framework (more parents to be placed in governmental bodies and LEA committees; LEAs were asked to produce education development plans; new school regulations as to establishment, finance, staffing, admission, and selection procedure).

Structure and Proposals
This White Paper addresses two main concerns: the low achievement rates in secondary schooling in comparison to primary education; and a perceived lack of diversity in Key Stages 4, which does not allow pupils to develop all of their talents and interests. The paper opens with a foreword by the new secretary,

---

[72] There is a remarkable overlap of age-groups covered by school education and further education. Compulsory schooling encompasses children from 5 to 16, further education from 14 to 19; hence it starts at the age of compulsory schooling. The starting point for this overlap was the Dearing Report of 1996. It suggested making the comprehensive 5-16 approach more flexible and introducing vocational courses in the 14+ period, hence in key stage 4. The following White Paper "Learning to Compete: Education and Training for 14-19 Year Olds" (DfEE, 1996), published by the Conservative government in 1996, marked the first time that the 14-19 age-group was considered as a period of its own (Young and Spours, 1998).
[73] English school education is segmented into 5 key stages. Key Stage 3 and 4 are the last two stages in compulsory schooling. Key stage 5 leads to A- levels.

followed by an introduction to the paper. Both sections are very interesting for the purpose of this research, as it is here where the visions and beliefs of the governments are expressed and the solutions – at an abstract level – are presented. The next six chapters (3-8) are focused on particular policy proposals, while the last chapter (9) covers the general implementation and legislation of the proposals.

Regarding the entire schooling period, the following proposals are made in the White Paper:

- an extension of beacon (schools which provide a benchmark for low-performing schools) and specialised schools;
- deregulatory measures and more autonomy in terms of curriculum, condition, and pay for "successful" schools, whereas falling schools should be "turned round" (8) through extra supervision and assistance;
- minimum performance target for GCSE attainment (at least 25 per cent of all pupils in one school should obtain five A*-C GCSEs by 2006);
- extension of literacy and numeracy lessons to secondary schooling;
- league tables for Key Stage 3 pupils;
- proposition for greater curriculum flexibility in Key Stage 4 that would allow pupils to pursue more individual tailored schedules, including vocational education courses;
- allowing more talented pupils to obtain qualifications faster;
- enhancing the status of vocational awards;
- target of at least 20 City Academies by 2005;
- proposals to allow for the creation of all-age City Academies in disadvantaged rural areas or as a substitution for failing schools;
- expansion of the private sector to assist failing schools if LEAs are unable to do so.

Analysing the Argument

Trying to grasp these proposals more abstractly, three aspects are striking: First of all, we see the proclamation of an extension of league tables for schools and achievements of pupils. League tables rank schools according to their performance, measured by the performance of pupils in the standardised exams. This quasi-market measure assists parents in choosing the right school for their children and places peer pressure on the bad performers, as these schools have to fear not only declining numbers of pupils but also run the risk of being exposed to stricter regulations.

The second striking aspect is the promotion of more flexibility at key stage 4. Although the paper clearly speaks of the merits of the comprehensive school system (16) and condemns the failures of the selective system (which was replaced at the end of the 1960s and beginning of the 1970s), a strict approach to the comprehensive system is abandoned with the introduction of more choice and flexibility in key stage 4 (consult footnote 72).

Thirdly, the increasing role of private actors is striking, not only in terms of the responsibilities they are allowed to assume but also regarding the role that is assigned to them. Private actors are "used" to create a sort of threat to state agencies. Thus, for example, in the case of failing schools within a Local Education Authority, the Authority has to consider partnerships for the school with the public, voluntary and private sector (51 f.).

The main goals for education appear on page five. Three goals are mentioned, the "twin goal" of achieving both "economic health and social cohesion of the country" and "personal fulfilment of children at school". The next paragraph (1.2) specifies the source of this transformative pressure, pointing out that it is the need to "prosper in the 21st century competitive global economy" that guides knowledge, skill, and education policies.

Thus, there is a clear reference to the concept of globalisation and the conviction that the loss of jobs through the transfer of low-skilled labour to newly industrialised countries can be offset only by pursuing a (high) skill strategy. This paragraph also applies these observations to the needs of children, stating that it is education that "equips them for work and prepares them to succeed in the wider economy and in society." Thus, almost immediately social cohesion and self-fulfilment are neglected as objectives that education should generate for children.

The paragraph also has some interesting grammatical aspects. It first uses the third person singular to demonstrate an inevitable process (a changing world) to which Britain has to adapt. It then changes to the first person plural in order to show that "we all" must tackle this situation.

The subsequent two paragraphs of the paper broadly describe the measures that are expected to address the challenges to school education: raising the numeracy and literacy standards and expanding these courses to secondary education; and introducing more choice, particularly in the last two years of secondary schooling, in order to develop pupils' talents.

Interestingly enough, paragraph 1.8 presents another set of objectives which are only implicitly related to skill standards in a competitive global economy. This paragraph is about the principles established by New Labour for public service reforms, which follows a different agenda, such as accountability and inspection; devolution of responsibilities for service provision; greater choice for consumers; and improving the working conditions for the staff (Doyle, 2003; Homburg, Pollitt and van Thiel, 2007). Thus, education and skill oriented goals have to be reconciled with goals about how to reshape the service sector. This double purpose approach is noticeable in the policies that the White Paper proposes, such as, for instance, the devolution of further competences, e.g. regarding the curriculum, which is accompanied by a greater discretion as to how to adapt the curriculum to pupils' talents. Another example is the expansion of league tables, which allows parents (consumers) to choose the right school for their children on the basis of educational attainment.

We observe here an approach that has become prevalent in many states and within many policy fields: namely the tendency to regulate rather than directly provide public services (Homburg, Pollitt and van Thiel, 2007; Osborne and McLaughlin, 2002, 9; Steer et al., 2007). In its purest form this means that the state privatises the production of goods and services and supervises the privately produced goods and services through regulations and special supervisory boards. Such practices have become prevalent in fields like telecommunications and railway services. However, these practices are increasingly being used in social and education policies as well. The English example, as rolled out in the White Paper, provides a good illustration of how these mechanisms are – at least partly – applied: peer reviews through league tables, devolution of area-specific responsibilities to "front-line" practitioners with the simultaneous establishment of strict achievement targets and a precise curriculum; and the substitution of failing schools with City Academies. Just to make one point clear, we are not talking about the privatisation of the whole education sector, just the school sector. However, referring to the section about possible ideas that might be relevant in education policy more broadly, we can see that neo-liberal ideas, i.e. the conviction in the prevalence of the market, are applied in this area as well.

The reference to this second set of indicators clearly highlights the fact that not only are "educational issues" tackled but that the policies and reforms coincide with other objectives that are only indirectly associated with educational policy. This means that educational policy not only facilitates the attainment of economic and social goals; the reference to public service reforms dictates the manner in which education shall be provided. Moreover, this means that we must consider an additional set of aims when we evaluate educational reforms.

Let us briefly consider both sets of aims contained within this paper. Policies that can be traced back to educational ideas are based mainly on the taken-for-granted assumption of a fast changing and globalising world that requires an ever higher standard of skills in the population. Apart from the fact that the number of low-skilled jobs is dwindling, no further evidence is given as to how the world is changing. Moreover, the paper does not consider how these changes impact different societal groups in various way that might make

5.2 Analysis of governmental papers in England 135

different measures necessary, instead of a 'one-size-fits all' approach to education and skills.

Nevertheless, the educational goals alone do not allow for one to derive concrete policy proposals regarding the structures to which educational initiatives should adhere. This obscure frame becomes clearer when considering the second set of objectives, namely those on public policy reforms.

To conclude the analysis of this White Paper, the underlying line of argumentation proceeds on the assumption that the world is changing and competition is growing due to globalisation. The generation of high skills will ensure that the country remains competitive. Education has to be oriented to this purpose, yet simultaneously must take into account the principles of public service reform.

5.2.5 White Paper "14-19: Opportunity and Excellence" (DfES, 2003a)

Context of the paper
This paper (DfES, 2003a) was New Labour's second White Paper that explicitly refered to the age period of 14-19. In particular, this period encompasses further education.

Structure and Proposals
There are two volumes of this White Paper. The first volume was drafted in the same mode as the previous White Papers: A foreword by the Secretary of State (David Blunkett) is followed by an "Executive Summary". The first chapter portrays problems, visions and solutions in further detail, before the following chapters turn to concrete policy proposals. A peculiarity that characterises the whole paper is the division into short-term and long-term goals. The second volume is devoted to the specific details of the proposals. Here, the intended measures are described in-depth, underpinned by surveys and inquiries. For the purpose of this chapter it suffices to concentrate on the first volume. The proposals set out in this volume are the following:
- the closer cooperation of all relevant education institutions in a local area in order to tailor the curriculum to local needs and fine-tune the different curricula of the educational institutions;
- the introduction of "hybrid" GCSE's that combines the traditional academic focused GCSE's and eight vocational GCSE's – though all GCSE's are to be labelled just as GCSE's without any attributes more flexibility in curricula through more choice and by "disapplying" elements of the National Curriculum that were previously compulsory;

- a new qualification framework that comprises both academic and vocational qualifications from the age of 14 onwards in order to facilitate for "parity of esteem";
- the announcement of the establishment of the 14-19 Working Group, chaired by Mike Tomlinson.

Analysing the Argument
Although this White Paper is devoted to the entire 14-19 age-group, it concentrates mainly on those young people within this group who do not pursue an academic path. Thus the paper is mainly concerned with the preparation of pupils for the labour market after their compulsory education. It is this focus that is striking and which distinguishes this paper from papers about higher education and school education, in that it does not even pretend to have another goal apart from serving labour market purposes.

This is also reflected by the paper's vision for the 14-19 phase (14 f.). A consistent vision does not guide the reader through the paper as was the case in previous papers. The vision is not defined in a coherent manner but rather as a list of items that have to be fulfilled in order to accomplish the vision. Instead, it is the challenge as outlined already in the foreword that is the central theme of the paper:

> "to create a clearer and more appropriate curriculum and qualifications framework for the 14-19 phase – one that develops and stretches all our young people to achieve their full potential, and prepares them for life and work in the 21st century" (2).

The participation rate of about 76 percent in post-16 education as of 2005 (the goal is to attain 90 percent by 2015; Hayward et al., 2006, 94) is perceived of as being too low to meet this challenge. The paper claims that "low staying on rates are caused by weaknesses of vocational offer" (4) in terms of quality and flexibility.[74] According to the paper, a similar situation was previously found in academic-oriented school education but was tackled by the "Curriculum 2000" reform, which allowed for more flexibility in A-levels (4 f.).

"Choice" is the major keyword to be introduced into the 14-16 phase and which is intended to help raise participation rates in post-16 education. The paper frequently mentions that according to OECD statistics its competitors have

---

[74]Moreover, low participation rates are connected to England's international competitiveness in the following way: low participation rates lead to a low overall skill level; low-skilled individuals are more likely to be unemployed and unemployment is not only a social issue, but is considered to damage national competitiveness (10).

higher staying on rates in post-compulsory schooling. Thus, it comes as no surprise that the targets by which the vision has to be achieved are mainly participation quotas (17).

Pupils should be able to choose an individually-tailored schedule, with less compulsory requirements and more options for specialised education. This is supposed to lead to a smoother transition into training or work (5). At the same time, the acquired skills should be integrated into a coherent framework that ensures a level playing-field for both those concentrating on academic pathways and those on vocational ones.

As this last sentence indicates, beside the concern about participation rates the issue of "parity of esteem" implicitly underpins the paper. In one of the few instances in which the paper explicitly talks about the divide between vocational and academic education it requests a new use of language that validates vocational education as an independent and renowned component of its own and not just the last resort of low achievers.

One pattern has already become evident in the previous papers and will remain apparent in upcoming ones: for the government "parity of esteem" essentially means to leave academic education (Curriculum 2000 is the exception that proves the rule) untouched whereas the non-academic education remains under permanent construction.[75] This area is exposed to a constant tension between stability, reliance and conformity, on the one hand, and change, flexibility, and the perceived need to deliver a "wide range of institutions" (3) on the other. It is, presumably, this lack of a comprehensive and coherent approach, as suggested by the Tomlinson working group (DfES, 2004a) one year later, that is one of the main impediments to "parity of esteem" becoming a reality.

Two further aspects have to be briefly mentioned to which later analyses will refer in more detail. Firstly, this paper again shows the prevalent "supply-led strategy", i.e. a strategy that stresses the supply of skills over the issue of demand for skills. This strategy is pursued through two approaches: one where skills are offered in order to prompt demand for them in the long run; another that seeks to satisfy employers' demand for particular skills in the short term. Once again employers are given only a passive role in generating skills, as they are asked to contribute to vocational education and training but are not obliged to do so. One might sarcastically ask why employers would contribute at all if the state is about to deliver what they demand.

Secondly, and of significance for the theoretical conclusion that will be drawn from this empirical analysis, is the continuous reference to the OECD league tables and the conclusion on pages eleven et seq. on the need to learn

---

[75] This applies even though the paper acknowledges that some young people "are lost in an apparent jungle of alternative courses and qualifications" (11).

from other countries. The OECD seems to place peer-pressure on England, particularly when it comes to intermediate skills, which England perceives itself being short of. This latter aspect provides an initial indication that policy diffusion between countries may be occurring here. The reform chapter will elaborate further on this issue.

5.2.6 White Paper "The Future of Higher Education" (DfES, 2003c)

Context of the paper
It was not until 2003 that New Labour publishes its first White Paper on higher education since coming into power in 1997, called "The Future of Higher Education" (DfES, 2003c). Until then initiatives had concentrated on school education and further education. The foreword and the first chapter of the 2003 White Paper show why this was the case: the government was convinced of the quality of England's higher education system and institutions, claiming that "British universities are a great success story" (2).

Distinct from the two other educational areas, reforms in higher education are intended to maintain its self-perceived world-class, "second to none" (DfEE, 1999) status by tackling the few existing problems – minor issues in comparison to failing schools or the question of consistent qualifications in further education. Charles Clarke was still the Secretary in charge and assumed responsibility for this paper.[76]

Structure and Proposals
The paper begins with a foreword by the Secretary of State, stating that English universities are high performers and that this state-of-affairs must be actively maintained. Nonetheless, he does mention challenges facing higher education. Specific challenges outlined were: preparing for expansion in order to achieve the target of a 50 percent participation rate in higher education by all young people aged 18-30 (7); better harnessing higher education outcomes for economic wealth creation; and ensuring fairer access to higher education regardless of a student's financial and parental background. The first chapter, which follows the Executive Summary, explains in more detail the need to take action. Chapters 2 to 7 turn to specific proposals. The proposals found in the paper are the following:
- creating stronger links between higher and further education through increasing recognition of degrees as higher education-entrance degrees;

---

[76]Charles Clarke has become famous for his arguement to cease funding the humanities because they were "unproductive" (see The Guardian, 2003).

5.2 Analysis of governmental papers in England

- the development of foundation degrees to be awarded by higher education institutions in work-relevant subjects;
- increasing flexibility in subject and course schedules to meet the diverse needs of the student body;
- fairer access to higher education through grants for students from low-income families, the possibility to defer payments of tuition fees, and grant-support for part-time students;
- the introduction of a tuition fee range between £ 0 and £ 3,000 for UK students;
- allowing universities to search for other revenue sources, e.g. endowment funds;
- creating stronger links between higher education institutions and the (regional) economy.

Analysing the Argument
As with most of the White Papers, this paper displays a vision that the government intends to pursue. This vision embraces the three most prominent discourses in education (21): higher education is meant to meet the demands of the economy in order to provide prosperity and economic wealth; higher education has a social mission to equip people with the skills needed to be successful in their jobs; and higher education provides the skills which "define our civilisation and culture", hence a goal that resembles the more 'traditional' aims of education. These threefold overlapping higher education discourses are reflected in the aims broken down in paragraph 1.45 (21 f.). These aims vary in the extent to which they have concrete applications. For instance, the aim to expand participation in higher education for young people aged 18-30 to 50 percent is straightforward. Others, by contrast, remain rather vague, such as the government's vision for a sector which:

> "recognises and values universities as creators of knowledge and understanding and as engines for applying that new knowledge for the benefit of all"

or

> "recognises their role in educating their students to live life to the full, through the acquisition of skills and through fostering imagination, creativity and contribution to society." (21)

The main three tasks, however, are summarised in the Secretary's foreword. These are, firstly, the expansion of higher education; secondly, progress in harnessing knowledge in order to achieve economic wealth; and thirdly, to ensure fairer access to higher education.

Though the government explicitly commits itself to being the main financial contributor to the higher education system, it proposes to charge students a fee for their studies, hence making them contribute to a system that must simultaneously become more attractive for even more students in order to achieve the 50 percent target. Given the goal of a 50 percent participation rate, access has to be facilitated and adapted also for those students that can not afford to take up full-time studies. It is in this context that "fairer access to higher education" has to be considered.

We might ask the question "why expand the sector in the first place?" Addressing this question leads us inevitably to the underlying assumptions of this paper. It is here that we are able to discover the main driving force behind higher education expansion. The paper presents a forecast according to which the number of higher level occupations will rise between 1999 and 2010 by over one and a half million. The "case for expansion" is also fuelled by a "comprehensive review of academic literature" (5.3) that shows that education increases productivity and that it is higher education above all which leads to economic growth and which is significantly related to per capita income growth. What appears to be uncontroversial becomes less obvious when examining the footnote attached to this paragraph, which says that "It should be noted, though, that there are both data limitations and methodological problems in isolating the contribution of any particular factor empirically." (FN 29, p. 58). This is exactly the issue the theoretical literature in this book points out: national institutions can not be examined in an isolated manner. They have to be examined in the context in which they are embedded. Only then are we able to estimate the propositions mentioned in the papers. For instance, the same argumentation would apply if university graduates would gradually squeeze out people in certain occupations where university degrees were previously not necessary for the job – but would this be the intended purpose?

We clearly see in this paper the economically-biased conviction that a knowledge-based economy is both the consequence of and the response to globalisation. Raising the skill levels of the people is meant to be the solution in order to keep step with "our economic competitors" (1.12, p. 13) in a competitive world. That is why expanding higher education is seen as an appropriate measure. The concluding section will further examine the perceived correlation between higher education and economic prosperity.

5.2.7 White Paper "21st Century Skills: Realising our Potential" (DfES, 2003b)

Context of the paper
This paper, issued in 2003, was the third White Paper (DfES, 2003b) published in this year, after "The future of higher education" and "14-19: Opportunity and

5.2 Analysis of governmental papers in England

Excellence". Whereas the previously analysed White Paper was not very rich in terms of visions and long-term aims, this is what "21st Century Skills" is all about. It is not focused on a particular educational area, e.g. school or higher education. Instead it puts the notion of "skill" at its centre and develops a skill-focused strategy by which the economic and social goals are to be achieved. The significance of this issue for New Labour, as outlined in this paper, is highlighted by the joint cooperation of no less than four departments[77], topped off with a co-authored foreword by the Prime Minister.

By referring to previous initiatives and papers, "21st Century Skills" sets up an overarching framework that strives for "high quality lifelong learning" (20) in England and highlights the coordinated endeavours it takes to realise this strategy. In fact, the coordination of all relevant deliverers and contributors to this strategy is exactly what marks one of the paper's main challenges. The inherent tension of the 14-19 period, embracing both school kids and post-compulsory schooling teenagers, becomes extremely obvious in this paper, as both groups are under the ambit of different regulations and institutional responsibilities.

Structure and Proposals
The paper begins with a foreword by no less than five authors, among which Tony Blair is the most prominent. The other four are the Secretaries of the respective departments and the Chancellor of the Exchequer Gordon Brown. After the Summary, called "Summary of the Skill Strategy", the first chapter elaborates further on the need for reform and on the intended initiatives. Chapters two to seven are devoted to discussing single proposals in more detail and chapter eight is concerned with the delivery and the implementation of the strategy. Five annexes, containing further information to which the chapters refer, accompany the text. The key proposals of this White Paper are the following:
1. as to the skill strategy:
- primary education: further emphasis on literacy, numeracy and ICT skills;
- secondary education: further introduction of work-based elements in Key Stage 4, expansion of specialised schools and academies;
- further education: strengthening apprenticeships, closer links and better responsiveness to employers' needs;

---

[77] Apart from the DfES, "21st Century Skills" is published by the Department of Trade and Industry, the Department of Work and Pensions and Her Majesty's Treasury. Thus, as Pring rightly points out, it can be said that the 'government' published the Paper, as four departments were involved (Pring, 2004, 105).

- higher education: practical oriented foundation degrees, better knowledge transfers;
- adult education: fostering life-long learning and easier access to obtain low-level qualifications for those with no qualifications;

2. others:
- closer cooperation of all relevant actors to meet the needs of employers and employees;
- creating a Skills Alliance.

Analysing the Argument
This White Paper sets out a skill strategy that comprises all relevant educational areas. Hence it encompasses school education, further education and higher education at the same time – a fact that renders this paper unique. This is highlighted by the references this paper makes to previously published papers on different educational areas, such as "Schools, achieving success", "14-19: Opportunity and excellence" and "The future of higher education". The word "skills" was always rather prevalent in the previous papers, but in this White Paper the concept is of paramount importance. The opening paragraphs of the foreword provide a good impression of the expectations that are attached to "skills":

> "The skills of our people are a vital national asset. Skills help businesses achieve the productivity, innovation and profitability needed to compete. They help our public services provide the quality and choice that people want. They help individuals raise their employability, and achieve their ambitions for themselves, their families and their communities.
> Sustaining a competitive, productive economy which delivers prosperity for all requires an ever growing proportion of skilled, qualified people. We will not achieve a fairer, more inclusive society if we fail to narrow the gap between the skills-rich and the skills-poor." (8)

This inevitably brings us to the following questions: what are 'skills?' And, what is a 'skill strategy?' There are no easy answers to these questions, and the paper does not answer in an explicit manner. "Skills" are meant to be the solution and the appropriate answer to the challenges a "knowledge-based economy" presents. Returning to the above raised questions, the "skill strategy" is meant to be a response to the "skill challenge". Hence, by working out the perceived failures that give rise to the challenge we can gain insight into what the strategy attempts to respond to. The paper is concerned with "skill gaps", such as:

"in basic skills for employability, including literacy, numeracy and use of IT; intermediate skills at apprenticeship, technician, higher craft and associate professional level; mathematics; and management and leadership." (12) However, despite "economic success [...] record low levels of unemployment [...] low inflation, and high investment to modernise public services [...] our economic productivity and competitiveness remain well below those of major competitor nations" (11).

The decisive reason for these deficiencies is – according to the paper – to be found in the gaps in skills. The "skill strategy" is therefore supposed to be the solution to ameliorate this state of affairs. The proposals of this "skill strategy" lead us closer to the first question raised in this section: what are skills? The paper suggests that skills are work and labour market-relevant proficiencies. This understanding of skills matches well with the main aim stated in chapter one, paragraph one on page 11:

"The aim of this national Skills Strategy is to ensure that employers have the right skills to support the success of their businesses, and individuals have the skills they need to be both employable and personally fulfilled." (11)

Indeed, once more taking a brief glance at the paper's proposals, the utilitarian objective of this skill approach becomes obvious. It is an approach that regards skills as a "vital national asset" (8) in which England must invest and which will provide a future profit for the entire political economy.

5.2.8 *White Paper "14-19 Education and Skills" (DfES, 2005a)*

Context of the paper
This White Paper (DfES, 2005a), published in February 2004 by the DfES under Ruth Kelly (her first White Paper as Secretary of State), was meant as a response to the "14-19 Curriculum and Qualifications Reform. Final Report of the Working Group on 14-19 Reform" (DfES, 2004a) issued in October 2004. This working group was chaired by Mike Tomlinson and the report is, therefore, commonly called the "Tomlinson Report" or "Tomlinson Review". The working group was commissioned to develop advice and recommendations for the development of programmes and qualifications in the 14-19 phase.

The recommendations of the Tomlinson Review suggest that the working group interpreted the commission's mandate broadly, in that proposals embraced the whole 14-19 phase, i.e. vocational and academic education. However, the governmental White Paper "21st Century Skills," which referred already to the forthcoming work of the Tomlinson group, emphasises its role more as "the development of more coherent vocational programmes" (75). At a first glance this seems to be a triviality; in fact, however, it turns out to be the crucial point when analysing the DfES response (hence the White Paper "14-19 Education and Skills") to the Tomlinson Review. The working group was concerned with creating an all-embracing 14-19 qualification framework, which implied the gradual phasing out of individual GCSE and A-level qualifications. Instead, it proposed a unified system of diplomas for the 14-19 phase at four levels: entry, foundation (roughly at level GCSE grades D-G), intermediate (approximately equivalent to GCSE grades A*-C), and advanced (at the level of A-levels or advanced vocational courses). What sounds like a mere re-labelling of existing qualifications was in fact meant to overcome the traditional structure's tendency to divide academic and vocational education.

This is highlighted by the suggestion not only to abolish GCSEs and A-levels but also to integrate the Modern Apprenticeship scheme into the Diploma framework. The idea behind this framework was to provide for a smooth transition between academic and vocational education, to eliminate dead-end qualifications with no further chances to progress, and to make a major step towards "parity of esteem". Rather than dealing with individual qualifications, this framework was supposed to work with building blocks from which pupils could choose based on content and how far they want to proceed. Beginning already in the last two years of compulsory schooling, the framework was intended to provide incentives for pupils to stay in education, preferably until the age of 19. This Diploma framework, considered as a "flexible ladder of progression" (Connor and Little, 2005, 56), was the core proposal of the working group.

The report was largely welcomed in the White Paper. Yet it was precisely this core proposal that was disregarded, not only by the paper but also in forthcoming policy initiatives. Scanning the paper for proposals and for basic assumptions, the adherence of the government to the traditional architecture of education in the 14-19 phase is obvious. The government clings to the distinction between vocational and academic education, reflected in different qualificational setups. Its main efforts were concentrated on vocational education while leaving academic education mostly untouched.

This attitude was highlighted by the fact that the government wanted to "retain GCSEs and A-levels as cornerstones of the new system" (6, 44). Hodgson and Spours rightly point out the main conflict in saying:

> "At the root of all the debates about 14-19 reform is a clash of education philosophies – New Labour is reconciled to managing a divided system and Tomlinson was intent, in the long term at least, to abolish it." (Hodgson and Spours, 2005, 6)

5.2 Analysis of governmental papers in England

While taking a pledge for continuing educational reforms in England, the White Paper also mentions the need for stability in the system after having just recently introduced the "Curriculum 2000" programme, which offered more choice at A-levels (6). Moreover, the White Paper criticises the lack of clarity and transparency in the 14-19 phase (14) and states that "we must not overburden the system with change" (11). Thus, in this context the announcement of a new qualification alongside the already existing ones must have come as a surprise, regarding not only the fact of a new qualification but also its name: diplomas.

Due primarily to its rejection of the Diploma Framework, the White Paper was subject to some harsh critiques. Hodgson and Spours sum it up in affirming that the paper:

> "signal[s] the continuation of the existing order: a divided and alienating system based upon a strong break at 16; a mechanical and selective approach to general education; and vocational education for the less able with no guarantee of a greater commitment by employers." (Hodgson and Spours, 2005, 1)

To conclude this section, this White Paper already referred to the next White Paper "Getting on in business, getting on at work" (DfES, 2005b), which was issued only three months later. Both papers stated that they should be seen in combination with each other, as taken together the two papers reveal the Skills Strategy the government is pursuing. Understanding these papers as complementary reveals, however, another indicator of New Labour's adherence to the academic-vocational education divide. Whereas the White Paper discussed above deals mainly with school-based aspects of the 14-19 agenda, the latter one "just" discusses the approach to vocational education in more detail.

Structure and Proposals
The obligatory foreword by the Secretary of State is followed by the equally obligatory Executive Summary. The introduction to the actual proposals, however, turns out to be longer than usual. After the Introduction chapter there is the chapter about "The challenges we must overcome", which depicts in further detail the most pressing problems in English 14-19 education. The third introductory chapter of this White Paper is called "Vision" and attempts to explain how the challenges are to be met. The main proposals – besides the rejection of the Diploma framework suggested by the Tomlinson Review – are the following:

- the introduction of specialised diploma qualifications (alongside existing qualifications) at levels 1-3 to be awarded in 14 vocational "lines";

- the reduction of compulsory A-level modules from six to four and allowing pupils to choose harder questions in A-level exams in order to provide a better selection basis for universities;
- GCSEs to be retained while reviewing Key Stage 3 curriculum;
- the introduction of a separate General Diploma for recognising the achievement of five GCSEs at levels A*-C.

Analysing the Argument
It was probably in anticipation of the criticism for rejecting the Diploma framework proposed by the Tomlinson working group that the government put the notion of "choice" even more at the centre of its considerations than it had previously done. The strongly inclusive and unified approach by Tomlinson is contrasted to an "approach of choice" in which everybody should have access to tailored education according to his/her needs. This reveals, in contrast to Tomlinson, an almost Durkeimian approach, where people become a constitutive and valuable part of a coherent society by becoming specialised in the areas in which they have talents. Realising, however, that the sharp divide between academic and vocational education hinders people from "travelling" between areas and thus potentially blocks them from discovering their real talents, New Labour introduced the specialised Diplomas as a kind of "bridge qualification" between the two areas. The choices of qualifications available are supposed to be the "routes to success for all" (6).

What "success" actually means remains unclear; but understanding "success" is vital for understanding the aims of this White Paper. The foreword gives us an initial idea when it refers to the "twin aims" of economic prosperity and social justice. The more we elaborate on the underlying aims, however, the more we become aware that the latter aim is gradually dropped. The chapter entitled "The challenges we must overcome" (paragraphs 2.5 to 2.11) reveals that "success" in mainly understood economically.

So again, what exactly is the underlying line of argumentation? Skills policy is construed as an appropriate response-device to ameliorate the pressures to which the country is exposed. This functionalistic approach is clearly expressed by reference to economic pressures that are challenging the existing structure: "in this interdependent world, currents of economic change in other parts of the world can quickly affect this country [...]." (15). Structural economic developments "mean that even service industries serving one country can be sited in another" (15) and, given the decline in low-skill, manual jobs, "make greater demands on a young person's capacity to communicate, present themselves, work in teams and understand diversity" (15). Thus the determination to act is due to:

5.2 Analysis of governmental papers in England 147

> "the need to offer every young person the opportunity to become educated and skilled [which] is not an economic imperative, but a moral one." (15)

The case for reforms is even highlighted by a graph showing that productivity rises with skill attainment. Again, the paper reveals in an extremely obvious manner the government's supply-led approach when it claims that a "critical mass of highly-skilled people will continue to attract [...] employers to this country." (16) The paper largely disregards the demand aspect of skills and clings to the belief that providing skills in high quantities and qualities will eventually lead to economic prosperity, in-part triggered by foreign investments. Assuming this to be a common belief among Western economies, we have to take a closer look at how the paper intends to achieve these aims. With respect to the structure of the paper, one has to elaborate on "the vision" that is to guide policies along the path. Chapter three is entirely devoted to developing this vision. The main vision, which is put down in paragraph 3.2 (22), is the following:

> "Our vision is therefore that our education system should provide every young person with a route to success in life through hard work and dedication."

This vision is to be implemented by providing a system that allows people to equip "themselves with the skills and attributes that employers need" (22). It is a system which is based on the extension to pupils and students of a choice between qualifications that have been established in close cooperation with employers.

The whole paper is based on two underlying assumptions that are taken for granted but are, in fact, far from being uncontested. One of these assumptions is that higher skills produce higher productivity. This is even highlighted by the figure 2.2 in the paper, which reflects productivity in terms of wages and shows that earnings increase with qualification levels. Though this is not the right place to criticise these assumptions, there is a need to at least briefly comment on this claim. The only correlation this figure shows is that better educated people tend to earn more. It does not, however, show that an increase in skills will inevitably follow this linear correlation. An additional unit of skill might just as easily lead to a relative decline in income.

We do not need to elaborate on this assumption in more detail in order to see that it is entirely based on the belief that higher skills will produce an economic surplus, while it disregards the demand for skills, in that enterprises might not have the willingness nor the necessity to hire higher skilled employees and to pay them higher salaries.

The second hidden assumption relates to the relationship between skills and international competitiveness, which is also supposed to be linear. The case for reforms in education is constantly justified by referring to the need to maintain and increase international competitiveness. The theoretical literature review of this work shows, however, that political economies do not compete simultaneously for all products and services on a global scale (Hall and Soskice, 2001). Rather it is the specialisation of political economies that provides them with a competitive position on the international market. It needs to be asked if such specialisation really requires the upgrading of an entire people's skills. Moreover, one needs to be clear about which products and services are competing on a global scale in the first place. When the White Paper mentions that even services can now be located abroad, this is only half of the truth. The vast bulk of low-wage, low-skill service jobs in England are neither exportable nor importable (Keep, 2007). Additionally, when the paper talks about attracting employers to the country by generating higher skills, it again leaves excludes numerous other aspects that might influence employers decisions to (re-)locate in England.

Further to this, as we have seen, England is determined to follow a supply-led strategy, i.e. increasing the quantity and quality of skills and expecting through this to induce positive economic results. Thus, the demand-side of skills is left to its own devices. That this strategy is not inevitably conducive to success is exemplified by countries such as Canada and Scotland, in which high societal skill levels did not automatically lead to better economic performances. It suggests that an overarching skills strategy needs to take into consideration how to stimulate also the demand-side. This, however, seems to be the "crunchpoint" in English politics, which is driven by a strong liberal and market-oriented approach. The question is thus how to stimulate the economy and encourage employers to use the supplied skills without intervening in the mechanisms of the market (Keep, 2007, 9; Keep, Mayhew and Payne, 2006; Lloyd and Payne, 2004, 3 ff.). I will elaborate further on this issue below.

Returning to the concepts that seem to impact on policy decisions, in this paper the notions of "choice" and of a system "tailored to the needs of the individual pupil" are most importance (22). Both are supposed to be conducive to New Labour's aim to prepare young people for a life in which they can "pursue their aspirations, and through hard work qualify themselves to succeed, equipping themselves with the skills and attributes that employers need." (22)

To sum up this section, it has to be said that this paper, in contrast to most of the previous ones, appears to be "devoid of a broad and forward-looking educational vision [...]" (Hodgson and Spours, 2005, 4). Considering this paper and the next White Paper together, one gains an even more strong impression that the papers' intentions are to react to the Tomlinson Review by providing self-affirmation that the academic-vocational divide in English education policies still makes sense.

5.2.9 White Paper "Getting on in business, getting on at work" (DfES, 2005b)

Context of the paper
Only three months after the publication of "14-19 Education and Skills" the DfES with participation of the DTI, the DWP and the HMT (hence the same departments as for "21st Century Skills: Realising our Potential") issued the White Paper "Getting on in business, getting on at work" (DfES, 2005b). As the previous paper indicated, this paper and its predecessor have to be understood in combination with each other, as both together outline the 14-19 skill strategy. The main difference is that this paper emphasised the vocational and practical component of this phase, whereas the predecessor was both a response to the Tomlinson Review and focused on the school component of the 14-19 period.

Structure and Proposals
Atypically, this paper is divided into three parts, with each being physically separated from the others. The first part explains in an abstract way what the Skill Strategy is about: making England "the best educated, best trained, best skilled country in the world" (2), of "making this country a world leader in skills" (5). Part II provides a more in-depth elaboration of the proposals whereas part III serves as a source of empirical evidence (a technical annex as it is called) to which the first two parts refer. The main proposals and targets of this White Paper are the following:

- the increase of participation in education rate at age 17 from 75 to 90 percent in the next 10 years;
- the increase of Apprenticeship completion rates by 75 percent between 2003 and 2008;
- the creation of a network of employer-led Skills Academies;
- the intensification of collaboration on all levels in order to match the supply of skills with the demand by employers;
- the creation of Regional Skills Partnerships;
- the announcement of the Foster Review due in autumn 2005 on the future role of further education colleges.

Analysing the Argument
This paper complements its successor in forming an entire "Skills Strategy". It is focused on the vocational, non-school education and training component of this Strategy. This strategy aims at nothing other than making the country the "world leader in skills" (5). Again, this paper immediately follows a common pattern seen in the papers. Where the foreword refers in its first paragraph to the "twin goals of social justice and economic success" (1), the remainder of the paper elaborates in detail on the latter of the two aims, while by and large neglecting the first one.

The section called "The Challenge" (5 ff.) reveals the underlying utilitarian approach of this "Skills Strategy". It is about equipping the country's people with the skills the need to be competitive in a global marketplace" of high value-added goods and services" (5). It goes on to describe the imminent danger that, for example, China and India, which have been competing on the basis of low labour costs, are "increasingly competing not just on cost, but on expertise", as the number of graduates are increasing in both political economies.

We encounter here also another typical pattern of the papers: a comparison with other countries. This comparison is made with two purposes in mind. The obvious one is to justify political action, as England is supposed to compete with these reference-countries on a global scale. Secondly, it is a method to create the "we", to close the ranks and to prepare "our nation" for the challenges it is exposed to in the increasingly globalised world.

However, there is something exceptional about this paper, namely its increased concern with the demand for newly generated skills, which can be seen in paragraphs 7, 19 and 20 of "Part I: Overview". First and foremost the White Paper commissions Lord Sandy Leitch to review and forecast the long-term skills needs up to 2020. Moreover, the paper speaks of the risk of a "low skills equilibrium" in which England run the risk of being trapped (6). The government (and again we can dare to say "government", as four departments were involved in the draft of this paper) expresses its conviction that "skills", i.e. their generation at a level of high quality, will help to overcome this low skills equilibrium. The paper says: "Lack of skills makes it harder for employers to introduce the innovations, new products and new working methods that feed improvements in productivity" (6). This statement thereby justifies and explains both the country-inherent supply-led approach to vocational education and training and the lack of employer involvement in the vocational education and training arena.

It is this perception that leads the paper to place at its centre the issue of how to ensure the supply of skills the English economy needs. Thus, central for this paper is cooperation with employers for, firstly, detecting the needed skills

5.2 Analysis of governmental papers in England

and, secondly, for generating the skills. Again we come across the underlying assumption that an increase in quantity and quality of skills correlates linearly with productivity. This statement is only slightly weakened by recognising the following:

> "Skills alone cannot guarantee economic success, social justice and fulfilling personal lives. But they are one necessary contribution which, if combined in the right way with other factors such as enterprise and innovation, make success more likely. All of our major competitors are investing in skills." (6)

The government's emphasis on the key role skills is again highlighted by the statement that:

> "Skills are the key to so many of our economic and social goals, in our personal lives, at work, and in our communities." (25)

Thus, while aware of the fact that "skills" alone are unlikely to change the situation in England, New Labour nevertheless assigns them a key role in tackling numerous economic and social issues. This deep belief in the enabling function of an increased stock and quality of skills is probably the main reason for New Labour's overwhelming commitment to education policy.

The Skills Strategy, however, has also its demand-led aspects. More precisely, as outlined in paragraph 23 on page 9, the government offers employers a system that allows them to voice their needs, providing information on the basis of which the government can act. In other words, the system is not demand-led to the extent that employers actively contribute to satisfying their own skill needs. It is still the supply of employees with already acquired skills that drives the system and employers take on the role of customers in the English "education and skill-store". This is the foundational and basic condition that is considered to have "market"-like qualities (Keep, 2006a). Where this market fails the government will exert extra efforts to ameliorate the situation (Keep, 2006a). To make this point very clear, this "market" is thus a "perverse market," as the supplier (the government) puts itself in the driving seat to produce skills the demander would like to have – and this at almost no extra cost for the demanders and ultimate users. Hence, it is the unwillingness and un-necessity of employers to become directly involved in the training of employees that determines the system.

5.2.10 White Paper "Higher Standards, Better Schools For All: More choice for parents and pupils (DfES, 2005c)

Context of the paper
After the reshuffling of the cabinet in 2004 due to the resignation of David Blunkett (himself a former Education Secretary, although by then he was Home Secretary) Ruth Kelly became the Secretary of the DfES. This White Paper was the first paper on schools for which she assumed responsibility (DfES, 2005c). The paper was highly contested. One of the main proposals emphasised in the paper was more individualised and differentiated learning for pupils, which was widely welcomed. The other core proposal, however, caused huge debate, namely the plan to introduce Trust Schools. Trusts were intended to have charitable and non-profit making status, though it would also allow enterprises to get involved. Assets like buildings and land would be transferred to trust ownership. The governance of these schools would to a great extent be left to the trusts' own devices, including staffing, finances, and admission. More concretely, these schools would be freed from the strict regulations concerning pupil admission that apply to state schools.

The White Paper triggered an alternative White Paper initiated by Members of Parliament of the Labour Party (Morris et al., 2005). One of the main figures of this counter-response which was backed by almost 100 Labour MPs was Estelle Morris, former Labour Education Secretary. This alternative paper uttered the concern that "the proposed development of a body of self-regulating schools without an effective system of accountability or measures to ensure that the interests of all pupils are protected and advanced" (Morris et al., 2005, 4) is not only a deviation from the mantra "standards not structures" but would above all be the first step down the road of a selective school system. In particular the relaxed admission regulations for the new breed of Trust Schools would lead to more social inequality. The authors are furthermore very reserved as to the increased involvement of parents in school governance, highlighting that only a small number is likely to be willing and able to be involved in schooling issues.

Eventually, it was a bill amendment which strengthened fair admission and thereby finally motivated the opponents of the White Paper to agree to the bill only three months after having drafted their alternative paper. Furthermore the notion "Trust School" was abandoned, though the idea was being mantled in "Foundation Schools" and "Voluntary Aided Schools".

Structure and Proposals
The paper commences with two forewords, one by Prime Minister Tony Blair and one by the by then Secretary of State for Education and Skills Ruth Kelly.

The former forward appreciates the reforms undertaken thus far by New Labour while at the same time proclaiming the need for further reforms in the sector in order to achieve "world class" (1). These two introductory paragraphs are followed by a brief history of school education in which Blair outlines developments from 1944 to 1997 and Labour's reforms since then. Kelly's foreword resembles Blair's – apart from the historical overview – in that it appreciates the steps taken since New Labour's assumption of government in 1997, while also pointing out challenges the school system still faces.

The subsequent Executive Summary summarises the policies proposed in the paper. The first chapter, called "The Challenge to Reform" deals more thoroughly with developments and initiatives undertaken since 1997, followed by an evaluation of the still unsolved problems and concluding with a final section about how these problems are to be tackled. The following eight chapters (2 to 9) turn to particular issues and proposals, such as "Personalised Learning" or "A New Role for Local Authorities". The following proposals are presented:
- the changing role of local authorities "from provider to commissioner" (11);
- the introduction of a new institution in the school landscape, the so-called Trust school;
- the increase in the amount of information available to parents on primary and secondary schools;
- the introduction of "dedicated choice advisors" to give less well-off parents assistance in examining and selecting their options;
- the further relaxation of controls and regulations on well-performing schools;
- allowing specialised schools to specialise even further;
- the expansion of individualised learning for pupils, such as one-to-one tutorials for underperformers and more choices for the most talented pupils;
- the extension of opportunities for after-school group learning in different subjects.

Analysing the Argument
This White Paper was relatively silent about overriding educational goals. Some cautious references were made to a "globalised world" that requires high educational standards (7); or the scale of economic challenges which leave no other choice than ambitiously pushing forward with the reforms first started in 1997 (20). Some references are also made to social policy goals such as social mobility (5, 7). Personalised education for low-performing pupils, which would allow them to catch up with others in their class, is meant to be a device to pursue both aims, rising standards and increasing social mobility. Yet, it is worthwhile to concentrate on the argumentation for the proposal that received

the most criticism. The introduction of "Trust Schools" represents less of an educational necessity. In fact, as the opponents of the White Paper point out, there is no evidence that low-performing schools could be "turned around" by transforming them into Trust Schools (Morris et al., 2005, 3,7). An educational-driven argument for Trust Schools is also missing from the White Paper.

Instead, Trust Schools seems to be an attempt to further privatise parts of the English education system – rather than providing services, the state regulates the provision of services. Local Authorities are assigned a crucial role in this transformation. As Blair puts it in his foreword to the White Paper:

> "The local authority must move from being a provider of education to being its local commissioner and the champion of parent choice" (1).

Parents are clearly understood as costumers who demand choice and excellence for their children. This is the kind of engaged parents the DfES had in mind when writing the White Paper and matches with the consumer-driven approach of New Labour in school education.

What in fact appears to have had the biggest impact on this White Paper's approach to structural reforms, such as the introduction of Trust Schools, are considerations about reforms in the public sector. Naturally, outsourcing and privatising the maintenance of public green spaces is easier than doing the same in education policy. However, Trust Schools are another step down the road to the greater involvement of private enterprise and the state's eventual shedding of responsibility for the direct provision of education and its transfer to other actors, as has been done to some extent with City Academies and Foundation Schools (which substituted grant-maintained schools).

5.2.11 White Paper "Further Education: Raising Skills, Improving Life Chances" (DfES, 2006)

Context of the paper
This paper (DfES, 2006), issued in March 2006 and signed by Ruth Kelly (Secretary of State), Tony Blair (Prime Minister) and Gordon Brown (Chancellor of the Exchequer), was an answer to the so-called Foster Review. This review was entitled "Realising the potential. A review of the future role of further education colleges". It was chaired by Sir Andrew Foster (Foster, 2005) and published in November 2005. It came out in favour of a clear emphasis of colleges on economically valuable skills, for more specialisation of colleges, for higher transparency of the performances of colleges and learners, and for

5.2 Analysis of governmental papers in England 155

strengthening common regulatory patterns. Hence, this Review is definitely more in line with the general governmental position on the issues than was the Tomlinson Review.

This paper was the third White Paper on further education within one year. The White Paper "14-19 Education and Skills" was a response to Tomlinson and a justification why the government did not want to embark on the main proposal the Review suggested, namely the comprehensive Diploma framework. Soon afterwards, the paper "Getting on in business, getting on at work," came out to clarify the particular Skills Strategy the government intended to pursue and setting some interesting achievement targets. This newest paper places a greater emphasis on the institutional shape of the sector, reflecting on the general setup needed to achieve the targets and aims set in the previous papers.

Structure and Proposals
As usual, the White Paper is divided into a Foreword, an Executive Summary, and an Introduction that clarifies the intention of the paper, followed by chapters (six of them) turning to particular initiatives and concluded by a chapter about implementation issues. Structured according to the six main areas with which the White Paper deals, the main proposals are the following:
- specialisation (extension of Centres of Excellence and National Skills Academies programmes, specialist networks between colleges, stronger Sixth Form College sector);
- meeting employers and learner needs (learner accounts programme, Train to Gain programme operated with specific brokers);
- a strategy for better teaching and learning (installation of a Quality Improvement Strategy, Continuing Professional Development programme, facilitated access for new providers);
- spreading success and eliminating failure (scoreboards indicating the quality of institutions and allowing for comparisons and special devices for poor performers);
- funding (free tuition for all 19-25 year-olds for the first level 3 qualification);
- a new relationship with colleges and other educational providers (public service reform).

Analysing the Argument
This paper has two unique aspects that are worth elaborating upon in detail. Firstly, we encounter a slight change in language. Secondly, the impact of considerations about public service reform is even more striking than in the previous papers.

To begin with the first point, the paper talks of a "new dynamism within the system" that will be achieved by a "clear economic mission" for all further education colleges (12, paragraph 46). The previous papers attempted to maintain at least the appearance that reforms were intended to meet the twin aims of social justice and economic success, while most also saw them as conducive to personal development as well.

Arguably, this paper is about further education and as such it does not come as a surprise that the economic value of education is specifically emphasised. However, the clear dedicationn to an "economic mission" (later on it is also called the "employability mission" (65, paragraph 6.1)) for education had never before been stated as unequivocally as in this White Paper. This mission reflects the government's ambitions to focus on the "employability and progression of learners" (5, paragraph 14). The paper puts it even more bluntly in paragraph 15 (6):

> "So we will put the economic mission of the sector at the heart of its role. That means defining its central purpose as being to equip young people and adults with the skills, competences and qualifications that employers want, and which will prepare them for productive, rewarding, high-value employment in a modern economy."

This mission is being pursued, in particular, by means of further specialisation of the schemes, as the proposals enumerated above show. The authors of the paper were aware that this clearly confined "economic" approach to further education might provoke criticism and attempted to tackle it in advance. Thus the paper stresses that the "economic mission" does not automatically equal "narrow vocationalism", as learners will be taught general education as well. The paper also mentions a "social mission", though it is not discussed in further detail (6, paragraph 19). "Social justice," which is one sibling of the twin aims, does not appear until the very end of the Executive Summary and the notion of social inclusion is mentioned only in the second half of chapter two, where the paper attempts to marginally rebalanced the overwhelming focus on the economic value of further education.

The "economic mission" expresses the belief of the government that:

> "Our economic future depends on our productivity as a nation. That requires a labour force with skills to match the best in the world." (1)

And it rests on the government's observation that "at present, Further Education is not achieving its full potential as the powerhouse of a high skills economy" (1). Again, the paper fails to define what exactly a "high skills economy" is. Additionally, the aspect of "skills demand" is in a way contradictory. The

5.2 Analysis of governmental papers in England

government attempted to do two things at the same time. On the one hand it sought to ensure the collaboration of providers, Learning and Skill Councils (LSC) and other actors with employers in order to identity the needed skills for the economy and to subsequently provide them. On the other hand, however, the government commissioned a working group, chaired by Lord Sandy Leitch, tasked to identify the required skills of tomorrow, and by "tomorrow" the government means up to 2020. Despite the scepticism that we might have about such a long-term forecast, this review affirmed the continuation of the Government's agenda and belief that the area has to be steered, that skills have to be anticipated, and that skills must be generated beforehand.

The second important aspect at stake in this paper is that the:

> "measures set out in this White Paper build on [...] the public service reform principles that the Government has adopted in other sectors." (5, paragraph 12)

That is not to imply that this kind of reference does not appear in the other papers examined. Nevertheless, this paper clearly visualises education policy as being not just about educational targets and aims that are often closely linked to economic goals. "Education" is also a public service. If it is not produced by the state then it is at least regulated and monitored by public authorities. Thus, reforms of the public sector also include educational policy. The usage of particular words in the paper again brings the language of "new public management" to mind. Words like "consumer" referring to the relation between providers on the one hand and learners and employers on the other (34, paragraph 3.1); "transparency and accountability" caused by close assessments of colleges (55); or "strategic commissioner" when describing the role of the Learning and Skills Councils (76) – all these notions, presented in the context of the constant use of "demand" and "supply," indicate that it is not only about education as such, but in fact also about the governance of education.

Along this line, we observe a tension throughout all the papers regarding the governance of education institutions, a tension that is typically inherent in the discourse about "new public management"[78] (Steer et al., 2007, 4 f.; Homburg, Pollitt and van Thiel, 2007, 4 f.; McLaughlin et al., 2002): devolution of competencies in service provision is reconciled with closer regulation and monitoring. In fact, this is one of the most striking underlying patterns of the English education system: privatisation where it is feasible, assigning responsibilities to lower levels where it is possible, applying a dense regulatory framework against which performances of education institutions (and learners)

---

[78] Moreover, the discourse about "partnership" among all relevant actors refers to the "New Public Management" debate (compare with Klijn, Edelenbos and Hughes, 2007, 73 f.).

are to be assessed, and intervening and re-delegating powers when needed to improve deficiencies. The language used is intended to emphasise that devolution opens up further options to the local level for obtaining the performance targets:

> "If the FE system is to be capable of responding to the challenges of 14-19 reform and improving adult skills as this White Paper proposes, then we need to reshape the relationship between central government (and its agents) and education and training providers to release more of their energy, initiative and dynamism." (77, paragraph 7.1)

To conclude, this paper shows even more strongly than the others the impact of administrative considerations on (re-)shaping the education system. It is neither solely "education" as such, nor the mere reference to an economic discourse about the economic value of education, which entirely explains the line of argumentation in these papers. They are also highly influenced by a discourse of how educational goals should be achieved in terms of structure.

5.3 Analysis of governmental papers in Germany

The German education policy landscape is considerably more fragmented than the English. The main reason for this fact lies in the German federalist system, with the states being responsible for educational policies. Moreover, the social partnership between employers and employees is the crucial backbone of the vocational education and training system, rendering the overall system even more complex. As a consequence, we cannot refer to one single source as we did in the English case with the department for education White and Green Papers. The problem of finding appropriate papers that meet the needs of this research is further aggravated by the fact that there is no White and Green Paper-culture in Germany as there is in England. Therefore, the selection of sources consists of different types of papers, among which there are government declarations, federal reports, government comments, and announcements of government actions. This patchwork nevertheless provides a coherent picture of how Germany perceives its own situation, problems and challenges with respect to educational policies. As it was with the English section, the purpose of this chapter is to understand the overall concepts which guide and accompany the educational discussion in Germany. The papers will be presented in chronological order.

5.3 Analysis of governmental papers in Germany

5.3.1 Government declaration by the Federal Chancellor Gerhard Schröder in Parliament (10.11.1998; Schröder 1998)

Context of the paper
This was the first government declaration of Chancellor Gerhard Schröder in November 1998, less than one month after the Social Democratic Party (SPD) had won the general elections and come into power by means of a coalition with the Green Party. This government declaration came in the form of a speech in the German Parliament and presented the major guidelines the new government intended to pursue. The most pressing social issue at this time was the high rate of unemployment (Schröder, 1998). This applied equally and even more so to youth unemployment, making the vocational education and training system of central importance (Schröder, 1998).

Structure and Proposals
The government declaration is by and large devoid of concrete policy proposals. Instead, it makes more superficial references to various issues such as unemployment, tax policy, labour market policy, industrial policy, European policy, and foreign policy. Schröder attempted to present some broad guidelines along which his government's policies should be oriented, along with accusing the previous government for some of contemporary Germany's deficiencies. In paragraph six Schröder turned to educational issues (Schröder 1998, paragraph 6). The main suggestions for educational policy as presented in the declaration were the following:

- the creation of an active labour market policy, including further education;
- the issue of an immediate action programme in order to ameliorate unemployment among young people;
- the strengthening of lifelong learning;
- the creation of new incentives for supporting an increase in the supply of apprenticeships;
- improved educational planning in order to match demand and supply for academics;
- achieving more market mechanisms in higher education.

Analysing the Argument
As already mentioned, this was the first official statement in Parliament by the new government and we have to understand its meaning against the background of high unemployment rates, including among young people. Schröder pointed out that the imperative for these times is to meet the challenge of a European knowledge society (Schröder, 1998, paragraph 6). Interestingly enough he

provides a brief definition of how he comprehends a knowledge society: for him a knowledge society means a qualification-society. Thereby he underlines that a knowledge-society it is not about generating a knowledge-elite but about qualifying the whole society. Thus, it is the leitmotif of a knowledge society that Germany is meant to pursue. In this first declaration of the new government the chancellor already sketched some paths for achieving this aim. Regarding vocational education and training, he announced closer cooperation with employers – in particular with large firms – to develop further apprenticeship openings in order to get as many young people in vocational education and training as possible, as well as financial incentives to enable young people to continue their educations.

On higher education he announced the introduction of more competitive mechanisms between higher education institutions and educational planning that matches demand and supply for academic workforces.

These considerations were underpinned by three aspects: firstly, one of Schröder's main concerns seemed to be to ensure equal opportunities. He stressed the importance of equal access to education regardless of parental, cultural or socio-economic background. Secondly, this paper indicates the significance of international comparisons for educational reforms in Germany. In making a comparison of European countries Schröder claimed that young people in Germany stay too long in education before taking on responsibilities in the occupational world (Schröder, 1998). In the same breath, however, he stated that shortening educational periods must not occur at the expense of educational quality. In what appears to be an attempt to square the circle, the Chancellor makes reference to a third aspect – "bessere Verteilung der Ausbildung auf die Lebenszeit", or what is commonly known as lifelong learning. He pledged to enhance lifelong education and further education through more flexible training regulations and qualification procedures.

This brief statement about educational policy in Germany already contains the main issues that we will encounter in the following sections: a knowledge society which is underpinned by the principle of lifelong learning; the crucial significance of international comparative data as a guideline along which policies are oriented; and the social aim of equal access to education. Yet, it remains to be shown below what Schröder meant by the reference to a knowledge society (as understood as a qualification society).

5.3.2 Mut zur Veränderung: Deutschland braucht moderne Hochschulen – Vorschläge für eine Reform (BMBF, 1999)

Context of the paper
This paper was the first government declaration by the Federal Minister for education and research, Edelgard Bulmahn (BMBF, 1999). It evaluated the educational situation in the country after 16 years of conservative/liberal government under Chancellor Kohl, and, turning explicitly to higher education and research, called for the "Courage to Change" (thus the officially translated name of the document). According to Bulmahn, change and reform were needed as there were undeniable signs of crisis in the German higher education system. The following were taken as indicators of this crisis (see BMBF, 1999, 1):
- underfunding of the system;
- underinvestment in buildings and equipment;
- long completion periods;
- high dropout rates;
- insufficient labour market orientations of higher education;
- decreasing attractiveness on an international level.

The paper was published in April 1999, hence only two months before the so-called Bologna declaration was signed by 29 European countries. Thus Bulmahn's call to restructure the higher education system coincided with "Bologna," which caused one of the most extensive higher education reform efforts in post-war Germany. Furthermore, this paper announced the establishment of a regular educational forum (Forum Bildung) in which politicians, academics and the representatives of the economic sector discuss recent developments and future requirements of the German educational system.

Structure and Proposals
After a short introduction in which she explains the difficult heritage left by the conservative government, Bulmahn stresses the importance of the higher education sector for the future viability of Germany and makes a case for reforms. She presents five leitmotifs along which higher education reforms should be oriented:
1. equal opportunities in terms of gender and social background;
2. creativity in higher education institutions through conferring autonomy on the institutions;
3. better transfer of knowledge to economy and society;
4. focus on research on sustainable growth;

5. understanding accelerated national and international structural change as a chance for action.

This is then followed by proposals that indicate how the government intends to reform higher education along the sketched leitmotifs. Bulmahn classifies her suggestions into four areas:
1. Guaranteeing equal opportunities:
- maintaining parity of esteem of vocational and academic education
- reform of the federal education assistance act

2. Supporting creativity and autonomy
- greater administrative autonomy for higher education institutions by means of global budgets (investment vouchers)
- regular performance evaluation of higher education institutions (enrolment rates, quality, supervision)
- reducing duration of study
- modularisation of studies and introduction of credit point systems
3. Strengthening research by means of cooperation:
- closer cooperation between universities and research institutions
- internationalisation by encouraging foreign students and researchers to come to Germany
- closer cooperation between economic and higher education institutions in order to economically harness research
- facilitating start-ups by graduates and researchers
4. Social responsibility of higher education
- increasing investment in higher education over the next five years

Analysing the Argument
This government document, though short on concrete and directly applicable proposals, offers a great number of thoughts on how a future higher education system in Germany should be shaped. We see that this document basically has four main elements: 1) governance and administration of higher education institutions; 2) access to higher education institutions; 3) cooperation with the economy and harnessing research more efficiently; and 4) the role of German higher education institutions in an international higher education and research environment. On the issue of governance and administration, we observe a common current trend, one which we have already encountered in the English case, namely the re-structuring of public administration according to principles that are commonly subsumed under the heading "New Public Management" (NPM). NPM is a mixture of conferring competencies to lower units while

5.3 Analysis of governmental papers in Germany 163

strengthening framework regulation, operating with global budgets that are distributed according to performance indicators and at the same time strengthening accountability of higher education institutions. This is exactly what Bulmahn is suggesting. Yet, we have to be reminded that the federal level is only a co-contributor to the higher education area, the main expenditures are borne by the Länder. At this time, however, the federal level still had great power over the regulation of higher education issues among all Länder through the German Higher Education Framework Act.[79]

The second main issue refers to access to higher education institutions. The German government, represented in this case by Bulmahn, is particularly aware of equality issue in terms of the genders and social backgrounds of students. In contrast to England, facilitating and ensuring equality of access to higher education in Germany was not lumped together with expansion more broadly. However, we will see further below that this has changed, as Germany has become increasingly aware of its low higher education participation rates in contrast to other OECD countries (compare with coming declaration "Bildung, Forschung, Innovation – der Zukunft Gestalt geben" (BMBF, 2002)).

Thirdly, the paper argues in favour of closer cooperation between the economy on the one hand, and higher education and research, on the other. Though Bulmahn denies that it is all about the efficient usage of higher education and research outcomes, it is exactly this aspect that is stressed in this declaration: a stronger practise-orientation of higher education (BMBF, 1999, 1), a stronger economic utilisation of higher education and research (BMBF, 1999, 17 f.), and stronger efforts in facilitating start-ups (BMBF, 1999, 17 f.).

Fourthly, and here we can already see a specific trait of the German higher education discourse, we observe how the German higher education system is being placed in an international context and how conclusions are drawn from this comparison. Apart from placing the German political economy in a globalised internationally competitive context, there are two particular aspects where the need to reform higher education is justified by pointing to foreign experiences. First, Bulmahn refers to international experiences with a more market-driven and autonomy-providing governance approach (BMBF 1999, 2; compare with first point in this section). She discusses, all in the same paragraph, the need to confer more autonomy on higher education institutions; the need to introduce competition among institutions and to allow them to develop their own profiles; the need to ensure accountability by the introduction of performance goals; and

---

[79]This act was abolished in 1997 in the context of the German federalism reform, which provided greater autonomy to the Länder in all higher education issues whilst at the same time the federal level gained powers with regards to the so-called Bologna process and for the implementation of the Initiative for Excellence (Exzellenzinitiative).

the need to make funding dependent on these performance indicators.

Second, Bulmahn criticises the long length of study in Germany in comparison to American universities (BMBF, 1999, 10). In fact, and as we will see later on, it is these two issues – competition and market mechanisms among higher education institutions and shortening the duration of study – that are the drivers of two of the main reforms in the German higher education area in the last decade, namely the two-stage degree system of bachelor and master degrees as recommended in the Bologna declaration and the so-called Initiative for Excellence. As we see, these two aspects suggest that international comparisons play a rather influential role in reforming the German system.

5.3.3 Regierungserklärung von Bundeskanzler Schröder zum Thema Bildung und Innovation (Schröder, 2002)

Context of the paper
This was the first government declaration by Chancellor Schröder that explicitly and exclusively turned to education in Germany. It was published just four months before the general elections (Schröder, 2002). This government declaration has to be seen in relation to the government paper published just four months later by the federal secretary for education and research, Bulmahn ("Rede der Bundesministerin für Bildung und Forschung Edelgard Bulmahn anlässlich der Aussprache zur Regierungserklärung des Bundeskanzlers" (Bulmahn, 2002)). Whereas Schröder opened up the discussion about education and set the general guidelines policies should pursue, and about the main aims and expectation educational policy should strive for (in the manner of a Green Paper), the speech by Bulmahn concentrated on the proposals and suggestions that were developed from Schröder's declarations during the four-month-long interlude.

Structure and Proposals
This government declaration outlines the general guidelines along which educational policy should be oriented. Schröder also referred to some initiatives already undertaken. Yet on the whole the paper is devoid of concrete proposals. These were instead delineated in the following government document by the federal secretary of education and research.

Analysing the Argument
Right at the beginning of the document Schröder stressed that education is one of the main themes of a modern social policy through which society equips itself

5.3 Analysis of governmental papers in Germany

for future challenges. He again emphasised the need to ensure access to education. He stated:

> "Bildung ist für mich das zentrale Thema moderner Gesellschaftspolitik und Zukunftsgestaltung. Der Zugang zu den Bildungschancen und die Qualität unserer Bildungsangebote – das ist die soziale Frage des beginnenden 21. Jahrhunderts. Bildungschancen sind stets Lebenschancen." (Schröder, 2002)

In the same breath he specified the reasons why, according to him, education should be a high priority:
- educational chances are life chances;
- education means safeguarding the individual's future and is therefore the best investment for the future;
- education is the decisive key for entering the labour market;
- education is conducive to positive social recognition;
- education is the best security against unemployment;
- education leads to responsible citizens because it transports norms and values;
- education leads to social integration and social participation.

The declaration consists of several discourses that are conducted almost simultaneously. First of all there is the discourse about equal opportunities. It does not come as a surprise that Schröder's declaration placed such a heavy emphasis on equal access to education, coming so soon after the first so-called PISA-study carried out by the OECD. According to this study, Germany's performance at the time was well below average both in terms of pupils' performances and in terms of chances for social mobility. In reference to this study, Schröder announced efforts to introduce country-wide full-time schooling and to ease eligibility for financial assistance for young people in order to provide incentives to stay in education (by means of an expansion of the Federal Education Assistance Act). These initiatives were considered to ameliorate the most severe shortcomings of the German education system as seen by PISA, namely that the educational success of children is heavily dependent on the social background in which they grew up.[80]

Another main finding of PISA was the comparatively low achievement rates of pupils in school, a point to which Schröder also referred. In this "quality-discourse" he explained the poor PISA results regarding quality and raised

---

[80] In the meantime this observation was reaffirmed by the United Nations Special Rapporteur on the right to education, Vernor Muñoz, who explicitly emphasised the "high correlation between social/migrant background of students and educational achievement" (Muñoz, 2007, 2).

concerns about the political and economic impact this result could have for a country with the cultural traditions of Germany:

> "Wir alle müssen uns kritisch und selbstkritisch fragen, warum ein Land mit der wirtschaftlichen und politischen Bedeutung und der kulturellen Tradition Deutschlands nicht in der internationalen Spitzengruppe mithält." (Schröder, 2002)

In order to tackle this problem he heralds the start of a new culture of teaching and learning, a learning that is practically-oriented; more focused on "learning how to learn" instead of learning facts by heart, which according to Schröder is one of the most important means for facing the challenges that the knowledge society presents. This new culture of learning would span the whole life course rather than just a particular period before an individual enters the labour market. He emphasises the need for high-quality education, which he defines as education that is conducive to people's creativity and self-responsibility, thus:

> "eine Bildung, die zum Ziel haben muss, die Fähigkeiten, die Kreativität und die Selbstverantwortung der Menschen zu fordern und zu fördern." (Schröder, 2002)

Another subject that Schröder broached in his declaration was the issue of youth unemployment. He very briefly referred to the "Training-Pact" (compare with chapter 4.2.2) between the government and its social partners and to programmes to fight youth unemployment through ensuring access to vocational education and training, especially apprenticeships.

A fourth discourse refers to higher education and research. In the declaration, Schröder saw the situation of German higher education and research in an international environment in which German institutions needed to be supported in order to remain internationally competitive. He pointed out that Germany had become the third most attractive country for research, after only the USA and Great Britain. Using the example of biotechnology he highlighted the attractiveness of Germany as a place for high-end research and innovation and, thereby, for investment.

More comprehensively, Schröder invoked a discourse about the values education should convey and about the administration of education as a public service. He highlighted throughout the declaration the significance of education for German society, as education contributes to equipping the population with the norms and values on which society is built:

> "Bildung muss auch Werte, Normen und Haltungen vermitteln, auf die sich unsere Gesellschaft mit guten Gründen geeinigt hat und auf die unsere Gesellschaft gebaut ist." (Schröder, 2002)

5.3 Analysis of governmental papers in Germany 167

Hence, education is necessary for ensuring tolerance; for living peaceful among and with other nations and foreign cultures; for attaining an "environmental competence" (ökologische Kompetenz); and for distinguishing right from wrong. The interesting aspect of this discourse is not that norms and values are considered to be valuable components of a good education; we have already seen that to some extent in the analysis of the English papers. Rather, most interesting is the abundance of cross-sectional tasks that education is supposed to tackle given the current challenges.

The last significant discourse in this paper deals with administrative and governance issues. Schröder announced the need for more competition between schools for innovative educational concepts and more assessment, while simultaneously relinquishing more autonomy to the individual schools and higher education institutions. Thus, we observe again the intention to introduce administrative reforms along the lines of "New Public Management."

Whereas England stressed the need for expansion, Schröder emphasised that the success of an education system cannot be assessed only by means of number of diplomas awarded to students. In England, by contrast, we have seen that attaining participation targets is of paramount importance. Yet, as we will see later on, since this paper "expansion" has gained in importance in the German discourse too.

5.3.4 Rede der Bundesministerin für Bildung und Forschung Edelgard Bulmahn anlässlich der Aussprache zur Regierungserklärung des Bundeskanzlers (Bulmahn, 2002)

Context of the paper
As was mentioned in the previous paper, this speech by the federal secretary of education and research complemented the government declaration by Chancellor Schröder in June 2002. In this speech Bulmahn presented the outcome of a four month long discussion that was initiated by Schröder's government declaration (Schröder, 2002; Bulmahn, 2002). It is, therefore, less focused on general guidelines and overarching ideas in educational policies and more on their concrete application. The speech was held approximately one month after the general election of September 2002, in which the government of Chancellor Schröder retained office.

Structure and Proposals
The first brief section of the speech was dedicated to emphasising the need for reforms in educational policies. In reference to PISA, Bulmahn aspired to

achieve a position amongst the top-five ranked countries in the PISA study. In section four she presents four guiding principles for educational reforms in Germany:
1. sustainable research;
2. modernise the educational system and making it fit for the future;
3. creating the best conditions for the new generation of academics;
4. best possible education for everyone in Germany.

Paragraphs two and three include rather concrete proposals as to how the school educational system should be reformed. A core concern was the expansion of full-time schools. It was implicitly argued that full-time schools help to provide a level-playing field among all children regardless of their cultural and socio-economic backgrounds. Serendipitously, pupils' performances would simultaneously be raised. Thereby full-time schools would tackle the two main points of criticism of the PISA study.

Secondly, she announced national education standards that would allow pupils and young people to easily move among the different Länder and thus facilitate flexibility. Thirdly, she made a case for an independent assessment authority in the area of education. Therewith, she supported an institution that she identified as one of the reasons for the high performances in other PISA-countries. These two aspects clearly show how Bulmahn intended to alter school education along a similar line as in England and consistent with the "New Public Management" approach (compare with conclusion to this chapter). Fourthly, a national educational reporting system and fifthly a "Foundation for Education" were envisioned to ensure the brisk detection of deficiencies and their quick amelioration.

In a second paragraph Bulmahn turned to vocational education and training. The aspiration in vocational education and training was to make the system more flexible through the introduction of modularised qualification-blocks, thereby allowing young people who have not finished or attained a dual apprenticeship to gain at least a partial qualification. She announced the government would propose a new vocational training act, which would allow for a greater combination options among different educational paths and for greater internationalisation. As we know now, these considerations eventually led to the amendment of the Vocational Training Act in 2005 (to this act in detail see chapter 6.2.2).

In a third paragraph Bulmahn exclusively deals with higher education and research. She states that above all Germany needs more academics and, more broadly speaking, more well-qualified people, be it through higher education or vocational education. Moreover, she speaks about creating "beacon-higher

5.3 Analysis of governmental papers in Germany

education and research institutions" ("Leuchttürme" der Wissenschaftslandschaft) in Eastern Germany which would have an international reputation for high quality teaching and research. Hence, we observe that structural policy considerations were used to justify educational policy projects.

Analysing the Argument
Regarding the foundational argument behind the proposals, the previous government declaration of Schröder provided the argumentative frame for the proposals by Bulmahn. This can be referenced in the appropriate section above.

5.3.5 Bildung, Forschung, Innovation – der Zukunft Gestalt geben (BMBF, 2002)

Context of the paper
This working paper outlined the main initiatives that the government intended to pursue in the oncoming legislative period.

Structure and Proposals
The introduction of the working paper announced the five central themes of the government for the legislative period then beginning (BMBF, 2002, 1). These were:
1. supporting talented people while ensuring equal opportunities;
2. modernising education and research structures to ensure internationally competitive quality;
3. supporting technologies for new markets and creating jobs for the future;
4. sustainable research for humans and environment;
5. promoting Eastern Germany through education research and innovation with a concentration on regional clusters.

One chapter is devoted to each issue, which are then further subdivided into aims that are considered to contribute to the relevant aspect. Each aim-section is divided into a paragraph that explains why the particular aim is important and another paragraph in which the paper suggests how to achieve this aim by means of policy proposals. The following proposals are contained in the paper:
- creating a new system of qualificational building blocks in vocational education and training;
- providing information about vocational options early on in school;
- facilitation of access to higher education;
- strengthening autonomy of higher education institutions;

- supporting women in research and economy;
- new accreditation and certification system in order to facilitate further education;
- introduction of a system by which to accredit informal skills;
- national achievement standards in education;
- all relevant educational actors should be part of tight networks that orchestrate educational initiatives.

Analysing the Argument
The first paragraph outlined the vision for a future-oriented Germany that is economically, socially and ecologically strong. In order to achieve this vision, the paper delineated three guiding principles for educational reforms, namely innovation, social justice and sustainability (BMBF, 2002, 1). The reform initiatives take into consideration two main challenges that Germany is (supposedly) exposed to: firstly, strengthening Germany's position in an international globalised world, creating employment, and maintaining and enhancing the standard of living; secondly, all activities have to be carried out in a sustainable, environmentally friendly way. Education and research policy was considered a key policy area for achieving these aims (BMBF, 2002, 1).

The introduction of the paper elucidates why education is assigned a pivotal role (BMBF, 2002, 2). The argument is that education and training determine an individual's life-chances because they are the key to accessing the labour market. Additionally, education and training ensure social participation and provide norms and values in a world that is becoming increasingly complex.

Moreover, the paper stated that qualified employees are the most important future resource for the state and society (BMBF, 2002, 2). This was one of the central themes of the paper. The need to increase the amount of intermediate and highly qualified people was justified by the claim that by 2015 the demand for qualified workers would increase by 2.4 million, of which at least one million people would need higher education (BMBF, 2002, 5). Hence, the forecast encompassed a period of no less than 13 years. Unfortunately there is no reference in the paper that indicates on which research this claim is founded. In the same breath, however, the paper refers to a study by the OECD that includes higher education participation rates. According to this data Germany was – at that time – well behind, with only 27.7 percent of young people of any given age cohort starting studies at higher education institutions, while the OECD-average was 44 percent.

We encounter a common pattern in the German papers, one that appears to be far more influential than in the English case, namely the influence of international benchmarks. This influence goes beyond the mere fact of

5.3 Analysis of governmental papers in Germany

Germany's localisation in an international context of globalisation and international competitiveness. International comparisons and benchmarks appear to have a direct effect on reforms in the German educational system. In school education, full-time schooling is to be introduced country-wide, a decision made in reference to the vast bulk of Western countries that follow this policy. School achievement rates are to be improved because of PISA; schooling periods and school enrolment are criticised for being too long and too late in comparison to other OECD countries; governance and administration of higher education institutions need to be oriented towards more competition and market mechanism as is done in other countries; performance assessment in higher education need to be enhanced as other countries have already proven; and vocational education and training has to be further internationalised and to be aligned with the Copenhagen process through modularisation and more outcome-oriented assessment – again with reference to experiences abroad. That is not to say that education policy in Germany is entirely determined by international influences, or that Germany embarks on strategies that follow the lines of simple policy diffusion processes or even "policy mirroring". Yet, it is also more than merely expressing the fact that Germany aligns its policies to international "standards."

Moreover, it may also mean that problem-definition is derived from these comparisons, which then propel political action. To illustrate this argument, the German higher education participation rate is considered as being too low. Two questions arise: firstly, too low for what? What purpose can only be attained by higher participation rates in higher education and not through other means? Secondly, the participation rates are too low with reference to what? Are they too low with reference to the demand for skilled higher education graduates? What we observe here is that the awareness of the problem has arisen by contemplating Germany in an international context, even if it is not decisively driven by it. In this international context, in which familiar keywords like globalisation and international competitiveness are omnipresent, Germany compares itself by means of data that entirely disregards the German environment (in terms of economic and social environment) in which German education is embedded.[81] Thus, what Germany did was compare its participation rates to those from abroad, which led to the realisation that their rates were lower, which led to the desire to increase its rates given that higher education is a prestigious area. It

---

[81] A comparison between the English foundation degrees and the German dual apprenticeship exemplifies how easily higher education participation rates can be misleading if they are used as an indicator for the competitiveness of a political economy. Moreover, as the political economy literature contends, the temptation to participate in an international competition for skills might be misleading, as political economies might not be able to make use of them.

thereby disregards questions about quality, just as it neglects the fact that a dual apprenticeship can be as valuable as a higher education qualification from abroad. The chapter on English foundation degrees will enlarge upon this issue (see chapter 6.1.3).

Thus one might suppose that the fact of comparatively low participants in German higher education has been transformed into a "problem" only because Germany feels obliged to compete with respect to international participation rates. Hence, international league tables influence German national educational policies. Putting it in other words that are more akin to the English situation, the case for expansion (expansion of intermediate and high skilled people) is justified against the background of a future perspective (increase of demand for qualified employees by 2015) and by referring to international league tables. The most obvious reason for expansion, however, is not mentioned, namely the actual demand for more qualified persons.

Another driving factor seems to be structural policy considerations. A whole chapter in the paper is devoted to Eastern Germany (BMBF, 2002, 29). Through the creation of scientific clusters in this region it is hoped that structural disadvantages will be ameliorated by inducing a demand-push through supply-led initiatives. The paper also portrays the picture of a knowledge society that makes a lifelong learning strategy imperative (BMBF, 2002, 8). Though not referred to as the main influences, the measures introduced for achieving this vision often resemble, to some extent, those from the experiences of countries such as England and/or from the recent portfolio of fashionable items that circulate under the heading of New Public Management (compare with BMBF, 2002, 8). These include guaranteeing high quality qualification-products by introducing a new accreditation and certification system that allow people to attain further qualifications more easily; certifying informal competences; regular and independent assessments of educational programmes; and a further modularisation of further education programmes.

This paper again shows how different driving factors impact educational policy making in Germany. If we attempt to weight these different factors, we discern one factor which is, if not the most influential, then certainly one of the leading factors driving German policy considerations. This is the German perception and comparison against an international context. This aspect seem not only to drive Germany's solutions but, moreover, it seems to determine to some extent what is even considered as a problem.

5.3 Analysis of governmental papers in Germany 173

5.3.6 Egoismus überwinden – Gemeinsinn fördern: Unser Weg zu neuer Stärke (Schröder, 2004)

Context of the paper
The governmental paper "Egoismus überwinden – Gemeinsinn fördern: Unser Weg zu neuer Stärke" by Chancellor Schröder does not explicitly turn to educational policy (Schröder, 2004). In this declaration Schröder outlined the so-called "Agenda 2010". However, the reforms covered under this title are meant to form a comprehensive social policy and societal policy concept that encompasses the area of educational policy as well. The "Agenda 2010" was and still is a fiercely controversial debate. This is mainly due to the fact that this reform represents a massive commodification of social policy (notion refers to Esping-Andersen, 1990), particularly in the area of social assistance.

Structure and Proposals
Except for a few brief references to recent and future policy initiatives in the area of education this paper does not present any proposals.

Analysing the Argument
The so-called Agenda 2010 by the social-democratic/green government outlines an overarching cross-sectional societal concept for Germany. This concept is most directly applicable to social and labour market policies, with its most prominent outcome being the so-called Hartz-legislation. For Schröder, Agenda 2010 takes into consideration two main challenges: globalisation and demographic developments. Thus, Germany is a "offene Volkswirtschaft, die sich Tag für Tag dem internationalen Wettbewerb zu stellen hat" and the imperative is to find a balance between facing and accepting the facts of international competition, on the one hand, while retaining basic social state principles on the other. Regarding the demographic development, Schröder speaks of the changing ratio of employees and pensioners, which will to a large extent determines the future of the German social state.

It is in this context that Schröder broaches the issues of education policy. According to him education is the key to progress and social security in a globalised world. Three facts underpin the central significance of education for Germany. Firstly, Germany has no considerable amount of natural resources on which economic endeavours could be focused. This makes investing in people even more important. Secondly, Germany, as a country with comparatively high labour productivity, can remain in its position only by reducing the shortage of qualified employees. According to Schröder, labour migration and working overtime can ameliorate the situation only in the short-term. In the long-run there is no alternative to investing in the education of children in order to increase the volume of labour in sectors with high skill-requirements.

Thirdly, Schröder perceives education from the perspective of family policy. Care facilities and full-time schooling would need to be expanded in order to allow for higher employment rates among parents (in particular women) while also thereby providing additional incentives for people to have children. Hence, demographic development plays a considerable role in German social policy broadly and German educational policy specifically, as we have seen before.

In addition, the chancellor underlined the fact that education, like health provision, cultural programmes and security, are public goods, and that it is the responsibility of the public authorities to maintain and ensure these services. We should keep this statement in mind for the later elaboration of the three reforms, as this statement was expressed in a time of privatisation, a time when much has been said and written about a 'regulatory state'.

5.3.7 Aufstieg durch Bildung – Qualifizierungsinitiative der Bundesregierung (BMBF, 2008a)

Context of the paper
This paper introduced the so-called "qualification-initiative" (Qualifizierungs-initiative). It consists of measures with which the federal government promotes education and the attainment of qualifications from crèches (day cares) to further education on the job (BMBF, 2008a). Hence, it is a paper about the German way of lifelong-learning. Yet, as the paper states, the implementation of this initiative is dependent on the cooperation with the Länder and the social partners.

Structure and Proposals
A short introduction explained the context of the "qualification-initiative" as proposed by the Federal Ministry of Education and Research (BMBF). This chapter was followed by a section that offered a short overview of the seven main strands of this initiative. These seven strands are subsequently mapped out in the rest of the paper. These seven areas are:
1. more educational opportunities for children below the age of six;
2. increasing completion rates;
3. social mobility by means of education;
4. facilitating the transition from school to higher education;
5. more attention to science and engineering;

6. enhancing opportunities for women;
7. further education and lifelong learning.

The most important proposals are the following:
- supporting disadvantaged young people by offering financial incentives to those employers who engage members of this group;
- better guidance for those who want to enter the labour market;
- piloting of vocational education and training-building blocks in order to foster the transition to a dual apprenticeship and to facilitate final examinations;
- attempt to modularise dual apprenticeships by offering similar core-qualifications for different sectors to be complemented by specially tailored occupational qualifications;
- increased usage of external (i.e. on-the-job) vocational education and training opportunities for those who are unable to and an opening as an apprentice;
- facilitating the transition from school to vocational education and training by harmonising school-standards among the federal countries;
- announcement of a renewal of the "Pact for training" (Nationaler Pakt für Ausbildung und Fachkräftenachwuchs);
- regional partnerships for ensuring further education;
- various financial incentives for taking up and staying on in education, further education,
- or higher education.

Analysing the Argument
This paper represented an attempt to create an overarching education strategy. Hence, it is not confined to a particular educational area but embraces all possible stages of education: pre-school facilities for children, school education, vocational education and training, higher education and the recurrent theme of 'lifelong learning'.

The introduction of this paper clearly shows the expectations that are place upon education, as expressed in the "qualification initiative" and developed under the headline "qualification now!" Education is seen as the means to future success because it is conducive to economic growth, social inclusion and cohesion, and self-fulfilment in vocational terms (BMBF, 2008a, 2). Again, we come across the three main aims that are associated with education: namely economic, social, and personal.

Regarding the economic goals it is argued that education and qualified employees ensure economic growth. This is true of both higher education graduates and apprenticeship holders. It was believed that future economic trend would further increase the demand for qualified employees due to rapid technological progress and increasing globalisation. Excellence in education is, therefore, a necessity for Germany. By extension, the "qualification-initiative" is also necessary in order to maintain and expand the quality and quantity of education. Later in the text we find a passage that to a large extent resembles the discourse which we encountered in the English papers, namely the contention that more higher education students are needed to sustain international competitiveness (BMBF, 2008a, 24).

Regarding the social aims, the belief that education generates social inclusion and cohesion dominates (BMBF, 2008a, 21). A whole chapter is devoted to this issue, not least because according to the PISA-study Germany's school education is well below average in terms of social mobility (compare with Schröder's remakrs in Schröder, 2002), in particular for young people from migrant backgrounds. Personal goals in terms of an individual occupational perspective are also mentioned very briefly (BMBF, 2008a, 2).

The "qualification initiative" is unfolding against the background of:

> "Globalisierung, Wissensbeschleunigung, demographischem Wandel und einem veränderten Familienbild." (BMBF, 2008a, 2)

Hence, the initiative is meant not only to pursue the "goal-troika" (economic, social, and personal aims) but to also ameliorate demographic pressures[82] and to respond to altered family structures.

Apart from these ambitious, if not overambitious, aims of the "qualification initiative," in the text we encounter another motivation for these policy proposals, namely international comparisons. On page five the paper states that educational endeavours by all actors need to be intensified and coordinated in the light of experiences in other OECD-countries. The paper again criticised the relatively low higher education participation rate of 36.6 percent, which is well below the OECD average (54 percent). On the one hand, this critique is understandable, as higher education participation rates are considered to provide evidence about the skill structure of a country. On the other hand, however, the critique is surprising because in the same breath the paper admits that the low German participation rate can be partly explained by higher education programmes in other countries that content-wise would be associated with and

---

[82]Though not explicitly mentioned, it is possible that lifelong learning, which is supposed to make the older generations more employable, is considered as a means of ameliorating demographic challenges, since this group would be, as a consequence of increased employability, able to pursue a profession until an older age (see BMBF, 2001, 4).

provided for in the German vocational education and training system (BMBF, 2008a, 24). As this research will show at a later stage, it is exactly this point of criticism that has raised objections against the English foundation degrees as being counted as a higher education programme when it is in fact hardly distinguishable from vocational education and training programmes in other countries. Yet, references to international comparative studies are not confined only to higher education aspects; further education is also considered to be well below the international average, a fact which is used to argue in favour of lifelong learning (BMBF, 2008a, 31).

To sum up, the initiatives proposed in this paper seem to have three main drivers: first of all they are about generating the skills that are required to achieve sustainable economic development. The reference to a perceived lack of qualified employees and higher education graduates (particularly in natural sciences) bears exactly on this point. Yet, the initiatives lack any statement that specifies which qualifications Germany is lacking. A second driver is a sort of self-perceived peer-pressure caused by comparing Germany with other countries. Yet, as the case of English foundation degrees reveals, a comparison of, for instance participation rates in educational areas among countries, can be misleading if educational contents are not properly taken into account. A third driver relates to the issue of social mobility, which is considered to be insufficiently provided for in the current the education system. This issue is fuelled by the PISA-study, which explicitly stressed this aspect.

5.4 Comparison

Before beginning the comparison, some terms that are of crucial importance for this section must be clarified. We need to align the key analytical concepts of the theoretical framework with prominent notions used in the papers (e.g. visions, aims). Obviously, when the papers refer explicitly to these notions, they are applied in the foreground of the political discourse. Moreover, we noticed that these notions used in the foreground are underpinned by assumptions, (public) philosophies and paradigms that sit in the background of a discourse. Therefore, the papers only implicitly relate to them. The forthcoming sections called "underlying assumptions" will address this background component of discourses. Hence, this chapter seeks to disentangle the foreground and background ideas of the discourse(s) in order to reveal the ideational drivers of policy initiatives.

In the papers we encountered notions such as visions, aims, principle goals or main aims, objectives and targets. The foreground of a discourse is theoretically described mainly by means of three concepts. These are policies, programmes and frames. Even though these concepts are further divided into cognitive and normative types of ideas, at this stage and for the sake of operationalisation, in this analysis this distinction will not be used. Yet, this foreground can also be subdivided according to those notions encountered in the papers. This distinction is not about different types of ideas, as it is with cognitive and normative ideas. Rather it is about deconstructing the causal chain of argumentation, i.e. deductively tracing arguments from visions to aims to concrete initiatives.

As to the notions used in the papers, and hence to the foreground of the discourse, "visions" relate to "aims" in that the former displays a desired long-term scenario whereas aims are the means by which to realise this scenario. Elaborating on visions, however, not only serves the purpose of revealing what kind of long-term goals the government pursues but, moreover, serves as a template against which aims and policy initiatives can be assessed in order to discover any ranking of these aims.

The notion of "main aims" refers to a high level of abstraction. It is an aim that can not be related to an even more abstract aim but only to a vision. As a metaphor we can use a triangle. At the top are the visions, the highest level of abstraction. The second, slightly more spacious level, makes room for main aims and major guidelines. The third layer includes the guidelines for a particular policy field and how it should be shaped. Finally, the fourth layer is devoted to concrete policy proposals.

Thus far we have been dealing mainly with foreground concepts and notions. The question now is how we can account for basic assumptions, for "paradigms" and "public sentiments", hence the concepts used in the background of a discourse? For the sake of simplicity the following analysis will combine these concepts into a single concept referred to as "underlying assumptions" (compare with Campbell, 2004, 94).

Underlying assumptions refer to the foundational and/or basic assumptions that accompany the policy making process. We begin with the proposal that these assumptions provide the pursuit of a particular vision/aim with momentum and therefore heavily influence policy outcomes. Moreover, we proceed on the assumption that it is basic convictions and underlying assumptions on which aims, main aims, and visions are based (compare with chapter 2.3.3). The notion of "underlying assumption" represents assumptions or presumptions of particular correlations and nexuses that accompany decisions, in this study, decisions in education policy. For instance, the goal to attain a 50 percent participation rate in higher education is driven by the underlying assumption that the amount of higher education students positively correlates with the economic performance of the English political economy. Referring to the abovementioned triangle metaphor, we can think of a circle around it in which we can place these basic assumptions/ideas because these assumptions impact the entire chain of argumentation (from visions down to concrete initiatives).

The visions will be outlined first, followed by the main aims, and finally by their less abstract applications, when particular reforms will be scrutinised. The procedure is of critical importance for detecting accompanying ideas and beliefs because visions and aims on a low level of abstraction are not necessarily correlated in a linear fashion. Rather it is the deconstruction of the line of argumentation that leads from one group of aims to another which will reveal the underpinning assumptions and, therefore, the guiding ideas on which government considerations are based. Hence, it is the precise evaluation of visions and aims that provides a look into the nature and character of the underlying assumptions that accompany policy considerations.

This section will be structured as follows:

1. First, the visions and main aims as outlined in the papers will be elucidated. This will provide an understanding of the explicitly mentioned drivers of education policy and hence of the foreground of the discourse.
2. Secondly, aims alone do not indicate how they are to be pursued and achieved. For instance, the appeal to foster employer involvement in vocational education and training can be attained by various means. Underlying assumptions accompany and guide the pursuit of an aim, influence the momentum of the process, and ultimately impact policy outcomes. These underlying, "background" assumptions will be displayed in this section.
3. Thirdly, as we have seen with the paper analyses, the area of education encompasses significant sub-discourses. The main aims – which will be outlined in the coming section – indicate these sub-discourses as they are contained in the overall educational discourse, e.g. economic and social aims. Hence, we need to rank these discourses according to their significance and intensity with which they are pursued (the so-called "order of discourse").
4. The fourth section critically evaluates the lines of argumentation that we encountered in the papers. Thereby, we will be able to understand how and why particular problems are defined and how they are meant to be solved.

5.4.1 Visions and aims: the discursive foreground

5.4.1.1 The English case

Describing the aims and goals of English educational policy is far from an easy task. The "twin aims" of economic success and social justice, which are the most apparent pursuits of policymakers, are not the only aims being pursued in this area. Lifelong learning, unlocking individual potentials, partnerships among all relevant actors, flexibility and choice, better performance according to international league tables, becoming the "world leader" in skills, public service reforms, establishing a new working ethos, introducing market elements, "vocationalism" – all of these are goals and components of the educational visions mentioned in the papers. The pivotal difference between these ideas lies in their level of abstraction, i.e. some are more abstract than others. The desire to support partnerships between all relevant actors exemplifies this situation. According to New Labour's reading of the issue, partnerships are to be facilitated because they generate more options for young people. More options mean more flexibility and choice, and choice is conducive to higher participation rates in post-secondary education (compare with e.g. DfES, 2003b). It is assumed that this leads to higher intermediate skill levels, which are critical to escaping the low-skill equilibrium. The pursuit of a knowledge-based society is an inevitable requirement for retaining international competitiveness. The relevant vision, as seen in the White Paper "21st Century Skills" (DfES, 2003b, 17), is to improve England's productivity, achieve sustainable growth, and attain a higher standard of living.

Hence, we see that the rather concrete aim of promoting partnerships is interwoven with a whole set of aims. These aims can be traced back to one of the "twin aims", namely economic prosperity, as it is the most abstract aim and one which fades into and connects with a long-term vision (e.g. DfEE, 1999; DfES, 2005a). However, this situation is even more complicated than just outlined. Even if we focus on just two particular elements of this argumentation-chain, some problematic issues emerge. Why are higher participation rates bound to occur as a result of the introduction of more choice into the system? Why do greater numbers of people with intermediate skills inevitably lead to a more competitive position in an international arena? The papers do not provide any clear answers to these questions.

These two examples show that objectives are guided by particular beliefs and underlying assumptions. Referring once more to this example, one might argue that it is underpinned by a belief in the market as the prevailing organising principle. This is a view that sees young learners as customers, searching and

5.4 Comparison

demanding educational programmes. The state in this view is seen as the supplier of more choice, meant to satisfy the customers in this market. Finally, it is the idea of a knowledge-driven economy which leads to the belief that competitiveness will increase once intermediate skills have been strengthened qualitatively and quantitatively, not to mention the deep conviction in a supply-led skills policy as the means to prompt demand for these skills (compare with e.g. DfES, 2005a).

Visions
To start with, we need to turn to the visions mentioned in the papers. "Visions" relate to "aims" in that the former displays a desired long-term scenario whereas the aims are the means to achieve this scenario. Elaborating on visions, however, not only serves the purpose of revealing what kind of long-term goals the government pursues, but, moreover, serves as a template against which aims and policy initiatives can be assessed in order to discover any ranking of these aims. The vision of the two papers issued in 1997 proclaimed a "Vision for the new Millennium":

> "Our vision is to build a new culture of learning which will underpin national competitiveness and personal prosperity, encourage creativity and innovation and help build a cohesive society" (DfEE, 1999, 6).

The core of this vision is a new learning culture. As the analyses showed, in most instances this culture refers to lifelong learning and a "passion" for learning (as for instance in DfEE, 1999). The aspects associated with this vision – national competitiveness, personal prosperity, and a cohesive society – seem to be on an equal footing; there is no apparent emphasis on one aspect at the expense of another (this is covered more in-depth in the next section). In the later papers this "visionary vision" is superseded by more "confined" and "practical visions". The White Paper in 2001 speaks of a vision of a school system "which values opportunity for all, and embraces diversity and autonomy as the means to achieve it" (DfES, 2001, 6) and of a "coherent and effective phase of 14-19 education" (DfES, 2001, 32). The higher education paper in 2003 refers to a vision that is focused on satisfying the demand for particular skills by employers in order to achieve economic wealth. However, in this context the vision also refers to the traditional, self-fulfilling aims of education that "define our civilisation and culture" (DfES, 2003c, 21). So far we have discussed New Labour's attempt to introduce a visionary approach to education policy right at the beginning of their term of office. Over time these visions gradually broke down into less visionary considerations about the future. It was not until 2003 in the White Paper called "21st Century Skills" that the government once again formulated a broad overarching vision about skills, education and their role within a future society. This paper is special because it is not concentrated on a particular area, such as higher education or further education. In this respect it is in keeping with the first Green Paper about educational issues by New Labour in 1997, as both demonstrate New Labour's all-embracing approach to the generation of skills and the purpose of education. "21st Century Skills" pledges a skill strategy which:

> "seeks to ensure that, across the nation, employers have the right skills to support the success of their businesses and organisations, and individuals have the skills they need to be both employable and personally fulfilled." (DfES, 2003b)

The underlying aims of this strategy, however, clearly indicate that it was the government's concern about England's economic performance that propelled the strategy. It is the employable citizen as part of the economic value chain who is perceived to be "personally fulfilled" (White Paper "Schools – Achieving success", DfES, 2001). We see in this strategy a slightly stronger emphasis on the economic goals of education than we did in the 1997 paper. The observation is supported by the Further Education White Paper issued in 2005, which proclaims the vision that: "our education system should provide every young person with a route to success in life through hard work and dedication" (DfES, 2005a, 22) and that in order to accomplish this vision people should be equipped with the skills employers need. Hence, the visions in the papers are dominated by economic considerations rather than those about personal fulfilment (beyond economic fulfilment) and a cohesive society (beyond a workforce society).

Main aims "Aims" as used in the papers is a very broad term. As it turns out, it is very difficult to distinguish between visions, main aims which accompany a vision and less-abstract aims that are derived from visions and main aims. Yet it is a necessary requirement to do so because it is the lines of argumentation that unveil the underlying assumptions. To attempt a start, we should first have a look at the list of aims mentioned in the papers:

- economic success
- integrated/included society
- international competitiveness
- a new culture of learning
- personal fulfilment
- better basic skills (numeracy and literacy)
- unlock individual potentials
- increasing employability

5.4 Comparison

- helping the most disadvantaged
- increasing quality and quantity of intermediate skills
- 'massification' of education
- lifelong learning
- supporting partnerships
- flexibility, choice and diversity
- strengthen private engagement
- high skill strategy
- public service reform
- 'parity of esteem'
- closing skill gaps
- enhancing productivity
- achieving higher scores in international league tables
- 'world leader in skills' and excellence

The "twin aims" (DfEE, 1997b, 1997a; DfES, 2001, 2005a, 2006) give us an initial idea of those aims sitting on the top floor: 1) economic success and 2) social justice. Indeed, these two aims are "main aims" in the sense that they can not be described any more abstractly. Yet, we can find other abstract objectives in this list. "Personal fulfilment" (White Paper "Schools: Achieving success", DfES, 2001) is a third frequently-mentioned aspect and again, while this is an aim, it is rather imprecise for a concrete "manual" for policy initiatives. Fourthly, and moreover, educational reforms do not place only education as such at the centre of considerations. The delivery of education – irrespective of direct impacts on educational aspects in their strictest sense – seems to be important contemplation of the government as well. Therefore "public service reforms", as mentioned in the papers, (DfES, 2001, 2003b, 2006) are also a main aim, though the criteria for successful reforms are very different from educational reforms. Fifthly, so far we have entirely disregarded educational aims that are neither functionalistic nor utilitarian, aims that do not serve a particular economic, social or administrative function. However, education as understood from a traditional perspective is assigned a purpose and value of its own, in reproducing cultural values, facilitating critical thinking and promoting future democratic citizens (e.g. Crouch, Finegold and Sako, 1999, 5; Doyle, 2003; about an "educational revolution" that should accompany the English "skill revolution" see Pring, 2004, 112 f.). Even though the papers barely referred to this type of aim, we should nevertheless keep it in mind.

What is striking is the plethora of strong aims that are associated with educational reforms and policies. The education system plays a pivotal role for New Labour. Education seems to be the crucial lever with which the society and the political economy are to be changed to respond to the challenges and pressures to which England is perceived as being exposed. Education and skills are meant to be the "panacea" for the most pressing social and economic challenges. This understanding of education is most likely to lead to an extremely utilitarian approach towards education, an assumption that will be assessed in the following sections (Grubb 2004, 1 f.; Doyle, 2003, 4 ff.; Keep, Mayhew and Payne, 2006).

5.4.1.2 The German case

Visions
The German visions and emphases differ from those in the English papers. Whereas England explicitly formulates visions that guide policy initiatives, German long-term goals need to be derived implicitly, as they are less outspoken and salient. Instead, visions are formulated in the context of the most pressing issues to which Germany is exposed. Hence, visions in Germany are to a large extent based on an evaluation of the status quo.[83] Examples of these kinds of "visions" are the endeavours to ameliorate unemployment, an issue of prime importance and one that is consistently mentioned in the papers. Dealing with demographic change or altered family structures (both mentioned in BMBF, 2008a) are two other aspects that, together with the "challenges of globalisation" and the "acceleration of knowledge", form the main basis of the "qualification initiative" of 2008 (BMBF, 2008a). This initiative exemplifies the fact that the German papers are mainly concerned with reacting to existing issues rather than with sketching desirable future scenarios.

We find only a few subtle references in the papers to broader visions that affect society on a large scale. In his first government declaration in 1998, Chancellor Schröder proclaimed the birth of the "knowledge society" (Schröder, 1998, paragraph 6). Yet, as he made clear shortly afterwards, the vision is not about knowledge *per se* but about qualifications. The "qualifications" discourse in German educational policy, however, mainly refers to vocational education and training and to the share of youngsters who are unable to find an apprenticeship opening. Thus, one might argue that the "knowledge society" in the reading of Schröder is less a vision and more a means to tackle recent employment problems.

It is in Schröder's government declaration of 2002, four months before the

---

[83]This is less so the case in England. There visions are sketched as future education scenarios in particular and societal scenarios in general. Thereby visions express a status which is desirable and are less concerned with feasibility than the German visions.

general elections, that we detect the closest thing to a vision. He speaks of education as the central theme for a modern and future-oriented policy, a policy which should stress educational opportunities and access to education as the crucial social issues of the 21st century because: "Bildungschancen sind stets Lebenschancen" (Schröder, 2002). In the same declaration the Chancellor heralds a new culture of learning that places an emphasis on the generation of creativity and on "how to learn". These statements have to be kept in mind when analysing the reforms in Germany in order to detect whether visions and political reality correspond or stand in stark contrast to one another.

Shortly thereafter, another paper sketched a picture of a future-oriented country that is economically and socially strong, and ecologically sound (BMBF, 2002). It provides some indication of the guiding principles along which Germany should develop. These are innovation, social justice and sustainability. In this context, education plays a very important role, as it is considered the key to progress and social security in a globalised world.

Yet if we consider education policy in more detail, we encounter the tendency to react to current problems, as described above. Visions in school education are heavily impacted by PISA and the good performers in this study. Vocational education and training is oriented towards its own model, as Germany remains convinced of value of the dual apprenticeship system and merely wants to adapt it to meet current challenges. It is in higher education that the German papers provide the most outspoken vision. However, here again it is the vision of a European higher education area that drives the debate on higher education and teaching issues; and it is the Anglo-Saxon predominance in research that propels considerations about, for instance, the initiative of excellence.

Main aims
As with the English papers, drawing a clear distinction between the visions, aims and basic assumptions/ideas mentioned in the German papers is not an easy task. To start with we should take a look at the aims mentioned in the papers. The list comprises the following items that are associated with education policy:
- tackling unemployment
- facilitating access to education
- best possible education for all
- complying with European standards
- achieving higher ranks in international studies such as PISA
- expanding higher education participation rate
- supporting excellence in higher education, including "beacon universities" and "research clusters"

- preparing more people for the first training market
- supporting infrastructure in Eastern Germany
- ensuring sustainable development
- promoting ecological policy
- shorter study periods and more practise-orientation in higher education
- fostering further education
- introducing market mechanisms in higher education
- implementing full-time schooling
- more competition among schools for innovative concepts
- strengthening quality in school education
- appreciating the cultural and civilising value of education
- social integration
- modularisation and flexibility in vocational education and training
- becoming one of the leading nations in education
- establishing national education standards
- promoting individual life chances
- facilitating the economy to create apprenticeship openings
- tackling demographic changes

We can see that the expectations associated with education in Germany are manifold. Yet throughout the papers' analyses two main aims are consistently mentioned and stressed: tackling unemployment and ensuring equal access to education. However, the former main aim seems to be the most important. All papers – particularly those which are not solely concentrated on higher education and research – are focused on improving the situation in both the labour and training market. Thus, fighting unemployment is of paramount importance. Several of the aims listed above can be subsumed under this main aim, such as, for instance, supply-oriented measures to facilitate the creation of apprenticeship openings, fostering further education, preparing young people from deprived backgrounds for the first training market, and infrastructure policies for Eastern Germany.

Equal access to education could also be subsumed under the main aim of decreasing unemployment. Given that family background heavily influences the educational chances of children (Muñoz, 2007) and that educational attainment heavily influences future job opportunities one might argue that facilitating access to education is also an initiative against unemployment. Nevertheless, it is worth considering this as a social aim while also acknowledging some connections exist with the first main aim, such as, for instance, preparing young people to enter the first training market. The lack of equality in educational chances is one of the main criticisms expressed in the PISA-study. We must

5.4 Comparison

consider this issue a social aim because it deals mainly with how to integrate as many young people as possible into the educational system in order to facilitate their social integration, even though it equates social integration to labour market integration.

Moreover, we have to consider this discussion against the background of a gradual devaluation of the lowest secondary school track (Hauptschule), which has high ratios of youngsters from deprived and migrant backgrounds and also high ratios of drop-outs. Offering these young people prospects in the education system can hence be understood as more of a social aim; it is in this vein that the claim for the best possible education for all has to be understood. Integrating this group into the labour market is another story. Furthermore, it is hoped that education will be one method among many that are available to tackle the severest demographic difficulties. Full-time schools are considered to kill two birds with one stone: providing incentives for parents to enter the labour market on a full-time basis and thereby providing incentives to raise the fertility rate (not to mention the pedagogical aspirations that are associated with this school form).

Administrative and governance issues constitute another important aim of the papers. This point, however, has to be considered in a nuanced manner, as this issue assumes different roles within the three educational areas. The papers' analyses have already revealed that the papers are relatively silent about school education, presumably due to a lack of competencies in this area, which is entirely and exclusively under the ambit of the Länder. Yet, the federal level suggests establishing national educational standards, a non-departmental assessment body to supervise these standards, and increased competition among school institutions for innovative concepts. Arguably these proposals might be seen as a step towards greater transparency and comparability between school education institutions in terms of their performances.

This applies also to higher education. The initiative of excellence is a major attempt to introduce financial incentives for research; the opportunity for higher education institutions to choose their masters students is tantamount to increasing competition between the students. After all, one might say that the "raison d'être" of a "beacon university" is to be a "beacon" among those institutions with minor luminosity. Thus, ideas such as marketisation, stratification and establishing rankings seem to fuel considerations about higher education.

Governance and administration questions in the dual apprenticeship scheme are traditionally dealt with by the social partners. Hence, as regards administrative issues, the papers address vocational education and training without the inclusion of the dual apprenticeships. Yet, vocational preparation programmes are conducted by vocational schools and vocational schools are –

once again – the responsibility of the Länder, which means that the administrative influence of the federal level is minor.

Furthermore, we encounter a set of aims that we might label as personal aims. These include supporting individual life chances and fostering social integration. Yet, like in the English case, these personal aims have to be comprehended economically. Hence, social integration means integration into the labour market and "individual life chances" could easily be replaced by "individual job chances". Moreover, the papers mention an ecological imperative (including sustainable development) when pursuing educational aims, in particular in research. Interestingly, this aim is only mentioned in the coalition agreements (presumably due to The Greens (in German "Bündnis 90/Die Grünen") which insisted on ecological mainstreaming in German policies) and not in the government declarations. There are also few references to education as an end in itself and as a means through which cultural, civilising and democratic values are communicated. However, only by referring to the underlying assumptions that underpin the pursuance of these aims can we discover the real drivers behind them. This is the main task of the following section.

Nevertheless, the papers' analyses have revealed that tackling unemployment is of paramount importance. Hence, ensuring equal access to education is not only a social aim but, based on the disproportionately large share of low educated people classified as unemployed, another measure to ameliorate tensions on the labour market.

5.4.2 Underlying assumptions: the discursive background

After having examined these rather outspoken aspects we must identify the implicit underlying ideas that guide education policy. Putting it in other words, what is it that is conducive to economic success, social inclusion and self-fulfilment in the context of a globalised world? Arguably education systems are embedded in an institutional context. Therefore, one can assume that issues and pressure points affecting political economies in general will affect education systems as well. The context in which visions and aims are embedded provides us with the contemporary 'commonsensual' assumptions, convictions and beliefs. There are two ways to reveal these ideas. The most obvious is to search the documents for direct and explicit references to them. Secondly, the way the line of argumentation is constructed, i.e. how one aspect is linked and leads to another, allows us to draw inferences about underlying ideas and convictions.

If, however, ideas exert influence on the choice of policy initiatives, then we can expect that ideas have an impact also on the definition of challenges and

5.4 Comparison

problems. Thus, in order to understand the selection of a particular policy option we need to trace it back to the context out of which it emerged in order to understand how the social problem was socially constructed and defined.

5.4.2.1 Underlying assumptions that guide pursuance of aims – the English case

The context in which England is considered to be embedded is characterised by two main conditions. Firstly, England is described as a country exposed to economic pressures prompted by globalisation and, secondly, as being exposed to the challenges faced by a "knowledge-based society". Thus there is a belief that the world is changing and that England has to adapt as smoothly and quickly as possible to these challenges. It comes at no surprise that the papers use the personal pronoun "we" when talking about the challenges to be overcome, thereby creating a sense of togetherness in order to activate the individuals and to stress the necessity that everybody has to contribute to these transformations.

Regarding the first aspect, the globalised and networked world is characterised by increasing international competition. The frequent reference to international league tables, such as those issued by the OECD, or the self-reference to countries such as India and China show that the English government perceives itself to be in this international competition.[84]

Among the remarks in the papers, one aspect seems to be most significant for the government: the comparatively low productivity rate. Accordingly, increasing the productivity rate is given high priority. The relative low productivity rate in comparison to England's main competitors is – according to the papers – the main obstacle to attaining a higher degree of competitiveness (White Paper "21st Century Skill: Realising Our Potential", DfES, 2003b). Strengthening the generation and quality of skills is supposed to be conducive to a higher productivity rate. "Skills" are considered a "national asset" (ib.) in which the government must invest:

> "The skills of our people are a vital national asset. Skills help businesses achieve the productivity, innovation and profitability needed to compete. They help our public services provide the quality and choice that people want." (DfES, 2003b, 8)

---

[84] It has to be said, however, that the papers do not distinguish between different competitors or different political economies. If and to what extent England is a direct competitor of China and India is far from obvious, as countries are specialised in the production of particular goods and services and thus are not necessarily competitors on all fronts.

The area of intermediate skills is identified as that which is lacking. When elaborating on the English educational reforms further below we will often come across the notion of "intermediate skills shortages".

The second contextual condition, the knowledge-based society, complements the picture. As understood in the papers this term describes two developments. The first encompasses the loss of low-skill and low-income manufacturing jobs to "newly industrialising countries" (Crouch, Finegold and Sako, 1999, 1) and the rising importance of the services sector. The second development the papers refer to is the increasing significance of knowledge in political economies. The conviction is that manual low-skill jobs are gradually being superseded by jobs that require higher degrees of knowledge.

Taking both aspects together shows the entire picture in which the government perceives the English political economy to be embedded: a country that is subjected to international competition which increasingly requires knowledge-based production processes. England has to face this situation and be forearmed for this competitive race through embarking on a high-skill strategy that will simultaneously allow it to escape both the low-skill equilibrium and the notorious low productivity levels. Therefore, education policy takes on a pivotal role in the government's considerations:

> "Our economic future depends on our productivity as a nation. That requires a labour force with skills to match the best in the world." (DfES, 2006, 1)

Thus, the belief that upgrading society's overall skills will improve the picture is all too obvious when analysing the papers. The "challenge" – as it is often called – leads to an abundance of reforms referred to in the analyses.

A manner by which to reveal some of the most significant and relevant underlying assumptions is to analyse the roles different actors assume or the roles which are assigned to them. Therefore, we shall distinguish between three different types of perceptions as displayed in the papers: 1) the perception of the individual person; 2) the perception about employers/the economy; and 3) perception about the function of the state and public authorities and its relation to other actors.

Perception about the individual person
What is the perception about individual persons that provides the foundation on which visions and aims sit? Though not giving an explicit answer, the White Papers are quite clear on this point: it is the idea that once equipped with a decent level of education an individual is able to sustain him or herself in the globalised world through flexibility and willingness to learn throughout his/her

whole life, thereby making them ready for the knowledge society (often underpinned by notions such as "love for learning", which is required to face current challenges, e.g. (DfES, 2006, 7). This will lead to a situation in which the individual is able to find the occupation which best fits his/her talents and interests. As a result, s/he will become a valuable part of the society and thus be socially included and self-fulfilled. It is this Durkheimian (communitarism) approach that allows the economy to then draw on a stock of motivated and ever more educated people, which allows employers to change gears and strategies in order to escape the low-skill equilibrium. The role of the state in this process is understood as one that enables, that "releases the energy" (DfES, 2006, 77), that lets societal actors operate at arms' length from the state, and as one that supervises rather than regulates. There is a salient belief that everyone should be put in their own driving seat in order to strive for their own fortune, while the state merely provides the seat and well prepared roads on which the drivers can operate in order to shortcut, bypass, or overtake others according to their proficiencies, talents, and aspirations (for an aeronautic metaphor see Keep, 2007, 17).[85] The White Papers implicitly begin from this underlying starting point. In essence, skills are claimed to be the mechanism through which the government can provide "equality of opportunity", which is regarded as being a prerequisite for economic, social and personal success (Lloyd and Payne, 2004; DfEE, 1999; DfES, 2001, 2005b, 2006, 5).

Perception about employers/the economy
In an education system that puts the economic purpose of education at its core, employers play a crucial role. Employers must indicate the skills that they need in order to harness the generated skills as efficiently as possible; that is arguably what a utilitarian approach to education policy is all about (on utilitarianism in education policy see Doyle, 2003; Grubb, 2004). Therefore, it is remarkable that employers play a rather passive role in the government's considerations. Instead, New Labour clings to the belief that upgrading the whole society to a higher educational level will lead to a "supply-push", i.e. employers will increasingly recognise and utilise the qualification stock available. The hope behind this assumption is to stimulate the economy and to eventually escape the low-skill equilibrium that the UK broadly and England in particular are supposed to be stuck in (also Lloyd and Payne, 2002; Finegold and Soskice, 1988, 374). As

---

[85]The academic literature is familiar with this line of argumentation. The notions of the "enabling state" (e.g. Gilbert and Voorhis, 2001) or the rather quick bloom of the "social investment state" comes closest to what New Labour is suggesting (Lister, 2002, 2004; Esping-Andersen, 2002; Newman and McKee, 2005; Sherraden, 2003; Perkins, Nelms and Smyth, 2004). It is in these two approaches that the notion of "human capital" (Coffield, 2000, 240) is broadly laid out.

already alluded to, the papers by and large avoid assigning employers specific roles or commitments. Instead, they encourage employers to cooperate as closely as possible, without, however, going into too much detail and without outlining any sanctions for non-cooperative employers.

This belief in the "supply-push" explains two further peculiarities of New Labour. Firstly, it allows the government to concentrate its efforts on education policy as the key component of a comprehensive and overarching economic and social policy. Secondly, it allows them to keep their hands off a "real" industrial policy, or even a re-strengthening of the institution of social partnership, as both aspects are traditionally contentious issues in England. However, education policy, understood as skill policy, is – as Keep formulates it – a rather neutral tool in the grand policy tool box for economic and social policy (Keep, 2006a). Suffice it here to say that the mantra of "education, education, education" reveals New Labour's conviction in the power, efficacy and the "panacea-effect" of skills.

In order to offer employers "the skills they need" (White Paper "21st Century Skill: Realising Our Potential", DfES, 2003b, 11) the government pursues a three-part strategy: massification, diversity, and excellence (Doyle, 2003, 4 ff.). These three aspects are to be pursued simultaneously. Massification is reflected in policies such as the extension of the higher education sector, the raising of the compulsory schooling age, and in the vast supply of different programmes and schemes intended to meet as many learners' interests and – even more importantly – employers' demands as possible. This last aspect brings us inevitably to the second guideline, which is diversity. The sheer number of options available to a youngster in England can been seen at best as offering "choice among a huge variety of options" but at worst as creating an incomprehensible and extremely fragmented qualificational jungle, in particular at ages 14-19. Finally, excellence is another one of the keywords. It stands in some contrast to massification and we will examine and evaluate in the next chapters if and how these two aims are reconciled.

Perception about the function of the state and public authorities
The function of the state in educational and skills policy matches perfectly the societal discourse about education, which perceives employers as passive profiteers of state policies and which is simultaneously quite demanding on current and future workforce. The perception is that of a market in which young people and employers are the customers and the state is the supplier. Yet there is a crucial difference between the two customers: young people are requested to accept an educational product, whereas employers might protest and complain about the skills-offer and refuse to acquire any of these skills. The state has put

5.4 Comparison

itself into the position of a supplier that must provide both the skills needed by employers and – as the Leitch Report does (Leitch, 2006) – forecast the future skill needs, through which it can design an industrial policy that steers the country towards a high-skill economy with higher production levels; in other words, exit the low-skills equilibrium.

"State," however, does not equal "state". We can see a tremendous difference between the self-perception of the central governmental authorities on the one hand and the local and non-departmental bodies on the other hand. It is the central authority that has the power to launch new initiatives and which has profoundly restructured the educational landscape, including the shape and mode of action of all relevant bodies. Moreover, it is the central government that has maintained and further expanded market elements in all areas of educational policy. School league tables, Beacon Schools, Research Assessment Exercise – just to name a few – serve the sole purpose of creating a market in the educational system. Elaborating on the governance of these educational markets, we have to face one critical aspect alluded to in the papers: educational policy is not only about educational issues and educational outcomes. Education is a public service. As it is a public service, education is subject to public service reforms. This kind of reforms occurs under the heading of "New Public Management" (NPM) and, here again, we enter a "minefield" when attempting to precisely define what NPM really is. However, one of its main hypotheses is that a market-oriented public sector performs with greater cost-efficiency than alternative models (Homburg, Pollitt and van Thiel, 2007, 4 f.; Doyle, 2003, 1; Steer et al., 2007). What we see in England is the following. Local units are given more discretion over the resources they receive. These local units compete in a market for learners, pupils, apprentices. At the same time they are accountable to superordinated bodies, with the Department at the top. The subordinated local unit is supervised by the higher unit. In the event of a local unit fails (for instance, in terms of low results in school tables) the higher unit is allowed to take action, up to and including the removal of the local provider and its replacement with another. Regarding colleges, their sword of Damocles is their replacement by a private actor. The department is the meta-supervisor. Funding is to a large extent dependent on performance and is thus a key steering device.

This reveals New Labour's underpinning belief in the market as the main social ordering principle. The government cedes responsibility for the generation of skills to the hands of lower units, whereas it assumes more supervisory power over this "market". Thus, the central government perceives its own function mainly as a regulator and supervisor who controls the delivery of education carried out on its behalf by lower units.

5.4.2.2 Underlying assumptions that guide pursuance of aims – the German case

According to the papers, Germany's educational policy is situated in a context of high unemployment rates and insufficient social security systems. The main reasons for unemployment, however, are not seen as being inherent in the German political economy. For the papers the main reason for higher unemployment is the weak world economy. The main tools to ameliorate this situation are seen as being supply-led incentives (compare with "Agenda 2010"). In this regard education is just one tool among many, with other examples including reforms in the social security system, changes in tax policies and labour market incentives. An increase in the quantity and quality of education is considered to be conducive to lower unemployment rates, since the economy is expected to make use of the increased portfolio of available skills.

Another important contextual factor that influences Germany's considerations on educational policies is the dense European and international context in which the papers situate Germany. The PISA-study for school education, the European Qualifications Framework (Copenhagen process)[86] for vocational education and training, and the Bologna-process for higher education demonstrate the huge influence European and other international benchmarks, such as those by the OECD, exert on German educational policy.

Perception about the individual person
German educational policies are difficult to understand without considering social policies as well. The commonly used slogan of "fördern und fordern" ("to boost and to challenge"; compare with Social Security Code, book two, SGB II) expresses this linkage. The so-called Hartz-legislation, which stems from the "Agenda 2010" (Schröder, 2004), has profoundly changed the relationship between state authorities and individuals, in that the latter are far more "challenged" by the former. This influences educational policies. Hence, in practise it is not a "new culture of learning" that stresses creativity and "learn how to learn" (compare with Schröder, 2002) that drives educational policy. Rather it is the social and labour market policy related aspects of educational policy that prevail. As Chancellor Schröder puts it, it is in this context that education is assigned a crucial role. This statement is exemplified and highlighted by the so-called G8-process, whereby higher secondary education is reduced by one year without adapting the syllabuses, and the Bologna-process, which dictates rather rigid and tight timetables.

---

[86] See http://www.bmbf.de/de/3322.php.

When combining this perspective on education policy with the one on social policy (including the Hartz-legislation) we encounter a situation for the individual which to a large extent resembles the English case. Education is perceived as the crucial lever to avoid becoming dependant on the state. The individual consequence of not making (not being able to) use of available educational opportunities is that the person will need to apply for low level residual assistance. Thereby pressure is exerted (usually negative financial incentives) to accept any job available. Individuals are exposed to a higher degree of commodification. Both, education policy and social policy contribute to this development. Analogous to England, the lowering of the residual net of social assistance is to be compensated for by an increase in educational provisions, preparing people to lead a "self-fulfilled life" (BMBF, 2008a).

Referring to one of the most prominent concepts in the comparative welfare state literature, famously applied by Esping, one might claim to find a lower degree of de-commodification in Germany (Esping-Andersen, 1990). Instead we see a situation that looks more like a liberal welfare approach. This observation is in accordance with recent analyses of the German welfare system in general and the social assistance structure in particular (see SKOPE-project).

Consequently, we observe some remarks in the papers that remind us of what has been called a "social investment state": investing in the education of the children in order to satisfy high-skill demands (Schröder, 2004) and education as the best investment in the future for individual life chances (Schröder, 2002). Arguably, it is only when reading the papers that these aspects shine through; yet, also education policies – considered against the background of the profound and transformative social policy reforms – reflect a changed perception of individual in the German political economy.

Perception about the economy/employers
The relation to employers and business is also one of "boosting and challenging" ("fördern und fordern"), though on a far less rigorous basis. The "Ausbildungspakt" is meant to challenge employers by, to use another phrase, offering "carrots and sticks," namely helping business to set up apprenticeship openings while simultaneously wielding the "sword of Damocles": namely the training levy. Yet, there are two developments that work against the government's attempts to maintain and obtain employers' support in training. Firstly, there is an upward tendency in school education. The devaluation of the Hauptschule has led to an ever greater number of pupils striving for the higher secondary school track. University and university of applied science degrees are increasingly attractive for pupils (FAZ, 2009) and, in some vocational areas, also more attractive for employers, relative to the alternative of apprenticeships

leading to eventual employment. Secondly, an ever larger proportion of low and middle secondary education school leavers are considered to lack "trainability" and thus enter the transition system. As a result of either of the two developments, the state increasingly puts itself in the driving seat and provides vocational education that previously was jointly provided for along with an employer in the dual system. This can have a tremendous impact on how employers and business perceive themselves and how they are perceived. It is not impossible to foresee a scenario in which Germany draws nearer England: why should employers care for something that they can get for free?

Thus the picture of employers that is drawn by the papers is ambiguous. On the one hand, the state attempts to assist the social partners in creating apprenticeship openings; on the other hand, if employers are not interested in training their prospective staff, they can turn to the labour market supply of trained young people who have gone through publicly provided training and education programmes (including universities of applied sciences). The main points of justification for this behaviour are supposed lack of trainability and the inability of the dual system to quickly adapt to new vocational challenges.

Perception about the function of the state and public authorities
In England we saw a clearly hierarchical structure: competencies for policy decisions are bundled at the governmental level. Consequently, in this "simple polity" (Schmidt, 2008), arriving at a decision is comparatively easy. By contrast, the German system is far more fragmented and numerous actors, such as states and social partners, have a tremendous impact on educational issues. Thus the federal government is less a supplier of educational services and more a supporter and "enabler" of other actors who provide these services. Again we have to distinguish between the different educational areas. A salient example of this observation is the "Ausbildungspakt" regarding vocational education and training. Here we see the state attempting to assume more responsibility, even though the responsibility lies with the social partners. State authorities try to mediate between employers and unions in order to ensure a sufficient amount of apprenticeship openings. At the same time, the state is launching school-based vocational education and training courses in order to address the miserable situation in the apprenticeship-job market. However, as we are talking about *schools* after all, these initiatives are under the ambit of the federal states.

In higher education, by contrast, Germany is pursuing a path which is familiar to us from the English case: namely, allowing for global budgets devoted to single institutions, for more market mechanisms in higher education (more competitions among institutions, among students, and within institutions) and at the same time adopting a slightly more rigid approach to how curriculums

5.4 Comparison

are organised and how courses of studies should be formally shaped (Bologna-process). However, education is still to an overwhelming extent perceived as a publicly provided service, which marks a noticeable difference from England. Schröder explicitly highlighted this fact by stating that education needs to be a publicly offered and administered service (Schröder, 2002).

We have already seen that education policy is sometimes used as a form of structural policy, especially in Eastern Germany. The idea behind this policy is to trigger a positive avalanche effect: supporting universities in particular regions in Eastern Germany to become "beacons" of research and teaching and thereby facilitating scientific networks to develop that will attract employers and business and thereby lead to a reduction in unemployment with all the positive side-effects this implies.

This example shows the instrumentalisation of education; how education policy is sometimes "disguised" as structural, economic, or social policy, not least because it is through these channels that the federal level can influence education policy; and the deep belief in supply-led policies, where educational policy initiatives are considered to be the initial seeds by which to create thriving regional economies ("blühende Landschaften").

Finally, we need to again look at the influence European and international benchmarks and comparisons have on Germany. We can see this influence on school education and higher education in particular, most prominently through PISA (OECD-study) and the Bologna-process. Paradoxically, it seems that it was not until the launching of these processes that the actual problems were defined. Is it really a disadvantage to not have as many higher education graduates as other OECD countries? Does PISA really tell us something about the prospective chances of young people on the labour market, especially given the importance of vocational education and training in Germany as a kind of almost compulsory post-secondary education? Can we not understand a higher education system without beacons like "Oxbridge" as actually having the advantage of being an egalitarian system, such as the German one used to be? The perception of the function of the state and public authorities seems, at least in these two educational areas, to be less self-confident than in England, in that achievements in European and international tests and benchmarks appears to be of eminent importance.

5.4.2.3 Summary of the English and German basic assumptions

What we see are educational initiatives which are supposed to enable individuals; initiatives which are utilitarian to the extent that the generation of skills has to satisfy the demand of employers; and initiatives which are disguised as educational but which also pursues a different agenda, namely to restructure the delivery of public services. Traditional values of education, such as educating future democratic citizens and facilitating critical thinking, are by and large neglected in a discussion which is driven by considerations of globalisation, international competitiveness and a cohesive society, i.e. a society in which people are an active part of the labour market. But about which country are we actually talking? In fact, most of the underlying assumptions in both counties resemble each other. The analysis of the order of discourse in the next section will shed light on how the emphases on these issues vary.

The previous few sentences refer mainly to the English case (compare with DfEE, 1997a, 1999). Of course, these inferences are generalisations and to some extent they should not be formulated as a critique. For instance, is training – by and large – not all about equipping young people with exactly the skills they need in order to succeed on the labour market? Is this not vocational education and training's main purpose? Are we not able to discern in the higher education paper indications that higher education is also about teaching the values that constitute Western society (DfES, 2003c; for a critical statement to this issue see Gibbs, 2002, 200)?

Even if we can answer these questions in the affirmative, we still have to notice the main ideational drivers that underpin considerations about educational policy in England. Firstly, there is a deep belief in a globalised and networked world in which concerns about international competitiveness through improved economic performance are of supreme importance. Moreover, there is a belief that everybody according to her/his talents is able to contribute to this improvement. There is also the idea that the market is the main organising principle for educational proposals. However, this belief ends at the doors of companies and factories, as employers utilise the skills they need and demand the generation of skills they require; and they demand these skills on a "market" which literally bears no risk for them. Regarding the perception of the individual person, considerations are driven by the idea of an individual whose resources and talents need to be released and canalised. It is the deep belief that everybody in principle is responsible for her/his own fortune that leads to the idea that the state should just offer "equality of opportunity" and that individuals have only to embrace the opportunities offered in order to lead a self-fulfilled life. The above remarks, however, leave us with some uneasy questions about the correlative argumentation used in the papers. These questions will be addressed and answered in the following chapter.

In the German case, we clearly see how Germany, like England, increasingly pursues a supply-led approach. The way education policy is connected to a policy to ameliorate the severest problems in terms of unemployment is based on the belief there will be a supply-push once people are better trained and educated. The references in the papers remind us of what is called a "social investment state" and reinforces this contention. The remarkable aspect of this is less that it, to a large extent, resembles the English case and more the unexpected emphasis on individuals. According to the common welfare state literature we would expect this in the English case but not in the German. Yet, educational policy has to be seen in the light of the German labour market reforms, and this is where the picture has changed: Germany is becoming more "liberal", in the sense of Esping-Andersen's typology, in that it offers fewer de-commodifying social measures and exposes the individual to more rigorous labour market mechanisms (e.g. "Zumutbarkeitsregeln"). As such, we might need to consider educational policy not only as complementary to social policy but also as a type of preventative social policy.

The role of employers and business is different in both countries and more ambivalent in Germany's vocational education and training scenery. Here employers are still – to a large extent – held responsible for the creation of the appropriate skills they need – thus a demand-led initiative. By contrast, in England – put simply – employers demand skills that are to be generated by means of public initiatives. In Germany there are some gradual developments in this direction. Moreover, there is not a genuine hard sanctioning mechanism to make employers cooperate (the same applies to England). It seems that supply-led policies are becoming ever more prevalent while at the same time graduates of universities of applied science are in increasing demand.

5.4.3 Order of discourse

The notion of "order of discourse" refers to Norman Fairclough's framework (compare with Fairclough, 2001). It describes how different discourses are ordered, i.e. if there is a dominant discourse. In Fairclough's words "order of discourse" is "the way in which diverse genres and discourses and styles are networked together" (Fairclough, 2001, 2). For the purpose of detecting this order we have to elaborate on how the educational discourse is conducted in the papers and thereby discover the prevailing and subordinated discourse(s). The overarching education-discourse consists of several sub-discourses. As discourses are the medium through which aims, aspirations, attributes, and visions are transmitted, we are able to discover the relevant sub-discourses by referring to the above mentioned main aims. Consequently, in order to identify the driving aims and ideas for change, we have to compare the discourses in which the relevant aims are hidden.

Solely ascribing the above listed goals to their relevant main aims, however, does not suffice to provide clear evidence for the "order of discourse". If it did, administrative aims would come last on the priority list of New Labour – an conclusion which is hardly convincing given the huge impact administrative issues seem to have on all areas of public services in England (e.g. Peters and Besley, 2006, 31). What we have to do instead is use the qualitative analysis above and further examine the textual context in which aims are mentioned in order to get an idea of the intensity with which the aims are pursued.

5.4.3.1 The English order of discourse

The introductions and executive summaries provide a first indication of how the educational discourse is ordered among its sub-discourses. I will use this preliminary order to structure the following five sections. In this regard, the economic purposes of educational policies seem to be very important. This preliminary assumption is based on two indicators: the place this aim is mentioned in the introductions and executive summaries (in this case the economic aims can be seen right from the beginning) and the number of times the documents refer to this aim (in this case very often). The second sibling of the "twin aims" is social justice (social integration), which is mentioned reasonably early, though fewer times. "Self-fulfilment" as a third main aim quite often complements the "twin aims". It seems, however, that it is not pursued with the same intensity, as it appears – if it appears at all – rather late and in only a few instances. The aim to reform public services is mentioned on even fewer occasions. Yet, it still may be rather influential if one takes into consideration the extent of institutional reforms undertaken by New Labour.

Economic aims
To start with, a brief glance at the above outlined list of aims shows that most of the mentioned "sub-aims" (see section above on "Visions and aims") can be subsumed under the broad aim of economic prosperity. Indeed, the economic purpose of educational policy is of paramount importance as a justification for policy reforms (see explicitly Peters and Besley, 2006, 76, 78). Right from the beginning of each paper the significance of skills and skill-generation for England's (British) economic success and development is stressed, as well as for its international competitiveness. This is best expressed by quoting two papers which embrace the whole period of analysis. The first analysed White Paper from 1997 already underlined the economic significance of education:

> "Priority is indeed being given to education, to employability and to investment for the future." (DfEE, 1997a, 4)

The Further Education White Paper issued in 2006 stressed the "economic mission" of education, saying that:

> "Our economic future depends on our productivity as a nation. That requires a labour force with skills to match the best in the world." (DfES, 2006, 1)

The social equivalent of the "economic mission", however, is not referred to in any further detail. Moreover, the analyses of the papers prove that this line of argumentation remains the prime determinant for justifying policy initiatives. The "hub" of this argumentation is the labour market. It is the labour market which is supposed to be an indicator of the usefulness of education and it is the labour market which serves as the pool for employers' recruitment endeavours – employers who are allotted the crucial role in shaping England's economic role, prosperity, competitiveness and economic wealth. In describing this nexus, in the academic literature we regularly encounter the notions of vocationalism and utilitarianism (Keep, 2007, 14; Peters and Besley, 2006, 76 ff.; Doyle, 2003; Grubb, 2004; Coffield, 2000).[87] In this context the notions refer to an educational approach that considers educational policies with respect to their usefulness for the labour market. Thus, education is grasped in economic terms.[88] It is less surprising to find utilitarianism and vocationalism as the driving forces behind vocational education. Schemes such as, for instance, apprenticeships or the "Train 2 Gain" programme, are all about a close connection to the labour market. Even the attempts to introduce a greater general education component into vocational education do not render the initial purpose of these schemes obsolete. However, it is harder to reconcile the use of a pure utilitarian and vocational approach to school education and higher education. Yet recently introduced schemes in these two areas, such as the young apprenticeship programme or foundation degrees, demonstrate the breadth of this development. Overall, the economic aims in educational policies seem to play an extraordinarily important role.

---

[87] However, the papers use the term "vocationalism" more cautiously: The White Paper "Further Education: Raising skills, improving life chances" explicitly states, that the "economic mission" of educational policies does not automatically equal "narrow vocationalism" (DfES, 2006, 6).

[88] In the literature this approach is contrasted to an approach where education is an "end of its own" (Crouch, Finegold and Sako, 1999; Doyle, 2003) or where education is meant to produce democratic and responsible citizens (see also Pring, 2004, 112 f.; Gibbs, 2002, 200).

Social aims
The primary social aim mentioned in the papers is social inclusion, also called social integration or social cohesion (see DfEE, 1997a; DfEE, 1999; DfES, 2005c; DfES, 2006). It is one sibling of what the papers call the "twin aims": i.e. the economic and social goals of education policy. Almost without exception, the introductions refer to this aim as one of the main drivers for reforms. When it comes to more concrete policy initiatives, however, it becomes less important and the economic purposes clearly prevail. Social integration/inclusion is understood simply as integration into the labour market; the term "social justice" is equated to equality of opportunity (DfEE, 1999, 7). Thus, social aims are not only subordinated to economic aims; moreover, they are actually disguised economic aims.

Public sector reforms
The discourse of "public sector reforms" is clearly subordinated to the economic discourse (see clear references to the issue of public sector reforms in education policy in DfES, 2001; DfES, 2003b; DfES, 2006). Yet its significance should not be underestimated. Educational reforms in England have to a large extent been structural reforms addressing the delivery of this "public good". Considerations about how to reshape the delivery of education are heavily underpinned by New Labour's concept of how the public sector should deliver its services. As such, this aspect contrasts the second aspect of "social aims": it is mentioned less frequently, but applied more rigorously. The topic of public sector reforms in education policy clearly accompanies education reforms. The issue becomes immediately significant when reforms affect the administration and governance of education (e.g. compare with deregulatory measures as proposed in DfES, 2001).

Self-fulfilment
The aspect of self-fulfilment is the weakest aim, i.e. it is seldom mentioned and hardly referred to at all when policy initiatives were presented (e.g. DfEE, 1997a; DfES, 2001). The context in which this notion does appear focuses, as with social aims, on labour market-purposes: it is skills and education that provide the individual with the essentials for a fulfilled (working) life (compare with Keep, 2007, 13, 17).

5.4.3.2 The German order of discourse

In the German case we encounter even more discourses that are linked to educational policy. Yet, and analogous to the English case, we observe a remarkable number of aims that are assigned to educational policies. The most prominent ones are labour market and economic related aims, social aims and personal aims (compare with BMBF, 2008a). However, and again analogous to the English case, the different aims have not been pursued with the same intensity, as the analysis of the relevant discourses will reveal.

Labour market aims and economic aims The labour market related discourse clearly dominates the first few papers. This does not come as a surprise, as high unemployment rates were the main issue in the 1998 election campaign:

> "Unser drängendstes und auch schmerzhaftestes Problem bleibt die Massenarbeitslosigkeit." (Schröder, 1998)

Not only in this period but also in the latter papers low education levels are associated with gloomy prospects on the labour market and are, thereby, seen as the main reason for high unemployment rates, particularly among young people (Schröder, 1998, 2002). All other discourses are clearly subordinated to this aim: social aims are practically equated with a policy that facilitates the creation of jobs; and personal fulfilment is to be obtained on and through the labour market. With regard to economic aims, the papers are mostly silent about school education. Higher education and vocational education, are treated differently in the papers. Vocational education is mentioned as an area in which Germany has to defend its comparative advantage of high productivity rates, which are considered a prerequisite for Germany's economic success, particularly in high quality manufactured goods (Schröder, 2004). Higher education is associated with either the need to increase participation rates to the level of international competitors (see the section about international discourse) or with the need to boost German research initiatives, as there are fears the country has fallen behind others, in particular against the Anglo-Saxon countries.

Less strong than in England, but still very salient, is the context in which Germany perceives itself as being situated: one of globalisation and international competition. Sustainable economic development is also heralded, for which education plays a crucial role (BMBF, 2008a).

Social aims
Social aims are emphasised throughout the papers, be it as a prerequisite for a sound and just educational policy or as a desirable outcome of such a policy. The goals are social inclusion and social cohesion, respectively. Even though aspects of equal access to and equal opportunities in education were mentioned already in the first paper (Schröder, 1998), these issues gained further impetuousness after the PISA study (Schröder, 2002). However, we need to consider two aspects of "social aims" separately. On the one hand, the aim of social inclusion has an economic flavour when it is understood as labour market integration. On the other hand, equal access and equal opportunities to education refer in particular to school education (see PISA) and higher education, as both areas exhibit a great degree of correlation with parental socio-economic backgrounds. Tackling this low degree of social mobility is actually one of the central goals of the government (BMBF, 2008a). Yet as discussions about the *Hauptschule*, tuition fees in higher education and the initiative of excellence reveal, politicians might pursue other priorities.

International discourse
At first glance it might be surprising to turn to the "international" discourse since "being international" does not necessarily seem to be an aim in itself. One would assume that international experiences and benchmarks matter most in instances where there is uncertainty about the appropriate reform option (compare with chapter 2). Yet this discourse has a huge impact beyond this function. Germany's self-perception as being part of and embedded in a globalised world seems to render international experiences and benchmarks extremely influential. It appears that this international context leads Germany to notice, or perhaps even to define, a social problem in the first place. Would Germany have been aware of its performance shortcomings if PISA had not happened? Is it not a fact that long durations of study are a problem because Germany perceives itself to be in competition with other political economies in which lengths of studies are shorter? "Internationality" itself becomes an aim if solutions are immediately derived from the international source of the problems.

In higher education this development is rather salient. The German pursuit of the goal for a European higher education area is supposed to kill two birds with one stone: to achieve greater comparability and transferability between different higher education systems by means of the Bologna process; and to thereby reduce the lengths of study, which is considered to be a particular German issue.

A similar situation is visible in school education. The PISA study revealed two of the most pressing problems in German secondary education: on the one hand, the lacking performance of pupils, on the other, the strong dependence of pupils' performance on their socio-economic background. Both issues were discussed and fully acknowledged in Germany only after PISA was published.

Personal aims
"Educational chances are life chances" (Schröder, 2002) – statements like this, which emphasis personal aims, are rather rare in the papers. Yet, when we encounter them they are in argeement with what has already been mentioned: life chances and a self-fulfilled life are grasped in vocational terms (BMBF, 2008a). As such, personal aims are clearly subordinated to labour market related aims and economic aims.

Administrative aims
In probably no other area are federal competences as confined as in education policy. The rhetoric of the papers, however, resembles to large extent that which we came across in England: strengthening competition among schools and higher education institutions, and devolving more competences in financial issues while simultaneously restricting competencies regarding content and qualifications (Schröder, 1998; BMBF, 1999; Schröder, 2002; BMBF, 2002).

Even though these are affairs that are under the ambit of the German states, there are some common developments in administrative issues: the implementation of the Bologna process, the initiative of excellence, the reduction of schooling years for higher secondary pupils, and the nationwide discussion about the role of the lowest secondary school track (Hauptschule) prove that there is an on-going intra-national diffusion process. One could see this occurrence as a further application of the policy diffusion literature.

Even though there are some analogies to the English case with respect to administrative aims, we nevertheless observe some differences in the contexts in which these aims are mentioned. Conviction in the power of the market and the prevalence of "New Public Management" seem less important as drivers of German policy. Instead, consideration and application of initiatives and experiences abroad seem to be the key factors.

Structural policy
It could be argued that educational policy, as a policy that pursues labour market related and economic aims, is structural policy as well (see e.g. BMBF, 2002). Yet in some areas this is more explicit than others. For example, ss the papers point out, the creation of beacon-universities and research networks is in particular targeted towards Eastern Germany, where it is hoped that these facilities will be an initial spark that ignites regional development.

Miscellaneous

In his government declaration of 2002, Schröder raised three other subjects that can be treated briefly, as they obviously do not play a crucial role in educational policy considerations. He underlined the fact that education serves the purpose of teaching values and norms on which society is built:

> "Bildung muss auch Werte, Normen und Haltungen vermitteln, auf die sich unsere Gesellschaft mit guten Gründen geeinigt hat und auf die unsere Gesellschaft gebaut ist." (Schröder, 2002)

Moreover, he points out the necessity to obtain "environmental competences" (Schröder, 2002) and move towards the provision of full-time education in order to allow both parents to pursue a regular working life (Schröder, 2004). This latter aspect is influenced by both the quality discourse centred on the PISA study and by altering family structures. All three aspects are not referred to any further, are not reflected within the policy proposals, and are clearly overshadowed by the other discourses.

5.4.3.3 Summary to the English and German order of discourse

As the analysis shows, the economic purpose of education prevails in the discourse in England. Moreover, not only does it prevail, but both the social aims and the self-fulfilment aim are largely defined in economic terms. Only the goal of reforming the public sector seems to be a goal in and of itself, though reforms in this vein are quite often economically justified themselves, as they are driven by efficiency and efficacy considerations rather than educational ones. Neither in England nor in Germany is education understood as an aim on its own. Apart from this important similarity we need to state that the economic harnessing of education assumes top priority in both countries, although with a slightly different emphasis: Germany has been mainly concerned with high unemployment rates, which education measures are meant to tackle, whereas England's considerations revolve around productivity rates and international competitiveness. The self-perception of Germany as being part of a globalised and economically integrated world, however, leads to a discourse that is far stronger than in England, namely the discourse about meeting international benchmarks. In Germany this latter discourse and the labour market related and economic discourse prevail; others are clearly subordinated. This applies also to the administrative discourse, which is largely embedded into the "internationality" discourse.

5.5 Critique of argumentation

So far the analysis has revealed the significance of some underlying assumptions as applied in the papers of both countries. The notion of (1) "knowledge-based society" for instance is commonly used in England and Germany for explaining why skills have increasingly gained in importance for political economies. The effects, consequences and roots, however, are not further queried; not even a definition of what "knowledge-based society" means in the first place is provided. The same applies to the (2) sketched correlation between levels of skills and economic performance. This is the basis from which (3) potential skill shortages are detected.

As we can see in an instant, the three aspects are far from being uncontested. Thus, this section will serve two major purposes. Firstly, it is a critical investigation of the main underlying assumptions that are used in both countries. Hence, it is about unveiling the main argumentative foundations on which the lines of argumentation are built. The second purpose is to establish a critical background against which the analysed reforms in the oncoming chapter can be assessed. The three issues will be scrutinised by means of theoretical literature and further evidenced mainly by referring to the English case. Yet, as will become evident, the arguments can be equally applied to the German case.

5.5.1 Knowledge-based society

When it comes to education policy, one idea or concept prevails in academic and political discussions, namely the "knowledge-based society/economy". Governmental papers are of no exception, though they use numerous different expressions: "learning age" and "knowledge and information economy" (DfEE, 1997b); "age of knowledge" (DfEE, 1997a); "knowledge and information economy of the future" (DfEE, 1999); "European knowledge society" Schröder, 1998; "knowledge society" Schröder, 2002; "knowledge-based economy" (DfES, 2003b); "knowledge-dominated age" and "knowledge economy" (DfES, 2003c); or "knowledge-intensive economy" (DfES, 2005b).

Irrespective of which expression the papers use, "knowledge-based society" (or equivalents) is employed as a synonym for a huge number of aspects that reflect the current zeitgeist as seen in the papers: the increasing significance of knowledge; the importance of knowledge for the production process; the declining significance of the industrial sector; increasing competitiveness propelled among others by the enhanced use of information technologies (IT); and the necessity to be more productive and internationally competitive. Thus, the increasing significance of knowledge is perceived as both a cause and a result. For example, the rising importance of IT has rendered knowledge more important and challenges the existing political economies, yet simultaneously the recipe for tackling this challenge is seen as being exactly what caused the challenge in the first place, namely in accepting and adapting IT as quickly as possible and by rendering "knowledge" the number one priority in educational policy.

The academic literature shows that the emergence of the concept of a "knowledge-based society" did not appear overnight; rather it was an evolutionary process which accompanied some major changes in the economic structure of western industrialised countries (Stehr, 2005, 300). One of the first individual to use this notion was Robert E. Lane in 1966 who talked about a "knowledgeable society" (compare Stehr, 2001, 118). The transfer of jobs with low skill requirements to new industrialised countries and ongoing technological progress have led to the belief that we are facing a shift from an industrial to a post-industrial society, or even to an economy based mainly on the services sector. The growing concern about knowledge accumulation and education systems is propelled by the loss of low-skilled manufacturing jobs and evidence that unemployment in western societies is highest among those with low levels of skills and education (Crouch, Finegold and Sako, 1999, 1). Hence, it does not come as a surprise that wage differentials between skilled and unskilled people have risen significantly (see Brown, Green and Lauder, 2001, 6; see also next section). The process of growing differences in returns, however, is twofold: It is due to the *increasing* importance of human capital and employability on the one hand and the *decreasing* value ascribed to jobs pursued by low-skilled workers on the other (Hansen and Vignoles, 2005, 33).

Nico Stehr takes the concept of a knowledge-based society even further. As he claims, until recently societies were perceived of in terms of property and labour. Nowadays, however, "knowledge" has become the main driver, the socially constitutive determinant and factor which stratifies societies (Stehr, 2005, 301). Knowledge as a productive asset is defined as the "capacity for action" (Stehr, 2005, 305). Thus, the wealth of companies in advanced societies is increasingly embodied in creativity and information, rendering knowledge an influential factor of production. This means that the economic value and capital of an economy relies evermore on its knowledge and on the way it manages and accumulates this factor of production. Stehr characterises this development as a shift from a "material economy" to a "symbolic economy" (Stehr, 2005, 312; compare with Brown, Green and Lauder, 2001, 5 ff.; Peters and Besley, 2006, 7 ff.). The former notion signifies economies' focus on size of workforce, amounts of labour time and amounts of physical capital, hence an economy

5.5 Critique of argumentation

whose manufacturing process is reliant on material inputs. Over time, the main traits of an industrial economy, such as demand and supply for primary goods, the role of manual work, the magnitude the international commodity market carries, and the meaning of place and time for the production process, have decreased in relevance, as opposed to the increasing significance of symbolic input (Stehr, 2001, 121). This symbolic and knowledge-based input has gradually become the determining factor for economic endeavour, prosperity, and expansion (Stehr, 2001, 312).

This does not mean that these issues have entirely replaced labour and property as the constitutive mechanisms of society, or that knowledge has never played an important role before. Yet knowledge is being added as a new principle, one which transforms and challenges traditional patterns, as information and creativity have become ever more important factors to an enterprise's success. Drucker even claims that the application of knowledge is the dominant wealth-creating activity in production and innovation processes, as opposed to the allocation of capital or the use of physical work (see Brown, Green and Lauder, 2001, 6). The area which possibly exemplifies and symbolises this process in its most extreme form is the fast and dynamic development in information technologies.

Knowledge is crucially important for the life chances, lifestyle, and social influence of individuals. It is also conducive to employability and is thus critically important for an individual's economic opportunity, vocational choice, and occupational status. But knowledge has not only become a significant factor influencing society. Knowledge has evolved into a factor of production just like labour and property. This holds true in particular for western political economies, which have been forced to embark on different economic strategies due to the decline of the labour-intensive industrial sectors, especially the transfer of low-skilled jobs to newly industrialised countries.

However, the growing significance of knowledge is not simultaneously reflected in working patterns, for two reasons. Firstly, the loss of employment opportunities in the industrial sector is not tantamount to a decline of its significance. Computerisation and automation can affect employment negatively, while having no impact – or even a positive impact – on the economic strength of the sector. Secondly, it is questionable whether low skilled workers formerly engaged in manufacturing professions can be compensated with a "knowledge-relevant" job (Stehr, 2001, 130; Coffield, 2000, 241).

The English papers in particular lack a further differentiation of this kind. The academic literature criticises the papers for perceiving the workforce as one homogenous entity that is treated with "blanket entitlements and simple, monolithic skills-supply programmes" (Keep, Mayhew and Payne, 2006, 550).

The papers barely take into account the different needs of different sectors, different product and service offerings according to different consumers, different market strategies even among organisations within one sector, and different strategies to achieve competitive advantage (Keep, Mayhew and Payne, 2006, 550). This is not about blaming the English approach as such, but about assessing its performance according to its own aspirations, namely to provide and ensure skills which render England the "best skilled country in the world" (DfES, 2005b, 2) and a "world leader in skills" (ibid. 5).[89]

Hence, contemplating of the academic literature leaves us with some uneasy questions about this parsimonious skill approach: How are these considerations transformed into an overarching skill strategy? What about components of the political economy which can not be subsumed under the heading of a knowledge-based working environment? More concrete, how is a knowledge-based high skill strategy applied to low-skilled groups within a society? And what about the jobs these groups have?

We are able to obtain a better idea of how "knowledge-based society" is understood by looking once more at the English "skill strategy". The approach towards skill generation is based on a rather one-dimensional human capital approach, one that is concentrated on upgrading the skills of the population while at the same time one that largely disregards both the demand-side of skills and alternative policy options for promoting prosperity. Moreover, the English government perceives the workforce as one homogenous entity and thereby neglects the necessity of treating groups of workers and employees in various sectors in a different manner (see Keep, Mayhew and Payne, 2006, 550 ff.). Summing this point up, the English response to the complex knowledge-based society challenge is a "skill strategy" that is based on a human capital scattershot, "one-size-fits-all" approach (compare Brown, 2001, 40; Peters and Besley, 2006, 78).

The academic literature provides a more sophisticated perspective in that it does not perceive national economies as a unitary block. Instead, it accounts for the fact that national economies consist of various sectors which contribute to the overall economic picture of a country. If we perceive a political economy as a unitary entity that is exposed to the challenges of a knowledge-based economy,

---

[89]Ashton and Sung provide a conceptual framework that facilitates the understanding of what skills employers actually need (Ashton and Sung, 2006). They draw on a case study undertaken for the Department of Trade and Industry (DTI). The authors distinguish between a technical and an interpersonal relation of production, the former referring to knowledge in the closest sense of the word, the latter referring to generic skills, motivation and commitment. They conclude that: "[f]or some employers (with their specific competitive strategy), training beyond the operation level is pointless and counter-productive. Resources devoted to such an 'undifferentiated' skills policy are likely to be wasteful." (Ashton and Sung, 2006, 17).

we are quite likely express conviction in what Brown et al. have called a "magnet economy", i.e. an economy which attracts national and international investment and thus pulls the whole economy to a higher level (Brown, 2001, 9).

Yet, if we open up this "black box", the sectors that immediately profit from a knowledge-based education strategy make up only a portion of the entire whole (Brown et al. speak of no more than 40 percent; Brown, Green and Lauder, 2001, 20). Moreover, and more specific to the educational issues at stake here, it is higher education and research which are seen as the main drivers of a knowledge economy (Peters and Besley, 2006, 54). This picture can be completed with reference to research done by Kevin Smith, who states that though new technologies are highly prestigious, "low tech" industries (as opposed to "high tech" industries), such as engineering, food, wood products and vehicles still make a significant, stable and reliable contribution to national economies.[90] Hence, this brief review shows the literature stresses the highly complex, multi-layered and evolutionary process that the term "knowledge-based society" attempts to denote. Moreover, the depictions of "knowledge-based societies" in the academic literature clearly emphasise one crucial issue: "knowledge" as a decisive factor has always existed and has only become more prominent through a long evolutionary process, but one which has not rendered the main features of "material economies" utterly obsolete (Stehr, 2001, 119). It is this smooth transition from one status to another that characterises contemporary western societies.

5.5.2 *About the correlation between skills and productivity*

The papers argue that there is a correlation between levels of skills and educational attainment, on the one hand, and economic performance (as in GDP), on the other. The major difference between England and Germany lies in the aspiration of the former to increase productivity rates, whereas the latter is mainly concerned with reducing unemployment rates (e.g. White Paper "21st Century Skill: Realising Our Potential", DfES, 2003b and White Paper "14-19 Education and Skills", DfES, 2005a; Coffield, 2000, 240; Keep, Mayhew and

---

[90]Smith highlights an additional aspect about the relation between "knowledge-creators" and "knowledge-users": "We can suggest that many so-called low-tech sectors are intensive in their use of scientific knowledge – industries such as food production, machinery, printing and publishing, wood products, and a range of services, have significant indirect science inputs. […] Thus, 'low tech' industries are knowledge intensive, and are frequently part of 'high tech' systems, and both scholars and policy-makers should be aware of their significance for growth. If the term 'knowledge economy' is to have any real significance it must take such processes and activities into account, not only as bearers and users of knowledge, but also as drivers of change." (Smith, 2002, 27).

Payne, 2006; Schröder, 1998; Schröder, 2002).

Yet the correlation between education, productivity and GDP is far from clear (Keep, Mayhew and Payne, 2006; Wolf, 2004). As to the first correlation, it is questionable whether people with a given degree of education and a particular earning level necessarily have higher productivity (Keep, Mayhew and Payne, 2006). The productivity differences between the services sector and the manufacturing sector could account for the unclear positive correlation. Secondly, the correlation between productivity and GDP is not straightforwardly either (Fernandez and Mayhew, 2008). An example illustrates this issue: comparing the US and Germany throughout the 1990s reveals that the US economy, despite having higher rates of GDP, has considerably lower rates of productivity. Furthermore, this example might even suggest that there is a negative correlation, in that lower rates of productivity are offset by longer working days and higher employment rates. However, this is not to suggest that productivity and the GDP are generally negatively correlated; it is just to point out that the "taken-for-granted" assumptions of a causal link between education/skills, productivity and GDP, as suggested by the policy documents, is far from clear and uncontentious. In fact, and especially interesting for the English case, there are examples that contradict this perception. Scotland has, arguably, already "accomplished the skill strategy" and possesses a more highly qualified workforce than England. Yet there is no evidence this has positively impacted its economic performance relative to England (Keep, 2007, 11; Keep, Mayhew and Payne, 2006, 545).

In addition, the papers assume a positive relationship between education and wage returns. This relationship is widely accepted. However, it must be mentioned that the growth in wage differentials is not caused only by an upward trend; low-skilled people tend to earn even less than they did in the industrial period. This means that the upward trend coincides with a downward trend for the low-skilled, thus leading to even greater differentials (Hansen and Vignoles, 2005, 33). Consequently, we should be sceptical of quasi causal liner argumentation models like: an enhancement in education and training efforts caused by technological change ultimately leads to higher skills which automatically lead to higher wages.

Moreover, it has to be kept in mind that this relationship might be based on a "replacement competition" (Keep, 2007, 21), as employers might require a level of employee skill in certain professions that formerly required lower skills. Thus we might see an upward development, as jobs will be filled by people with higher formal qualifications than those who had worked there before. This is a development which is actively promoted by, for instance, the Report of the House of Lords in England, which states: "To increase the stock of skills in the

5.5 Critique of argumentation 213

UK requires flows of better-qualified young people to replace those retiring workers who have lower skills" (House of Lords – Select Committee on Economic Affairs, 2007b, paragraph 19). Taking this argument as it is, it seems bizarre to embark on a high-skill strategy if people with a higher qualification level are supposed to assume a job that was formerly carried out by someone with a lower level.[91]

This observation might lead one to ask how better economic performance is to be achieved if higher skilled workers just take over the same job from lower skilled workers. The answer is that it is up to the employer to recognise the abundance of skills that are available to them, to reflect on her/his production strategy and to consider changing it in order to best utilise the skills resources available. This reconsideration will – according to the papers – lead to better economic performance. Hence, we see again the significance of a supply-led approach to education policy. This approach is even more prevalent in England than in Germany.

5.5.3 Skill levels and education participation rates

Both countries have criticised their low participation rates: England moans about a lack of intermediate skills whereas Germany complains about low higher education participation. For example, the White Paper "21st Century Skills" published in 2003 discusses the "skill gaps" from which England is supposed to be suffering. The gap is:

> "in basic skills for employability, including literacy, numeracy and use of IT; intermediate skills at apprenticeship, technician, higher craft and associate professional level; mathematics; and management and leadership." (DfES, 2003b, 12)

Thus, England is seen as being short of skills – but too short for what? Is it a "current" shortage that fails to provide employers now with the skills they need? Or is it a "putative" shortage, one which can only be estimated against the backdrop of a vision about how the government wants the future to be (Keep, 2006b, 4)? Thus we need to examine two time horizons in order to see whether this issue is considered one for the present or one for an anticipated future.

On the short time horizon, neither countries points out particular economic

---

[91] There is an inconsistency in that the supply-led approach is not only about meeting the needs of the labour market but above all about a calculated over-supply of skills that is meant to trigger demand for them and substitute people with lower skill levels – an approach which runs the risk of generating a large pool of over-educated people (Keep, 2006b, 6).

areas that are affected by the lack of skills or low participation rates; rather they refer to international benchmarks and comparisons (e.g. OECD) in order to highlight the (self-)perceived issue. However, the theoretical literature about the varieties of capitalism teaches us that such references can easily lead to a comparison of "apples and oranges" (Hall and Soskice, 2001). It is problematic to compare only different outcomes of different skill systems while disregarding the diverse conditions of the political economies in which education systems are embedded. In other words, is it not possible that a country can have an overall lower skill level and in spite of this fact, or even because of it, still be internationally competitive? It is the particular economic and political orientation of a political economy that constitutes its distinctiveness and it is this distinctiveness which constitutes its international competitiveness, i.e. which renders the production and generation of particular goods and services more efficient in one political economy than in another. This contemplation, however, reveals again the deep belief of the English government in the efficacy of a "skills strategy". There is the conviction that this item alone can improve England's place in a globalised world (Keep, Mayhew and Payne, 2006). The same applies to the belief that closing the "skills gap" will improve England's productivity rate, an aspect which has already been dealt with in the previous section. In both cases, when complaining about low higher education participation rates references are made to international studies, while a similar economic justification for the "qualification initiative" appears in the German papers (e.g. BMBF, 2008a).

On the longer time horizon, anticipating the requisite skills for accomplishing a future scenario entails some risks (compare with Leitch, 2006; Keep, 2007). On an abstract, visionary level, it is an internationally competitive knowledge-based economy that the English government has in mind. This vision is backed by referring to past experiences of structural economic change – the rise of the services sector, wage differentials between high and low educated people, just to name a few – from which inferences are drawn for the future. The government obtains information about the skill needs of the economy by means of a "National Employers Skills Survey". This survey serves the purpose of recognising the skills that employers need for their endeavours. However, one must ask whether the answers really reflect the current needs or if employers, being offered the chance to choose the best product on the "skill-rack" at no additional cost, are giving inaccurate and/or unrealistic answers. Moreover, the accuracy of these forecasts is vulnerable to financial and economic crises, as exemplified by, for instance, recent difficulties for the automotive industries in Germany in particular and unpredictable developments in the field of new technologies in general.

5.5 Critique of argumentation

"Skill shortages", the pledge for higher participation rates, and the idea of a knowledge-based society each pretend that everybody, once being skilled, will be able to work in a "knowledge-environment". Yet evidence from England reveals that this perception is over-simplistic.

The picture of a knowledge-based society as presented in the papers disregards the possibility that low-paid jobs pursued by low-skilled people are not merely a shortcoming of a society but a constitutive component of a Western political economy. The English government commissioned Sir Sandy Leitch to estimate future skill needs up to 2020. The Leitch Review turned out to be one of the clearest statements of the expectations associated with skills and educational policies:

> "Our nation's skills are not world class and we run the risk that this will undermine the UK's long-term prosperity. Productivity continues to trail many of our main international comparators. Despite recent progress, the UK has serious social disparities with high levels of child poverty, poor employment rates for the disadvantaged, regional disparities and relatively high income inequality. Improving our skill levels can address all of these problems." (Leitch, 2006, 1)

Leitch's, as well as New Labour's, belief in a knowledge economy is based on the conviction that "knowledge" is causing a massive change in the structure of employment, as the amount of jobs with higher skill requirements increase while the low-skilled working class is about to vanish. Leitch proves this development empirically through several figures, showing that jobs with few qualification requirements will have almost disappeared by 2020. However, as Keep and the Centre for Enterprise point out, this forecast is based on the expected supply of skills, not the potential demand by employers (Keep, 2007, 10; Lloyd and Payne, 2004, 3 f.; Keep, 2006b; Mason, 2004). Thus, one might query the inferences that Leitch has drawn from these figures. Again we see here a thoroughly supply-led approach, one which "Leitch" was initially intended to overcome.

Moreover, figures for England by Delorenzi and Robinson indicate that an increase in the number of positions with high skill requirements does not inevitably correlate with a decline in low-skill jobs (Delorenzi and Robinson, 2006). From 1982 and 2002, the decline in the percentage of jobs at the lower end of the skill range was marginal (from 39.3 percent in 1982 to 36.3 percent by 1992 and to 35.2 percent in 2002) and is anticipated to remain nearly stable at 34.5 percent through 2012. According to the same dataset by Delorenzi and Robinson, the development of the field of high-skill occupations takes place at the expense of intermediate skill jobs. As a consequence, speaking of a high-skill "knowledge-based society" when roughly half the workforce remains in occupations with intermediate– or low-skill requirements overstates the significance of "knowledge" in education and skills policy. The Learning and Skills Council confirms this development by noting a "polarisation in the jobs market", in that there is a tendency for a growth in jobs which require either a high or a low skill level[92]; future jobs-growth on the intermediate skill level, by contrast, is estimated to remain modest (Learning and Council, 2007, 73 f.) if not decline (Delorenzi and Robinson, 2006).

Leitch's and the government's argumentation tend to simplify the situation when claiming that an up-skilled society is the main condition for tackling the challenges of globalisation. Not only are most low-skilled service sector jobs not exportable, but moreover, investments in education, especially further education, are greatest for already high-skilled people, who need these skills to compete internationally, and not for low-skilled people, who might need further "skill-investment" more desperately (Keep, 2007, 27; Coffield, 2000, 242). Hence, appeals for higher participation rates and concerns about skill shortages need to be carefully considered in their context and one must scrutinise what aims are actually being pursued by such policies.

---

[92]Moreover, the Learning and Skill Council (Learning and Council, 2007, 24), while acknowledging the increasing significance of knowledge, highlights the still huge importance – in terms of scope and extent – of low-skill jobs, and thereby the importance of the sectors in which they are placed, for the present and the future economy.

6 Educational reforms: process tracing and evaluation

In this chapter the reforms made to the English education system will be traced and evaluated. This task represents the core of this book for one major reason: the reforms will be evaluated against the background of all available information that this book has thus far explored. Thereby, this chapter will pull together the evidence gathered in the previous chapters. The historical outlines provide us with the main traits that characterise every system. Putting this in words of historical institutionalism, the evidence from this chapter delineates the path along which developments are supposed to have occurred.

The theoretical framework provides us with tools with which we can scrutinise the reform initiatives. These tools allow us to account for "unexpected changes"; how ideas – in terms of Schmidt (2008) – are used in different contexts and at different points in a reform process (Blyth, 2002); what kind of theoretical drivers might trigger reforms processes; how reforms relate to existing policies; and how reforms are implemented and to what extent ideas and discourses play a role in this process.

The paper analysis showed how education discourses are constructed. The discourses reveal the possible drivers of policy action in the educational arena against which reforms can be evaluated. Moreover, the analysis reveals the aims and expectations that are associated with particular reforms.

The forthcoming chapter takes this a step further and shows how reforms are discussed, how they are linked to the policy discourse, and how they are ultimately implemented. It is because we are tracing the reform processes that we are able to make statements about how successful reforms operate in a given institutional context. In so doing, we can make some important observations about the way in which the reforms alter the institutional design in a manner we would not have expected if we were to adhere to the historical institutionalism and varieties of capitalism literature.

Last but not least, "evaluation" means pulling together these pieces of evidence and considering them in the light of the questions formulated at the beginning of this study. These are:

1. What drives institutional change?
2. What role do concepts such as institutional complementarity and path-dependency play within the reform endeavours?
3. How profound are the reforms? Are they "path-breaking"?

A major problem with evaluating the following six selected reforms is that these are recent changes and that although some of them have *begun* to have an impact, they have not yet made their full force felt. Therefore, the analysis has to be conducted carefully, because an evaluation that embraces a comprehensive analysis of intended and unintended effects and which provides conclusive evidence as to the success and deficiencies of a particular reform might run the risk of overstating its findings at this early stage. Yet, given the context of what this research argues we can draw inferences and hypothesise about the future development of a particular reform in its institutional setting.

The intention of the evaluation is twofold. On the one hand, we will compare reform outcomes with the core arguments of the historical institutionalism and varieties of capitalism literature. This will enable us to discover if and to what extent the reform deviates from the path in the relevant area. For this task, the main traits of a particular educational field within the examined country will be contrasted with those features that characterise the reform.

On the other hand, the evaluation serves as a detailed analysis of the driving factors behind a reform. "Ideas" will thereby play a crucial role, as will international benchmarks. These influences will be set in contrast to the theoretical assumptions of the historical institutionalism and varieties of capitalism literature.

As to the procedure, each of the following six sections will be subdivided into five parts. Firstly, in order to understand the reform in its entirety we need to describe the problem or deficiency which the reform is supposed to tackle. Thereby we discover the discursive starting point of the reform. Secondly, the policy formulation procedure and the adoption of the initiative will be traced. At a third stage, the discourse that ultimately led to the implementation of the reform will be outlined according to the concepts outlined in the theoretical chapter (see chapter 2). Fourthly, the post-implementation critique of the reform will be presented in order to provide further information against which the reform can be assessed. The fifth stage is devoted to an evaluation and assessment of the reform. Thirdly, the reform will be evaluated in five steps: (1/5) I will briefly outline the paths along which we expect reforms – in a given area in one of the two countries – to evolve. This will serve as a template against which (2/5) it will be shown why the relevant reform has the potential to qualify as a "deviator" from the expected path. In a third step (3/5), by means of the theoretical framework and the explanatory-power of discursive institutionalism, the underpinning ideas, expectations and aims that assist our understanding of how this "path-breaking" policy proposal came about will be discussed. Fourthly (4/5), the theoretically-understood discourse will be contrasted to the implemented version of the reform in order to detect the prevailing ideational drivers. Thereby we will find an answer to the question of when ideas are manipulated, confined, stressed, or abandoned during the implementation of a policy proposal in a given national context. Fifthly (5/5), the reform process will be contemplated it its entirety in order to make a statement as to how "path-breaking" the reform actually turned out to be.

6.1 Policy reforms in England – three cases and their selection

This chapter will concentrate on three particular reforms that have been undertaken in England (Curriculum 2000, apprenticeships, foundation degrees). As a reminder of what was discussed in the first chapter, here again are the three criteria used to select the reforms:
1. the reforms must have passed an entire policy cycle. This applies to all three reforms;
2. the reforms must have a significant role and importance in the educational discourse of a country. As the paper analyses have shown, this is the case with all three selected reforms, which play a crucial role in the English educational discourse;
3. the reforms should have the potential to alter the institutional setup. This requirement is certainly applicable for apprenticeships and foundation degrees and even for "Curriculum 2000".

The "Curriculum 2000" reform in the area of school education provides an excellent example both for comparing the aspirations in this area with the actual outcome and for a comparison with the German equivalent, the so-called "Abitursreform". This reform was an attempt to further modularise the post-compulsory curriculum, promote vocational-oriented school education, and broaden the supply of courses. Moreover, and this is proven by the papers' analyses, it is an endeavour to achieve a "levelled playing field" for academic and vocational education.

When analysing "apprenticeships" it is difficult to pick a specific reform because the whole scheme seems to be in constant flux. Thus, the analysis is focused on how this scheme has developed and how the intentions which accompanied the processes have evolved over time. Thereby we unveil the main problems, pitfalls and deficiencies of the whole English further education system. For this book the English apprenticeships scheme assumes critical importance for at least three reasons: firstly, with an intended participation target of 28 percent (by 2005; DfES, 2005b, 8) the government wants apprenticeships to become the second main route for post-compulsory education after A-levels (DfEE, 1999, 17). Thus, one might understand this target as complementary to the 50 percent target in higher education. Secondly, apprenticeships are thought to provide a considerably higher degree of standardisation among the vocational education and training qualifications in England. In the same vein, apprenticeships are meant to provide a clearer occupational orientation rather than a mere qualificational one, though without altering labour market regulations. Thirdly, employer involvement in the scheme has always been a major aim of English education policy. One could presume that once a substantive engagement of employers has been achieved the whole system will gain a more demand-led character, rather than the prevailing supply-led, state-driven character it has taken thus far.

The foundation degree is an interesting scheme for various reasons. It displays the influence of "vocationalism" on higher education and is intended to contribute to the goal of achieving 50 percent participation in higher education by any given age cohort by 2010. Moreover, it seeks to contribute to "parity of esteem" between academic and vocational education.[93] Thereby, foundation degrees tackle one of the two "stratification levers",[94]. This part of the analysis will be accompanied by the question of how and where to a draw the line between higher education and further education.

All three reforms (changes in schemes) are dealt with in the papers. Thus we can consider these developments in the context the papers provide. In this chapter the concrete contexts in which these reforms are mentioned will be identified alongside the tracing of the whole reform context and discourse.

---

[93]Officially foundation degrees are higher education qualifications; however, they are shaped similar to a FE qualification.
[94]The other one refers to the difference in esteem between different higher education institutions, i.e. Ox-bridge at the top and the rest below.

6.1.1 School education: Curriculum 2000

> "Earlier this year in the light of our Qualifying for Success consultation we announced important changes to the qualifications system to reflect our goals for young people. The changes were particularly designed to increase the range of choice available to young people so that they can follow the learning pathway best suited to their aspirations and abilities." (DfEE, 1999, 47)

1) Agenda setting, problem identification

"Curriculum 2000" is not a reform that came about all of the sudden. Though not implemented until 2000, its roots can be traced back to the 1996 "Dearing Review of Qualifications for 16-19 Year Olds" (Dearing, 1996) which was commissioned by the Conservative government. At this time participation and performance targets set by the National Advisory Council on Education and Training Targets (NACETT) had already been applied but their achievement without further reforms seemed to be highly unlikely (Hodgson, Spours and Savory, 2003, 17; for targets and their accomplishment-rates in 1995 and 1996 see Mag, 1996; Mag, 1997). This problem coincided with criticism by Ofsted about the implementation of GNVQ and a general discontent with the effectiveness of different post-16 qualifications (Hodgson, Spours and Savory, 2003, 17). Commissioning Dearing to review the system was based on these pressures to which the system was exposed. Among its 198 recommendations, the Dearing Committee suggested the establishment of AS-levels as halfway qualifications with regard to the full A-level; the introduction of key skills; more flexibility in the school curriculum, particularly in secondary education and applied and vocational courses for pupils in Key Stage 4 (aged 14 and onwards); a national framework for qualifications at four levels; and to consider the introduction of an overarching certificate for this phase (Dearing, 1996; Oancea and Wright, 2006, 22; Hodgson, Spours and Savory, 2003, 17 f.). Nearly simultaneously, in 1996 Labour published its plans for changing the 14-19 curriculum once they came into power. The document was called "Aiming Higher: Labour's plans for reforms of the 14-19 curriculum" (Labour Party, 1996). Whereas the Dearing review had one benchmark around which the proposals revolved, namely the traditional academic A-levels which were by and large left untouched by the review, "Aiming Higher" pursued a more integrated approach: an overarching certificate and modularisation of a coherent 14-19 curriculum and qualifications framework (Labour Party, 1996; Hodgson, Spours and Savory, 2003, 18 f.).

The proposals in this paper mainly concentrated on reforming the post-compulsory schooling period. Reforming the A-level takes up a major part of these considerations. Changes are justified with reference to the recent global economy, in which education is pivotal to national prosperity. It is argued that "at advanced levels of education and training we have fallen far behind our competitors" (Labour Party, 1996, 2). As to A-levels, two aspects are striking. Firstly, as Dearing noted and "Aiming Higher" returns to, a typical course of three A-levels in England involves 18 taught hours per week; in France and Germany, by comparison, the usual number of hours taught per week for the A-level equivalent is around 30 (Dearing, 1996; Labour Party, 1996, 10). Thus, New Labour argues in favour of a longer learning time (not in terms of years spent in school but in terms of hours per week; this issue is interesting to consider in the context of German initiatives to shorten the teaching period on the way to an Abitur). Secondly, a further problem seen is that "present A-levels offer too narrow a specialisation too early" (Labour Party, 1996, 1) and that this limited base of knowledge does not match the requirements of a rapidly changing economic environment. Keeping in mind the theoretical considerations of the varieties of capitalism literature, we will need to further elaborate on this issue later in this study when trying to answer the question: is a specialised A-level still "general" enough for placing England among those countries that focus on general skills, given that nearly 50 percent of any given age cohort attains A-levels?

2) Policy formulation, adoption and path-deviation
Instead of applying the proposals of "Aiming Higher", after having taking office in 1997 New Labour launched a consultation document called "Qualifying for Success: A Consultation Paper on the Future of Post-16 Qualifications" (DfEE, Office and DENI, 1997). One might assume that this consultation paper would follow the pledge of a unified system as seen in "Aiming Higher"; in fact it draws heavily on Dearing in suggesting a tracked approach that also offers linkages between these tracks, basically between vocational and academic education (DfEE, Office and DENI, 1997, 4). Thus, the initial proposal for a unitary system was abandoned. This consultation document already included the main proposals for reforming the post-compulsory secondary school sector – the reform which in 1998 was eventually labelled the Curriculum 2000 reform (Higham, 2003, 10 f.). As a consequence, references from this period that talk about the "Qualifying for Success" reform refer to what was later called Curriculum 2000. Despite all the above, the main rhetorical drivers for launching the consultation document remained the same as for "Aiming Higher": referring to a global economy which requires England make the A-levels broader, more flexible, and more tailored to the needs of the pupils.
The core recommendations of "Qualifying for Success" are the following:

6.1 Policy reforms in England – three cases and their selection 223

- the introduction of key skills (communication, information technology, and the application of numbers);
- the introduction of an Advanced Subsidiary Level (AS-level) half way to the A-levels;
- a new vocational-oriented qualification that also leads to an A-level, called Advanced Vocational Certificate of Education (AVCE) to replace Advanced GNVQ;
- an overarching certificate embracing all qualifications attained at the advanced level;
- and the development of a single qualifications framework in which all qualifications apart from higher education qualifications were intended to fit.

The primary driving factors behind the launch of "Qualifying for Success" can be found both within the system itself (as the above mentioned targets imply) and in contextual factors that generated pressure points on the system.
As to the system-inherent driving factors, "Qualifying for Success" was about:
- easing the transition from GCSE to A-levels;
- broadening the curriculum and ensuring more breadth of studies at the advanced level by encouraging students to pursue more than the three subjects routinely taken at A-level;
- better aligning general and general vocational qualifications and allowing students to pursue a mix of academic and vocational subjects in upper secondary education;
- ensuring greater consistency of standards among different qualifications at the advanced level;
- and creating a secondary school pathway intended to facilitate the achievement of a 50 percent higher education participation by all people aged 18-30 by 2010 (DfEE, Office and DENI, 1997; Hodgson, Spours and Savory, 2003, 28).

With "Qualifying for Success" New Labour left the academic A-levels untouched, despite that the party had harshly criticised the previous government for doing the same. The intended reform steps would retain the core architecture of the English 14-19 curriculum and qualifications framework. Changes were to be rather incremental in comparison to what was first championed, namely the unified approach.

At the end of the day Curriculum 2000 represents little more than the introduction of a few new qualifications. Thus, we can hardly talk about the replacement of an existing scheme; rather new qualifications were put alongside the existing architecture. Therefore we might describe the reform as a layering-mechanism. Nonetheless, the expectations that were placed on this reform initiative remained high. It is not the institutional structure *per se* which was to be fundamentally altered. Rather the reform was intended to change perceptions of the school system and in doing so would deviate from one of the system's most traditional traits. Namely, Curriculum 2000 introduces more choices into the A-level curriculum including the introduction of vocational subjects and thereby represents an attempt to revalue vocational education. Thus, attaining "parity of esteem" was a main aim of this reform and it therefore deviates from that path that we would expect.

Furthermore, Curriculum 2000 is supposed to narrow the divide between academic and vocational education by providing modularised qualifications in both areas that can be combined with each other under one roof. Another aim of this reform is to increase teaching hours per week, as England many of its pupils are not obtaining the same breadth of studies as students in countries with longer teaching hours per week.

3) Theoretically grasping the discourse

So how did this reform come about, given that it is a reform that not only attempts to fundamentally alter the esteem-structure of English school education but which could also eventually lead to a change in the overall skill pattern (i.e. share of vocational education)? Curriculum 2000 is driven mainly by two underlying ideas. On the one hand, there is the paradigm that says that more breadth and choice leads to superior outcomes, both educational and economic, and, moreover, that parity of esteem is the objective to reach in order to ameliorate the cleavage between academic and vocationally-oriented education.

Yet, on the other hand, we observe a deeply-rooted normative belief in academic A-levels, a conviction that eventually led to the turn from "Aiming Higher" to "Qualifying for Success".

A-levels have long been highly respected in England, among students, parents, higher education institutions and employers. Altering these qualifications, let alone their abolishment altogether, was likely to provoke broad resistance, in particular among the middle class (Hodgson, Spours and Savory, 2003). Yet, if the above-listed aims of "Qualifying for Success" were to be achieved, changes were inevitable. The solution was to leave A-levels as they were and add new qualifications. Now, however, the issue of voluntarism[95] becomes relevant, because as long as students, schools and colleges, and higher education institutions did not demand the new qualification, the system would

---

[95] For elaboration on this issue see the critique-section of this chapter.

remain more or less the same. Hence, funding incentives and inspections were increased as a means of ensuring the broad application of the new reforms. As Hodgson and Spours express it, the reservations about fundamentally changing the A-level structure was one of the main reasons why a "real" curriculum reform, instead of incremental qualification alterations, was almost impossible. Thus, the communicative discourse is dominated by the need to provide "parity of esteem," whereas on a cognitive level we implicitly recognise that this parity of esteem has to be achieved by "lifting" vocational qualifications without altering the "gold standard". The voluntaristic gloss shows the dominance of an English understanding of the issue.

In the background of this paper we can observe another known driver of policy. This is the goal of reaching the 50 percent participation target in higher education. However, in the context of Curriculum 2000 the participation target itself is revealed only by intensely examining the papers. Hence, although in the higher education context it is explicitly spelled out, here it resides as a background normative idea.

Furthermore, we need to look at the contextual factors behind the reform. Firstly, qualification and curriculum reforms are propelled by general considerations on how to deliver public services. These "New Public Management" influences are further expressed by the nationally set targets for student participation and student achievement, and the double-movement of increased devolution to lower and private units accompanied by stricter accountability measures (Tomlinson, 2002, 37). Hence, administrative goals need to be considered, as they represent a fundamental paradigm shift not only in education but also in other public services in England.

Secondly, England was perceived as having deficiencies in its upper secondary education system, both in terms of the breadth of the curriculum and compulsory hours in schools. On the one hand, the Curriculum 2000 reform can be understood as a reaction to a discourse that highlights employers' needs for greater a breadth of knowledge of school leavers. On the other hand, however, we very seldom encounter in the English context such a clear reference to the experiences of other countries as we do for this issue. France and Germany are exemplified both for longer teaching hours per week and more breadth in (compulsory) curricula (The Guardian, 2005). In both countries pupils have to take up to 30 hours of courses per week, while in England pupils have to attend only 15 to 18 hours on average, an amount which is thus perceived as being to low by to international standards (Dearing, 1996; Labour Party, 1996, 10; The Times, Educational Supplement, 2001b). This coincided with a perceived lack of breadth in studies. The English curriculum was considered as being narrow, inflexible and over-specialised, especially in comparison to other European countries such as France or Germany. Moreover, "breadth of studies" – as was being argued – is what employers and higher education institutions are asking for (Labour Party, 1996, 10). Hence, regarding this aspect we see a clear case of policy diffusion. The idea of "learning from success" is alos applicable here, as the reference to Germany and France is tantamount to the perception these two countries perform better in this respect. Yet considering this aspect against the backdrop of the varieties of capitalism literature we observe a peculiar situation: England is perceived as being dominated by a general skills pattern and yet it is embarking on a strategy in order to attain the breadth and generality of subjects as seen in Germany, a country that is supposed to be dominated by specific skills. Moreover, the international examples, such as France and Germany, are used as weapons to de-legitimise the current system. The French system in particular serves as a template for considerations about a baccalaureate (The Guardian, 2005), a topic that is again being hotly debated in the context of the so-called "diplomas".

A third contextual factor refers to the rising numbers of students in full-time education at the advanced level who are simultaneously employed part-time (Hodgson and Spours, 2003, 21 f.; Hodgson and Spours, 2001). The increase in part-time employment among 14-19 year olds was an additional reason both for the establishment of the half-way AS-qualifications and the opportunity to re-sit modules and exams (DfEE, 1999, 46 ff.; Higham, 2003, 11).

If we refer to the "aim-troika" of expansion, diversity, and excellence (Doyle, 2003, 4 ff.), which is supposed to be conducive to the generation of the skills needed by the labour market, we see that Curriculum 2000 is closely connected to them. Flexibility, choice and diversity are to be ensured through the introduction of qualifications half-way to A-levels, the broadening of subjects on offer, and the introduction of key skills. It is hoped that this diversity will attract additional pupils for A-levels to facilitate reaching the 50 percent higher education target (DfES, 2003c, 7; The Times, Educational Supplement, 2006b). Excellence is to be achieved by offering vocational A-levels on an equal footing with the academic ones.

4) Post-implementation critique on mode of operation
It comes as no real surprise that the reactions to the "Qualifying for Success" proposals were mixed: schools and sixth-form colleges enthusiastically welcomed the reforms in that they appreciated the introduction of greater breadth in the curriculum, though there were some reservations about how end-users (e.g. higher education institutions and employers) would make use of this (Hodgson and Spours, 2000, 11 f.). Most concerns revolved around the implementation of the reforms. The introduction of key skills, AS-levels and

6.1 Policy reforms in England – three cases and their selection 227

AVCE, and the resulting greater assessment needs would require considerably more staff and financial resources (The Guardian, 2000b; The Times, Educational Supplement, 1999b). Furthermore, it was pointed out that detailed information for students and parents about the reforms was missing, as was thorough preparation for teachers. In this context, criticism was put forward that the government rushed into the reform without having piloted and evaluated it properly beforehand (The Guardian. 2001b).

Only ten months after Curriculum 2000 had come into effect, the Secretary of State for Education and Skills in the newly founded DfES, Estelle Morris, responded to increasing complaints about the reforms by ordering an inquiry (QCA, Qualifications and Curriculum Authority, 2005; The Times, 2001d). Even the White Paper "Schools, Achieving Success" mentions implementation problems with Curriculum 2000, without, however, discussing them in further detail (DfES, 2001, 32).

One of the most controversial areas was the introduction of Key Skills into the post-compulsory curriculum. They are rejected by advanced students as a "waste of time", as they concentrate on issues that these students should have already attained. Secondly, they are not chosen voluntarily by students, as they already have to deal with an increased workload due to the A-level reform-component of Curriculum 2000. Thirdly, given that high-achieving schools and students have rejected them, their value is far from clear (The Guardian 2001a; The Times, Educational Supplement, 2002a).

The reactions of higher education institutions were as diverse as the institutions themselves. Nonetheless, by and large the reactions were hesitant, a rather understandable attitude given that the first applicants to universities to run through the new system were not expected until two years after the implementation of the reforms. The voluntarist approach is expressed not only by the fact that higher education institutions were not required to acknowledge the new qualifications (Hodgson, Spours and Savory, 2003, 33), but moreover, in the widely varying messages by the universities about which qualifications, grades and UCAS-points the expected future students would need in order to be admitted (Hodgson and Spours, 2000, 13). One could claim that the unregulated demands of Curriculum 2000 qualifications not only left students and parents without any clear idea of the real value of the new qualifications but ultimately led to one of the largest shortcomings of this reform package.

Critics are concerned that what was initially intended to provide more breadth and parity of esteem will eventually turn out to preserve the divide both between academic and vocational education, and between prestigious 'selecting' universities and less prestigious 'recruiting' universities. Thus, the question which has to be answered is whether higher education institutions will pay attention to studies with great breadth or whether they will cling to three academic A-levels with A grades as the main entrance route to higher education? As the chief executive of the Association of Colleges expressed it in 1999:

> "Would the older 'selecting' universities, as opposed to the 'recruiting' newer universities, give students with broadened, 'pick and mix' qualifications, as much attention as those with three A-levels?" (The Guardian, 1999b)

The issue revolves around the notion of "voluntarism" (Hodgson, Spours and Savory, 2003, 137 f.).[96] It is not just "compulsory schooling" that stands as one of the main characteristics of the English education system; the transition from compulsory schooling to post-compulsory schooling denotes a dividing line between two entirely different logics. Whereas the former is compulsory and choices for those involved are relatively small, post-compulsory schooling (hence also A-levels) is marked by a high degree of voluntarism. Voluntarism in English post-compulsory schooling – and Curriculum 2000 has to be understood in this vein – means that this period is characterised by choices by all relevant actors: learners can choose the qualifications they strive for; schools and colleges have a large extent of discretion on which qualifications and programmes they offer; and employers and, most notably, universities have freedom in what kind of qualifications they demand from their future employees or students (Hodgson, Spours and Savory, 2003, 137). Furthermore, this latter logic is characterised by being qualification-focused and even more market-oriented.

In other words, not only was the post-compulsory schooling curriculum been altered with Curriculum 2000 in order to offer more choice and more breadth of studies without ascribing a clear value to these qualifications, moreover, "end-users" – and this means above all higher education institutions but also employers – were not obliged to recognise increased breadth through or grades in additional subjects (Hodgson, Spours and Savory, 2003, 33). As a consequence, higher education institutions hesitated to change their traditional admission policy (mostly three A-levels in traditional subjects, such as in science, arts or humanities), which undermined the value of the reforms even further. Thus, though it attempted to provide "parity of esteem" among a variety of subjects (including more applied subjects) with the AVCE-qualification, critics expressed scepticism, claiming that that in reality and in terms of

---

[96]Although England ranks as a 'liberal market economy' with a corresponding welfare system, it possesses two systems that are highly solidary and comprehensive. These are the so-called "holy cow" of the National Health Service (NHS), on the one hand, and the compulsory and comprehensive school system on the other, though the latter does not exist in a pure form (compare with Green, Preston and Janmaat, 2006, 138).

6.1 Policy reforms in England – three cases and their selection 229

appreciation the system would remain selective and fragmented.[97]

At the time of "Qualifying for Success" also employers remained comparatively silent and indifferent (Hodgson and Spours, 2000, 14 f.). This is surprising, as the reforms were intended to meet employers' needs (see The Times, Educational Supplement, 2001c). Given that the potential "end-users" (employers, universities) were puzzled about the reform and its future merits, it is hardly surprising that this attitude extended equally to students and parents.

Politicians were mostly concerned about the reputation of A-levels and were thus by and large in favour of this reform, as opposed to a more path-breaking one (Hodgson, Spours and Savory, 2003, 32 f.). Students are allowed to take vocational A-levels, which are – at least in theory – on equal footing with their academic counterparts. Moreover, they are allowed to re-sit exams to refine their course choice after the first year (mainly by means of a 'half-way' qualification called Advanced Subsidiary Level). On the basis of the strict modularised shape of this post-compulsory area students are permitted to sit an AS-level exam (which would normally mark the end of the first year of sixth form) at the end of the second year and can thereby accumulate more points in the UCAS-tariff system, which is used as a basis for university admission.

Doubts have been raised about the real qualitative gains for students from a reform which was first and foremost oriented to expanding the programmes quantitatively (The Times, Educational Supplement, 2001a). In this vein, the critique has been made that additional subjects at AS-level tend to be complementary rather than achieving genuine depth (The Times, Educational Supplement, 2001b). Thereby, it is thought that the reputation of the highly regarded A-levels could be damaged. As to the vocational sibling of the classic academic A-level, as early as 2001 Hodgson and Spours already accused the AVCE as being to complicated to administer and inflexible in assessment. At the same time, the value and purpose of the AVCE remained unclear and therefore there were calls for it to be fundamentally reviewed (The Guardian, 2001a).

Interestingly enough, among the few to promote a unified system was the secretary of the DfEE at that time, Baroness Blackstone. She favoured a French-style baccalaureate in order to ensure a wider range of subjects could be taken by students under the umbrella of an overarching certificate (The Times, Educational Supplement, 1999a).[98] This would have also been more in

---

[97] What is missing from this perspective is a "real" curriculum reform, one which influences also the demand for pupils. Instead Curriculum 2000 is about adding qualifications and providing more choice. That is why the reforms have sometimes been re-dubbed by academics as "Qualifications 2000" instead of "Curriculum 2000" (Hodgson, Spours and Savory, 2003, 31).

[98] The considerations about the introduction of a French-style baccalaureate have up to now always revolved around the question of whether England should give up A-levels or not. Recently, on the basis of the so-called Tomlinson Report, the discussions about a unified approach re-emerged. This

agreement with New Labour's initial suggestions for a more unified approach, as stated in the Party Manifesto with which they contested the Conservative government under John Major (Hodgson and Spours, 2002, 39; The Times, Educational Supplement, 2001b). In contrast, the suggestions of the Dearing Review, upon which Curriculum 2000 was ultimately based, essentially preserved the distinctions between academic and vocational qualifications in that it favoured a tracked phase-based approach, one grounded in the academic-vocational education divide and a clear distinction between phases (14-16 and 16-19; see Hodgson and Spours, 2002, 38 f.).

Yet, "unifiers" were cautiously optimistic about Curriculum 2000, as they saw in this reform a possible first step towards a unified system (Hodgson and Spours, 2002, 38 f.). In fact, Curriculum 2000 attempts to square the circle in that it attempts to combine the tracked and the unified approach: it allows for a variety of options among different academic subjects, vocational subjects, and key skills, but in clear tracked routes (for a further formulation see Hodgson and Spours, 2002, 42 f.). Thus, the reform preserved the academic A-levels while altering the qualifications scenery around them. As for the Conservatives, they remained relatively silent, as most of the proposals to a large extent resembled what the Dearing Committee had suggested, a Committee they had commissioned when they were still in power (The Guardian, 2001b).

It took almost three more years and a new label (from "Qualifying for Success" to Curriculum 2000) before the reforms were implemented and applied in September 2000. Apart from the proposal to establish an overarching certificate, which was finally abandoned, all the above-mentioned proposals of "Qualifying for Success" were implemented. Additionally, "world class tests within the A-level system to stretch the most able" (DfEE, 1999, 47) were piloted with the implementation of Curriculum 2000. This kind of A-levels, however, was not implemented until 2002, after which time is has been called "Advanced Extension Award" (AEA). AEAs are aimed at the top 10 percent of English students in A-levels.

It came as no real surprise that the reform was particularly criticised for 'sitting on the fence'. Some wanted a more unified approach that ensured a broad curriculum which facilitated a mix of academic and vocational education and which ameliorated undesirable elitist tendencies. Others were apprehensive about a loss of value in the "gold standard" of English school education, which had

---

time it is called a unified Diploma-approach. It must be said, however, that like the baccalaureate, Diplomas as an overarching qualification that embraces academic and vocational education and which therefore substitutes A-levels will not be realised in the short-term. Instead New Labour plans to introduce a 'specialised Diploma', a new qualification which students can attain alongside A-levels (Stanton, 2005).

served for decades as a valuable discriminator for university admission procedures.

All in all one might state that expectations of Curriculum 2000 were cautiously optimistic. Most criticism was with respect to implementation problems and to a lack of information about how qualifications and breadth of study would be recognised by the so-called end-users. However, within the first half year after its implementation a whole cornucopia of criticism was put forward against Curriculum 2000. The next section will deal with these points of criticism.

5) Evaluation
From a cynical perspective, one might say that the "success" of Curriculum 2000 is expressed by the fact that ever since its issuance discussions about baccalaureates and diplomas in an overarching and coherent 14-19 period have never ceased (i.e. The Times, Educational Supplement, 2005, 2006a). Diplomas have recently been piloted and rolled out and thereby ensued the Curriculum 2000 reform. But why is it that the initial proposal as spelled out in "Aiming Higher" and the eventual outcome of Curriculum 2000 stand in such stark contrast?

Breadth and higher esteem – these were the main aims of the reform. Yet, as it has turned out, Curriculum 2000 has so far failed to provide either of these: the proportion of 16 and 17-year-olds attaining vocational education decreased between 2000 and 2002 from 42 percent to 36 percent, with students still preferring academic A-levels (The Times, Educational Supplement, 2004); the proportion of pupils defined as "specialist" (specialists take all their A-levels from the same domain of either science, social science or arts) increased from 30 percent to 35 percent in the first three years of Curriculum 2000 (The Times, 2003b); most universities do not accredit extra AS subjects or key skills (The Times, Educational Supplement, 2005); colleges are lacking the financial resources to sustain the supply of extra AS subjects (The Guardian, 2005); the credibility of A-levels has been contested (The Times, Educational Supplement, 2007a); and the reforms have not succeeded in bridging the vocational-academic divide and academic A-levels remain the dominant qualification (The Times, 2007b; The Times, Educational Supplement, 2008).

One of the crucial reasons for the failure of the reform lies in the high degree of voluntarism that characterises the English system. It is the voluntary decision of the student to increase the breadth of his/her learning, and it is the universities' and employers' decision to accept and appreciate this breadth. In other words, in the discourse of the analysed documents the government stresses the urgency to increase teaching hours and breadth in knowledge; the initiative, however, leaves the basic structure untouched, with academic A-levels as the calibration point, and instead rests only on supplying additional voluntary qualifications.

Yet, why did the reform not alter the acknowledgement structure accordingly, by rendering Curriculum 2000-components compulsory? Curriculum 2000 was meant to replace the old system. Paradoxically it did replace it, without replacing it: the reform succeeded in providing a new modularisation structure, the introduction of key skills, an Advanced Extension Award, and new vocational education incentives. Yet, the reform failed in its main aim, namely to provide "parity of esteem". Curriculum 2000 did not succeed in transferring the high esteem ascribed to academic A-levels over to vocational qualifications. Hence, when considered against the background of the discourse, the half-hearted manner of the reform is rather surprising.

Elaborating on the discourses that accompanied this reform initiative, we very clearly see a tension between the parlance about the topic, on the one hand, and the actual undertaken actions, on the other hand. We see how the reform was easily manipulated to accommodate the dominate existing structure of the English school system and thus why it has not resulted in vocational qualifications becoming qualifications on an equal footing with A-levels.

Discursive institutionalism provides us with useful tools to account for a discourse that deviates from what we would expect. Yet, it provides us also with the appropriate toolby which to unveil the causes of Curriculum 2000's failure: the power of the normative, background and underlying assumption (as in public sentiment) of the need to preserve the "gold standard" – hence academic A-levels – has rendered the reform a toothless tiger. Considering the acknowledgement structure (the cleavage between academic and vocational education) as an institution, we can see how path-dependent the English school system really is. This informal yet powerful "esteem-institution" is the background against which reforms such as baccalaureates and diplomas must be assessed.

6.1.2 Further Education: Apprenticeships

> "Our vision of the Learning Age is to build a new culture of learning and aspiration which will underpin national competitiveness and personal prosperity, encourage creativity and innovation and help build a more cohesive society. [...] The strengths of the past apprenticeship and craft system need to be replicated in a new age, while meeting the challenge of a rapidly changing competitive economy." ("Learning to Succeed", DfEE, 1999, 13)

6.1 Policy reforms in England – three cases and their selection

1) Agenda setting, problem identification

In order to attain a clear understanding of how apprenticeships work and their main problems and deficiencies we need to review how apprenticeships initially came about. "Classical" apprenticeships had a long tradition, yet vanished nearly entirely during the 1960s and 1970s. For reasons that were already discussed in the historical chapter, these employer-led apprenticeships declined both in terms of reputation (being seen as too long, too focused only on 'time-serving' instead of competencies, too inflexible) and, in consequence, also in participation.

Thus, the Conservative Government established the Youth Training Scheme (YTS) in 1983. This initiative was supposed to counter the decline of traditional apprenticeships. Additionally, and even more importantly, the YTS was considered an initiative for tackling youth unemployment. The scheme (a level 2 qualification; in the meantime re-branded "Youth Training", YT) was to be complemented by a level 3 qualification called "Modern Apprenticeship", which were piloted in 1993 and rolled out in 1994. The label was chosen with deliberation, referring to the traditional apprenticeships on the one hand and emphasising the difference to YTS/YT in that, firstly, these apprenticeships would lead to a level 3 (intermediate/technical) qualification; secondly, that apprentices would be given an employed status rather than being linked with training providers; and, thirdly, that Modern Apprenticeships would be targeted at those with good GCSE attainments, yet who were not willing or able to pursue GCS A-levels (Huddleston, Unwin and Keep, 2005, 5).

In 1997 Modern Apprenticeships were complemented by Foundation Modern Apprenticeships (FMA). This scheme was directed towards those interested in Modern Apprenticeships but not as yet capable of pursuing one. Thus, FMA were provided at level 2 and the requirement that apprentices must have employed status was relaxed. If we now take a quick glance back at the distinguishing features of MA and YT, we notice that those features used as a justification for introducing FMA were those that were explicitly done away with by the MA. In other words, and as claimed in the academic literature, FMA are by and large the direct successors of YT, with the mere difference of having a different label (Fuller, 2004, 2).

2) Policy formulation, adoption and path deviation

Ever since 1993 the Youth Training scheme and Modern Apprenticeships have been subject to a plethora of adaptation, reform and rebranding. It is difficult to pick only one particular reform to discuss, while obviously their first introduction in 1993 is clearly outside the period of analysis of this book. Yet, this scheme perfectly reflects some peculiarities of the English further education sector, such as its state-programme driven character and the strong emphasis on the supply of skills rather than demand for skills.

The analysed White Papers make a strong case for apprenticeships. "Learning to Succeed" talks about building a "new culture of learning and aspiration which will underpin national competitiveness and personal prosperity, encourage creativity and innovation and help build a more cohesive society" (DfEE, 1999, 13). It is in this context that apprenticeships are mentioned because it is this rapidly changing environment (such as the fast changing competitive economy in the digital age) that renders on-site learning in small and medium sized companies necessary. Moreover, it is argued that there is a social need to up-skill those with few skills in order to tackle unemployment. Therefore, apprenticeships are part of a policy that seeks to ensure social cohesion and to avoid social exclusion (DfEE, 1999, 13). Thereby, we once again encounter the twins of economic and social goals. The White Paper stresses the need to close the (self-perceived) skills gaps (DfEE, 1999, 17). These skills gaps were identified in reference to skill patterns in other countries, especially in Germany and France. The German case is taken as a template that demonstrates how apprenticeships can increase skills and qualifications at the intermediate level (DfEE, 1999, 13).

Already in 2001 the whole apprenticeship scheme was reviewed by the Modern Apprenticeships Advisory Committee chaired by John Cassels, hence commonly called the Cassels report (MAAC, 2001). The main reasons for commissioning this report were (compare with Fuller and Unwin, 2003b, 5; Nuffield Review of 14-19 Education and Training, 2008b, 8):
- low completion rates;
- a lack of common standards;
- a need to frame compulsory elements of apprenticeships;
- and a lack of employer demand, involvement and commitment.

Interestingly enough, these issues have been fairly persistent problems up to today (compare with House of Lords – Select Committee on Economic Affairs, 2007b). The critique section in this chapter will further elaborate on some of these core issues. A consultation paper in 2000 and the Cassells report in 2001 came to the conclusion that the two apprenticeship schemes needed to be complemented by a technical certificate and that an overarching certificate was needed to approve the fulfilment of all components.

By then "apprenticeships" were a rather loose concept for people attaining Key Skills and NVQs. As GSCEs could be partly or entirely used to fulfil the Key Skills requirement and employers were more concerned that their apprentices learn the relevant on-the-job skills, Key Skills were large neglected

6.1 Policy reforms in England – three cases and their selection

as a constitutive component of apprenticeships.[99] As a consequence, dropout rates were and still are higher in comparison to other countries, as often on-the-job attained NVQs suffice to pursue a profession. The overarching certificate was introduced in order to offer an incentive for apprentices to finish the entire apprenticeship skill-package programme. Technical certificates were considered to valorise apprenticeships by complementing on-the-job skills and genuine skills. Furthermore, the combination of Key Skills and technical certificates was supposed to strengthen the transferability of an apprenticeship given that these are not employer-specific skills, unlike those obtained through on-the-job training.

Technical certificates had by then already been applied in the more prestigious apprenticeship frameworks, such as engineering. The Cassels report now recommended their incorporation in all frameworks (MAAC 2001). Apart from this proposal, the report recommended the following changes to the system (compare with MAAC, 2001, 41 ff.):

- a concise framework for all schemes labelled "apprenticeships";
- an apprenticeship diploma which attests to the passage of all relevant qualifications;
- pre-apprenticeship course for those not yet ready to enter a regular apprenticeship programme, called "Entry to Employment" (E2E);
- an entitlement for an apprenticeship for those aged 16-17 who have five GCSEs or those who are assessed suitable by pre-apprenticeship courses (E2E);
- "programme-led apprenticeship" (PLA) which allow for the pursuit of Key Skills and technical certificates first in a college and, thereafter, to achieve the missing NVQ for fulfilling the framework through on-the-job training as an apprentice;
- and that the DfES should assign the prime responsibility for managing and funding apprenticeships to the Learning and Skill Council (LSC), which in turn should be accountable to the department.

---

[99] Key Skills (genuine skills such as problem solving, working with numbers, communication, improving own learning, IT, and teamwork) were piloted and introduced into the 16-19 qualifications framework in 1997 as a response to the Dearing report in 1996 "Review of Qualifications for 16-19 Year Olds" (Dearing, 1996). Eventually Key Skills were added to the apprenticeship framework at level 2 and 3 in 2000 under the Curriculum 2000 reforms. Critiques of Key Skills started right from the beginning: though having been demanded and welcomed by employers in general, some sectors were sceptical about the profits and costs for employers these skills would bring (The Times, Educational Supplement, 2001c; The Times, Educational Supplement, 2003a). Moreover, Key Skills were accused of being over-specified and of being one of the main reasons for both low completion rates and low employer demand (The Times, Educational Supplement, 2002b; The Times, Educational Supplement, 2001c).

The White Paper "14-19: Opportunity and Excellence", issued in January 2003, even while complaining about low completion rates and the low quality of the scheme (DfES, 2003a, 11), announced a participation target of 28 percent of 22 year olds by 2004 (DfES, 2003a, 17). Subsequently the paper presents some reforms for the apprenticeship scheme which are meant to lead to higher quality, higher participation and higher completion rates. Noticeably, it seems there was deep impact on the policy making process by the Cassels report, as most of the initiatives are directed towards the Modern Apprenticeships Advisory Committee: "Entry to Employment", programme-led apprenticeships, and measures to facilitate employer involvement (DfES, 2003a, 28 f.).

In February 2003 the government announced the establishment of a National Modern Apprenticeship Taskforce. Its main aims are to encourage employers to take on apprentices, to increase the diversity of employers and sectors in which apprenticeships are offered, and to advise the government and the Learning and Skills Council.[100]

The White Paper "21st Century Skills", issued in July 2003 (hence half a year after "14-19: Opportunity and Excellence") complements the picture with the underpinning expectations and ambitions. This paper delineated a national skill strategy, of which apprenticeships were to be a major component. The skills strategy is supposed to:

> "ensure that employers have the right skills to support the success of their businesses, and individuals have the skills they need to be both employable and personally fulfilled" (DfES, 2003b, 11).

The larger picture painted is one of globalisation, economic productivity and competitiveness, all of which makes investment in skills imperative and does not allow for skill gaps (DfES, 2003b, 11), particularly because

> "economic productivity and competitiveness remain well below those of major competitor nations. One reason is that there are some serious gaps in our national skills base." (DfES, 2003b, 11)

The main areas of concern are the perceived gaps in intermediate skills at technician, higher craft and associate professional levels (DfES, 2003b, 12), perceptions due in part to references to countries such as France and Germany. The following line of argumentation is applied: these two countries have a higher output per work hour and this coincides with a workforce with a higher

---

[100]Compare with http://www.hm-treasury.gov.uk/newsroom_and_speeches/press/2003/press_24_03.cfm. The Taskforce consists of representatives from public authorities and private actors.

6.1 Policy reforms in England – three cases and their selection

percentage of intermediate qualified individuals (according to the paper 28 percent in the UK, 51 percent in France and 65 percent in Germany). The inference that is drawn stresses the significance of intermediate skilled workers and their contribution to higher productivity rates and thus to greater economic strength (DfES, 2003b, 12, 19).

Moreover, the White Paper turns to two particular issues which were then of significance in the public discourse: Key Skills and the age cap, which limits participation to those aged 24 and below (DfES, 2003b, 81). On the second aspect, the paper announces the intention to abolish the age cap in two steps in order to allow more senior people to begin and finish an apprenticeship. Therefore, structures would need to be made more flexible because these people are supposed to already have a higher skill-base than junior apprentices (DfES, 2003b, 81).

This whole issue would appear to be of minor importance, but in fact it reveals one of the crucial differences to the German system, where an apprenticeship is the entry qualification for a job on the first labour market. In England, by contrast, apprenticeships are not reserved only for school-leavers. Also people who already work in the first labour market can decide to 'top-up' their qualifications with an apprenticeship. Thus the scheme has become a central part of vocational further education.

In May 2004 the DfES, in cooperation with the LSC, published the review paper called "21st century apprenticeships – End to End Review of the Delivery of Modern Apprenticeships". The name "End to End Review" mainly indicates that the two strands were given new labels in which the word "modern" was relegated: Foundation Modern Apprenticeships (the ones on level 2) became Apprenticeships and the Advanced Modern Apprenticeship (the ones on level 3 which were initially named Modern Apprenticeships) turned into Advanced Apprenticeships. This paper is highly interesting because it suggests some far-reaching amendments:

- to eventually remove the age cap of 25;
- to introduce a Youth Apprenticeships for 14-16 year olds.

In addition, the paper champions a flexible apprenticeship design in order to allow sectors with a less of an apprenticeship tradition (e.g. retail and hospitality) to apply the framework more flexibly (DfES and LSC, 2004, 15). This marks a sharp deviation (to which the so-called "Blueprint" will refer) from the Cassels report, which highlighted the need to give the framework a clear compulsory structure and thereby ensure a consistent pattern of required learning across all sectors.

In 2005 the DfES published the White Paper "Skills: Getting on in business, getting on at work", which called for a 75 percent apprenticeship completion rate by 2008 (DfES, 2005b, 9). In the same year, another initiative to provide apprenticeships with a unique and consistent structure was put forward. In September 2005 the LSC released its brochure "Blueprint for Apprenticeships" (LSC, 2005). At a first glance the paper seems to replicate the idea of an apprenticeship framework that essentially consists of three compulsory components: a competence element, a knowledge element and transferable key skills.[101] If, however, we take a closer look as to how the knowledge based component *can* be fulfilled, we see a clear weakening of the commitment to technical certificates. Thus some sectors[102] are allowed to integrate the technical certificate as a "clearly identified and assessed part of the NVQ" (LSC, 2005, 13). By relaxing the requirement of a clearly distinguishable and separately taught and assessed knowledge based component, the government finally abandoned one of the key suggestions of the Cassels report, namely making technical certificates a compulsory component of apprenticeship frameworks (Nuffield Review of 14-19 Education and Training, 2008b, 9 f.). This thwarts the attempt to provide a consistent pattern amongst all relevant sectors. Moreover, this procedure would render apprenticeships more specified to the needs of particular companies while at the same time it marks a departure from the principle of transferable vocational knowledge (Nuffield Review of 14-19 Education and Training, 2008b, 11). As the report of the House of Lords states:

> "By 2005, shortly after it had been introduced, the Technical Certificate had effectively become optional and in a number of sectors there is now no separate assessment of the knowledge-based element outside of the NVQ." (House of Lords – Select Committee on Economic Affairs, 2007b, 36)

As a consequence, the consistency of apprenticeships varies from economic sector to another and according to the level on which the apprenticeships are delivered.

Already in 2007 the whole scheme came again under review. This time it was the House of Lords that published the report "Apprenticeship: a key route to skill" (House of Lords – Select Committee on Economic Affairs, 2007a). Right from the beginning of this report the significance of apprenticeships for the English economy is stressed:

---

[101] In fact, the paper even adds a fourth component, namely an introduction of employment rights and responsibilities (LSC, 2005, 10).
[102] This refers to Sector Skills Councils representing training issues in a particular sector.

> "Productivity in Britain continues to lag behind that of our main European competitors. One important reason is the large number of workers in Britain who have low skills and, consequently, low productivity and low pay." (House of Lords – Select Committee on Economic Affairs, 2007a, 7)

Apprenticeships should "be established as the main route to skills below graduate level" (House of Lords – Select Committee on Economic Affairs, 2007a, 17), something that the earlier White Paper "21st Century Skills" had already called for (DfES, 2003b, 75). Furthermore, the report identifies four main areas of failure in which reforms have not been followed through (see House of Lords – Select Committee on Economic Affairs, 2007a, 35):
- broadening and strengthening the content of the apprenticeship framework;
- engaging employers;
- progression within apprenticeship and from apprenticeship to foundation degree;
- and improving the basic skills of numeracy and literacy of school leavers.

The first two aspects are points of criticism that we have encountered throughout this chapter. They appeared in the latest version the Cassels report, which had already clearly stated that the lack of binding and compulsory components within the frameworks discredits apprenticeships and which stressed the importance of engaging employers more in the design, delivery, and management of the scheme.

The latest governmental publication on apprenticeships, issued in 2008, revisits the main issues. In line with the tried and tested approach, the paper, entitled "World-class Apprenticeships: Unlocking Talent, Building Skills for All", notes the importance of apprenticeships for meeting the challenges of the global economy and postulates that in order to meet these challenges participation rates in apprenticeships need to be considerably increased (DIUS, 2008, 3). As a benchmark, the paper refers to the Leitch review, which forecasted that the apprenticeship scheme would need to host 400,000 apprentices by 2020. One way of achieving this ambitious aim is by entitling young people with a particular level of education to an apprenticeship for (compare with Cassels report). This paper also again announces the introduction of a completion diploma (DIUS, 2008, 6), again seeks to boost employer involvement; and again concludes that the quality and consistency of the scheme are at stake (DIUS, 2008, 7). In this context, the Programme-led Apprenticeships (PLA) were to be subject to regulations on the minimum necessary on-the-job experiences. Employer involvement and supply were to be encouraged through financial incentives for those companies taking on apprentices, on the one hand,

and by participation targets in the public sector, on the other (DIUS, 2008, 7).[103] The paper clearly states that apprenticeships are a priority for the government, as they are important for the economy and business, for individual aspirations for promising wage returns and for the pursuance of social integration policy (DIUS, 2008, 9). Yet, we find a thus far unmentioned aspect, namely the status-problem with apprenticeships as a route of vocational education as opposed to academic education (DIUS, 2008, 17).

The depiction above has not concentrated on a particular reform, as is the case with the other two English reforms examined in this research. Rather the great number of amendments, adaptations and rebranding initiatives we have encountered display a consistent attempt to deviate from the path and alter the main characteristics of the system. These are above all: to increase employer involvement; to ensure stricter input requirements (e.g. compulsory elements of the apprenticeship programme); to provide the system with a higher level of esteem, in particular vis-à-vis academically-based education; and to supply the English economy with more specific skills on the intermediate level.

3) Theoretically grasping the discourse

How did this scheme come about and how is it possible that its intentions so clearly deviate from the expected path? The discourse in vocational education and training in England is multifaceted. Apprenticeships are the outcome of several concerns. As the analysis is not concentrated on one reform or amendment in particular, but rather on a general process, we encounter different mechanisms at play here.

Though apprenticeships can be traced back to the YTS, we discern a recent redirection of the scheme towards new goals, in other words we see "conversion".[104] Apprenticeships are no longer mainly about tackling youth unemployment but about supplying the English economy with intermediate skills. Apart from the fact that the papers display the frame (in terms of Campbell) of "the more intermediate skills, the better" (particularly those that are considered to be in short supply), they refer also to more hidden, cognitive ideas. As the chapter that critiqued the underpinning lines of arguments elucidated (see section 5.5.2), the "taken-for-granted" connection between productivity rates and skill levels is much looser than the papers lead us to believe. On the other hand,

---

[103] Attaining higher participation rates by recruiting more apprentices for the public sector is an aspect which now and then shows up in the papers (for example DfES, 2003b, 80). We will encounter this pattern also with "foundation degrees". This aspects represents further state involvement in the attempt to realise English skill-aspirations.

[104] We could even claim that the "drift" mechanism applies here, to the extent that youth unemployment has become less of an issue in England.

because it is taken-for-granted, countries with higher productivity rates are used as templates for how English education should develop. However, "learning from success" in this case does not imply that England should adopt an entire scheme. Higher productivity rates are linked to higher skill levels, including at the intermediate skill level. Matching the best skills in the world is the imperative, as low productivity rates are considered to be the main hindrance to attaining higher degrees of competitiveness.

In order to ensure that the right skills are generated, the discourse within the papers stresses employer involvement to an extent that had been absent since the "traditional apprenticeships" vanished. Nonetheless, employer involvement is an issue only in the communicative discourse, with hardly any impact on concrete policy initiatives. We hereby discern the underlying philosophy that sits at the background of the discourse, namely the supply-led approach to skills, i.e. it is hoped that by providing an abundance of skills employers will ultimately make use of them and thereby lift England onto a higher production level.

Moreover, we notice two conflicting discourses. One revolves around the quality of the scheme, as the debates about the technical certificate and an apprenticeship diploma exemplify. The other discourse revolves around the issue of quantity and thus is about participation rates. Examples that reveal these issues are the new sub-schemes (E2E, PLA) and the flexibility with which apprenticeships can be designed (compare with Blueprint). It is here where one of the crucial background normative ideas shines through, one which we have already seen with the YTS: the more apprentices the better. This idea is cognitively backed by the hope that once apprentices have finished their training, they are more easily able to find a job and to contribute to a new (and better) overall skill pattern level. We see that the programmes devoted to the quality issue are subordinated to the quantity issue: neither the technical certificate nor the diploma are compulsory elements of an apprenticeship that could provide a sustainable character to the scheme.

It is the constant re-calibration and the scheme's development over time that renders this case so interesting. Thus, the apprenticeship-schemes assume different characters within a rather short period of time: Initially meant to counter the YT scheme's low-quality and low reputation, then the incorporation of YT into the scheme, the impacts caused by the case of expansion, and the ongoing "programmeatisation" of the scheme continuously changed the character of apprenticeships and the understanding of what apprenticeships actually are.

4) Post-implementation critique on mode of operation
This section elaborates on two points of criticism that have broached in the

previous section: the demand of employers and concerns about the "label" apprenticeship.

a) Expansion and the demand of employers

When considering the overall education picture in England, with the envisaged 50 percent target of 18-30 year olds in higher education by 2010, apprenticeships serve a crucial role as the second pillar. The government has adopted a target of 28 percent participation with the objective of making them the main non-degree route to vocation. Taking the actual figures into account (see Nuffield Review of 14-19 Education and Training, 2008a), we can see that expansion is a high priority for the government (see papers' analyses). According to the government's own aim, apprenticeships should be employer-led and thereby meet employers' demand.

In particular, the linking of the scheme to employers has triggered a lot of criticism. The report by the House of Lords is one of the most openly critical documents. The report's conclusions on this point, and their judgement of the DfES, are devastating, as they question one of the key assumptions on which the apprenticeship scheme is based: namely the close relationship between employer and young people:

> "The DfES acknowledged that neither they nor the LSC collect data on the number of young people interested in or actively seeking an apprenticeship. [...] The DfES also made clear that no data are collected on employer demand for apprentices, nor is there any central or local record of businesses that employ apprentices." (House of Lords – Select Committee on Economic Affairs, 2007b, 26)

The validity of this criticism was even acknowledged by the accused department in a response paper to the House of Lords' report (DIUS, 2007, 10; House of Lords – Select Committee on Economic Affairs, 2007b, 103 ff.). It appears odd to proclaim an employer-driven programme when employers are not substantially involved, being "little more than passive partners" (Nuffield Review of 14-19 Education and Training, 2008b, 15) and there is no data collected on the extent to which employers actually demand apprenticeships. If we change perspectives for a moment and observe the situation through a 'German-lense' we might argue that there is no need to obtain these figures, as demand (apprentices) and supply (employers) of apprenticeships will find a natural equilibrium. The situation, however, changes entirely when we consider the English context. The background against which discourses about apprenticeships are conducted is one about expanding the system in order to achieve the 28 percent target, about expanding the system in order to provide the skills employers' demand, and about expanding the system in order to attain a

6.1 Policy reforms in England – three cases and their selection   243

higher level of economic wealth. It is in the context of an almost entirely supply-driven system that the lack of data on potential apprentices and interested employers comes as a great surprise. As Unwin and Fuller put it:

> "Furthermore, government (through the DfES, LSC or local LSCs) does not keep any records of employers involved in government-funded initiatives. This is very curious given the central role that government wishes employers to play in its skills strategy." (House of Lords – Select Committee on Economic Affairs, 2007b, 21)

Hence, it is not only difficult to understand what might persuade employers to take on apprentices (House of Lords – Select Committee on Economic Affairs, 2007b, 16); but moreover, the House of Lords Committee was told by the LSC that they worked on the assumption that the purchased apprenticeship places reflect the demand for apprenticeships (House of Lords – Select Committee on Economic Affairs, 2007b, 90 ff.). This lack of data has been widely criticised (Cassels in Fuller, 2004, 13; Nuffield Review of 14-19 Education and Training, 2008a,b; Keep, 2004; Fuller, 2004, 13 ff.). The same critique holds true for information about prior qualifications of apprentices (House of Lords – Select Committee on Economic Affairs, 2007b, 23).[105] In fact, as Huddleston, Keep and Unwin note, that the apprenticeship scheme is considered to take place in the educational arena and not in the labour market. Moreover, recruitment is by and large handled by training providers (in most cases), who search for places where apprentices attain their on-the-job practise (Huddleston, Unwin and Keep, 2005, 6). Unwin and Fuller, when consulted by the House of Lords for the report, say:

> "The providers sit at the heart of the VET system and concentrate on securing the number of apprenticeship placements (still referred to as "starts" in the DfES and LSC statistical databases) identified for them by their local Learning and Skills Councils (LSCs). These numbers are based on the annual PSA target set by Treasury and not on the needs of businesses for apprentices. As such, many employers have no connection with the qualification requirements of the VET programme as they are handled by the training provider." (House of Lords – Select Committee on Economic Affairs, 2007b, 21).

Hence, the state may promote expansion for reasons beyond actual employer demand. The picture this section has drawn suggests that the main driving force behind apprenticeship policies is not necessarily one about the generation of high-quality intermediate skills that serve employers and help close the skill gaps

---

[105] A recent study showed that almost half (45 percent) of those in apprenticeship programmes were already employed with the same employer when they started the programme (House of Lords – Select Committee on Economic Affairs, 2007b, no. 64).

(Nuffield Review of 14-19 Education and Training, 2008b, 15). Rather it seems that expansion has turned into an end in itself and that more emphasis has been placed on quantity rather than quality. This contention is further supported by two facts: firstly, the public sector tries hard to promote the scheme by setting up apprenticeships in the public sector itself (Nuffield Review of 14-19 Education and Training, 2008a, 2); secondly, it is particularly the introduction of Programme-Led Apprenticeships (see next section) that supports the assumption that apprenticeship policy is first and foremost about expansion and not about meeting employer demand. If employer demand is taken into account then it appears to be driven by a belief that is centred on "idealised projections of a future knowledge driven economy wherein all will be highly skilled knowledge workers […]" (Keep, 2004, 3).

b) Stretching the "label"

The House of Lords repeated what the government had already said on several previous occasions:

> "Apprenticeship should be established as the main route to skills below graduate level." (House of Lords – Select Committee on Economic Affairs, 2007b, 17)

But for what does an apprenticeship actually stand? Can we speak about it as of a scheme sui generis in the first place? Is it a programme for those who are already on the job or for those intending to enter the labour market afterwards? Is it a scheme led by employers or a state-driven scheme? Does the label "apprenticeship" indicate similarities as to the formal content of apprenticeships?

There are no definitive answers to these questions: the schemes do intend to provide a first vocational education for school-leavers, but they also offer options for those people who are already employed and want to complement their skills; the scheme is sometimes driven by employers, but even more often it is driven by the state; and occasionally apprenticeships resemble each other between sectors, but often they are distinctive regarding their National Qualification Framework Level (1, 2 and 3) and whether technical certificates are a compulsory component or not; and sometimes they are perceived as a quasi qualification, for instance in engineering (though the completion certificate is still to be introduced), but high dropout rates suggest that parts of the apprenticeship framework often suffice to take on a regular job without having finished the whole programme.

Thus, talking about apprenticeships requires talking about a form of vocational-based education and training as the least common denominator. The debate of how to integrate theoretical knowledge within the apprenticeship

6.1 Policy reforms in England – three cases and their selection

frameworks exemplifies the considerations between structure on the one hand and flexibility on the other. 'Apprenticeship' is used as a badge for programmes with various shapes. Hence, the notion 'apprenticeship' reveals little about their common features in terms of quality and structure:

- there is no compulsory framework-structure, with technical certificates having a quasi optional character in some of the frameworks (House of Lords – Select Committee on Economic Affairs, 2007b, 14);
- there is no overarching completion diploma (House of Lords – Select Committee on Economic Affairs, 2007b, 37) which could increase the value attaining of all relevant certificates; a lack which leads to high dropout rates (Fuller, 2004, 3) and to apprentices and employers choosing the qualification they assign value to while leaving other out (e.g. Key Skills);
- there is no regulation about the length of an apprenticeship, rendering the programme inconsistent (Fuller, 2004, 3);
- there is no regulation as to how close to employers' needs apprenticeships are allowed to become or how general they have to be kept, which raises the question of why the state should finance a vocational training that is of use only to one employer (Huddleston, Unwin and Keep, 2005, 6);
- there is uncertainty about the exchange value of a completed apprenticeship according to sectors and regions (Fuller, 2004, 4);
- there is no coherence in status of the apprentices – some being employed directly with an employer, many being contracted with training providers – hence a situation remains which was meant to be resolved after the introduction of Modern Apprenticeship (and the gradual phasing out of YTS) and which is likely to be reinforced if an entitlement is implemented, as is intended (Nuffield Review of 14-19 Education and Training, 2008b, 5);
- there is no stable governance structure, as the form of apprenticeships have often changed, as have the various bodies involved in their administration (House of Lords – Select Committee on Economic Affairs, 2007b, 35, 40);
- and there is a lack of governmental commitment to minimum standards of education and training in apprenticeships (Ryan in House of Lords – Select Committee on Economic Affairs, 2007b, 97).

The so-called Programme-Led Apprenticeships are the latest member of the apprenticeship-family. Apprentices in this programme are recruited by learning providers and start their training with the theoretical component and Key Skills before they obtain on-the-job training with an employer. It is the provider's responsibility to find an employer willing to take on a programme-led apprentice and provide the apprenticeship component.[106] For this reason the Nuffield Review Issue Paper on Apprenticeships posed the following question:

> "To what extent is it acceptable to include programmes such as Programme Led Apprenticeship as apprenticeship provision? Does this dilute the broader understanding of what apprenticeship is/should be, and what is the implication of this for the important role traditionally played by learning at the workplace in apprenticeship provision?" (Nuffield Review of 14-19 Education and Training, 2008a, 12)

As this quotation and other references prove, there seems to be some reservations about the fact that this programme is also called an "apprenticeship ". It is feared that this might further lead to a change in the nature of the relationship between employers, learners, training providers and the state (Nuffield Review of 14-19 Education and Training, 2008b, 5 f.). Again, the Nuffield Review Issue Paper on Apprenticeships appeals for binding standards in apprenticeships, claiming that:

> "Without this kind of regulation, there is a danger that the term 'apprenticeship' could be stretched so far as to be meaningless, lacking clarity about its aims and purposes [...]" (Nuffield Review of 14-19 Education and Training, 2008b, 2).

5) Evaluation of apprenticeships

Apprenticeships have an ambiguous overall form. On the one hand, we see consistent attempts to deviate from the path and alter the main characteristics of the system: to increase employer involvement; to ensure stricter input requirements (e.g. compulsory elements of the apprenticeship programme); and to provide the system with a higher esteem in particular vis-à-vis academically-based education and supply the English economy with more specific skills on the intermediate level. The discourse as sketched above reveals the high significance which is attached to this scheme, both with respect to the generation of intermediate skills and participation rates.

Yet is it a "path-breaking" reform? Probably not. Tracing the reform process reveals how initial ideas and aims were increasingly adapted, shaped, or even abandoned once placed in the concrete institutional context. Employer involvement, a stricter input-regulation, a concluding certificate, or a commonly accepted value of the scheme – all these elements were intended to not only establish a vocational education route which is ultimately conducive to higher productivity rates but also to promote vocational education's esteem. What has happened, in fact, is the establishment of a rather obscure label that adheres more

---

[106] The main target group are young people who are not able to find an "Employer-led Apprenticeship" (LSC, 2007).

6.1 Policy reforms in England – three cases and their selection

to the mechanisms that we expected in the first place: an output-orientated, supply-led, low esteem system with a low degree of standardisation. Thus, at best apprenticeship frameworks are more flexible (than for instance the German ones); at worst, however, they lack a strict, clear and obligatory theory grounded structure, which renders the label "apprenticeship" ambiguous.

Moreover, in terms of participation the apprenticeship scheme hardly qualifies as a success story. As the Nuffield Review of apprenticeships points out, in 2005 fewer than one in ten 16-18 year olds were participating in apprenticeship programmes in England (Nuffield Review of 14-19 Education and Training, 2008a, 5). Only 7.5 percent of this age-group participated in work-based learning – an all time low, decreasing from 11.3 percent in 1994. Within the work-based route, around five percent were enrolled in apprenticeships at level 2, 2.7 percent in apprenticeships at level 3 and only 1.3 percent in E2E (see Nuffield Review of 14-19 Education and Training, 2008a, 5). Hence, the target of 28 percent of young people up to 22 years of age participating by 2004 (compare with DfES, 2003a, 17) has clearly been missed. Against this background one may be sceptical of the extent to which apprenticeships can contribute to meeting the target of 90 percent of 17 year olds in education and/or work-based learning by 2015 (DCSF, 2008, 2; Nuffield Review of 14-19 Education and Training, 2008a, 5).

Attempts to ensure stable and committed employer engagement have failed, as have attempts to produce greater reliability and recognition of the scheme. "Employer engagement" is one of the most frequent notions circulating when it comes to apprenticeships. In fact, however, the latest amendment to the scheme, the so-called programme-led apprenticeships, is just the newest evidence that the scheme is far form being employer-led. It is a state-led, state-supplied, and state-controlled scheme that is entirely integrated into the educational scenery in England.

The idea of programme-led apprenticeships, unveiled and elaborated upon entirely in "A Strategy for Programme-led Apprenticeships in England 2007-2010" published by the LSC in 2007 (LSC, 2007), highlights once again the crucial importance of LSCs in the provision of apprenticeships and the rather passive role taken on by employers. Furthermore, we observe the tendency for what could be called the increasing "programme-atisation" of apprenticeships, namely a deviation from a 'real' employer-led scheme towards a programme that is largely provided by the state, similar to school education and higher education.

Beginning with the YTS and including its successors, the whole apprenticeship scheme has been characterised by strong direct state involvement, which renders contemporary apprenticeship a mainly state-driven scheme. Moreover, the initial linking of apprenticeships with a scheme intended to support the most disadvantaged has had a lasting effect on the reputation-divide between academic and vocational education, in that the latter is viewed as being intended only for the least-talented.

We have come across some major areas of tension that characterise the issues of apprenticeships in England. There is first and foremost the tension between considerations about a programme that is intended to generate high-quality intermediate skills on the one hand and the case for expansion on the other. Expansion, and this is another common pattern in the English education system, is to be achieved, above all, by diversification of the scheme. Along the same lines, secondly, we observe some friction between providing a clear consistent structure and the desire to ensure flexibility. In order to facilitate expansion (main route to vocational skills, participation targets) the government tries to square the circle: it attempts to sell apprenticeships as a high-quality vocational-based education and training scheme with high standards and requirements and clear routes of progression. At the same time, however, in order to attract employers to engage apprentices, especially in sectors that formerly had no apprenticeship tradition, the government allows for exceptions with regard to the requirements that need to be fulfilled.

A third area of tension revolves around the issue of "parity of esteem". Although attempting to become an esteemed educational route, apprenticeships have not been able to entirely shrug off their reputation as a scheme that is intended only for low-achievers (Fuller, 2004, 17). One of the reasons for this situation is to be found in the perceived cleavage between academic and vocational education. Another reason stems from the fact that one of the predecessors of the apprenticeship scheme is the Youth Training Scheme, which was indisputably a scheme for low-achievers and nothing else. It seems even today that the apprenticeship scheme has still not succeeded in getting rid of the stigma that it is a programme offered to the least talented whereas the more talented will either simply find a job or pursue a higher education route.

Discursive institutionalism helps us to understand how this development – a scheme which was ascribed many expectations and aspirations, and which was supposed to break from the traditional training path in England – came about. The discourse shows that England is indeed considering its position in an international market-environment as varieties of capitalism would predict, yet with another outcome than we would theoretically expect: England is trying to alter its skill pattern in the direction of more specific skills. Theoretically we would expect general skills to be strengthened, as this is supposed to contribute to England's specific institutional advantages. The implementation of, and the various amendments to, apprenticeships tell a different story, not so much about skill patterns but about the general aim of apprenticeships. The aim to provide a unique scheme that generates concisely defined skills is watered down for the sake of expansion.

In the end, however, we can see why the system has failed to achieve the significance which was initially assigned to it. The reasons for this failure can be found in the basic structure of the system. In other words, the English training institutions show a great degree of inertia and resistance; developments proceed path-dependently.

6.1.3 Higher Education: Foundation degrees

"If we are to create a more inclusive society and unlock the potential of our workforce, we must also increase the number of routes into and through higher education [...] we need to create a continuum of learning where people can expect to move in and out of education throughout their lives. At the centre of this new approach will be the new Foundation degree [...]." (DfEE, 2000, 2; David Blunkett, Secretary of State for Education, 2000)

1) Agenda setting, problem identification

Although the initial spark for foundation degrees cannot be traced back to one of the earlier examined White Papers, their mention in the latter of these papers justifies the choice of foundation degrees as the higher education reform on which I will elaborate in-depth. The Bologna process has had a huge impact on higher education in many European countries. This does not, however, apply in the English case, which – arguably – was taken as a template for "Bologna". In terms of qualificational reforms it is, therefore, not the introduction of bachelors and masters degrees but of foundation degrees which qualifies as the main reform initiative in higher education.

The Dearing Report, issued in 1997 after New Labour had already come into office but commissioned by the preceding Conservative government, is said to have marked the birth of the foundation degree (Wilson, Blewitt and Moody, 2005, 112; Foskett, 2005, 353 f.). The Dearing Committee advised the government to introduce a "sub-degree" to generate intermediate occupational skills that are linked directly to the needs of the labour market and thereby ensure a closer link between vocational and academic education (Dearing, 1997).

The idea of a foundation degree-scheme finally materialised in a consultation document which followed a speech on higher education by the then Secretary of State for education David Blunkett at the Maritime Greenwich University in February 2000 (Blunkett, 2000). This speech marked the first official mention of "foundation degrees" and thereby followed-up on the suggestion of the Dearing Report to introduce a "sub-degree". Thus we must examine the precise wording of this speech in further detail and then supplement this with evidence from relevant statements in the White Papers.

2) Policy formulation, adoption and path deviation
This speech is highly important, as it was the first comprehensive elaboration on higher education by the DfES after Labour came to power in 1997 and after the Dearing Report was published.[107] This speech provides us with the perfect starting point for tracing the reform-process involved in the creation of foundation degrees because it conveys the driving ideas, aims and targets which have been associated with this scheme.

In the speech Blunkett made a prediction about the future trajectory of higher education in the light of "new constraints caused by the rapidity of change" (Blunkett, 2000, paragraph 7). He centred the issue around the notion of globalisation, which would require high levels of education with higher education at its heart (Blunkett, 2000, paragraph 10). He spoke about a "profound change [which; J.W.] has taken place in the global environment" (Blunkett, 2000, paragraph 8), such as the internationalisation of trade and production, which is tightly linked to altering global financial markets and the increased mobility of capital. The whole process is decisively fuelled by the development of information and communication technologies. He argued that this new global economy is driven by the "powerhouses" of skills, innovation, and knowledge (Blunkett, 2000, paragraph 9). Therefore, higher education has to be placed at the centre of this development because it provides the excellence in knowledge and innovation need for an economy that wishes and is determined to act on a global scale (Blunkett, 2000, paragraph 6).

According to Blunkett, the pressures of globalisation on higher education must be met by a threefold strategy: first, introducing new modes of virtual learning and new international alliances; second, providing more diversity in higher education; and third, strengthening the cooperation of businesses with higher education institutions. This strategy is supposed to achieve the following objective:

> "Our objective is expansion with diversity and excellence throughout the sector, so that we secure wider participation in a higher education system valued for its quality as a whole." (Blunkett, 2000, Paragraph 29)

However, there is some tension between the attempt to support expansion and diversity at the same time. Anticipating a critique along these lines, in

---

[107] Just as a reminder, the first White Paper that was explicitly focused on higher education was not published by New Labour until 2003.

6.1 Policy reforms in England – three cases and their selection

paragraphs 27-29 Blunkett explicitly emphasised the importance of the quality of the English higher education system (Blunkett, 2000). In paragraph 28 of his speech Blunkett turns directly to this point and makes the pledge that "standards in higher education must not be sacrificed to expanded access."

In this context he describes the experiences of other countries with a two-year qualifications in higher education (unfortunately without naming them, paragraph 32)[108], while in the following paragraph (33) he finally refers to the term "foundation degree". The foundation degree as a new qualification reflects the above discussed tension, as this degree is perceived as being attractive to young people who have not yet been in higher education (hence expansion) and of providing intermediate higher education skills. In other words the foundation degree has to be understood as an attempt to fulfil the demanding aim of having 50 percent of all people aged 18-30 in higher education by 2010, the target set in 1999 by Prime Minister Tony Blair (The Guardian, 1999a).[109]

In this speech Blunkett specifies the main drivers behind the introduction of foundation degrees. In the first place he advocates "expansion with diversity and excellence throughout the sector" (paragraph 29) in the same breath as pointing out the shortage of people with intermediate skills, in particular highly qualified technicians (paragraph 32). Therefore, new entry routes to higher education have to be created which are "oriented strongly to the employability skills" (paragraph 32). The White Papers displayed why "massification" and "diversity" in higher education play crucial roles (compare with Doyle, 2003, 4 ff.): diversity is supposed to lead to higher participation rates which lead to higher skill levels in society and which is thereby conducive to strengthening international economic competitiveness. This line of argumentation is presented in White Paper "The Future of Higher Education" (DfES, 2003c, chapter 5) under the heading "Expanding higher education to meet our needs", where "needs" is defined in terms of economic needs. Also the White Paper "21st Century Skills" discusses the advantages of foundation degrees for meeting the higher level skill needs of the economy (DfES, 2003c, chapter 26). This argument is again put forward in the White Paper "Getting on in Business, Getting on at Work":

> "We must ensure that HE programmes are designed and delivered in a way that best helps students gain the skills that employers need. We will do that by expanding Foundation Degrees, designed in partnership with employers." (DfES, 2005b, Paragraph 19)

---

[108]Grubb shows that the foundation degree emulates the US Associate Degree (Grubb, 2004, 20, 35).
[109]The White Paper "The Future of Higher Education" published in 2003 emphasises this point even further in stating that one of the main drivers for the implementation of this scheme is to fulfil the higher education participation target of 50 percent among those aged 18-30 by 2010 (DfES, 2003c).

Returning to Blunkett's speech, the notion of "diversity and excellence" finds its expression in a two-year degree that is supposed to close "our historic skills deficit in this country [which; J.W.] lies in the shortage of people with intermediate skills" (paragraph 32). Thus, the case for foundation degrees is not about excellence; at best it is about "excellent intermediate skills" or "intermediate higher education qualifications" (compare with The Times, 2001).

The establishment of this higher education degree is meant to narrow a perceived historical shortage of intermediate skills and hence to provide skills which are, in for instance Germany, predominantly generated through vocational education. Consequently, foundation degrees are about expanding higher education at the lower skill end of the spectrum. In the higher education White Paper we see that the government eventually accepted and supported the gradual substitution of Higher National Diplomas (themselves being higher education qualifications, though not degrees) with foundation degrees (DfES, 2003c, 43).

In his speech at Greenwich University Blunkett states that foundation degrees shall increase employability and thus "offer clear routes into the labour market or further learning" (Blunkett, 2000, paragraph 35). Students who study for a foundation degree are supposed to be:

> "fully equipped with the skills and abilities they will need for effective engagement in the knowledge economy – so that they are enterprising and creative, familiar with the world of work, and possess a sound base of ICT and other key skills as well as specialist knowledge" (paragraph 35).

Again we can draw on the White Papers in order to elaborate upon an interesting aspect that should keep in mind for the evaluation of this scheme. When the papers refer to "employers" and a "knowledge economy", these references are not confined to "employers" in the private economy. Especially the White Paper on higher education stresses the significance of foundation degrees for public sector workers (DfES, 2003c, 88). It remains to be seen as to what extent the public sector will turn to foundation degrees as a means of attaining the 50 percent higher education target.

Apart from closing the skill-gaps and the provision of intermediate skills, foundation degrees are supposed to contribute to the amelioration of other issues. Following from Blunkett, one might speak about another perceived "historical deficit". The notion of "parity of esteem" refers to the endeavour to provide a level playing field between vocational and academic education. Since a foundation degree is a degree, i.e. a formal academic higher education qualification lying between honours degrees and non-degree-qualifications such as Higher National Diplomas (HND) and which consists of a vocational component, it is supposed to bridge these areas. Until the foundational degree,

6.1 Policy reforms in England – three cases and their selection

academic and vocational education had been rather separate spheres. "Parity of esteem" (paragraph 34ff) means first and foremost the differences in reputation and hence the differences in terms of occupational options on the labour market. Academic education, i.e. the classic honours degrees (bachelor and master), are not only ascribed a higher value; moreover, vocational based further education has been regarded as education for school low-achievers. Foundation degrees are supposed to put an end to these perceptions.

Furthermore, lifelong learning can also be facilitated through foundation degrees. As Blunkett pointed out in the consultation document and the HEFCE in its "Foundation degree prospectus", this qualification is believed to be conducive to lifelong learning, as it might attract not only people from under-represented groups but also mature learners who wish to upgrade their skills without abandoning their job ("earn and learn", HEFCE, 2000, 5). The scheme-design explicitly allows and facilitates part-time and distance learning in order to encourage this group's participation – an attempt which might eventually lead to higher overall participation rates. People possessing Advanced Apprenticeships or vocational A-levels are also a target group for foundation degrees.

Another important trait of foundation degrees is their "stepping stone" feature. The scheme has been constructed as an easy way to honours degrees (paragraph 36). It is also an attempt to provide a more flexible and transparent system that more easily allows individuals to climb the educational ladder, to link different qualifications and also to provide better pathways for progression (DfES, 2003c, 7).

These drivers are embedded in a context of globalisation, which renders skill-enhancement an imperative for sustaining competitiveness in the international global economy (Wilson, Blewitt and Moody, 2005, 113). For the government, however, "skill-enhancement" is mostly understood in terms of quantity and diversity rather than quality. Foundation degrees play a pivotal role in the government's endeavours to achieve the 50 percent aim in higher education.

The expectations and aims associated with foundation degrees are far from modest. They are introduced along the priorities of excellence, diversity, and expansion. In concrete terms this means providing intermediate higher education skills of which the economy is considered to be short, striving for the 50 percent target, and contributing to the "learning age", including the necessary component of lifelong. Foundation degrees represent a major attempt to provide employer-tailored vocational education on a higher education level recognised by a degree. These foundation degrees thus stress industry-specific if not firm-specific skills. This is an interesting aspect, as it is counter both to England's affiliation with those political economies that are focused on general skills and to some of the main traits of the English higher education system (two-years degree, business-tailored, parity of esteem).

3) Theoretically grasping the discourse
How did this policy proposal, which ostensibly deviates from what would be expected, come about? The foundation degree, as one of the major higher education initiatives in England in the last decade, is based on a communicative discourse that in the foreground of the debate stresses "expansion with diversity and excellence throughout the sector" (Blunkett, 2000, paragraph 29). Yet excellence and the pledge for intermediate skills might conflict somewhat with each other, as we have already seen. Nonetheless, the cognitive driver stems from the perceived shortage of exactly these skills.

The more hidden factors and aspects – in other words the philosophies or paradigms – which propel this discourse are the following: only an expanded higher education area will be able to meet future demands for well-skilled employees on an intermediate level and thereby to tackle the (perceived) notorious low productivity level in England and maintain/facilitate international competitiveness; a supply-led approach which assumes that employers will eventually make use of the skills generated by the education system; and a perceived lack of highly-qualified and skilled employees.

The normative side of the coin is driven by the conviction that "the higher the participation rate, the better". It is perceived to be a public duty to expand and thereby allow as many people as possible to enter higher education. The orthodox belief in a supply-led approach to education policies, which is also reflected in foundation degrees, appears to reduce uncertainty regarding how to cope with the challenges recent developments are exerting on the English economy. However, there is no clear institutional blueprint for foundation degrees, apart from vague references to an American scheme.

Instead, the drivers for the scheme are the conviction that there will be reputational payoffs from greater higher education participation rates and the "taken-for-granted" belief that higher participation rates *per se* will eventually lead to better performance by the English political economy. Foundation degrees are layered on the existing institutional structure; they are not a formal substitute for a current scheme. However, in practise they displace HND.

4) Post-implementation critique on mode of operation
After the introduction of foundation degrees, heavy criticism was not long in coming. This section outlines the major points of criticism.

a) Terminology, value FD vs. HD

Representatives of higher education institutions were particularly apprehensive about a possible devaluation of the traditional honours degree by labelling a two-year sub-honours and work-based qualification a "degree". As the National Association of Teachers in Further and Higher Education (NATFHE) claimed in 2000, the purpose of an academic "degree", which teaches people to be critical and reflective, would be rendered unrecognisable, as foundation degrees have strictly instrumental purposes. Furthermore, NATFHE was concerned that foundation degrees would become a "bogus qualification to provide expansion on the cheap" (The Times, Higher Education Supplement, 2000f). Also the Conservatives criticised New Labour's initiative, arguing that foundation degrees would devalue honours degrees and that there should remain some minimum of a gap between academic honours degrees and vocational-based education. This critique must be seen in the context of the high national and international reputation of the English higher education system and its qualifications and the desire to preserve the unique value of academic degrees.

Thus, opponents such as representatives of prestigious universities, NATFHE and the Quality Assurance Agency for Higher Education are concerned about confusions, at worst a devaluation of British degrees from the perspective of international students, caused by a "degree" that has hardly nothing in common with the prestigious honours degrees apart from the name (The Guardian, 2000c). It is argued that eventually foundation degrees could therefore harm English competitiveness in the higher education market.[110]

Another criticism draws on the attempt to strive for "parity of esteem" by means of foundation degrees. The English vocational education system tends to provide post-compulsory schooling education for those considered too intelligent to enter the labour market directly at the age of 16, where they would be employed in low-skilled jobs, but at the same time not smart enough to enter directly into universities. Foundation degrees are meant to bridge this gap by providing both a higher education-option for those not yet qualified for university entrance and a clear route of progression after having obtained a foundation degree. Hence critics claim that the selection process which characterises the English higher education system is being watered down, at the cost of its high reputation and quality. Moreover, it has been claimed that foundation degrees could devalue four-year vocational degrees, mostly offered

---

[110] In his Greenwich speech Blunkett acknowledges the international attractiveness of this economic sector (Blunkett, 2000, 14): it is based both on a worldwide renowned academic system, with the "Oxbridge" beacon-universities being synonymous with quality in terms of teaching and research rather than for qualifications centred on vocational education, and on the importance of English as the global language, which attracts international students from all over the world (Gibbs, 2002).

by former polytechnics, as most students may opt to pursue only two-year degrees (Mayhew, Deer and Dua, 2004, 78; The Guardian 2000c; The Guardian, 2000a; The Times, Higher Education Supplement, 2000e).

Another criticism turns explicitly to option of using foundation degrees as "stepping stones". Foundation degrees do not merely provide a qualification; instead, foundation degrees can also be used as a "stepping stone" to honours degrees, which would entail just another 15 months of university study. This is one of the main differences between a foundation degree and a Higher National Diploma.[111] Since, however, academic degrees are held in high esteem, whereas the real economic value of a foundation degree is not yet clear, people have argued that foundation degrees could be used by people solely for its "stepping stone" function. This would clearly thwart the initial intention of the programme, i.e. to provide a high quality mix of vocational and academic education tailored to employers' needs and thus providing direct access to employment (Little, 2005, 138). A development like this could undermine its "raison d'être" as an intermediate skill generating qualification. Thus, the intention to provide a closer and denser qualificational framework that allows people to "travel" between different schemes and allows for various ladders of progression might have a major flipside because of the fact that the "esteem-structure" is so clearly in favour of honours degrees.

Furthermore, the close partnership-approach behind foundation degrees has been criticised. The scheme represents another major initiative to link universities, further education colleges, and employers (compare with Wilson, Blewitt and Moody, 2005, 115). Yet in practise, the partnership between universities and further education colleges is often only for formal reasons: further education colleges have no degree awarding power. Thus, even though around 50 percent of off-the-job training is carried out by further education colleges, they need to have "partner-universities" that award the final degrees. Consequently, a formal degree mainly obtained through a further education college has led to concerns about the quality of the scheme, as for instance seen in the report by the "Foundation Degree Task Force" (DfES, 2004b, 6), and raised questions about whether foundation degrees really qualify as a *degree* (compare with Mayhew, Deer and Dua, 2004, 78 f.; The Times, Higher Education Supplement, 2000d).

Concluding this section, we should take a look at foundation degrees from the perspective of the so-called Bologna process. The English qualification

---

[111]Foundation degrees can be easily complemented with an additional year of university studies to obtain a bachelor degree. A Higher National Diploma, by contrast, offers only access to universities. The "Diploma" as a certificate, however, is not accredited. Thus, the foundation degree-path to a bachelor lasts three years while a bachelor following a Higher National Diploma lasts five years.

structure was to a large extent used as a template for this process. Interestingly enough, however, of all degrees covered by "Bologna", foundation degrees have been subject to the most scepticism as to whether they comply with the Bologna standards. The main criticism along these lines revolves around the duration of only two years, given that according to the Bologna declaration all degree qualifications should involve a minimum of three years of full-time studies. Thus, one could claim that it is the country from which the template originated that is now undermining "Bologna" (The Times, Higher Education Supplement, 2000d; The Times, Higher Education Supplement, 2000c; Gibbs, 2002, 201).

b) FD vs. HND, re-branded

Additionally, the criticism of foundation degrees has been fuelled by a lack of clarity and distinction between foundation degrees and Higher National Diplomas (HND) (compare with discussions in DfES, 2004b, 5). Content wise these two qualifications seem to be mostly congruent, also regarding access requirements. Quite often Higher National Diplomas have been "re-branded" as foundation degrees (compare with Wilson, Blewitt and Moody, 2005, 115, 118; The Times, Higher Education Supplement, 2000d; The Times, Educational Supplement, 2000b). Moreover, both qualifications sit on the same level within the National Qualifications Framework. [112]

Yet, there are three main differences in the setup of foundation degrees as opposed to Higher National Diplomas. One of these is in their "stepping stone" function, which allows for different options of progression (compare with previous section).

Secondly, another main difference is meant to be the work-based element of foundation degrees. However, this requirement is enforced less strictly than one might suppose. For full-time students the work-based requirement is fulfilled by an internship and is, therefore, far from being a clear gateway into occupation with an employer (compare with DfES, 2004c, 4).

A third major difference between foundation degrees and Higher National Diplomas lies in the fact that the former is particularly constructed to attract people who are already employed and wish to pursue further education. It is in this context that one has to understand the criticism of the "50 percent target", as foundation degrees are supposed to attract additional part-time students.

Thus, one might conclude that this scheme is intended to attract additional students to higher education who previously would have pursued a further education or Higher National Diploma pathway, or not continued in education at all. Yet representatives of the Associations of Colleges are concerned that

---

[112] See http://www.edexcel.org.uk/VirtualContent/75727/Revised_NQF_incl_NVQs_KS_FHEQ.pdf.

foundation degrees' students might just substitute existing qualifications with foundation degrees, as is likely to be the case with the Higher National Diplomas (The Times, Higher Education Supplement, 2000f).

With respect to the announcement to gradually replace Higher National Diplomas with foundation degrees one might raise the question "what must a degree substantially consist of"? This question is also raised in a European context, as critics claim that foundation degrees fall short of European standards (The Times, Higher Education Supplement, 2000d). Moreover, with respect to the fact that in the 2006-07 academic year 54 percent of foundation degree students were taught in further education colleges (HEFCE, 2007, 4), and that in these instances there had to be a validating university which is allowed to award degrees (though this has recently started to change), one might raise the question of where to place the dividing line between further education and higher education. What can be perceived as "just" further education and what as higher education? In other words: can we expect a qualitative difference between Higher National Diplomas and foundation degrees or are we merely witnessing a rebranding of qualifications within the qualificational area of higher education, possibly even at the expense of the sector's reputation? Indeed, when speaking in its "Report to Ministers" about whether foundation degree should be ascribed to the further education area or the higher education area, the "Foundation Degree Task Force" stated that:

> "The trouble is that at present they [foundation degrees; J.W.] sit uncomfortably between the two [further education & higher education; J.W.]" (4).

It is this dilemma in which foundation degrees seem to be caught.

c) Double-demand

The issue of "double-demand" for foundation degrees refers to two different demands which will determine the success of this new scheme: the demand of employers and the demand of students. Both demand situations are closely linked and are likely to correlate, i.e. if employer demand is high one could assume that student demand for the scheme is also rising.

Regarding the demand of employers, a survey of the members of the Confederation of British Industry (CBI) presents a rather ambivalent picture. It showed that 77 percent of the firms could see a value in foundation degrees. In the same breath, however, CBI stated that due to a lack of market research there is no clear evidence that "skills shortages are systematically greater among those recruiting at sub-degree level." Moreover, the CBI was not able to identify any evidence that employers' demand for skills at this level will rise in the future –

6.1 Policy reforms in England – three cases and their selection 259

one of the core assumptions of New Labour (The Times, Higher Education Supplement, 2000e). Not only is the main employer organisation indifferent towards the new scheme, the HEFCE is simultaneously both supportive and suspicious. Like the CBI, the HEFCE is unsure about demand for foundation degrees:

> "The foundation degree is being introduced against a background of declining higher national diploma recruitment and without prior market testing. The council strongly recommends some attempt to evaluate student and employer demand for the foundation degree before any major growth is channelled through this qualification route." (The Times, Higher Education Supplement, 2000f)

Both the CBI and the HEFCE question the need for more employees holding a sub-degree qualification. Firstly, particularly employers in those sectors with highly regarded HNDs do not see any added value from foundation degrees. Secondly, the demand for higher-level qualifications, hence honours degrees, seems to be greater than for intermediate higher education qualifications like the foundation degree (The Times, Educational Supplement, 2000a). Furthermore, it is claimed that foundation degrees will complicate the further education qualification jungle and that foundation degree graduates may prefer continue on to an honour degree rather than use their foundation degrees for entry into the labour market (The Times, Educational Supplement, 2000a; The Times, Higher Education Supplement, 2000g). This confusing picture is complemented by a rather unclear picture about employer engagement, which is supposed to be one of the corner stones of the scheme (Gallacher, Ingram and Reeve, 2006, 8 f.). To sum up, a statement by a professor from Liverpool University pinpoints what is possibly the main driver for foundation degrees:

> "Is there going to be a real demand from employers for them? Much of the expansion of higher education is supply-side expansion – politicians thinking it would be good for more people to go to university." (The Guardian, 2000a)

As to the demand for foundation degrees from students, one might assume that it is highly dependent on the value this new scheme has on the labour market. Hence, student demand is dependent on employer demand and therefore we can speak about a double-demand problem (The Guardian, 2000c). Needless to say, some key points of scepticism mentioned in the paragraphs above apply equally to the demand situation of students: further complication of the sub-honours degree qualification jungle[113]; lack of clear distinctiveness from HND in terms of

---

[113] According to newspapers, students and employers are confused by the 7,000 sub-degree

content;[114]; and a lack of knowledge about the status of foundation degrees as compared to honours degrees.

5) Evaluation

The idea of "expansion" dominates higher education initiatives. Yet expansion is subject to two further specifications when it comes to policies: expansion of diversity and expansion of excellence. As has been argued above, foundation degrees serve the purpose of expanding the system by introducing more options – thus the system becomes more diverse. Excellence does not play any role here. The communicative discourse bears witness to this fact, as the main critiques revolve around the fact that foundation degrees are "expansion on the cheap" (The Times, Higher Education Supplement, 2000f) and that they are thwarting excellence rather than contributing to it. The coordinative discourse is mainly conducted in the corresponding consultation document, which is – by and large – of minor importance for the process itself (for the consultation document see DfEE, 2000).

The figures show that participation in foundation degrees in absolute terms has risen rapidly since they were launched in 2001. In the 2003/04 academic year 21,000 students were enrolled in foundation degree programmes in the UK (Hayward et al., 2006, 175). In 2007/08 the figures amount to 72,000 registered students (HEFCE, 2008, 2). The Higher Education Funding Council for England (HEFCE) expects participation numbers to nearly hit the 100,000 threshold by 2010 (HEFCE, 2008, 2). Moreover, with the increase of foundation degrees there has been a corresponding decline in HNDs (compare with Hayward et al., 2006, 175; Higher Education Statistics Agency, 2009), a fact that underpins the claim that foundation degrees have the tendency to squeeze out HNDs.

In order to advance this analysis we should compare foundation degree registration figures with overall higher education participation figures.[115] In

---

qualifications on offer (The Times, Educational Supplement, 2000a; The Times, Educational Supplement, 2000b).

[114]This applies also to the work-based learning element, which is not new to the further education area in England (Mason, 2001). The Quality Assurance Agency for Higher Education (QAA) stated in its 2005 review that employer involvement in the design and provision of foundation degrees, promoted as one of the key characteristics of this scheme and thereby providing attractiveness for students, is "not overtly strong" (QAA, 2005, 16).

[115]If we are to make a statement about the national skill patterns we need to raise some preliminary observation that are specific to England: the UK in general and England in particular are characterised by a huge share of foreign (overseas) students, attracted both by the higher education system and certificates, and by the language. The share of overseas students, however, drops considerably when we look at foundation degrees: there are only four percent overseas students enrolled in foundation degree programmes (EU and non-EU), with the remaining 96 percent being UK-students (compare with HEFCE, 2008, 26). The share of overseas student in the total number of

6.1 Policy reforms in England – three cases and their selection 261

2006/07 around 2,000,000 students were enrolled in the higher education system in the UK (Higher Education Statistics Agency, 2009). In the same time period 60,580 foundation degree students were enrolled (HEFCE, 2008, 11), thus a share of around 3 percent. Participation numbers are expected to rise in the coming years, whereas overall student numbers are expected to slightly decrease (compare with Universities UK, 2008). Nonetheless, the relevance for the overall higher education system is modest.

Interestingly enough, ever since foundation degrees were introduced they have to some extent been subjected to what we might call a Streeck and Thelen "conversion" (Streeck and Thelen, 2005, 26): as a survey of foundation degree qualifiers conducted six months after they obtained their qualification shows that a majority of qualifiers continue in higher education, either on a full-time or part-time basis. Only 26 percent entered employment on a full-time basis (HEFCE, 2008). One might contend that the stepping stone function of foundation degrees seems to prevail, whereas the function of providing an employer-tailored higher education qualification is pertinent for only around one-quarter of all foundation degree qualifiers. This "stepping stone" function is probably the pivotal aspect that determines the "real" value of foundation degrees and ultimately their success: the more students that use it as a stepping stone, the lower seems to be the value of foundation degrees as qualifications in their own right. In this sense foundation degrees are a scheme in a higher education transition system.

Hence, by contrasting the English higher education discourse with foundation degrees we clearly detect the prevailing importance of expanding the system in order to provide additional study options for additional students. "Excellence" is by and large not an issue. The same applies to foundation degrees as instruments for enhancing the overall skill patterns of the population and thereby increasing productivity levels, because to a considerable extent foundation degrees just squeeze out already existing qualifications (such as HND), essentially simply giving a new label to a similar content.

As already outlined in this chapter, discursive institutionalism provides us with tools by which we can understand changes that are unexpected according to the concept of path-dependency. Moreover, the aim of foundation degrees is to provide something new, a non-existent bridge between higher education and vocational education, an(other) attempt to obtain "parity of esteem". Furthermore, one could argue that considerations along the lines of the varieties of capitalism literature are equally disproven. In terms of maintaining and supporting international competitiveness, one might expect there would be

---

students in UK higher education is almost 15 percent. Hence, if we want to draw inferences about English skill patterns and the significance foundation degrees have assumed in the higher education area and for the English political economy, we need to be cautious not to underestimate this scheme.

efforts to preserve the status of English degrees, as England has been very successful on the international higher education market and attracts a great number of foreign students. For England higher education is not only a means to an end but a market in itself. Instead we discover a rather functional-driven reform that is meant to ameliorate a perceived skills deficit at the intermediate (associate professional and technical) level (Gallacher, Ingram and Reeve, 2006, 4) but simultaneously has the potential to damage the reputation of English degrees.

So far so good, the discourse about the reform shows an unexpected outcome. However, is this reflected by a profound change in the institutional landscape? Maybe in the future it will turn out to have a profound character, but up to now the effect of the reform has been modest. A core reason for this incremental development lies in the acknowledgement structure of the English educational system, with honours degrees at the top of the scale. On the other hand, the English educational reform seems to have become a victim of its own endeavours. The rapid changes of educational institutions and qualifications in England make it extremely difficult to relate foundation degrees to existing qualifications and thereby fit them into the acknowledgement structure at the correct level. In fact, especially given initiatives in the vocational education and training area with apprenticeships as the "spearhead", one might wonder where to place foundation degrees in the overall picture. With respect to foundation degrees this situation is aggravated by the fact that the purpose, namely expanding the system, was the father of the initiative. Thus the additional value of foundation degrees has not been considered adequately.

6.2 Policy reforms in Germany – three cases and their selection

This chapter turns to policy initiatives in the German educational area. Similar to the analysis of England, one particular reform from each educational area will be examined. Also as with the English case, the three reforms must comply with the three criteria outlined in chapter 6.1. Educational policy is, in general, under the ambit of the German states. Whereas the federal level still has a few competencies and/or options to influence the policies of the states in vocational and higher education, this possibility is extremely limited in school education. Yet, interestingly enough, the German school landscape is less fragmented than one might expect. The reduction of schooling years in higher secondary education (commonly called G8) is an example of both how policies are driven by contemplating the international environment and how policies can domestically disseminate throughout the federal states. The reform matches the overarching discourse about German education periods (including those in vocational education and higher education) being too long in comparison to the international average. The reduction of the number of higher secondary education schooling years needed to obtain a higher education entrance qualification, which has been applied and implemented in almost all German federal states, serves as an example of how policies can suddenly become liable to "fashions". To what extent we can speak about a "path-breaking" reform will be further discussed in the relevant section.

The section on vocational education and training will scrutinise the various attempts to provide alternatives to the dual apprenticeship system. This adaptation is quite amazing, as the dual apprenticeship system, one of the main educational pillars of the German political economy, is characterised by a high degree of employer involvement and thereby by high degrees of employer-tailored skill specifity. By strengthening the school-based pillar of vocational education through the amending the Vocational Education and Training Act, both these characteristics are likely to diminish. In its pure form, this approach would more resemble the English approach to vocational education and training. The relevant section will clarify this issue by elaborating on the amendment law passed in 2005 and on its impact on the German training "gold standard".

For the higher education sector the initiative of excellence (Exzellenzinitiative) is analysed. One might argue that this initiative only implicitly touches on education in the strictest sense of the word, as the initiative is concerned mainly with research in higher education institutions. Yet, I argue that this policy initiative – in particular in combination with the Bologna process – has led to a "paradigm shift" in German higher education (Hartmann, 2006) because it combines a far more European standardised degree-structure with a remarkable attempt to stratify and marketise the education system. As the relevant section will demonstrate, this initiative has assumed an important central role in the German higher education discourse. Given that the first two rounds of funding have been completed we can already draw some inferences about the effects this reform has had on the system.

6.2.1 School education – G8

"Was für eine Aufregung um eine Angleichung an den europäischen Standard!" (Die Zeit, 2008b)

1) Agenda setting and problem identification
Arguably, elaborating on reforms in school education in Germany is very

challenging, if it is feasible at all. In almost no other area are the competences so clearly assigned to the states as in school educational matters. While vocational education and training is at least partly under the ambit of the federal level (stipulations about the training site of the dual apprenticeship system), and while it also, even after the federalism reform, has a few "points of impact" in higher education (Bologna process, initiative of excellence), school education matters remain entirely under the ambit of the states. Given these conditions, it is surprising that the system is not characterised by extreme heterogeneity. Instead, there is a noticeable similarity of the school systems among the states. Nevertheless, there has not been a 'single' reform in the strictest sense of the word; rather there have been potentially 16 reforms that may have taken a similar direction in all 16 states. Therefore, it is difficult to detect the "initial spark" for the reform that eventually disseminated throughout Germany.

The main justification for embarking on a 12 (eight) year strategy instead of a 13 (nine) year strategy stems from consideration of, and resulting apprehension about, school education in the main economic competitors of Germany, primarily European states such as France and England (wdr.de, 2008a). It was feared that the comparatively long schooling period, in combination with comparatively long studying periods (for males one needs to take into account also the military or social service period), might lead to a competitive disadvantage for German applicants in the burgeoning internationally integrated labour market (wdr.de, 2008a).

The G8 reform was undertaken in accordance with the concerns as expressed in the governmental papers: the fact that German pupils and students are comparatively older than their international competitors in the international labour market (compare with Schröder, 1998; BMBF, 1999; Schröder, 2002; BMBF, 2002). As a consequence they would suffer from a comparative disadvantage. Therefore, and in order to render the overall German education system more competitive, educational periods would need to be shortened.

2) Policy formulation, adoption and path deviation
The reduction of higher secondary schooling years from 13 to 12 years is one example that does show heterogeneity with respect to the timing of the reform.[116] There are even states for which this policy programme was hardly a reform *per se*, as they have mandated 12 years of schooling for several years. Two states (Saxony and Thuringia) never changed the GDR-based 12 years of schooling after reunification, whereas Saxony Anhalt and Mecklenburg Western Pomerania returned to 12 years of schooling after using the Western system for only a short

---

[116]Secondary school in higher secondary schooling, hence in the *Gymnasium*, was reduced from nine to eight years; thus the term G8.

6.2 Policy reforms in Germany – three cases and their selection 265

period. Thus, of the Eastern states, only Brandenburg adopted the 13 year schooling system, though the city of East Berlin also adopted the 13 year system as used in West Berlin.

It was only around 10 years after reunification that reduced schooling in higher secondary education became an issue in the Western states. In 2001/02 the Saarland was the first West German state to switch to a 12 year system. Given the legal independence in this area, it is striking that all states – though at different points in time – embarked on the same strategy by using the same rhetoric.[117]

This applies also to the statements made about G8 in the press and other media, which resemble each other even though they are confined to particular states. A member of the school ministry in North Rhine-Westphalia, for instance, hoped that G8 would be conducive to quicker schooling, quicker studies and quicker success in the labour market (wdr.de, 2008a). Thereby, Germany could considerably reduce the age of labour market entrants (wdr.de, 2008a).

The German school education system is characterised by a high degree of stratification. Furthermore, school enrolment is comparatively late and the schooling period for higher secondary education, which leads to a university entrance qualification, is comparatively long. Furthermore, the German school system is characterised by part-time schooling, a fact that matches the pattern of a conservative welfare state system (Esping-Andersen, 1990; Castles and Mitchell, 1993; Ebbinghaus and Manow, 2001; Clasen, 2005; Ferrera, Hemerijck and Rhodes, 2001).

Why can we classify the G8 reform as deviation from the above sketched path? The reform obviously has no impact on the stratification of the German school system. The same applies to the issue of school enrolment ages. Against the background of the theoretical framework the alterations to the sketched path are rather modest. As the minimum hours for pupils to attain an Abitur are set and likely to stay fixed at 265 taught hours per year in higher secondary education[118], there is hardly any impact on the generality of skills attained by the pupils, as curricula has remained unaltered. Hence, the literature on the varieties of capitalism is not of any help here.

Reducing schooling years in higher secondary education does not appear to be a path-breaking reform in any respect. Whether a country pursues a 13 year strategy to a university entrance qualification or merely 12 years has hardly any

---

[117]For an outline of the different endeavours and stipulations of the states in introducing G8 see the following web page of the Kultusministerkonferenz www.kmk.org/schul/Schulzeitam Gymnasium.pdf.
[118]There is a discussion to reduce them from 265 to 260. Yet, this is unlikely to undermine the general argument.

impact on issues such as stratification, standardisation or the distinction between general and specific skills. Yet if we contemplate this reform in the light of an overall incremental change, not only in school education but also in social policy, the G8 reform complements a picture that is increasingly deviating from what we would expect according to the comparative welfare literature.[119]

So, the reform exhibits some path-breaking tendencies if we consider the effects it has on the schooling structure. Shorter schooling years lead to longer schooling days in all the states that pursue the so-called G8 strategy [120]. This is consistent with the aspiration to establish full-time schools. Full-time schooling, however, is not only a prerequisite or consequence of G8. Moreover, it is an initiative which is based on a consideration that indicate a slight deviation from the "path" that we would expect. This (re-)consideration is that the male-breadwinner model, according to which a working man sustains the household and a woman cares for the household, has become increasingly obsolete. In this model the housewife would also care for the children – the pupils coming home from part-time schools. It is this male-breadwinner model on which the idea of the conservative welfare state is rooted. If we now go a step further and consider the main indicator which distinguishes liberal, conservative and social-democratic welfare states, namely de-commodification (compare with Esping-Andersen, 1990), we notice that commodification has become much more of a guiding principle for German social policy, not least since the so-called Hartz-reform. G8 is a puzzle-piece that fits the overall picture of an overarching attempt to further commodify society by relieving women of their responsibilities in the home.

We can thereby contest the underlying theoretical approach which we query in this research: namely historical institutionalism. If we understand historical institutionalism as the basis for both the varieties of capitalism and comparative welfare state literature à la Esping-Andersen, we can contest one of these approaches by contesting the underlying basis which both have in common. Thus, if we consider Esping-Andersen's crucial concept for his categorisation, i.e. de-commodification (see Esping-Andersen, 1990), we can notice changes in German social policy (e.g. so-called Hartz-legislation in social assistance, introduction of funding mechanisms in pension). The G8 reform obviously does not directly contribute to these developments, yet it complements the "sidelines"

---

[119] The conservative welfare model is characterised by modest degrees of commodification and is based on a male-breadwinner perception and, thereby, on a perception of a housewife that cares for the family in general and the children in particular (for this categorisation see Esping-Andersen, 1990).

[120] As elementary schooling takes four yours, another eight years of Gymnasium are needed to obtain the university entrance qualification; hence, G8.

of the overall picture in that it faciliates the further commodification of women/mothers on the labour market and a further anticipated commodification of pupils, consider as the future workforce. The inclination to further commodify the members of the society and the deviation from the male-breadwinner model indicates an incremental change in a German welfare model that had traditionally been considered as a conservative model.

3) Theoretically grasping the discourse
The G8 reform is to a large extent consistent with the rhetoric used in the government papers. The desire to shorten educational periods in both school and higher education is reflected by this reform (compare with Schröder, 1998; BMBF, 1999; Schröder, 2002; BMBF, 2002). Needless to say, shortening educational periods is not an end in itself but serves the purpose of adapting them to OECD standards (BMBF, 2002). Hence, school education is critically assessed against an international context. Regarding the ideational component of the discourse, we notice that G8 is only one policy initiative in the broader programme of reducing education periods for future graduates.[121] This is underpinned by the normative idea and deep conviction, which is also detectable in higher education, that shorter educational periods in school education (and higher education) are needed to face competitive challenges. At the same time there is also the cognitive idea that long education periods are the main hindrance for young people in international labour markets, as they are expected to compete with other applicants who are considerably younger. Hence, the appropriate remedy is considered to be shortening the time spent in higher secondary education and higher education.

Thus, the foreground of the debate on a normative level is determined by the conviction that the German educational periods are too long to sustain international competitiveness. This conviction serves also as a cognitive blueprint to solve the problem. Meanwhile, experiences abroad serve as "weapons" to de-legitimise the current system.[122] The main diffusion driver on a domestic level are what Simmons and Elkins call "common norms" and the

---

[121] The higher education section will reveal that these concerns mainly refer to the academic career. Shortening periods is an issue for both higher secondary education, hence for pupils striving for a higher education entrance qualification, and for higher education (apart from contributing to a European higher education area, the implementation of the Bologna process is justified by the hope it will help to shorten study periods in Germany). Although the federal level has no formal and legal competences to influence the states' decisions in school education, the statements in the governmental papers reflect the efforts that were undertaken by the states.
[122] Interestingly, since the Saarland introduced G8 in 2001/02, the reform has now disseminated throughout Germany, not to mention the four Eastern states which, after examining the pros and cons, did not implement the 13 year system 15 years ago.

"taken-for-grantedness" of the advantages of shorter periods. Taking the perspective of politicians, one would need to emphasise "learning from success", as they considered shorter schooling periods abroad to be preferable and more successful with respect to educational policy and labour market policy. From an international perspective, the reform was introduced with the hope of catching up with international competitors and thereby attaining material payoffs.

The reforms were generally introduced by "layering" G8 over the old G9 stipulation. Yet, the aim was to displace the old system altogether. Transitional periods have been rather short and the introduction of G8 slightly abrupt (compare with footnote 119).

4) Post-implementation critique on mode of operation

The Turbo-Abi and the economisation of school education
The sometimes harsh criticism of G8 is somehow surprising, as four out of 16 states have applied this type of higher secondary schooling for almost 20 years. Most critiques turn on the issue that schooling periods have changed *time-wise*, but not *content-wise*; in other words, the same content that had been taught in nine years of higher secondary schooling are now condensed into eight years (BR-online, 2008; wdr.de, 2008c). Critics speak about overloading children, about a lack of leisure time, and occasionally even about a loss of childhood (Die Zeit, 2008a; Die Zeit 2008c; wdr.de, 2008c; wdr.de, 2008b).

The rhetoric on which the reform is based has been heavily criticised. Opponents note that G8 is mainly concerned with German international competitiveness and does not stem from educational or didactic considerations. As Gaschke understands it, G8 is an ideology that stresses concepts like competition, contest and economic welfare and that the reform pursues economic aims above all, rather than educational or didactic aims (Die Zeit, 2008a; wdr.de, 2008c; wdr.de, 2008b). Furthermore, it is argued that G8 serves the purpose of reducing expenditures, in particular payroll costs for teacher (Die Zeit, 2008a; BR-online, 2008). Critiques in this vein claim that notions such as personal maturity, discernment and character are increasingly squeezed out of the discourse, which is instead dominated by concerns about velocity, globalisation and competitiveness (Die Zeit, 2008a).

Moreover, the president of the German teacher association, for instance, speaks of a dilettante implementation of the reform, in particular because the curricula have not been adapted to shorter schooling periods (wdr.de, 2008c). At the same time, he fears exactly this adaptation, as he believes it would come at the expense of teaching quality (wdr.de, 2008c). The parents' council of Hesse argued along the same line, namely that children and their families suffer from the overload of pupils and that schools often lack adequate infrastructure longer teaching periods, such as school lunch or leisure activities for breaks (hr-online, 2007). Pupil representations have also objected to G8 as being too economically-oriented while neglecting personality development (wdr.de, 2008b).

265 Jahreswochenstunden
Critics claim that 265 taught hours per year to attain a higher secondary school degree are too much, that they overload the pupils. They therefore champion a reduction of this figure (Die Zeit, 2008d). This critique has caused some surprise (sueddeutsche, 2008). Two-hundred sixty-five taught hours per year were stipulated by the Standing Conference of the Ministers of Education (Kultusministerkonferenz) in the beginning of the nineties, when most of the Eastern states opted for a 12 year system. The Western states saw school standards jeopardised by the four Eastern states and therefore introduced the minimum threshold of 265 hours. Only now that the remaining 12 states intend to adopt this threshold, the 265 hour minimum provision has been called into question (Die Zeit, 2008a; sueddeutsche, 2008).

5) Evaluation
The reform matches the general discourse, which calls for a greater velocity in education in order to attain a greater competitiveness. Yet, we are missing a quality discourse here, one which turns to curricula and teaching contents, a discourse which was decisively kicked-off by the PISA-study. The great significance of PISA is highlighted by numerous references to this study throughout the governmental papers (Schröder, 2002; Bulmahn, 2002; BMBF, 2002, 2008a). Admittedly, PISA is not focussed on higher secondary education, but secondary education within the compulsory schooling period. Nonetheless, it is surprising that the curricula and quality discourse is by and large disregarded in the G8 discourse. Remarks such as Schröder's that shortening educational periods must not happen at the expense of educational quality (Schröder, 1998) are largely neglected, as the complaints about the implementation of the reform clearly show.

Referring to the distinction between specific and general skills or using the concept of stratification does not assist us in understanding G8. In order to comprehend the extent of this reform we need both to refer to historical institutionalism in its basic-version and to contemplate the reform against the background of overarching changes in the German political design. G8 does not only match an altered understanding of educational policy but also of family and social policy, and the equivalent rhetoric. The parlance of the discourse reflects the *zeitgeist*, which is concerned with economic notions such as European competition and international competitiveness, both of which pupils will have to face once they enter the labour market. The reform also helps the German efforts to introduce full-time schooling. The condensed schedules inevitably lead to longer school days. Full-time schooling is championed not merely because of educational or didactic reasons; moreover, it accounts for a development and expectations that both parents are active in the labour market. Thus, one might argue that full-time schooling serves the purpose to further commodify the members of the society. Although it is only a small piece of the overall puzzle, the policy initiative "G8" (which is part of the programme to reduce education period) and its political justification fit into the picture of an overall development that is aligned with these notions.

Moreover, it shows and proves the tremendous impact international benchmarks and competitors have on educational considerations. Despite the previous paragraph, one could question whether this reform would have come into effect if the international environment had been disregarded. Not only the drivers but also the identification of the problem in the first place lie outside the purely domestic self-perception. Hence, it is only by perceiving Germany in its international context that we can understand this reform.

6.2.2 Vocational education and the dual apprenticeship system

> "Das duale System der beruflichen Bildung ist weltweit anerkannt und [...] sichert [...] der Wirtschaft den Fachkräftebedarf der Zukunft und trägt damit entscheidend zur Wettbewerbsfähigkeit und zum Wohlstand Deutschlands bei." (Federal Ministry of Education and Research, http://www.bmbf.de/de/1644.php)

1) Agenda setting and problem identification
Regardless of the discourse we consider, the public or the political one, the dual apprenticeship system is assigned the utmost importance. In discussions about non-academic secondary education, this scheme serves as a reference point around which initiatives and reforms revolve. Yet, in fact, recent developments do not support the confidence in the scheme: a trend to higher education, the structural changes to a bifurcated services economy (Eichhorst and Marx, 2009, 7 f.), low educational proficiencies of lower secondary school leavers which render a direct engagement in the dual apprenticeship system difficult (threshold one), and missing routes of progression to further and additional educational options; these are only a few aspects which exert pressure on the system as it is and render alternatives more important. The dual apprenticeship is clearly – to use a common expression in this book – the "gold-standard" of non-academic post-secondary school education in Germany. Yet its merits are increasingly

6.2 Policy reforms in Germany – three cases and their selection

becoming its handicap, because the relationship between supply and demand for dual apprenticeship places indicates that a burgeoning number of young people face massive problems in finding an opening in the dual system. Therefore, the German vocational education system has been equipped with preparatory schemes (the transition system) that are supposed to facilitate entrance into the dual system. The amendment of the Vocational Training Act of 2005 (Berufsbildungsgesetz, BBiG) is yet another attempt to ameliorate the situation in this area.

So what is it exactly that the law is attempting to respond to? What is it that prompted this reform? The significance of the dual apprenticeship system for the German vocational education system is based on two aspects. On the one hand, "quality", as the dual apprenticeship system generates a future workforce with a considerably higher level, plus the chance to get employed with the training company. The merits and the quality-aspect of dual apprenticeships are stressed in the governmental papers, as we have seen. On the other hand, we have "quantity", because until the middle of the 1990s the system had provided vocational education for almost every second German youngster.

Nevertheless, the dual system is in a 'double crisis' at 'threshold one' as well as at 'threshold two' (Deissinger and Hellwig, 2004, 162). The origins of this 'double crisis' are manifold:

- new industrial and service sectors are not able to offset the dramatic loss of training places in declining traditional sectors (Deissinger and Hellwig, 2004, 164);
- new occupational profiles, for example in the IT-sector, are increasingly complex and involve greater theoretical understanding and knowledge;
- new low end service occupations require minimal general educational requirements (Eichhorst and Marx, 2009);
- employers criticise a lack of training maturity among school leavers (Deissinger and Hellwig, 2004, 164);
- among the high-performers from school, universities of applied science have become increasingly more preferred over dual apprenticeships;[123]
- insecurities for potential apprentices because of constantly changing occupational designs, changes rooted in the above mentioned macroeconomic processes (Deissinger and Hellwig, 2004, 164);

---

[123] Between 1994 and 2004 the number of new higher education entrants in Germany increased from 265.952 to 358.704. Particularly remarkable was the rise in entrants in universities of applied science. In the same period, the number in this area rose from 84.407 to 118.963; Federal Statistical Office Germany, http://www.destatis.de/presse/deutsch/pk/2005/hochschulstandort_d_2005i.pdf. This trend not only threatens to weaken the reputation of the apprenticeship scheme but furthermore can not offset the decline in training openings (Deissinger and Hellwig, 2004, 164).

- regional and occupational imbalances.[124]

Yet, and referring to the quantity aspect, recent participation figures tell another story.[125] The development of the supply of dual apprenticeship openings is erratic: between 1999 and 2006 there was a downward tendency, from 654,454 to 591,540 (compare with KIBB, 2008).[126] Yet, the years 2004 and 2006 are exceptions, as openings numbers increased in relation to the preceding years. Moreover, there was a considerable increase from 2006 to 2007 (KIBB, 2008). In 2007 the openings amounted to 644,057 places, an increase of nearly nine percent, mainly due to upward tendencies in the economic and labour market. A similar unsteady process can be observed within the demand figures for dual apprenticeships.[127] However, there is one constant tendency observable across time: the ratio between demand and supply has been consistently unfavourable for those searching for an apprenticeship. Eichhorst et al. call it a suffered loss of collectivist quality (Eichhorst and Marx, 2009, 6). The figure of un-placed applicants reached a peak of about 49,453 in 2006 and dropped considerably in 2007 to 29,053 (KIBB, 2008).

In 2006, among all applicants for a dual apprenticeship, the share of those who had already applied for a place during the previous year(s) was 40 percent (Ulrich and Krekel, 2007).[128] In other words, only 60 percent of the applicants applied for the first time.[129]

---

[124] E.g., the construction sector (a sector that has traditionally employed many low school achievers) has been in a constant downturn since the 1990s. Exemplifying a regional imbalance, youngsters in eastern Germany generally have more problems in finding an apprenticeship in their local area, a fact which again confirms the huge dependence of the system on the general economic situation.

[125] Compare with Baethge, 2007, 44: participation figures for dual apprenticeship system in 1995 were at 51.2 percent, in 2004 at 43.3 percent, while participation in the transitional system in 1995 was at 31.9 percent; 2004 at 39.5 percent.

[126] The development is complemented by an increasing number of school leavers, from 760,000 in 1992 to 950,000 in 2005; see Federal Statistical Office Germany, http://www.destatis.de/basis/d/biwiku/schultab16.php.

[127] In the last decade the absolute figures range from 595,706 in 2002 to 660,380 in 1999; KIBB, 2008.

[128] In 2006, 371,500 of 763,000 registered job and training seekers started an apprenticeship in the dual system. About 49,500 (6 percent) found neither a place in vocational education and training nor in the labour market, which is the highest number since the reunification. Around 45 percent of all registered seekers pursue a vocational education outside the dual scheme (Engelbrech and Ebner, 2006, 1 f.).

[129] In absolute terms: 302,100 of a total 762,800 applicants; Ulrich and Krekel, 2007, 1. It is here where we encounter one of the key issues in German vocational education statistics, namely the so-called supply-demand-relation (Angebot-Nachfrage-Relation, ANR), a tool used to express the relation between the supply of apprenticeship openings and the demand for them. Yet we need to handle this tool with caution. As Ulrich points out, this tool disregards at least two groups that need to be included in order to obtain a comprehensive picture: those registered but not actively searching

6.2 Policy reforms in Germany – three cases and their selection

One of the strongest arguments in favour of a school-based vocational education system on an equal footing with the dual system stems from closely considering the above-outlined figures. The rise of vocational education on a school basis has led to an amelioration of the lack of places on the apprenticeship market; yet, it has neither tackled the problem sustainably, nor has it filled the gap entirely. Therefore, the transition system has considerably increased in significance over the last one and a half decades (Antoni et al., 2007)[130] without, however, improving its status. In other words a course in the transition system – as the word implies – is meant to be complemented by "real" vocational education.[131]

Thus, as overall places in the dual apprenticeship scheme do not match their demand and as the transition on threshold one (from school to vocational education and training) has become more difficult (which has caused a massive increase in the transition scheme)[132] full-time school vocational education has been assigned a crucial role. Yet, most of these courses are outside the BBiG and consequently are not approved or examined by the chambers. Hence, their "real value" in terms of acceptance on the labour market is meagre. Therefore, the amendment law is a major attempt to strengthen vocational school education by allowing it to obtain a status equal to dual apprenticeships.

2) Policy formulation, adoption, path deviation
The amendment of the Vocational Training Act of 2005 (Berufsbildungsgesetz,

---

for a dual apprenticeship because they are in the "transition system", but who in fact wish to enter a full-value vocational education; and those who for various reasons are not registered at all with the Federal Employment Agency (see Ulrich, 2006). The first group counts in the statistics as people who have been placed in some kind of non-academic post-secondary school education; in fact, however, the overwhelming majority would be unlikely to pursue one of these programmes if they were accepted in the dual system. Thus, for most young people the "transition system" is nothing more than a "wait loop". Based on data from 2005, Ulrich shows that when accounting for these two disregarded groups the ANR is not 95.2 but 81.1, resulting in a lack of openings of around 142,000 instead of 28,300 (see Ulrich, 2008, 9).

[130] As Ulrich (2008, 4), shows the participation share in this scheme grew by around 120 percent between 1992 and 2006.

[131] It is transitional in the sense that it is supposed to assist those school leavers who do not succeed in entering the first training market with vocational preparatory courses. Often these young people are labelled and stigmatised as "deprived youth" (benachteiligte Jugendliche). These courses do not provide a fully-valid vocational education – which gives them the transitional character – but pursue the aim of bringing these young people into the first training market. Thus it comes as no real surprise that this system is perceived as a "wait loop" or "parking area" for low-achievers (Ulrich and Krekel, 2007; Ulrich, 2008). As a consequence, the transition system hides youth unemployment (Greinert, 2006, 50).

[132] The situation on the first training market improved considerably in 2007. Some argued that evidenced the influence of the training pact. This is hard to prove. It seems clear, however, that improvements on the labour market have an impact also on the training market.

BBiG) marked a noticeable reconsideration of the German vocational education scenery.[133] The law is a reaction to a situation in which more and more school leavers are compelled to opt for courses in the transition system or for vocational education outside the ambit of the BBiG and who thereby lack the chance to be examined and certified by the chambers. Chamber examinations are still critical for obtaining a "vocation". This vocation is of vital importance for entering the first labour market, the "qualificational space" (Maurice, Sellier and Silvestre, 1986). Allowing young people to pursue full-school vocational education programmes that are certified by the chambers – as suggested by the law – is considered to facilitate both the acceptance of these "non-dual" programmes and their participants' entrance into the labour market. This law deviates from the expected path, as a supply-led orientation of the system challenges the corporatist shape of the system. Moreover, the system would no longer be characterised by its two learning sites. Yet it could render state-provided vocational education more accepted.

Broadly speaking the aim of the amendment law is twofold. On the one hand, the legislation is supposed to facilitate further modularisation. For instance, periods abroad during a vocational education programme or vocational preparatory courses shall be taken into account and be accredited (see articles 7). Moreover, as article 45 BBiG states, even former working experiences can allow for an accreditation towards final exams conducted by the chambers – a clear indication towards a more competence-based approach rather than the traditional input and curriculum-based approach. Thereby these stipulations comply with the so-called Copenhagen declaration, which seeks to establish a European vocational education area equivalent to the Bologna process in higher education. Hence, the government brings modularisation efforts into alignment as a further step to internationalise the German vocational education system (BMBF, 2002). As such, the governmental papers regularly state the advantages of a more modularised system and, therefore, herald further steps in this direction (compare with BMBF, 2002, 2008a).

On the other hand, the provision is an attempt to introduce a second vocational education pillar based on full-time schooling and which is on an equal footing with the dual apprenticeship system in order to emancipate non-academic post-secondary schooling education from the dual system. The reason for this attempt lies in the fact that the training market situation for dual apprenticeships is highly dependent on economic trends and, consequently, also on the labour market situation. In other words, a weak economy has an impact on available openings in the dual system, as the governmental papers already elucidated

---

[133]Commonly the vocational education scenery in Germany is subdivided into three categories: dual apprenticeships, full-time school vocational education, and transition system.

(compare for instance BMBF, 2008b). The establishment of an equivalent school-based track could help to tackle these shortages by offering a steady supply of training places regardless of the situation on the dual apprenticeship market.

The share of applicants who have already applied for a place in the first training market in previous years is high. Contemplating this situation from a different angle, we might contend that these young people can be understood as being unemployed, as they rather likely would enter the first training market if they could.[134] Thus the transition system is accused of concealing youth unemployment. The predatory competition for dual apprenticeship openings leads to high participation rates in the transition system (compare with Ulrich, 2008, 4). According to this standpoint, the amendment law would offer those young people who get caught in this "wait loop" a chance to obtain a recognised occupation and thereby will reduce youth unemployment. Yet the issue of how school-based vocational education is to be matched with the demand for it is not further problematised.

The amendment of the Vocational Training Act of 2005 (Berufsbildungsgesetz, BBiG) allows for full-time vocational education courses to be finished by exams conducted by the chambers, which are held in high esteem (article 43, para. 2 BBiG). This privilege is traditionally reserved only for dual apprenticeships. Thereby, the initiative touches upon a quasi-sacrosanct symbiosis between the highly regarded dual apprenticeships and the chamber exams. The main aim that is being pursued with this initiative is the amelioration of youth unemployment and ensuring social integration and labour market participation (Schröder, 1998, 2002; BMBF, 2002, 2008a).

Unsurprisingly, this reform provoked fierce reactions. Educational discourses in Germany often reflect the conflict over competencies between the federal level and the states. This applies also to vocational education. In addition, however, the social partners and the chambers are included in the discourse as well. This renders the discourse even more complex and reforms more difficult. As a consequence, the initial version of the amendment law that was promoted by the federal government was highly contested among all parties in Parliament, including the governing ones. Articles 7, 43 and 45 were criticised in particular, as they included a legal entitlement for full-time vocational school pupils to be certified and examined by the chambers.

The reactions in Parliament reflect this controversy. Most statements heralded the "success story" (Brase, SPD, in Plenarprotokoll, 2004, 12351) of the dual system and simultaneously expressed concerns about sacrificing the dual

---

[134] As apprenticeship contracts count as employment contracts – and fall under the ambit of labour law – apprentices are registered as employed persons.

scheme, namely that the increased value placed on school-based programmes would automatically lead to the devaluation of the dual system (Hartmann, FDP, in Plenarprotokoll, 2004, 12346). The debate reveals the common understanding of the dual system: the dual system as a locational advantage for Germany (Schummer, CDU/CSU, in Plenarprotokoll, 2004, 12342); the merits of the scheme for tackling youth unemployment; or the apprehension about a "change of paradigm" if another scheme was introduced on a levelled playing field (Brase, SPD, in Plenarprotokoll, 2004, 12351).[135]

These parliamentary reactions are complemented by those of the social partners, which are – by and large – along the same lines. Both the employer organisation DIHK and the German Federation of Trade Unions (DGB) oppose the formal equalisation of school-based vocational education and the dual system (compare Greinert, 2006, 59). Additionally, the division of competencies between the federal level and the states triggered harsh criticism from the states, as they saw the federal level as encroaching upon their right to stipulate the site of school learning in the dual system (Greinert, 2006, 60 f.).

The first draft law, which intended to ensure a common federal procedure for the new initiatives, was rejected. Instead, the crucial new provisions were placed under the ambit of the states. These have to decide, in close cooperation with the state-commissions for vocational education (Landesausschüsse für Berufsbildung) in which the social partners have the voting majority, how and to what extent they make use of the options the amendment entails (compare with Greinert, 2006, 56). The justification for the ultimate modification of the amendment law was that the law does not intend to introduce a new school-based vocational education scheme on equal footing with the dual apprenticeship system, but rather to provide an approximation of the former to the latter. Yet, though these provisions are limited in duration (until August 2012), some states have begun to make use of them.[136] For these states, this process involved rather long and cumbersome negotiations with the state commissions for vocational education about the exam standards, while the chambers' monopoly on conducting examinations was maintained (Bellaire and Brandes, 2007).

---

[135]In this context Greinert speaks of a "grotesque lack of contact with reality" (Greinert, 2006, 58) when MPs argue that the dual apprenticeship system leads to lower youth unemployment rates (yet, as we have seen, there is hidden youth unemployment) and that the "academia-isation and school-isation" of vocational education would lead to a sustained loss in quality, to more bureaucracy, higher costs, and a disadvantageous decoupling of general education and work-based experience.

[136]Bavaria, Hesse, Mecklenburg-Western Pomerania, Lower Saxony, North Rhine Westphalia and Thuringia enacted directives in order to allow admission to chamber examinations. Rhineland-Palatinate and Schleswig-Holstein depend on voluntary agreements with the chambers (compare with Bellaire and Brandes, 2007, 6 ff.).

3) Theoretically grasping the discourse
The discourse is a mixture of confidence about the dual system and its merits (for instance Plenarprotokoll, 2004, 12340 ff.), on the one hand, and, on the other, about some major deficiencies that revolve around dual apprenticeships. As the dual system is conceived of as the backbone of the German vocational education area and remains, therefore, unaltered in its core structure, the efforts to strengthen school-based vocational education can be understand as an act of "layering", as it is neither meant to displace the existing system nor is the existing system exhausted (compare with Streeck and Thelen, 2005, 20 ff.). Instead, the option for the states to allow for vocational school-based programmes to be evaluated by the chambers has been established alongside the dual system. Therefore "layering" is the appropriate tool for describing the mode of change in this area.

Yet we can speak also of a "drift". This does not, of course, apply to the reform, but to the dual system that the reform is supposed to complement. As Streeck and Thelen say: "the world surrounding an institution evolves in ways that alter its scope, meaning, and function" (2005, 25). The dual system was once the functional complement to higher education: apart from those pupils in higher secondary schools who went onto higher education institutions, the dual system was a socially integrating education scheme pooling those young people from middle and lower secondary school tracks and providing them with vocational education, status and identity. What we observe in Germany nowadays, however, tells another story. Roughly speaking, one-third of an age cohort goes onto higher education, slightly more than one-third is in the dual system, and another one-third is neither in higher education nor in the dual system.[137] This last third are "outsiders" to the system of recognition, esteem and status.[138] "Drift" applies in the sense that the dual apprenticeship system is not able to provide a vocational education to all those young people below the higher education school track who are willing to do an apprenticeship. They are, thereby, deprived of the merits the dual system generates: the "concept of vocation", status, and occupational self-fulfilment (compare with Ulrich, 2006; Ulrich and Krekel, 2007; Ulrich, 2008).

To take the analysis further, the mechanisms for change reveal a paradoxical situation: the slight loss of scope of the scheme (generation of employer-tailored skills by means of the dual apprenticeship) has led to situation

---

[137]Share of freshmen enrolled in higher education institutions was 37 percent (Bildungsberichterstattung, 2008, 7) with another 30.5 percent in the dual system (Bildungsberichterstattung, 2008, 96).

[138]The exceptions are vocations in the social, care and child-care area, which are traditionally taught outside the dual system.

in which fewer people are socially and occupationally integrated. The remedy for the latter is to be achieved by fostering the former. Cause and effect are turned upside down. Thereby, the amendment law reveals a tendency of "conversion", as the aim of training for the sake of participatory principles supersedes the purpose generating specific skills.

Clinging to the dual apprenticeship system, is not merely a matter of conviction but serves also for the "reduction of uncertainty" (compare with Blyth, 2002). All the pressure points the dual system is exposed to seem to make actors unsure about the appropriate steps to tackle the situation. Relying on what has up to now had "high esteem" and "international reputation" reduces uncertainty (compare with theoretical framework in chapter 2.4). Therefore, the dual system in its basic structure remains untouched. The communicative part of the discourse, as displayed in the papers, attempts to stress the merits of the system, the coordinative part is guided by the attempt to come to an agreement with employers to supply more apprenticeship openings, something which ultimately led to the so-called "Training Pact" of 2004. Interestingly enough, it is the dual apprenticeship system itself which served as a kind of blueprint for the new reform. Yet, the "blueprint", in the terms of Blyth (2002), does not so much refer to the system in terms of content and curricula; rather the amendment law (BBiG) is concerned with the valuation and preservation of the status of dual apprenticeships. School-based vocational education must undergo similar procedures in order to be recognised at the same level as the dual system: it is the exams conducted by the chambers that are supposed to confer status and vocation and, thereby, set in motion integrating effects in the labour market.

If we try to grasp the discourse with the ideational matrix based on Campbell and Schmidt (compare with chapter 2.3.3) we see a deeply rooted belief and underlying assumption in the background of the debate which equates the dual apprenticeship system with high productivity rates, high export shares and high profile manufactured goods. In terms of cognitive ideas – based on the prior underlying assumption – we notice the acknowledgement that youth unemployment is too high and that efforts should be undertaken to ameliorate the situation (for instance Schröder, 1998, 2002). However, as for "frames" and "public sentiments", hence the normative-led discourse, we see implicit and explicit attitudes and statements in the Parliamentary debate (Plenarprotokoll, 2004, 12340 ff.) that clearly stress the merits of the system "as we know it" and, thereby, declare it both sacrosanct and as a reference point for every other reform in the field.

Now, what drives this reform? The amendment law also contains additional steps for a further modularisation of vocational education, thereby allowing for easier "travelling" between different educational options, right up to allowing for a cumulative exam procedure. Of course, however, it is also an effort towards a more competence-based approach that stresses certified educational building blocks over entire "vocations". Thereby, this effort is a major attempt to comply with the so-called Copenhagen process, the equivalent in vocational education to the Bologna process in higher education. Copenhagen seeks to promote greater job-mobility among the members through a European Credit (Transfer) System for Vocational Education and Training (ECVET). As the Copenhagen declaration is non-binding, we might speak here of a policy diffusion driver, such as "learning through communication".

Yet, as with the initial attempt to establish a vocational school-based scheme on a levelled playing-field with the dual apprenticeship system, exogenous drivers are more difficult to detect. In fact, we observe a functional necessity to adapt the system to an ever bigger social problem, namely that many young people striving for an apprenticeship opening without success are being placed in a "wait loop" in the transition system or drop out of the statistics altogether. This aim is tantamount to what we have seen in the governmental documents: decreasing youth unemployment and ensuring social and labour market participation and integration (Schröder, 1998, 2002; BMBF, 2002, 2008a). As a consequence, youth unemployment on the one hand and a – perceived – lack of qualified employees which threatens Germany's high labour productivity on the other hand (compare with papers BMBF, 2002; Schröder, 2004; BMBF, 2008a) have led to the proposal to allow vocational school leavers access to chamber exams. Even the ultimately less radical amendment law cannot belie the fact that it contests the omnipresence of the dual apprenticeship system.

4) Post-implementation critique on mode of operation
This section will elaborate on two particular points of criticism in further detail.

Quality, participation and esteem
Doing a dual apprenticeship not only leads to a vocational certificate; it defines and determines to a large extent the social status and social integration of an individual and, thereby, the degree of "self-fulfilment" – as understood by the papers. The burgeoning transition system and school-based vocational education sector, both of which do not lead to a full-value and fully recognised vocational education, lead to a situation in which the dual apprenticeship system is not sufficient for providing these extra-vocational items. Thus scholars advocate the establishment of a second vocational education pillar, one which is school-based and formally on equal footing with the dual apprenticeship (compare with initial draft law in Greinert, 2006, 58). In other words, the vocational education system

would need to become more independent of economic trends and the job market.

Opponents, however, have reservations that this development will occur at the expense of the high quality and high esteem that the dual apprenticeship scheme enjoys (for instance Schummer, CDU/CSU, in Plenarprotokoll, 2004, 12342). It is feared that the standards will be watered down if people who were not able to find an opening on the first training market are accepted to sit chamber exams. This concern applies in particular to the group of young people who lack "trainability". This view is complemented by concerns that rendering higher education more easily accessible (for instance by bachelor degrees) would deprive the scheme of the more talented youngsters and, thereby, further lead to a devaluation of the dual apprenticeship system.

Detachment from practical learning site and labour market regulation
Criticism is also raised about a possible decoupling of off-the-job skills and general skills, on the one hand, and work-based experiences, on the other. As the above mentioned reactions in Parliament illustrate, it is feared the amendment will spark a "change of paradigm" that undermines a core characteristic of the dual system, namely the unity of both learning sites in one scheme. Moreover, the supply-led character of the amendment law could ultimately lead to a mismatch of supply and demand for particular vocations.

5) Evaluation
As we may recall, the amendment law was passed despite considerable concerns about the quality of the scheme and a putative loss of international competitiveness (compare with statements in Parliament, Plenarprotokoll, 2004). Hence, we may suspect that additional "other considerations" weighed on the decision, considerations that go beyond varieties of capitalism's concerns about international competitiveness.

Yet, what are these "other considerations" according to the governmental documents and how are these considerations met by the reform? They are about providing highly qualified future employees, about apprehensions regarding a mismatch of supply and demand on the labour market, and above all about ameliorating the situation for young persons on the training and labour market (Schröder, 1998, 2002). Yet, and even more importantly, the difference between the first version of the law and the version that passed the two legislative chambers was driven mainly by concerns about the scheme itself (Greinert, 2006). It is here that we detect that the debate is not about the dual apprenticeship scheme as such; the crucial point actually lies in the admission to sit final examinations conducted by the chambers. Thus, on the one hand we observe that apprehensions and considerations about international

6.2 Policy reforms in Germany – three cases and their selection 281

competitiveness are subordinated to social policy and labour market policy issues, as the varieties of capitalism literature would predict. On the other hand, however, when it comes to the issue of chamber exams the German vocational system appears to be rather stable, robust and esteem-oriented, if not to say "path-dependent": it is the chambers that have the "vocation awarding power" and these vocational certificates are the entrance cards to the qualificational space (see Maurice, Sellier and Silvestre, 1986), to social participation and integration. Hence, even given a profound change prompted by the reform, the discourse about the BBiG amendment law and its ultimate output retain the uncontested and prominent anchor of the vocational education and training system, namely chamber examinations on the way to attaining a vocation.

We now need to turn to the impact of the reform. The amendment law consists of three strands: the accreditation of vocational preparatory courses in the transition system so that the count towards a full-time, full-value vocational education (as for instance through a dual apprenticeship) according to section 7 BBiG; the admission for leavers from vocational school-based programmes to be approved by the chambers according to section 43 (2) BBiG; and the admission to final examinations conducted by the chambers if a person produces evidence that s/he worked in a specific occupation for a given time according to section 45 (2) BBiG.

The success of the stipulation of section 43 (2) BBiG is not yet clear. In 2006 only 4,641 persons were admitted to final exams after having passed full-time vocational school programmes (see BMBF, 2008b, 149). One reason for the modest use of this provision lies in the shape of this section: it is basically under the ambit of the states to make use of it. According to the vocational education report issued in 2008, only two states applied the stipulation of section 43 (2) BBiG (in North Rhine-Westphalia and Thuringia, BMBF, 2008b, 195).[139]

The stipulations of section 45 (2) BBiG resemble more of a competence- and output-oriented approach. If a person produces evidence of having worked in a particular occupation for at least one and a half times as long as is prescribed as being the period of initial training, s/he shall be admitted to the final examinations by the chambers. Putting it in less legal terms, a person working this period in an occupation is considered to have obtained enough work experience and occupational competences to be allowed to sit the exams. This is a major deviation from the rigorous input- and curriculum based German approach to vocational education. The German vocational education report issued in 2008 provides some evidence as to what extent this provision was applied in 2006, with 24,617 persons admitted to final examinations according to

---

[139] For further information about how the different efforts of states by applying the BBiG see Bellaire and Brandes, 2007.

section 45 (2) BBiG (see BMBF, 2008b, 149).

The greater modularisation provide for in section 7 BBiG – let alone the longitudinal effort to pool core qualifications of different occupations in one certificate or the option of cumulative examinations instead of one single final examination – also evidences a slightly altered approach from strict curriculum focus. The 2008 vocational education report finds that eight states passed regulations based on section 7 BBiG BMBF, 2008b, 195; compare with outline in Bellaire and Brandes, 2007).

In comparison to those 551,434 young people who started a dual apprenticeship in 2006, the 29,258 – hence a share of 5.3 percent – who bypassed the dual system and yet were admitted to final exams appears to be a very small group. Yet, and despite the fact that the amendment law will expire on August 2012, we might suspect that the significance of this reform will increase in the coming years for the following reasons:

1. The transition system has grown ever since it was created, and it has especially increased its significance during periods of economic declines and a tight labour market. Figures from the national education report issued in 2008 confirm this observation. With the exception of 2006 – an exception which proves the rule – the transition system has grown from 341,137 (31.9 percent of all those people in vocational education) in 1995 to 503,401 (39.7 percent) in 2006 (Bildungsberichterstattung, 2008, 96). One might want to supply these young people additional possibilities than just the hope of becoming employed at some point in the future with an employer within the dual system.
2. The dual apprenticeship system itself exerts pressure on the vocational education system. It cannot absorb all those willing to do an apprenticeship because the dual apprenticeship system has constantly been taken as a reference point along which other vocational education and training measures are assessed. Therefore these measures mostly fall behind the dual system in terms of esteem and acceptance.
3. Paradoxically, the reform itself can lead to further pressure on vocational education as bandwagon effects do not seem to be unlikely. That means that employers could dis-engage and thereby divest from the dual system because of the temporarily more risk-free and cheaper options the reforms offer.
4. As the vocational education report from 2008 anticipated, there are negotiations going on in additional states to those which have already applied the new "room for manoeuvre" the amendment law offers. As various actors are involved – among them business and chambers, which are by and large rather unreceptive to the reform (in particular because they fear a loss in

quality) – negotiations are cumbersome and take a long time (compare with Bellaire and Brandes, 2007).
5. After all it will take some time to convince businesses of the merits of vocational education certificates that are not obtained through the "regular" dual apprenticeship pathway even if approved by the chambers. In particular the last two aspects point to some possible hindrances to the entire development of the reform. Time will show whether these obstacles can be overcome.

The reform represents a deviation from what we might expect based on the indicators that were described in the historical chapter. The strict input- and curriculum-based approach has been loosened. The work-based training site – one of the two sites of the dual apprenticeship system – is now complemented by a work-based competence-obtaining work experience site (section 45 (2) BBiG) that does not require attending vocational schools (the second site). As the figures show, usage of the stipulation of the reform are modest so far (Bellaire and Brandes, 2007). This is also related to the fact that in 2006 and 2007 the training market improved somewhat. It might be expected that figures will rise considerably when the economy again weakens. However, the deviation from some of the core backbones of the system indicates a transformative even if gradual change in the perception of vocational education due to functional adaptation processes.

The sustainability of the 2005 BBiG reform is difficult to assess. The dual apprenticeship system remains the "gold standard". Therefore, attempting to assess the reform leads us inevitably to anticipate future developments of the dual system. As Walden predicts, on the basis of recent figures there will not be an easing of tension in the training market before the middle of the next decade unless there is a significant economic upturn – as the year 2007 to some extent showed (Walden, 2006, 44 ff.). Therefore, the mismatch between the supply and demand of apprenticeship openings is likely to continue.

However, some questions should be raised before we attempt to use these pieces of evidence to make inferences about the overall skill patterns in Germany. Estevez-Abe, Iversen and Soskice (2001) claims that the German skill patterns are specialised, that either firm or at least industry-specific skills prevail over general skills. One of the main pillars of this argument is the existence of the dual apprenticeship system. Yet, as the figures in the section about the Vocational Training Act reform show, only around 40 percent of an age cohort passes the dual system – hence 60 percent do not. If we now take into account the English attempt to provide industry-specific skills[140] we might be tempted to

---

[140] Remember that these initiatives are not only confined to the vocational education and training area but extend into the higher education area, e.g. foundation degree.

question the distinction between Germany as a firm- and industry-specific skills based political economy, on the one hand, and the general skills focused English political economy, on the other. This is even more true given the increasing significance of the service sector, which displays an ongoing bifurcation with a raising stress on general skills (compare with Eichhorst and Marx, 2009, 6 ff.).

If we start from the facts about ratios and participation numbers and consider them against the background of the theoretical and political discourse, some doubts arise over the significance of the dual apprenticeship system. Yes, the significance is still huge, but is it large enough to allow inferences concerning the skill patterns of the whole society? Moreover, it is clear that the reform is fuelled by considerations about a functional-driven adaptation to problems rather than a solution in terms of institutional competitiveness that emphasises considerations about institutional complementary. The Vocational Training Act of 2005 (Berufsbildungsgesetz, BBiG) exemplifies this development.

6.2.3 Initiative of excellence

> "Es könnte sein, dass sich dieser 13.Oktober rückblickend als eines der wichtigsten Daten der deutschen Universitätsgeschichte erweist. Der Exzellenzwettbewerb hat die Universitäten, ja das ganze Wissenschaftssystem in Bewegung gebracht." (Ernst-Ludwig Winnacker, President of the German Research Foundation in: Die Zeit, 2006.)

1) Agenda setting and problem identification
The German higher education system had been characterised by an astonishing equity among higher education institutions and the unity of research and teaching. Until the launch of the initiative of excellence there had been no "Oxbridge", no "beacon universities", and no Ivy-League universities (compare with Hartmann, 2006). The initiative of excellence is a first attempt to institutionalise a stratified system and to stress excellence and diversity (Hornbostel, Simon and Heise, 2008, 101).

Yet, the initiative of excellence (Exzellenzinitiative) is not the only major change and reform in Germany's higher education area. Introducing tuition fees, the "Bologna process" and a new university-pact that is hoped to ensure sufficient university places for an expected increase in student numbers form the context in which the initiative of excellence is situated. In this list, the initiative seems to be just one additional item that indicates a remarkable and comprehensive alteration in higher education.

Together with the conversion of "Diplom" and "Magister" degrees to

6.2 Policy reforms in Germany – three cases and their selection

bachelor and master degrees, the initiative of excellence is likely to be conducive to two major path-deviating developments: competition between higher education institutions and a loosening of the unity of research and teaching.

Using the concepts of stratification and marketisation helps us to understand the ongoing developments. The initiative of excellence uses the latter to attain the former. The purpose and politically desired effect of the initiative is to stratify the German research scenery in order to obtain cutting-edge and innovative research outcomes (see president of the science council (Wissenschaftsrat) in forschung, 2005; compare also Hornbostel, Simon and Heise, 2008, 97 ff.). An application tender that places higher education institutions in competition with each other is the means by which to achieve stratification. Hence, the initiative qualifies as a potential deviator from the path German higher education is supposed to follow (compare with chapter 4.3.2).

Interestingly enough, it was the social-democratic chancellor Schröder that proclaimed already in 1998 (the year the SPD won the general elections) the need to focus on excellence in higher education and to introduce competition (Schröder, 1998; compare with Focus, 2007).[141] Already one year later, Bulmahn highlighted this appeal (BMBF, 1999). Yet, it took five more years before the government initiated the programme "Brain up! Deutschland sucht seine Spitzenuniversitäten" (Germany searches for its top universities), announced by Bulmahn in January 2004 (BMBF, 2004).

In her speech on the occasion of the congress "Deutschland. Das von morgen." Bulmahn discussed for the first time the programme that eventually became the initiative of excellence. She highlighted the central importance of innovation ("Innovationen sind das Lebenselixier einer Gesellschaft" BMBF, 2004), teaching and research for a society and criticised Germany for failing to invest in education and research in the 1980s and 1990s. Though on an abstract level she refers to both research and teaching, when she outlines the steps that Germany has to take we clearly see a focus on research.[142] Moreover, as she points out, research is not an end in itself; rather, research should be concentrated on those areas that ensure high returns both in terms of jobs and economic prosperity. It goes almost without saying that the context in which Bulmahn perceives Germany to be embedded is one in which globalisation dictates the rules of the game, in which high investments in research and development lead

---

[141] Several scholars trace the initiative back to a speech held by the Federal President Roman Herzog in 1997. He appealed to the public that a "Ruck durch Deutschland" (a jolt trough Germany) was needed (see Hornbostel, Simon and Heise, 2008, 5).

[142] Probably, the focus on research is due to the complicated competence structure between the federal level and the states, because according to the *Grundgesetz* the federal level has a slightly greater impact on research than on teaching in higher education.

to economic growth, in which action is required because competitors are perceived to be "catching up", and one in which Germany needs to be forearmed to defend its position as an export-champion (compare with chapter 5.4 for an elaboration on these lines of argumentation).

Three major guidelines are at the centre of Bulmahn's outline (BMBF, 2004, 3):
1. More expenditures for research, but also more research for the money invested (Mehr Geld für die Forschung, aber auch mehr Forschung für's Geld!)
2. Support must prioritise job creation (Gefördert wird, was Fortschritt und Arbeit schafft.)
3. Creating top universities for attracting the most intelligent researchers (Mit Spitzenuniversitäten die klügsten Köpfe gewinnen.)

It is mainly about harnessing research for economic and labour market purposes. Bulmahn reveals she has a very technology-centric understanding of this process:

> "Technologien und Forschungsfelder der Zukunft für die Arbeit und den Wohlstand von morgen – das sind für mich Informations- und Kommunikationstechnologien, die Bio- und Nanotechnologie sowie die Gesundheits- und Nachhaltigkeitsforschung. [...] Kurz, wir fördern das, was Fortschritt und Beschäftigung schafft!" (BMBF, 2004)

We will see later on that this "technological understanding" will be applied to the initiative of excellence as well. Crucial guidelines for recalibrating the German higher education system are the introduction of more competition, better networking, more chances for new talents, and less bureaucracy (BMBF, 2004, 5 f.). These remarks culminate in the evidence that Germany lacks top universities:

> "Was uns fehlt, sind Spitzenuniversitäten, die weltweit strahlen und die klügsten Köpfe anlocken." (BMBF, 2004, 9).

2) Policy formulation and adoption

In the same speech and soon after the above statement Bulmahn proclaims the competition "Brain up! Deutschland sucht seine Spitzenuniversitäten! Ich möchte mit deutschen Spitzenuniversitäten die klügsten Köpfe gewinnen!" (BMBF, 2004, 10). This title, which too closely resembles that of game shows, was abandoned shortly afterwards. The term "top university" was substituted by excellence – a concession to traditional social-democrats for whom equity among universities is the leading *sacred cow* (Barlösius, 2008). A year and a half later the federal level and the states agreed on a compromise for what has since been called the "initiative of excellence". As we will see later on, the content of the initiative has been even more tailored towards research than "Brain up! "; however, the initiative emphasises and further elaborates on the main aspects of the initial paper.

An agreement on the programme was not easily achieved. The initiative of excellence was concluded during a period that was dominated by debates about restructuring German federalism. In general, the states gained full competencies over higher education issues. Hence, the initiative of excellence is the exception to the rule. Approximately 1.9 billion Euros are being awarded for the duration of the four-year programme, of which the federal level bears 75 percent and the states 25 percent.[143] Since the federalism reform came into effect, the federal level has been relieved of responsibility, and thus expenditures, for the extension and maintenance of universities. Now the money is mainly devoted to the initiative of excellence (Der Spiegel, 2007d).

The initiative of excellence consists of three different lines of funding (compare with Hornbostel, Simon and Heise, 2008, 97 f.; Sondermann et al., 2008, 122 f.). The first is for graduate schools and promotes and supports PhD-students. Secondly, so-called excellence clusters are sponsored. The purpose of this line of funding is to support research clusters of universities and leading German research institutes and business. Thirdly, so-called future-concepts are sponsored. Universities can apply for this line of funding with an innovative approach to teaching and research. The type of application can range from administrative innovation to substantive developments of teaching and research. However, for the last funding component only those universities which have at least one excellence graduate school and one excellence cluster are eligible.

Until 2011 universities are asked to apply annually. So far two rounds of funding have taken place. Funding decisions were made by a joint committee consisting of members from the German Council of Science and Humanities (Wissenschaftsrat) and the German Research Foundation (Deutsche Forschungsgemeinschaft) on the basis of reports by referees, mainly international referees.

In the public debate the initiative was generally welcomed (see Hornbostel, Simon and Heise, 2008, 97). One of the biggest proponents of the initiative of excellence was the president of the German Research Foundation, who championed the day of the proclamation of the initiative as "one of the most important dates for German higher education history" (Die Zeit, 2006). Others herald the fact that equity among higher education institutions is squeezed out in

---

[143] Yet, only those states have to contribute whose higher education institutions are awarded with one of the lines of funding; Hornbostel, Simon and Heise, 2008, 98.

favour of competition, which is believed to be desperately needed in the system. There are those who hope to profit from the initiative and assign it major importance for the future of German higher education (Die Zeit, 2004; Die Zeit, 2005; Die Zeit, 2006; Cicero, 2006). For some scholars the initiative is only a first and necessary step on the way to a transformation of the German research landscape (e.g. Hans Weiler in Deutschlandradio, 2005).

By and large, however, the issue of teaching is almost absent. This is surprising as the – rather general – rhetoric of the initiative of excellence comes up in a context that stresses high productivity rates and high export rates, the need to compete within an international environment, and a debate that criticises the comparatively low participation rates of students in reference to OECD-data. If the goal is to provide excellence and to further facilitate access – let alone to ensure equal access to higher education institutions – in order to reach the OECD-average in student entrance rates (BMBF, 1999, 2002), then the initiative of excellence is only one side of the coin. As outlined in the coming section, this critique illustrates the public and ultimately also the institutional resistance the initiative has to overcome.

3) Theoretically grasping the discourse
In this section the initiative of excellence shall be subsumed under the concepts and tools that were outlined in the theoretical chapter (see chapter 2). We can call the initiative a change in paradigm, in terms of Hall a third-order change (Hall, 1993, 283 ff.). What has occurred in the German higher education area represents a profound change in ideas as "public philosophies" (compare with Schmidt, 2008, 307): the introduction of market mechanisms as a prerequisite for and result of a major step towards stratification. The initiative itself – which can be ranked as either a programme or a concrete policy – reflects straightforwardly the change in public philosophies.

The normative ideas are dominated by an understanding that a higher education system that is based on equality among higher education institutions is no longer sufficient for generating internationally competitive cutting-edge scientific research outcomes. Market mechanisms are seen as a superior solution through their provision of incentives for better performances. The cognitive side of the ideational coin reflects exactly this mindset: the lack of competition is held responsible for Germany's rather modest ranking in international league tables assessing national research endeavours.

As for the interactive components of the discourses, namely coordinative and communicative discourses, and "background ideational abilities" and "foreground discursive abilities", we can state the following: a strong coordinative discourse between the federal level and the states is unavoidable in

6.2 Policy reforms in Germany – three cases and their selection

Germany once educational issues appear on the agenda. Yet we also observe a strong communicative discourse with the public, basically referring to the normative and cognitive ideational aspects of the initiative. The distinction between "background ideational abilities" and "foreground discursive abilities" can help increase our understanding of how the "unexpected changes" come about (compare Schmidt, 2008, 314 ff.). The "foreground discursive abilities" can explain that in launching the initiative of excellence the German actors closely regarded the situations abroad in order to define the benchmarks along which the initiative should be oriented and attempt to emulate the main traits of foreign successes (in this case, the main contributors to the success of the Anglo-Saxon model is considered to be the more marketised and stratified higher education scenery).

Therefore, it comes as no real surprise that the United States and the UK are taken as blueprints for the reforms – or at least this is the intention. Moreover, as Blyth states, ideas can also be used as "weapons" to de-legitimise current institutions and policies (Blyth, 2002, 34 ff.). As we have seen in the elaboration of the reform, this was the case here.

In the political discourse, the public discourse and the scientific discourse it is argued that incentives like those provided by the initiative of excellence are needed in order to allow for more competitive and innovative research outcomes. Thereby, the current system – one which is based mainly on equality of higher education institutions – is being contested and made partly responsible for the only modest performance in international rankings and for effects such as the "brain-drain". This, of course, is underpinned by references to experiences abroad – whereby we can turn to the policy diffusion literature.

We can detect at least two of the diffusion mechanisms offered by the policy diffusion literature that are at work behind the initiative of excellence and its drivers. Most evidently, the initiative is based on what is called "learning from success": countries that are perceived of as being successful – in this case, above all the United States and the UK – offer prescriptions on how success can be achieved.[144] Furthermore, "common norms" play a crucial role. Adopting market measures and introduce stratification and selection procedures seems to be the primary solution offered for higher education systems, as the "winners" incidentally create the norms by which this success has occurred. Of course these are not objectively identifiable criteria, as they depend on how actors interpret the situation. German actors detected a lack of market-based incentives by

---

[144]One might suggest that epistemic communities are operating here as well, defining the problem and providing solutions. In this case we would speak about "learning through communication" – one of the basic diffusion mechanisms the Bologna process rests upon. Yet, indications or evidence for the work of a international epistemic community on how to organise research could not be found.

comparing the domestic system to the "successful ones" and thus attempted to adopt the same tools for success.

The initiative of excellence does not displace the current system (compare with chapter 2.7). The process by which the reform has been implemented is through what Streeck and Thelen call "layering" (2005, 22). Only in the perception of the actors is the current system described as being partly "exhausted"; yet, the system is only further complemented with this initiative, not replaced by it.

4) Post-implementation critique on mode of operation

The reform has to be considered in the context of the other profound – not to say transformative – changes: the introduction of tuition fees, the Bologna process, and increased opportunities for universities to select students. Thus, the following critique of the initiative of excellence cannot be regarded isolated from other developments in this area. The first round provoked huge discussion and criticism for mainly two reasons: regional disparities and discipline disparities.

Excellence versus social sciences and humanities?

Boosting excellence comes at a price which is beyond the amount of money spent for a programme such as the initiative of excellence. Excellence means that there must be "normality" or non-excellence. That this would apply to universities which are not awarded with a line of funding was clear in advance. Yet the disappointment of some institutions after having been disregarded in the first round was exceeded by the shock for whole areas of studies, mostly social sciences and humanities. Among the 17 excellence-cluster that were awarded, only one had a clear social science programme; of the 18 promoted graduate schools only four applied with a concept that touches upon social sciences and humanities; and the three universities that were awarded for their future concept – remember that a requirement for this line of funding is at least one graduate school and one excellence cluster – applied with natural sciences topics (compare with Hartmann, 2006, 451; BMBF, 2008d; Focus, 2007). The second round attempted to compensate for this somewhat, but the prevailing emphasis on sciences remained.

Thus, in particular the first round revealed and highlighted Bulmahn's initial appeal as expressed in "Brain up! ": namely to promote the natural sciences as they promise to be most conducive to economic progress and have positive labour market effects (BMBF, 2004). Thereby, the initiative of excellence perpetuates existing imbalances in funding between sciences on the one hand and social sciences and humanities on the other (Hartmann, 2006, 450 f.), though the latter fields have been massively used to ensure wider access

6.2 Policy reforms in Germany – three cases and their selection

to universities or even to serves as "parking lots" in order to obscure youth unemployment Plümper and Schneider, 2007).

Excellence in the south versus the rest of Germany?
Moreover, it is feared that the so-called "principle of Mathäus" (Mathäusprinzip), i.e. the richer become richer whereas the poor remain in poverty, will exert its influence on the initiative. To some extent, it is argued, this effect was already observable in the results of the first round of the initiative of excellence: the well-off states in the south are more capable of providing an already well above-average scientific infrastructure with close connections to politics and business (Der Spiegel, 2007b; sueddeutsche, 2007b; Focus, 2007) and thus more likely construct convincing proposals and attract additional funding. Indeed, the north-south cleavage, in particular after the first round, was considerable (compare with Hartmann, 2006; Sievers, 2008; Der Spiegel, 2006a).

The quarrel flared up because of the three universities which were awarded for their future concept two are in Munich and one is in Karlsruhe, whereas promising candidates such as Heidelberg, the Freie University in Berlin or the RWTH in Aachen were not successful in their bids (Die Zeit, 2005; Der Spiegel, 2006a; Der Spiegel, 2007c).

Excellence in research versus excellence in teaching?
Another critique which was already raised at the beginning of the initiative of excellence was the mismatch between the increased investments into research and innovation and the lack of further investment in teaching. This fact is even more amazing given the significance attached to teaching as a method of redressing the comparatively low student entrance rates, which are perceived as a major German deficiency (sueddeutsche, 2007a).

The German Council of Science and Humanities has suggested the introduction of criteria to measure and estimate teaching performance at German universities (compare with Hahn, 2007). Hence, as Hahn puts it, what is missing in the initiative of excellence is an "initiative of excellence for teaching" (Hahn, 2006; Die Zeit, 2007). The initiative of excellence runs the risk of being responsible for a development which ultimately leads to a clear division between high esteem "research universities" and those occupied merely with teaching.

Excellent outcomes versus mediocre outcomes?
Some critics claim the initiative will only create positive feedback loops within certain institutions, while not having spill-over effects on the wider research community. Münch, for instance, shows that big universities are more likely to submit an application for a project that requires a line of funding simply because

of the greater manpower to which they can refer (Münch, 2006). Moreover, these universities are, due to their infrastructure and quantity of staff they employ (including professors), more likely to have close relations to politics, business and eventually also to those who decide upon assigning funding (Münch, 2006). The regression analyses he runs prove that the amount of publications – the currency of academia – is not necessarily related to the funding universities get for particular projects from, for instance, the German Research Foundation. He argues that the initiative of excellence fails to the extent that excellence in academia is normally not associated with a university but with particular scholars who happen to be, at a given time in a given place, those scholars with the most cutting-edge research (Münch, 2006; in the same vein Markl in FAZ, 2008; Der Spiegel, 2007a).

Excellence versus mass?
"Excellence" not only tells us something about the work which is perceived to be excellent; excellence goes hand in hand with its reference point, namely ordinariness. For a higher education system such as the German one, which is traditionally based on equality of institutions, this fact alone is almost like an earthquake for the prevailing attitude towards the system. As such, it is a measure to stratify the system. Arguably, the initiative of excellence is primarily focussed on research. Yet, as some first evidence shows, the label "university of excellence"[145] attracts students, regardless of the topic they intend to study and regardless of the profits they intend to gain from this label (Die Zeit, 2008e.). Impacts on the labour market in terms of stratification are not yet observable but seem to be likely to emerge (Sievers, 2008, 24 ff.).

This development comes with increased competencies for the higher education institutions to select their own students. Therefore scholars regard this development as an attempt to introduce a great deal of social selectivity into the system (Hartmann, 2006; Münch in Der Spiegel, 2007a).

5) Evaluation
When contemplating and assessing the reforms against the general educational aims as expressed in the governmental documents we are able to forecast potential developments. This is a feasible task given the evidences we have so far gathered. We can detect four aims in the documents that are related to higher education: ensuring equal access to educational options, ensuring educational chances, shorter duration of studies, and attaining world-class research outcomes. Clearly, only the last aim is directly related to the initiative of

---

[145]"University of excellence" is very close to the original term used in the "Brain up!" programme, which was about finding the "top universities".

6.2 Policy reforms in Germany – three cases and their selection

excellence. As for the benefits of this programme in terms of improving research performances the expectations are high (compare with Die Zeit, 2008f; Cicero, 2006; Die Zeit, 2006; Deutschlandradio, 2005; Stadlbauer, 2006a,b; BMBF, 2004), though some, for instance Münch, are highly critical and sceptical about the quasi-causal relation that drives the programme: the more money, the better the results (compare with Münch, 2006; Der Spiegel, 2007a; FAZ, 2008; Hornbostel, Simon and Heise, 2008, 97 ff.).

As the initiative is focused on research, it is difficult to draw inferences on how the other aims are affected by the reform.[146] As already indicated, the intended purpose of stratifying research endeavours might be accompanied by the unintended effect – or at least as effect that is not explicitly mentioned – of creating stratifying the teaching scenery. Some evidence from newspapers about the effects of the initiative of excellence for students reinforce this assumption (Die Zeit, 2008e). This, however, might thwart the government's aim to ensure equal access to educational options, as the most demanded universities have already introduced or are about to establish selection procedures. Of course demand is highest among those universities that are awarded the initiative of excellence. "Stratification is a political decision" – whether this aspiration is consciously applied also to the teaching side of higher education institutions can not be proven by the evidence in this analysis; yet, regardless of intentions, the unintended effects will quite likely lead to stratification.

The initiative of excellence is transformative in character and is taking effect rather abruptly (Hornbostel, Simon and Heise, 2008, 97 ff.). In particular, the concept of stratification can elucidate the current changes. Stratification comes with higher demands from students for places at high-performing higher education institutions. Selection procedures have already been established or are likely to be established in order to deal with the amount of applications (Die Zeit, 2008d). It is too soon to speculate whether these developments will eventually lead to the existence of some research-intensive universities with high esteem while other universities mainly supplying only teaching.

Moreover, we see a complementary picture of reforms when referencing aspects of the systems in the Anglo-Saxon countries: a stratified system with top universities with top research on the one end and teaching-based universities (universities of applied science reflect this distinction already today) on the other; a system in which student selection becomes the rule and not the exception; a system which attempts to introduce market mechanisms and therefore needs common degrees to enable the comparison of universities; and last but not least a system in which universities gain more administrative power

---

[146]For some preliminary inferences on the three lines of funding, see Sondermann et al., 2008, 122 f.

including raising tuition fees. Furthermore, we find in both countries great tensions between the aspirations to provide both universities for the masses and universities that produce cutting-edge research. One might call it an "identity crisis" for universities, which are caught between generating research on the one hand and, on the other, providing non-research intensive education by means of the bachelor degree for nearly one-half of an age-cohort.

If we perceive these developments against the background of other changes within the German higher education system, one could argue that the initiative of excellence in particular and the whole range of higher education reforms in general are leading to profound, transformative and "path-breaking" changes. There is probably no area in this research in either of the two countries which has been subject to such fundamental reforms as the German higher education area.

In terms of the historical institutionalism literature this development is difficult to explain; the change exhibits none of the characteristics of a "crucial juncture". The distinction between specific and general skills as described in the varieties of capitalism literature about vocational education and training is not of any help in this context either. It is discursive institutionalism that can help us to understand and account for these changes. The discourses show quite clearly – and they do it emphatically in the German case – that the point of reference is not the domestic institutional design and its institutional complementarity. Rather the point of reference is foreign experiences and international benchmarks, underpinned by the common belief in a higher education system that needs to be organised in a stratified manner and needs to comply with the principle that competition and markets lead to superior outcomes.

While in the historical chapter of this research we found the German and the English system to be rather different, we now have to state that they have become more alike – and that this is mainly due to the German reform initiatives rather than the English ones. We are able to understand why change occurs in this fashion only if we accept that a country sometimes "looks over the rim of the tea cup" and adopts ideas that do not necessarily comply with domestic commonsense understanding; the historical institutionalism and varieties of capitalism literatures cannot assist us in accounting for the initiative of excellence reform.

7 Conclusion

"An imperative to adjust?" Referring here to the title of this book, we are now able to answer this question. England and Germany perceive themselves as being exposed to a situation that renders action both necessary and inevitable. The research has provided some indication as to what extent these imperatives are socially constructed (compare in particular with chapter 5.5). Yet, in one way or another, skill formation in England and Germany is hotly debated, fiercely contested and has led to numerous political actions. However, accounting for changes in this area is not as straightforward as the theoretical starting point of this research might have implied. Neither are developments of a path-dependent variety, as historical institutionalism would suggest, nor do these developments comply with the dichotomy between general and specific skills, as provided by the varieties of capitalism literature. Following from this, some major theoretical and empirical arguments will be put forward in what follows.

Educational system analyses require detailed in-depth studies.

Among all the evidence collected in this book, one overarching consideration appears to be of vital importance: we need to apply a rigorous and differentiated view on the topic in order to understand recent developments in educational policy. This careful and detailed consideration comprises at least the following aspects. Firstly, it does not suffice to merely glance at a country or political economy as a whole in order to draw conclusions or make predictions of how and why reforms are launched and implemented. What is required instead is a careful elaboration that appreciates, among other things, that "education" needs to be further subdivided into at least three different educational areas in order for an analysis to be conducted.[147]

Secondly, there is not only one type of institution. As the empirical evidence revealed, we have to distinguish between at least two different types of

---

[147] It goes without saying that these areas can be further subdivided, such as, for instance, with further training and adult education. Taking a comprehensive perspective, all areas that are assigned to lifelong learning could be subsumed under education.

institutions: namely the formal, legally-based ones, which can be opposed to informal, reputation-based ones. Without this distinction the reasons for the successes and failures of reforms might remain hidden. The formal institutional reform Curriculum 2000, for instance, did not fail because it could not prevail over the formal institution of academic-oriented A-levels. Quite the contrary, it was the informal, reputation-based side of the coin, namely the esteem which is ascribed to academic-oriented A-levels, which prevented Curriculum 2000 from becoming equally accepted. The schemes offered by the reform never attained a similar recognition.

Thirdly, different stages and different levels of reforms have to be taken into account. An analysis by means of a policy cycle model turns to the cycle's stages. The cycle ranges from problem identification and agenda setting to implementation and evaluation and, thereby, allows us to contrast initial drivers with the outcome of a reform. Occasionally we encounter reforms that meet the initial aspirations (such as the initiative of excellence) or reforms which miss them (for example Curriculum 2000 and to some extent foundation degrees). Levels, by contrast, refer to horizontal layers, ranging from the abstract ideational level to the concrete implementation process of a distinct policy initiative. Thus, as has become clear, reform processes do not just begin with a concrete proposal and they are not finished once they are implemented. Rather, reforms are embedded in a discursive and institutional context. It is discursive institutionalism that facilitates our comprehension of how and to what extent this context matters. The conceptual tools offered by this approach allow us to unveil the interaction between the discursive and ideational context (especially the first few stages of the policy cycle) on the one hand and the institutional context (the latter stages) on the other.

We can elucidate these aspects by relating them to the theoretical point of departure we started with, hence the literature about varieties of capitalism and historical institutionalism.

The distinction between general and specific skill patterns cannot account for developments in English and German educational policy.

Drawing on the introductory chapter and then considering the acquired evidences, the rather rigid differentiation between political economies with a general skill-focus and those emphasising specific skills has to be challenged. If we consider the discursive level, we do not find many indications that the educational system of the English political economy is general-skill biased as opposed to specific skills in Germany. Apart from the still great tendency for specialisation in higher secondary education despite the Curriculum 2000 reform, there have been long lasting efforts to stress specific skills and even employer-tailored skills by means of apprenticeships and by establishing foundation degrees.

The German picture displays some modest steps in the opposite direction. Developments in higher secondary education – such as G8 and the increasing introduction of centrally organised school leaving examinations, efforts to further modularise vocational education and training, and the slight revaluation of school-based training by means of the BBiG – point to a strengthening of the general-skill component as opposed to specific or employer-tailored skills. This observation is supported by the increasing importance of the services sector, which is increasingly bifurcated (Eichhorst and Marx, 2009). Only in higher education do we observe a tendency to further specialise, as bachelor and master degrees are – by and large – less general than Diplom and Magister degrees. Yet this is not a development which accounts for a distinction with England.

Contemplating these developments on an institutional level, i.e. analysing the reforms in their implemented version when they start to have an influence, displays a slightly different scenario than the strictly discursive level. Frequently an initiative runs up against the existing institutional structure, in many cases a very resistant one. Often this institutional inertia lead to the failure of an initiative, as Curriculum 2000 exemplifies. Nevertheless, the picture as outlined above with respect to skill patterns persists: ranking Germany as a specific-skill focused political economy merely because of the existence of the dual apprenticeship scheme in the area of vocational education and training while disregarding school education and higher education, which are traditionally broad in terms of curricula and thus equally important for defining an overall skill pattern, appears to be as exaggerated as pooling England among the "generalists" mainly due to the non-existence of any dual scheme. The varieties of capitalism literature is a viable starting point for this research; yet, for understanding major developments in educational policy it is of little use.

Path-dependency is not as strong as historical institutionalism suggests.

Historical institutionalism, the main proponent of the concept of path-dependency, has some major points of relevance to this analysis, yet in a different form as one might have expected. Curriculum 2000 and the amendment of the Vocational Training Act (Berufsbildungsgesetz, BBiG) exemplify this contention. Both reforms were introduced and layered alongside existing institutions; hence, there is no displacement mechanism. Thus, both reforms contribute to the existing picture instead of substituting it. Moreover, both reform initiatives seek to maintain the prevalent institutional structure, namely the two "gold standards": A-levels and dual apprenticeships with chamber examinations, respectively. What we observe, however, is that by leaving the institutional "gold standards" untouched the acknowledgement structure, which is centred on these standards, is reproduced, i.e. reforms are assessed with reference to existing institutions. That is the main reason why Curriculum 2000 arguably failed to establish "parity of esteem" and why the BBiG has had considerable problems developing its potential.

In other words, and stressing this seemingly paradoxical point, by attempting to upgrade a new scheme to the level on which the commonly-perceived "gold standards" reside, the reform initiatives are likely to fail. Historical institutionalism can account for this situation, but it does not do so by directly addressing the inability of an initiative to displace a current institution or to become acknowledged as a new scheme in an institutional vacuum. Rather historical institutionalism supplies an explanation for the underlying acknowledgement structure, informal rules but nevertheless institutions, which to a great extent determine the success and/or failure of reforms.

However, we have also found developments for which historical institutionalism cannot account. The radical change in German higher education, for instance, is all but path-dependant. The slight decoupling of vocational education and training from direct employer involvement by means of the amendment law BBiG, the "Anglicisation" of the German economy (growth of low end, low esteem and low skills service jobs; Eichhorst and Marx, 2009), and the great alteration in family structures and working life patterns, of which the G8-reforms are a part, all challenge the concept of path-dependency. The same applies to the English efforts to emphasise the generation of specific skills through apprenticeships and foundation degrees. In the pre-implementation phase we see some considerable tensions with expectations of historical institutionalism, tensions which are perpetuated once reforms are implemented.

Ideas account for unexpected discourses and changes in educational policy.

Discursive institutionalism complements the theoretical picture in that it allows us to explain path-deviant reforms. This approach is particularly strong because it focuses on the policy cycle phases of agenda setting (problem identification), policy formulation and adoption. When the reform arrives at the last two stages, namely implementation and evaluation, two potential scenarios arise. Firstly, a reform which was path-deviant in its discourse remains path-deviant in its

7 Conclusion 299

implemented version. The alterations in German higher education exemplify this scenario. Secondly, and by contrast, the reform may eventually become path-dependant even though it was meant to deviate. In this case – for which Curriculum 2000 is an example – discursive institutionalism helps to discover intentional drivers. Thereby it creates a template against which the reform can be ultimately assessed. Historical institutionalism serves as a calibration point with which as assessment of the eventual impact of a reform on an institutional structure is rendered feasible – either it accounts for it or not.

Discursive institutionalism, however, allows us to trace a reform initiative back to its origins and to elaborate on the ideas and drivers which underlie the initiative.[148] Hence, the ideational component of the discourses allow us to detect commonalities and differences in the self-perception and the perception of the environment of both political economies: the talk about knowledge-based societies, for instance, impacts strongly on both domestic discourses; the utilisation of educational policies for goals in other policy areas such as economic policy, social and labour market policy; the devaluation of education as a value in its own right; the disregard of low-skill jobs that are resistant to socio-economic developments; and the huge impact of international benchmarks and the performances of other, potentially competing, political economies.

Yet, it is also interesting to employ discursive institutionalism in order to analyse how the above-sketched ideas, as in paradigms and public sentiments (or philosophies), are applied, adopted, bent or even ignored once they take the form of concrete policy measures. In England, for instance, one of the most important levers for achieving England's aims is by offering choice, namely choice of schemes, choice of qualifications, choice of certificates, and choice of individually-tailored educational paths. In Germany the aspirations to meet the above-sketched aims has culminated in policy strategies and actions – exemplified in school education and higher education – that are best explained by the policy diffusion literature. We encounter constant references to experiences and initiatives abroad and to international assessments (e.g. PISA) and, frequently, it is only with reference to these that a status quo is perceived as a problem requiring political action in the first place (hence problem identification and agenda setting).

However, evidence from both countries shows that ideas in concrete policies often lose their vigour the closer they are woven into a traditional institutional design. This contention is exemplified by the Curriculum 2000 reform, which failed mainly due to the highly stratified acknowledgement

---

[148] As a rule, the drivers and "initial sparks" of a reform are more easily spotted in England. This is due to the stronger emphasis on the communicative discourse in – as Schmidt calls it – "simple polities" such as England (Schmidt, 2008).

structure in favour of academically oriented A-levels; by foundation degrees, which for most students are a "through station" to honours degrees; and by the resistance to the first draft of the German BBiG because of fears it might impair the credit in dual apprenticeships.

Education systems need to be analysed in their institutional context.

As to the empirical conclusions of this research, we have seen that educational systems are given a crucial role in political economies. Frequently education is ascribed prime importance, yet only as a means to attain objectives in other policy areas, such as economic, social and/or labour market policy. In this context the harnessing and utilitarian character of education becomes salient in England as well as in Germany.

However, as already stated, a detailed elaboration does not allow for education to be treated as a black box, as the varieties of capitalism literature to an extent seems to suggest with it focus on only vocational education and training. It is for this reason that school education and higher education have to be taken into consideration if we are to make a general point about education and its position, function and shape in a political and potentially institutional complementary environment. Yet by attempting nevertheless to make such a general point, we have noticed that a "general point" runs the risk of being too simplistic if it disregards the various levels of an education system.

In fact, and putting the cart before the horse somewhat, "education" is as diverse as are the jobs where these acquired skills are applied: a German engineer, medical practitioner, banker, plumber, civil servant, retailer or porter all have in common the fact that they passed the German education system. So what? Can we really draw inferences, such as "specific skills" versus "general skills", from that?

There are further issues to be regarded once we apply a differentiated view that is not confined to education only but also encompasses a concise elaboration and precise appreciation of its institutional environment. As, for instance, the notion of a knowledge-based society implies, education is seen as just one component which a modern society is supposed to consist of. It reaches other policy areas as well, most apparently economic policy and labour market policy. However, as the concluding section to the paper analysis chapter showed, the perception of a knowledge-based society tends to disregard those secondary and tertiary sectors that have a tendency to be impervious to knowledge-based developments or are at least considerably less affected by them.

That is not to say that knowledge has not challenged traditional economic and labour market patterns. Yet we observe a tendency to neglect almost one-half of the workforce, namely that part which is neither employed in a knowledge-dominated working environment, nor likely to be engaged in it in the future. Hence, the reference to this kind of society in the papers once again reflects well what Keep, Mayhew and Payne have called a "one-size-fits-all" skill strategy with an expected panacea-function (Keep, Mayhew and Payne, 2006, 552).

This ambiguous picture is also reflected in a rather heterogeneous education system that renders parsimonious distinctions and typologies nearly infeasible: in both countries we find odd tensions between the aspirations to provide both universities for the masses and universities that produce cutting-edge research. One might call it an "identity crisis" of universities, torn between generating research, on the one hand, and providing vocational-oriented education, on the other. In vocational education and training both countries aspire for greater involvement by employers (arguably from different starting positions). Meanwhile, both embark on a strategy to expand the system through more choice and schemes, something that could be called a further "programme-atisation". In school education we observe a tendency to economise the system, with the primary aim of creating a qualified future workforce as quickly as possible. If there is one trait that characterises the English and the German education systems best then it is likely to be multifariousness.

England and Germany differ in their impetus to educational reforms.

Nevertheless, there is one decisive difference between the two countries, that of their "reform-impetus". Germany displays a somewhat greater propensity to orientate itself off the experiences of other countries and to refer to international assessments. Germans actually show a slightly lower self-confidence and self-security than is the case in England. The possible merits of the equality-based higher education system are as inconsiderately ignored as the possible advantages of Magister and Diplom-degrees or a thirteen-year schooling period for attaining the Abitur. It is only in vocational education and training, and even within this area it is the dual apprenticeship scheme specifically, which is fully appreciated. England, by contrast, is more conscious of the merits generated by its education system: A-levels, honours degrees, even apprenticeships. In the English context international comparisons are far less influential than they are in Germany.

The question arises, why this is the case? Two possible answers come into mind. First of all, since education policy in Germany is characterised by the involvement of different and numerous actors, references to education policies abroad could be used both as "weapons" to de-legitimise the current system and to thereby offer additional justifications for change and as "blueprints" for new institutions that might be easier to agree upon. Yet as even more likely reason for the difference in impetus is that the English education system is used as a common template for German initiatives. The Bologna process is only the most obvious example: the initiative of excellence attempts to emulate the Anglo-Saxon stratified higher education structure; modularisation in vocational education and training can be thought of as aligning the system with the Copenhagen process, which promotes a competence-based and output-oriented system like the English one; and shortening schooling periods in Germany is justified with reference to shorter periods abroad, of which England is just one example.

Summing all this up, most initiatives are propelled by various drivers, of which economic and social considerations (such as strengthening productivity, lowering unemployment, equipping the economy with skills which are considered necessary to meet contemporary economic challenges) or adapting systems to international standards are only the most prominent. Yet, as both counties pursue an overall supply-led approach to education, both put themselves in the driving seats for producing these skills. It is therefore the case that England and Germany feel exposed to an imperative to adjust; in doing so skill formation has become a pivotal instrument.

8 Bibliography

Allmendinger, Jutta, 1989: Educational Systems and Labor Market Outcomes, in: European Sociological Review 5, 231–250.

Antoni, Manfred, Hans Dietrich, Maria Jungkunst, Britta Matthes Hannelore Plicht. 2007: Die Schwächsten kamen seltener zum Zug, in: IAB Kurzbericht 2, Nürnberg.

Ashton, David N., Jonny Sung, 2006: How competitive strategy matters? Understanding the drivers of training, learning and performance at the firm level, SKOPE Research Paper, Oxford.

Baethge, Martin, 2007: Qualitative und quantitative Veränderungen im Berufsbildungssystem und politische Handlungsoptionen, in: Zukunft des Sozialstaats – Bildungs- und Familienpolitik, Bonn.

Bailey, Bill. 2003: 14-19 Education and Training: Historical Roots and Lessons, in: Nuffield Review of Review of 14-19 Education and Training 3.

Barlösius, Eva. 2008: Leuchttürme der Wissenschaft, in: Leviathan, 36, 149–169.

Baumert, Jürgen, Petra Stanat, Rainer Watermann, 2006: Herkunftsbedingte Disparitäten im Bildungswesen - Vertiefende Analysen im Rahmen von PISA 2000, Wiesbaden, 95–188.

Bellaire, Edith, Harald Brandes, 2007: Das Duale System anders organisieren! – Kombinationsmodelle der Ausbildung an Berufsfachschulen und in Betrieben, Bundesinstitut für Berufsbildung, Bonn.

Bennett, Andrew, Colin Elman, 2006: Qualitative Research: Recent Developments in Case Study Methods, Annual Review of Political Science, 9, 455–476.

Bessy, Christian, 2002: Certification of occupational competencies in the UK – comparison with the French experience, Centre d'Etudes de l'Emploi, Paris.

Bildungsberichterstattung, Autorengruppe, 2008: Bildung in Deutschland 2008 – Ein indikatorengestützter Bericht mit einer Analyse zu Übergängen im Anschluss an den Sekundarbereich I, Bielefeld.

Bildungsberichterstattung, Konsortium, 2006: Bildung in Deutschland, Ein indikatorengestützter Bericht Bildungsbericht, Bielefeld.

Blair, Tony, 1996: "Education, education, education", speech given at Ruskin College, Oxford, December 16th 1996, http://www.leeds.ac.uk/educol/documents/000000084.htm.

Blunkett, David, 2000: Speech on Higher Education at Maritime Greenwich University, 15 February 2000, London: DfEE.

Blyth, Mark, 2001: The Transformation of the Swedish Model – Economic Ideas, Distributional Conflict, and Institutional Change, in: World Politics 54(1), 1–26.

Blyth, Mark, 2002: Great Transformations: Economic Ideas and Institutional Change in the Twentieth Century, Cambridge.

Blyth, Mark, 2003: Same as it Never Was: Temporality and Typology in the Varieties of Capitalism, in: Comparative European Politics (1), 215–225.

BMBF, 1999: Mut zur Veränderung: Deutschland braucht moderne Hochschulen – Vorschläge für eine Reform, by Edelgard Bulmahn, Berlin.

BMBF, 2001: Berufsbildungsbericht 2001, Bundesministerium für Bildung und Forschung, Berlin.

BMBF, 2002: Bildung, Forschung, Innovation – der Zukunft Gestalt geben, Bildungs- und forschungspolitische Schwerpunkte des Bundesministeriums für Bildung und Forschung in der 15. Legislaturperiode, Bundesministerium für Bildung und Forschung, Berlin.

BMBF, 2004: Rede der Bundesministerin für Bildung und Forschung Edelgard Bulmahn anlässlich des Kongresses "Deutschland. Das von morgen." Berlin.

BMBF, 2006: Berufsbildungsbericht 2006, Berlin.

BMBF, 2008a: Aufstieg durch Bildung – Qualifizierungsinitiative der Bundesregierung. Bundesministerium für Bildung und Forschung, Berlin.

BMBF, 2008b: Berufsbildungsbericht 2008, Bundesministerium für Bildung und Forschung, Berlin.

BMBF, 2008c: Exzellenzinitiative, http://www.bmbf.de/de/1321.php, Berlin.

Braun, Dietmar, Fabrizio Gilardi, 2006: Taking'Galton's Problem'Seriously: Towards a Theory of Policy Diffusion, in: Journal of Theoretical Politics, 18: 298–322.

Brown, Phillip, 2001: Globalization and the Political Economy of High Skills, Oxford.

Brown, Phillip, Andy Green, Hugh Lauder, 2001: High Skills – Globalization, Competitiveness, and Skill Formation, Oxford.

Brzinsky-Fay, Christian, 2006: Lost in Transition: Labour Market Entry Sequences of School Leavers in Europe, in: WZB Discussion Paper, Berlin.

Bulmahn, Edelgard, 2002: Rede der Bundesministerin für Bildung und Forschung Edelgard Bulmahn anlässlich der Aussprache zur Regierungserklärung des Bundeskanzlers, Berlin.

Campbell, John L., Ove K. Pedersen, 2007: The Varieties of Capitalism and Hybrid Success: Denmark in the Global Economy, in: Comparative Political Studies, 40 307–322.

Campbell, John L, 1998: Institutional analysis and the role of ideas in political economy, Theory and Society, 27, 377–409.

Campbell, John L, 2002: Ideas, Politics, and Public Policy, in: Annual Reviews in Sociology, 28, 21–38.

Campbell, John L, 2004: Institutional Change and Globalization, Princeton.

Campbell, John L, 2006: Institutional Competitiveness: A broad Perspective on the Danish Case, Copenhagen.

Campbell, John L., Ove K. Pedersen, 2001: The Rise of Neoliberalism and Institutional Analysis, Princeton.

Castles, Francis G., Deborah Mitchell. 1993. Worlds of Welfare and Families of Nations. New York.

Clark, Damon, Gavan Conlon, Fernando Galindo-Rueda, 2005: Post-Compulsory Education and Qualification Attainment, Princeton.
Clark, Tony, 2006: Country Report: United Kingdom, Organisation for Economic Co-operation and Development, Paris.
Clasen, Jochen, 2005: Reforming European welfare states: Germany and the United Kingdom compared, Oxford.
Coffield, Frank, 2000: Lifelong learning as a lever on structural change? Evaluation of white paper: Learning to succeed: a new framework for post-16 learning, in: Journal of Education Policy, 15, 237–246.
Connor, Helen, Brenda Little, 2005: Vocational ladders or crazy paving? Making your way to higher levels – Research Report, Learning and Skills Development Agency, London.
Crouch, Colin, David Finegold, Mari Sako, 1999: Are skills the answer? The political economy of skill creation in advanced industrial countries, Oxford.
Culpepper, Pepper D, 2007: Small States and Skill Specifity: Austria, Switzerland, and Interemployer Cleavages in Coordinated Capitalism, in: Comparative Political Studies, 40, 611–637.
DCSF, 2008: Participation in education, training and employment by 16-18 year olds in England, Department for Children, Schools and Families, London: HMSO.
Dearing, Sir R, 1996: Review of Qualifications for 16-19 Year Olds, London.
Dearing, Sir R, 1997: Higher Education in the Learning Society: report of the National Committee of Inquiry in Higher Education, London.
Deissinger, Thomas, 2002: Apprenticeship systems in England and Germany: decline and survival, in: History of Vocational Education and Training in Europe in a Comparative Perspective, 2002, Florence, Italy, 28-40.
Deissinger, Thomas, 2004: Germany's system of vocational education and training: challenges and modernisation issues, in: International Journal of Training Research, 76–99.
Deissinger, Thomas, Silke Hellwig, 2004: Initiatives and strategies to secure training opportunities in the German vocational education and training system, in: Journal of Adult and Continuing Education, 10, 160–174.
Delorenzi, Simone, Peter Robinson, 2006: Choosing to Learn: Improving participation after compulsory education, London.
DfEE, 1996: Learning to Compete: Education and Training for 14–19 Year Olds, London.
DfEE, 1997a: Excellence in schools, London: Stationary Office.
DfEE, 1997b: The learning age: a renaissance for Britain, London: Stationary Office.
DfEE, 1997c: The learning age: a renaissance for Britain - A Summary, London: Stationary Office.
DfEE, 1999: Learning to Succeed: A New Framework For Post-16 Learning, London: HMSO.
DfEE, 2000: Foundation Degrees, A Consultation Document, London: DfEE.
DfEE, Welsh Office DENI, 1997: Qualifying for Success: a consultation paper on the future of post-16 qualifications, London: DFEE.
DfES, 2001: Schools: Achieving success, London: DfES.
DfES, 2003a: 14-19: opportunity and excellence, London: DfES.

DfES, 2003b: 21st Century Skills: Realising Our Potential, London: HMSO.
DfES, 2003c: The Future of Higher Education, London: DfES.
DfES, 2004a: 14-19 Curriculum and Qualifications Reform: Final Report of the Working Group on 14-19 Reform, London: DfES.
DfES, 2004b: Foundation Degree Task Force report to Ministers, Nottingham: DfES.
DfES, 2004c: Foundation Degree Task Force report to Ministers – A Summary, Nottingham: DfES.
DfES, 2005a: 14-19 Education and Skills, London: HMSO.
DfES, 2005b: Getting on in Business, Getting on at Work, London: DfES.
DfES, 2005c: Higher Standards, Better Schools for All, Norwich: Stationery Office.
DfES, 2006: Further Education: Raising skills, improving life chances, London: DfES.
DfES, LSC, 2004: 21st Century Apprenticeships-End to End Review of Delivery of Modern Apprenticeships, London: DfES.
DIUS, 2007: The Government's response to the House of Lords Select Committee on economic affairs fiffth report of session 2006-07 on apprenticeships, Department for Innovation, Universities and Skills, London.
DIUS, 2008: World-class Apprenticeships: Unlocking Talent, Building Skills for All. Department for Innovation, Universities and Skills, London.
Doyle, Mike, 2003: Discourses of Employability and Empowerment: Foundation Degrees and 'Third Way' discursive repertoires, in: Discourse: Studies in the Cultural Politics of Education, 24, 275–288.
Ebbinghaus, Bernhard, Philip Manow, 2001: Studying varieties of welfare capitalism, London and New York.
Eichhorst, Werner, Paul Marx, 2009: From the Dual Apprenticeship System to a Dual Labor Market? The German High-Skill Equilibrium and the Service Economy, in: IZA Discussion Paper No. 4220, Bonn.
Engelbrech, Gerhard, Christian Ebner, 2006: Lehrstellenmangel - Alternativen müssen Lücken schließen, in: IAB Kurzbericht 28, Nürnberg.
Ertl, Hubert, 2002: The Concept of Modularisation in Vocational Education and Training: The Debate in Germany and Its Implications, in: Oxford Review of Education, 28, 53–73.
Esping-Andersen, Gosta, 1990: The three worlds of welfare capitalism, Cambridge.
Esping-Andersen, Gosta, 2002: Why we need a new welfare state, Oxford.
Estevez-Abe, Margarita, Torben Iversen, David Soskice, 2001: Social Protection and the Formation of Skills: A Reinterpretation of the Welfare State, in: Varieties of capitalism: the institutional foundations of comparative advantage, ed. Peter A. Hall, David Soskice, Oxford, 145–183.
Fairclough, Norman, 2001: The Discourse of New Labour: Critical Discourse Analysis. In Discourse as Data: A Guide for Analysis, ed. Margaret Wetherell et al, London, 229–266.
Fairclough, Norman, 2003: Analyzing Discourse: Textual Analysis for Social Research, London.
Fernandez, Rosa M., Ken Mayhew, 2008: Human Capital Theory: Use and Abuse, Oxford.

Ferrera, Maurizio, Anton Hemerijck, Martin Rhodes, 2001: Recasting European welfare states for the 21st Century, London, 151–170.
Führ, Christoph, Carl-Ludwig Furck, 1998: Bd. VI: 1945 bis zur Gegenwart, in: Handbuch der deutschen Bildungsgeschichte, München.
Finegold, David, David Soskice, 1988: The failure of traning in Britain: analysis and prescription, in: Oxford Review of Economic Policy (4), 21–53.
Foreman-Peck, James, 2004: Spontaneous Disorder? A Very Short History of British Vocational Education and Training, 1563-1973, in: Policy Futures in Education (2): 72–101.
Foskett, Rosalind, 2005: Collaborative Partnership in the higher education curriculum: a cross-sector study of foundation degree development, in: Research in Post-Compulsory Education, 10, 351–372.
Foster, Sir Andrew, 2005: Realising the Potential: A Review of the Future Role of Further Education Colleges, http://www.dfes.gov.uk/furthereducation/index.cfm?fuseaction =content.view\&\\CategoryID=20\&ContentID=18, London.
Frommberger, Dietmar, Holger Reinisch, 2002: Development of disparate structures of Dutch and German vocational education, Magdeburg, 75–87.
Fuller, Alison, 2004: Expecting too much? Modern Apprenticeship: Purposes, Participation and Attainment, in: Nuffield Review of 14-19 Education and Training Working Paper 10.
Fuller, Alison, Lorna Unwin, 2003°: Creating a 'Modern Apprenticeship': a critique of the UK's multi-sector, social inclusion approach, in: Journal of Education and Work, 16, 5–25.
Fuller, Alison, Lorna Unwin, 2003b: Fostering Workplace Learning: looking through the lens of apprenticeship, in: European Educational Research Journal (2), 41–55.
Fuller, Alison, Vanessa Beck, Lorna Unwin, 2005: The Gendered Nature of Apprenticeship: Employers' and young people's perspectives, in: Education and Training, 47, 298–311.
Gallacher, Jim, Robert Ingram, Fiona Reeve, 2006: Differing national models of short cycle, work-related higher education provision in Scotland and England, http://crll.gcal.ac.uk/docs/HN_FD%20comparativepaper%20final.pdf, Glasgow.
George, Alexander L., Andrew Bennett, 2004: Case studies and theory development in the social sciences, Cambridge.
Gerring, John, 2004: What Is a Case Study and What Is It Good for?, in: American Political Science Review, 98, 341–354.
Gerring, John, 2006: Case Study Research: Principles and Practices, Cambridge.
Gibbs, Paul, 2002: Who Deserves Foundation Degrees?, in: Journal of Further and Higher Education, 26, 197–206.
Gilbert, Neil, Rebecca Van Voorhis, 2001: Activating the Unemployed: The Challenge Ahead, in: Activating the Unemployed – A Comparative Appraisal of Work-Oriented Policies, ed. Neil Gilbert, Rebecca A. Van Voorhis, New Jersey, 293–306.
Gorges, Michael J, 2001: New Institutionalist Explanations for Institutional Change: A Note of Caution, in: Politics, 21, 137–145.
Gospel, Howard, 1995: The decline of apprenticeship in Britain, in: Industrial Relations Journal, 26, 32–44.

Green, Andy, John Preston, Jan Germen Janmaat, 2006: Education, Equality and Social Cohesion: A Comparative Analysis, Basingstoke.

Greinert, Wolf-Dietrich, 2006: Defensive Modernisierung – die Chance einer zukunftsfähigen Transformation unseres Berufsbildungssystems durch das neue "Berufsbildungsgesetz" wurde vertan (Eine polemische Skizze), in: Berufsbildung heißt: Arbeiten und Lernen verbindet: Bildungspolitik – Kompetenzentwicklung – Betrieb, ed. Uwe Elsholz, Julia Gillen, Rita Meyer, Gabriele Molzberger, Münster, New York, München, Berlin, 49–65.

Grubb, W. Norton, 2004: The Anglo-American Approach to Vocationalism: the Economic Roles of Education in England, in: SKOPE Research Paper, Warwick.

Haas, Peter M, 1992: Introduction: epistemic communities and international policy coordination, in: International Organization,46(1): 1–35.

Hahn, Eckhart G, 2006: Gute Lehre, schlechte Lehre-was ist besser für eine Elite-Universität?, in: GMS Z Med Ausbild, 23, 4.

Hahn, Eckhart G, 2007: Empfehlungen des Wissenschaftsrats zu einer lehrorientierten Reform der Personalstruktur an Universitäten – Beginn einer Exzellenz-Initiative für die Lehre?, in: GMS Z Med Ausbild, 24, 24.

Hall, Peter A., Kathleen Thelen, 2006: Institutional Change in Varieties of Capitalism, in: Presentation to the Europeanists Conference, Chicago.

Hall, Peter A, 1993: Policy Paradigms, Social Learning and the State, in: Comparative Politics, 25, 275–96.

Hall, Peter A., Daniel W. Gingerich, 2004: Varieties of Capitalism and Institutional Complementarities in the Macroeconomy: An Empirical Analysis, MPIfG Discussion Paper 04/5, Köln.

Hall, Peter A., David Soskice, 2001: An Introduction to Varieties of Capitalism, in: Varieties of capitalism: the institutional foundations of comparative advantage, ed. Peter A. Hall, David Soskice, Oxford, 1–68.

Hannan, Damian F., David Raffe, Emer Smyth, 1996: Cross-National Research on School to Work Transitions: An Analytical Framework, www.econ.upf.edu/~montalvo/sec1034/school_work_ocde.pdf.

Hansen, Kristine, Anna Vignoles, 2005: The United Kingdom Education System in a Comparative Context, Princeton, 13–36.

Hartmann, Michael, 2006: Die Exzellenzinitiative - ein Paradigmenwechsel in der deutschen Hochschulpolitik, in: Leviathan, 34, 447–465.

Hartwig, Lydia, 2004: On the Edge: A German perspective, Bristol.

Hatcher, Richard, 2006: Privatization and sponsorship: the re-agenting of the school system in England, in: Journal of Education Policy, 21, 599–619.

Hay, Colin, 2001: The "Crisis" of Keynesianism and the Rise of Neo-Liberalism in Britain: An Ideational Institutionalist Approach, in: The Rise of Neoliberalism and Institutional Analysis, ed. Ove Kaj Pedersen, John L. Campbell, Princeton, 193–218.

Hay, Colin, 2006: Constructivist Institutionalism... Or, Why Ideas into Interests Don't Go, in: Annual Meeting of the American Political Science Association, Philadelphia, PA, August.

Hayward, Geoff, Ann Hodgson, Jill Johnson, Alis Oancea, Richard Pring, Ken Spours, Stephanie Wilde, Susannah Wright, 2006: The Nuffield Review Annual Report 2005-06, University of Oxford Department of Educational Studies, Oxford.
HEFCE, 2000: Foundation Degree Prospectus: Invitation (00/27), Bristol: Higher Education Funding Council for England.
HEFCE, 2007: Foundation degrees: key statistics 2001-02 to 2006-07, Bristol: Higher Education Funding Council for England.
HEFCE, 2008: Foundation degrees: key statistics 2001-02 to 2007-08, Bristol: Higher Education Funding Council for England.
Hellwig, Silke, 2005: The competency debate in German VET research: implications for learning processes based on vocationalism, in: Australian Vocational Education and Training Research Association Conference: 8th, 2005, Brisbane.
Higham, Jeremy S, 2003: Continuity and discontinuity in the 14-19 curriculum, in: Nuffield Review of 14-19 Education and Training, Working Paper 4.
Higher Education Statistics Agency, 2009: Students and Qualifiers Data Tables, http://www.hesa.ac.uk/index.php?option=com_datatables&Itemid=121&task=show_category&catdex=3\#quals".
Hodgson, Ann, Ken Spours, 2003: Beyond A-levels: Curriculum 2000 And The Reform Of 14-19 Qualifications, London.
Hodgson, Ann, Ken Spours, 2005: Building a strong 14-19 phase in England? The Government White Paper in its wider system context, Nuffield, Oxford.
Hodgson, Ann, Ken Spours, 2000: Qualifying for Success, Towards a Framework of Understanding, in: Broadening the advanced level curriculum IoE/Nuffield Series Number One, Oxford.
Hodgson, Ann, Ken Spours, 2001: Part-time Work and Full-time Education in The UK: the emergence of a curriculum and policy issue, in: Journal of Education and Work, 14, 373–388.
Hodgson, Ann, Ken Spours, 2002: Curriculum, learning and qualifications 14-19, in: Papers arising from a seminar series held at the Nuffield Foundation December 2001- January 2002, Oxford, 38–47.
Hodgson, Ann, Ken Spours, Chris Savory, 2003: What Do We Mean by a Broader Curriculum? : Curriculum 2000, Breadth and 14-19 Reform, School of Lifelong Education and International Development, Institute of Education, University of London.
Homburg, Vincent, Christopher Pollitt, Sandra van Thiel, 2007: Introduction, in: New Public Management in Europe: Adaptation and Alternatives, ed. Vincent Homburg, Christopher Pollitt, Sandra van Thiel, Basingstoke, 1–9.
Hornbostel, Stefan, Dagmar Simon, Saskia Heise, 2008: Exzellente Wissenschaft: Das Problem, der Diskurs, das Programm und die Folgen, Vol. 4 iFQ-Working Paper.
House of Lords - Select Committee on Economic Affairs, 2007a: Apprenticeship: a key route to skill. House of Lords, London: The Stationery Office.
House of Lords - Select Committee on Economic Affairs, 2007b: Apprenticeship: a key route to skill, Volume I: Report. House of Lords, London: The Stationery Office.
Howarth, David R., Aletta J. Norval, Yannis Stavrakakis, 2000: Discourse Theory and Political Analysis: Identities, Hegemonies, and Social Change, Manchester.

Howorth, Jolyon, 2004: Discourse, Ideas, and Epistemic Communities in European Security and Defence Policy, in: West European Politics, 27, 211–234.

Huddleston, Prue, Lorna Unwin, Ewart Keep, 2005: What might the Tomlinson and White Paper proposals mean for vocational education and work-based learning, in: Nuffield Review of Review of 14-19 Education and Trainin, Discussion Paper 33.

Hüfner, Klaus, 2003: Governance and Funding of Higher Education in Germany, in: Higher Education in Europe XXVIII, 145–163.

Iversen, Torben, 2005: Capitalism, Democracy and Welfare, Cambridge.

Iversen, Torben, David Soskice, 2001: An Asset Theory of Social Policy Preferences, in: American Political Science Review, 95, 875–893.

Jongbloed, Ben, 2003: Marketisation in Higher Education, Clark's Triangle and the Essential Ingredients of Markets, in: Higher Education Quarterly, 57, 110–135.

Keep, Ewart, 2004: Reflections on a curious absence: the role of employers, labour market incentives and labour market regulation, in: Journal of Education Policy, Vol. 20, No. 5, 533-553.

Keep, Ewart, 2006a: Market failure in skills, in: SSDA Catalyst, London, 16–32.

Keep, Ewart, 2006b: State control of the English education and training systemplaying with the biggest train set in the world, in: Journal of Vocational Education and Training, 58, 47–64.

Keep, Ewart, 2007: Skills and the labour market's role in delivering economic performance and social justice; competing visions for 2020, in: Seminar Paper at Cardiff University, 6th June.

Keep, Ewart, Ken Mayhew, Jonathan Payne, 2006: From Skills Revolution to Productivity Miracle - Not as easy as it Sounds?, in: Oxford Review of Economic Policy, 22, 539–559.

Kenworthy, Lane, 2006: Institutional coherence and macroeconomic performance, in: Socio-Economic Review, 4, 69–91.

KIBB (Kommunikations-und Informationssystem Berufliche Bildung), 2008: Ausbildungsangebot und -nachfrage für Hessen, die alten Bundesländer und das Bundesgebiet, Bonn.

King, Michael R, 2005: Epistemic Communities and the Diffusion of Ideas: Central Bank Reform in the United Kingdom. in: West European Politics, 28(1), 94–123.

Klijn, Erik-Hans, Jurian Edelenbos, Michael Hughes, 2007: Public-Private Partnership: a Two-Headed Reform. A Comparison of PPP in England and the Netherlands, Basingstoke, 71–89.

KMK, 2007: Allgemein bildende Schulen in Ganztagsform in den Ländern in der Bundesrepublik Deutschland - Statistik 2002 bis 2005, Sekretariat der Ständigen Konferenz der Kultusminister der Länder in der Bundesrepublik Deutschland, Bonn.

KMK, 2008: Allgemein bildende Schulen in Ganztagsform in den Ländern in der Bundesrepublik Deutschland - Statistik 2002 bis 2006, Sekretariat der Ständigen Konferenz der Kultusminister der Länder in der Bundesrepublik Deutschland, Bonn.

Küpper, Hans-Ulrich, 2002: Management Mechanisms and Financing of Higher Education in Germany. www.controlling.bwl.uni-muenchen.de/files/workingpaper/huk_2_2002.pdf, München.

Labour Party, 1996: Aiming Higher: Labour's plans for reform of the 14-19 curriculum. Labour Party, London.
Labour Party, 1997: Labour Party Manifesto, London.
Labour Party, 2005: Education and Skills, London.
Learning Skills Council, 2007: Skills in England 2007: Volume 1: Key Messages, Coventry.
Lee, Chang Kil, David Strang, 2006: The International Diffusion of Public-Sector Downsizing: Network Emulation and Theory-Driven Learning, in: International Organization, 60, 883–909.
Legro, Jeffrey W, 2000: The Transformation of Policy Ideas, in: American Journal of Political Science, 44, 419–432.
Leitch, Review of Skills, 2006: Prosperity for all in the global economy – world class skills, Final Report, Norwich, HMSO.
Liefner, Ingo, Ludwig Schätzl, Thomas Schröder, 2004: Reforms in German Higher Education: Implementing and Adapting Anglo-American Organizational and Management Structures at German Universities, in: Higher Education Policy, 17, 23–38.
Lister, Ruth, 2002: Investing in the citizen-workers of the future: New Labour's 'third way' in welfare reform, Working Paper #5, Boston.
Lister, Ruth, 2004: The Third Way's Social Investment State, in: Welfare State Change: Towards a Third Way?, ed. Rebecca Surender Jane Lewis, Oxford, 157–181.
Little, Brenda, 2005: Policies towards work-focused higher education – are they meeting employers' needs?, in: Tertiary Education and Management, 11, 131–146.
Lloyd, Caroline, Joathan Payne, 2004: "Idle Fancy" or "Concrete Will"? Defining and realising a high skills vision for the UK, in: SKOPE Research Paper, Oxford.
Lloyd, Caroline, Jonathan Payne, 2002: Developing a Political Economy of Skills, in: Journal of Education and Work, 15, 365–390.
LSC, 2005: Blueprint for Apprenticeships, Coventry: Learning and Skills Council.
LSC, 2007: A Strategy for Programme-led Apprenticeships in England 2007 for 2010, Coventry: Learning and Skills Council.
Lynggaard, Kennett, 2007: The institutional construction of a policy field: a discursive institutional perspective on change within the common agricultural policy, in: Journal of European Public Policy, 14, 293–312.
MAAC, 2001: Modern Apprenticeships: the way to work (Cassels report), DfES.
Machin, Stephen, Anna Vignoles, 2006: Education Policy in the UK, Centre for the Economics of Education, London School of Economics.
Marsden, David, 1999: A Theory of Employment Systems. Micro-Foundations of Societal Diversity, Oxford.
Mason, Geoff, 2001: The Mix of Graduate and Intermediate-level Skills in Britain: what should the balance be?, in: Journal of Education and Work, 14, 5–27.
Mason, Geoff, 2004: Enterprise Product Strategies and Employer Demand for Skills in Britain: Evidence from the Employers Skill Survey, in: National Institute of Economic and Social Research, WP, London.
Maurice, Marc, Francois Sellier, Jean-Jacques Silvestre, 1986: The social foundations of industrial power: a comparison of France and Germany, Cambridge and London.

Mayhew, Ken, Cécile Deer, Mehak Dua, 2004, The move to mass higher education in the UK: many questions and some answers, in: Oxford Review of Education, 30, 65–82.

McLaughlin, Kate, Stephen P. Osborne, Ewan Ferlie, 2002: New Public Management Current Trends and Future Prospects, London and New York.

McLean, Martin, 1988: The Conservative Education Policy in Comparative Perspective: Return to an English Golden Age or Harbinger of International Policy Change?, in: British Journal of Educational Studies, 36, 200–217.

Meyer, Rita, 2006: Besiegelt der Europäische Qualifikationsrahmen den Niedergang des deutschen Berufsbildungssystems, in: Berufs-und Wirtschaftspädagogik-online 11.

Misko, Josie, 2006: Vocational education and training in Australia, the United Kingdom and Germany, NCVER, Adelaide.

Müller, Walter, Yossi Shavit, 1998: From School to Work: A Comparative Study of Educational Qualifications and Occupational Destinations, Oxford.

Münch, Richard, 2006: Wissenschaft im Schatten von Kartell, Monopol und Oligarchie. Die latenten Effekte der Exzellenzinitiative, in: Leviathan, 34, 466–486.

Morris, Estelle, John Denham, Alan Whitehead, Nick Raynsford, David Chaytor, Angela Eagle, Martin Salter, 2005: Shaping the Education Bill – Reaching for Consensus, London.

Muñoz, Vernor, 2007: Report of the special Rapporteur on Education, Vernor Muñoz, on his mission to Germany, http://www.netzwerk-bildungsfreiheit.de/pdf/Munoz_Mission_on_Germany.pdf.

Newman, Janet, 2002: The New Public Management, modernization and institutional change, London and New York, 77–92.

Newman, Janet, Bob McKee, 2005: Beyond the New Public Management? Public services and the social investment state, in: Policy & Politics, Vol. 33, No. 4, 657–674.

Nuffield Review of 14-19 Education and Training, 2008a: Apprenticeship I – Prospect for growth, in: Nuffield Review of 14-19 Education and Training Working Paper, Issue Paper 3.

Nuffield Review of 14-19 Education and Training, 2008b: Apprenticeship II – A high-quality pathway for young people?, in: Nuffield Review of 14-19 Education and Training Working Paper, Issue Paper 4.

Oancea, Alis, Susannah Wright, 2006: Policies for 14-19 Education and Training in England, 1976 to the present day: a chronology, in: Nuffield Review of 14-19 Education and Training.

OECD, 2007: Education at a Glance 2007 - OECD Indicators, Paris.

Osborne, Stephen P., Kate McLaughlin, 2002: The New Public Management in context, London and New York, 7–14.

Perkins, Daniel, Lucy Nelms, Paul Smyth, 2004: Beyond neo-liberalism: the social investment state?, in: Social Policy Working Paper No. 3.

Peters, Michael, Tina Besley, 2006: Building knowledge cultures: education and development in the age of knowledge capitalism, Lanham.

Pierson, Chris, 1998: The New Governance of Education: The Conservatives and Education 1988-1997, in: Oxford Review of Education, 24, 131–142.

Pierson, Paul, 2000: Increasing Returns, Path Dependency, and the Study of Politics, in: The American Political Science Review, 94, 251–267.

8 Bibliography

Plenarprotokoll, 15/135, 2004: Deutscher Bundestag Stenografischer Bericht, 135. Sitzung, Berlin.
Plümper, Thomas, Christina J. Schneider, 2007: Too much to die, too little to live: unemployment, higher education policies and university budgets in Germany, in: Journal of European Public Policy, 4, 631–653.
Pratt, John, 1992: Unification of Higher Education in the United Kingdom, in: European Journal of Education, 27, 29–44.
Pring, Richard, 2004: The skills revolution, in: Oxford Review of Education, 30, 105–116.
QAA, 2005: Report of a survey of Foundation Degrees converted from existing Higher National Diplomas since 2001, Mansfield: Quality Assurance Agency for Higher Education.
QCA, Qualifications and Curriculum Authority, 2005: Annual Review 2005, Coventry.
Rueschemeyer, Dietrich, 2006: Why and how ideas matter, in: The Oxford Handbook of Contextual Political Analysis, ed. Robert E. Goodin Charles Tilly, Oxford, 227–313.
Ryan, Paul Lorna Unwin, 2001: Apprenticeship in the British 'training market', in: National Institute Economic Review, 178, 99–114.
Schmidt, Vivien A, 2005: Institutionalism and the State, in: The State: Theories and Issues, ed. Colin Hay, David Marsh Michael Lister, Basingstoke, 98–117.
Schmidt, Vivien A, 2006a: Bringing the state back into the varieties of capitalism and discourse back into the explanation of change, in: Annual meeting of the American Political Science Association, Philadelphia (August 31st September 3, 2006).
Schmidt, Vivien A, 2006b: Give Peace a Chance: Reconciling Four (not Three) "New Institutionalisms", in: Presentation at the Annual Meetings of the American Political Science Association (Philadelphia, PA, Aug. 31-Sept. 3, 2006).
Schmidt, Vivien A, 2008: Discursive Institutionalism: The Explanatory Power of Ideas and Discourse, in: Annual Review of Political Science, 11, 303–326.
Schröder, Gerhard, 1998: Regierungserklärung von Bundeskanzler Gerhard Schröder vom 10. November 1998 vor dem Deutschen Bundestag, Bundesregierung, Berlin.
Schröder, Gerhard, 2002: Regierungserklärung von Bundeskanzler Schröder zum Thema Bildung und Innovation, Bundesregierung, Berlin.
Schröder, Gerhard, 2004: Egoismus überwinden – Gemeinsinn fördern: Unser Weg zu neuer Stärke – Regierungserklärung von Bundeskanzler Schröder, Bundesregierung, Berlin.
Sharp, Caroline, 2002: School Starting Age: European Policy and Recent Research, London.
Sherraden, Michael, 2003: From the Social Welfare State to the Social Investment State: Asset Building Policy, http://www.nhi.org/online/issues/128/socialinvest.html.
Sievers, Marco, 2008: Die Exzellenzinitiative – ein Schritt in Richtung deutsche Eliteuniversitäten?, München.
Simmons, Beth A., Frank Dobbin, Geoffrey Garrett, 2006: Introduction: The International Diffusion of Liberalism, in: International Organization, 60, 781–810.
Simmons, Beth A., Frank Dobbin, Geoffrey Garrett, 2007: The Global Diffusion of Public Policies: Social Construction, Coercion, Competition, or Learning?, in: Annual Review of Sociology, 33, 449–472.

Simmons, Beth A., Frank Dobbin, Geoffrey Garrett, 2008: The global diffusion of markets and democracy, Cambridge.
Simmons, Beth A., Zachary Elkins, 2004: The Globalization of Liberalization: Policy Diffusion in the International Political Economy, in: American Political Science Review, 98, 171–189.
Smith, Kevin, 2002: What is the'Knowledge Economy'? Knowledge intensity and distributed knowledge bases, http://www.intech.unu.edu/publications/discussion-papers/2002-6.pdf, Maastricht.
Smithers, Alan, 2001: Education Policy, in: The Blair Effect, ed. Anthony Seldon, London, 405–426.
Smithers, Alan, 2002: Vocational Education, in: Comparing Standards Academic and Vocational, 16-19 Year Olds, ed Sheila Lawlor, London, 135–146.
Sondermann, Michael, Dagmar Simon, Anne-Marie Scholz, Stefan Hornbostel, 2008: Die Exzellenzinitiative: Beobachtungen aus der Implementierungsphase, iFQ-Working Paper, Vol. 5, Bonn.
Stadlbauer, Ernst A, 2006a: Exzellenzinitiative: Humboldt in Zeiten der Globalisierung, in: GIT, 50, 666–667.
Stadlbauer, Ernst A, 2006b: Umpolung durch Exzellenzinitiative: Von Gleichheit der Hochschulen zu Differenzierung und Elite, in: GIT, 50, 984–985.
Stanton, Geoff, 2005: The proposals for a new system of specialist (vocational) Diplomas, in: Nuffield Review of 14-19 Education and Training, Working Paper 32.
Stavrakakis, Yannis, 2004: Passions of Identification: Discourse, Enjoyment, and European Identity, in: Discourse Theory and European Politics, London, 68–92.
Steedman, Hilary, 2001: Five Years of the Modern Apprenticeship Initiative: An Assessment against Continental European Models, in: National Institute Economic Review, 75–87.
Steedman, Hilary, 2005: Apprenticeship in Europe: 'Fading' or Flourishing?, London.
Steer, Richard, Ken Spours, Ann Hodgson, Ian Finlay, Frank Coffield, Sheila Edward, Maggie Gregson, 2007: "Modernisation" and the role of policy levers in the learning and skills sector, in: Journal of Vocational Education & Training, 59, 175–192.
Stehr, Nico, 2001: Wissen und Wirtschaften: Die Gesellschaftlichen Grundlagen der Modernen Ökonomie, Frankfurt am Main.
Stehr, Nico, 2005: Knowledge Societies, in: Society and knowledge: contemporary perspectives in the sociology of knowledge and science, ed. Nico Stehr and Volker Meja, New Jersey, 299–324.
Steinmann, Susanne, 1999: The Vocational Education and Training System in England and Wales, in: International Journal of Sociology, 28, 29–56.
Streeck, Wolfgang, Kathleen Thelen, 2005: Introduction: Institutional Change in Advanced Political Economies, in: Beyond Continuity: Institutional Change in Advanced Political Economies, ed. Wolfgang Streeck Kathleen Thelen, Oxford, 1–39.
Taylor, Stephanie, 2001: Locating and Conducting Discourse Analytic Research, Thousand Oaks, 5–48.
Tomlinson, Mike, 2002: Inquiry into A Level standards: final report, London: Department for Education and Skills.
Tomlinson, Sally, 2001: Education in a post-welfare society, Buckingham.

Tomlinson, Sally, 2003: New Labour and Education, in: Children & Society, 17, 195–204.
Tomlinson, Sally, 2005: Education in a Post-Welfare Society, Buckingham.
Ulrich, Joachim Gerd, 2006: Wie groß ist die "Lehrstellenlücke" wirklich? Vorschlag für einen alternativen Berechnungsmodus, in: BWP – Berufsbildung in Wissenschaft und Praxis (3), 12–16.
Ulrich, Joachim Gerd, 2008: Jugendliche im Übergangssystem – eine Bestandsaufnahme, in: bwp@ Spezial (4), 1–21.
Ulrich, Joachim Gerd, Elisabeth M. Krekel, 2007: Zur Situation der Altbewerber in Deutschland, in: BIBB-Report 1/07, Bonn.
Universities UK, 2008: The future size and shape of the higher education sector in the UK: demographic projections, London.
van Thiel, Sandra, Christopher Pollitt, 2007: The Management and Control of Executive Agencies, Basingstoke, 52–70.
Walden, Günter, 2006: Wenn sich der Ausbildungsmarkt verändert, in: Vollzeitschulische Berufsausbildung – eine gleichwertige Partnerin des dualen Systems, ed. Arnulf Zöller, Bielefeld, 36–47.
Walford, Geoffrey, 2005: Introduction: education and the Labour Government, in: Oxford Review of Education, 31, 3–9.
Whitty, Geoff, 2005: The State and the Market in English Education Policy, Paper presented at Beijing Normal University.
Wiborg, Susanne, 2009: Education and Social Integration: Comprehensive Schooling in Europe, Basingstoke.
Wilson, John P., John Blewitt, Daphne Moody, 2005: Reconfiguring higher education: the case of foundation degrees, in: Education+ Training, 47, 112–123.
Wolf, Alison, 2004: Education and Economic Performance: Simplistic Theories and their Policy Consequences, in: Oxford Review of Economic Policy, 20, 315–333.
Wright, Susannah, Alis Oancea, 2005: Policies for 14-19 education and training in England, 1976 to the present day: a chronology, Briefing paper for the Nuffield Review of 14-19 Education and Training.
Young, Michael, Ken Spours, 1998: 14-19 Education: Legacy, Opportunities and Challenges, in: Oxford Review of Education, 24, 83–97.

Journalistic sources

BBC, 2006a: Kinnock criticises city academies, http://news.bbc.co.uk/1/hi/uk_politics/4917808.stm.
BBC, 2006b: Teachers condemn city academies, http://news.bbc.co.uk/1/hi/education/4904410.stm.
BBC, 2007: School leaving age set to be 18, http://news.bbc.co.uk/1/hi/education/6254833.stm.
BR-online, 2008: G8-Abitur: Wo bleibt der Realitätssinn?, by Martin Wagner.
Cicero, 2006: Befreit die deutsche Universität!, by Konrad B. Schily.
Der Spiegel, Online, 2006a: Schulreform: Die Hauptschule ist nicht mehr zu retten.
Der Spiegel, Online, 2006b: Weg damit – Keiner mag die Hauptschule, by Klaus Hurrelmann.
Der Spiegel, Online, 2007a: Der Elite-Wettbewerb schwächt die Hochschulen, interview with Richard Münch.
Der Spiegel, Online, 2007b: Elite-Unis: Jubel in den Südstaaten, by Jochen Leffers.
Der Spiegel, Online, 2007c: Exzellenzinitiative – Sechs Hochschulen werden Elite-Unis, by Jochen Leffers.
Der Spiegel, Online, 2007d: Schwer von Begriff – Was ist eigentlich... die Exzellenzinitiative? In der Bildungspolitik wimmelt es von Begriffsungetümen, by Thomas Darnstädt.
Deutschlandradio Kultur, dradio.de, 2005: Hochschulreformer: Die Exzellenzinitiative ist zu wenig, interview with Hans Weiler.
Die Zeit, Online, 2004: Der lange Marsch zu den Gipfeln.
Die Zeit, Online, 2005: Aufstiegshoffnung – Die Universität Heidelberg rechnet fest damit, im Elitewettbewerb zu reüssieren. Scheitern wäre eine Katastrophe, by Martin Spiewak.
Die Zeit, Online, 2006: Uns fehlt Fantasie: DFG-Präsident Ernst-Ludwig Winnacker will mehr Vielfalt an den Hochschulen: Neue Beschäftigungsmodelle, mehr Internationalität und mehr Frauen auf Lehrstühlen.
Die Zeit, Online, 2007: Exzellenz auch für die Lehre, by Martin Spiewak.
Die Zeit, Online, 2008a: Neoliberalismus im Klassenzimmer, by Susanne Gaschke.
Die Zeit, Online, 2008b: Pariser Tempo, by Alfred Grosser.
Die Zeit, Online, 2008c: Pädagogische Bulimie, by Reinhard Kahl.
Die Zeit, Online, 2008d: Turbopolitik und Lehrplanwirtschaft, by Reinhard Kahl.
Die Zeit, Online, 2008e: Uni-Elite – Gefühlte Exzellenz, by Kilian Kirchgessner.
Die Zeit, Online, 2008f: Wir sind zu kleinmütig – Der bedeutendste Umbau der Universitäten steht erst noch bevor, by Wolfgang Frühwald.

8 Bibliography

FAZ, Frankfurter Allgemeine Zeitung, 2008: Deutschland in der Exzellenzrhetorikfalle, by Hubert Markl.
FAZ, Frankfurter Allgemeine Zeitung, 2009: Zahl der Erstsemester auf Rekordstand.
Focus, 2007: Exzellenzinitiative – Leuchttürme ohne Basis?, by Johannes Balve.
forschung, 2005: Die Exzellenzinitiative: Hoffnung auf den großen Wurf, by Ernst-Ludwig Winnacker.
hr-online.de, 2007: Verkürzte Schulzeit: Eltern kritisieren G8.
Mag, T, 1996: A rocket for NET targets, by Hugh Lloyd Jones.
Mag, T, 1997: Skills For 2000?, by Hugh Lloyd Jones.
sueddeutsche, 2007a: Die geistige Elite, by Tanjev Schultz.
sueddeutsche, 2007b: Meinung: Die geistige Elite.
sueddeutsche, 2008: "Mathematik und Deutsch sind tabu", by Christine Burtscheidt.
The Guardian, London, 1999a: Blair's revolution for learning; Plan for huge rise in university numbers, by John Carvel.
The Guardian, London, 1999b: Universities challenged; David Gibson thinks dons are spoiling Curriculum 2000's chances of success, by David Gibson.
The Guardian, London, 2000a: Education: Further: Fancy a quickie?: Is the foundation degree just another confusing qualification, by Simon Midgley.
The Guardian, London, 2000b: Guardian Education Pages.
The Guardian, London, 2000c: A small degree of danger; Australia is tempting our students one way, America the other, as overseas universities line up for our best young minds. We're fighting back with two-year degrees, but will they work?, by Lee Elliot Major.
The Guardian, London, 2001a: About turn: Teachers and pupils have been saying it all year. Now the education minister is saying it too: the new sixth-form curriculum is a mess. As the official review begins, we ask the experts what should be done to put it right, by John Dunford, Dr Ann Hodgson and Dr Ken Spours.
The Guardian, London, 2001b: It's not cricket: Why didn't anyone speak to colleges before meddling with AS-levels, by Conor Ryan.
The Guardian, London, 2003: Will Charles Clarke have his place in history?, by Jeevan Vasagar and Rebecca Smithers.
The Guardian, London, 2005: Principals fear curriculum cuts: Students may be restricted to three AS-levels under new funding proposals, college heads say, by Peter Kingston.
The Guardian, London, 2007a: Brown sets out plans to keep pupils in school or training till 18.
The Guardian, London, 2007b: Leader: Give children a chance, not a lottery.
The Times, Educational Supplement, 1999a: Curriculum 2000 battles against the clock, by Julie Read.
The Times, Educational Supplement, 1999b: The pick 'n'mix generation, by Rosie Waterhouse.
The Times, Educational Supplement, 2000a: 700,000 extra students by 2002 and 7,000 sub-degree awards, by Ian Nash and Simon Midgley.
The Times, Educational Supplement, 2000b: Foundation degree may add to course 'confusion', by Harvey McGavin.

The Times, Educational Supplement, 2001a: Another Level -but Is It Worth It?, by Alison Brace.
The Times, Educational Supplement, 2001b: Can The Gold Standard Keep Its Currency?, by Kate Taylor.
The Times, Educational Supplement, 2001c: The State Must Stay In The Driving Seat, by Ian Nash.
The Times, Educational Supplement, 2002a: Another Year Of As Chaos?, by Phil Revell.
The Times, Educational Supplement, 2002b: Colleges Build On The Basics.
The Times, Educational Supplement, 2003a: Can Key Skills Be A Barrier To Success?, by James Harrison.
The Times, Educational Supplement, 2004: Reform Backfires As As Proves Favourite, by Michael Shaw.
The Times, Educational Supplement, 2005: An A-level In Stupidity, by John Dunford.
The Times, Educational Supplement, 2006a: England plans to give bac, by Jonathan Milne and Warwick Mansell.
The Times, Educational Supplement, 2006b: Universities are losing faith in A-levels.
The Times, Educational Supplement, 2007a: English teachers can think for themselves, by Trevor Fisher.
The Times, Educational Supplement, 2008: Diplomas: just a sticking plaster for A-level reform, by Stephen Jones.
The Times, Higher Education Supplement, 2000c: Bologna Foundation, by Tessa Blackstone.
The Times, Higher Education Supplement, 2000d: Degree Is Short Of European Standard, by Alison Goddard and Tony Tysome.
The Times, Higher Education Supplement, 2000e: Industry wary of sub-degrees, by Alison Goddard and Tony Tysome.
The Times, Higher Education Supplement, 2000f: Lecturers fear new degree is a sell-out, by Phil Baty.
The Times, Higher Education Supplement, 2000g: 'Hang On To Your Hnds', by Tony Tysome.
The Times, Higher Education Supplement, 2001: Great Idea – Shame About The Cold Feet, by Tony Tysome.
The Times, London, 2001d: A-level reforms were not properly tested, by John O'Leary.
The Times, London, 2003b: AS levels 'fail to achieve basic aim', by Glen Owen.
The Times, London, 2007b: A sensible gamble, or an admission of failure?, by John O'Leary.
wdr.de, 2008a: "Alle gefordert", Staatssekretär Günter Winands of the NRW school ministry, http://www.wdr.de/themen/wissen/bildung/schule/abitur/winandsjhtml?rubrik enstyle=wissen.
wdr.de, 2008b: "G8 geht gar nicht", pupil representative Horst Wenzel.
wdr.de, 2008c: "G8 wurde dilettantisch umgesetzt", Josef Kraus, Präsident des Deutschen Lehrerverbandes.

VS Forschung | VS Research
Neu im Programm Soziologie

Tilo Beckers / Klaus Birkelbach /
Jörg Hagenah / Ulrich Rosar (Hrsg.)
**Komparative empirische
Sozialforschung**
2010. 527 S. Br. EUR 59,95
ISBN 978-3-531-16850-0

Christian Büscher /
Klaus Peter Japp (Hrsg.)
Ökologische Aufklärung
25 Jahre ‚Ökologische Kommunikation'
2010. 311 S. Br. EUR 39,95
ISBN 978-3-531-16931-6

Wolfgang Berg /
Aoileann Ní Éigeartaigh (Eds.)
Exploring Transculturalism
A Biographical Approach
2010. 180 pp. (Crossculture) Softc.
EUR 34,95
ISBN 978-3-531-17286-6

Wilson Cardozo
Der ewige Kalte Krieg
Kubanische Interessengruppen
und die US-Außenpolitik
2010. 256 S. (Globale Gesellschaft und
internationale Beziehungen) Br. EUR 39,95
ISBN 978-3-531-17544-7

Erhältlich im Buchhandel oder beim Verlag.
Änderungen vorbehalten. Stand: Juli 2010.

Gabriele Doblhammer /
Rembrandt Scholz (Eds.)
**Ageing, Care Need and
Quality of Life**
The Perspective of Care Givers
and People in Need of Care
2010. 243 pp. (Demografischer Wandel –
Hintergründe und Herausforderungen)
Softc. EUR 34,95
ISBN 978-3-531-16626-1

Dorothea Krüger (Hrsg.)
**Genderkompetenz
und Schulwelten**
Alte Ungleichheiten – neue Hemmnisse
2010. ca. 230 S. (Kultur und gesellschaftliche Praxis) Br. ca. EUR 29,95
ISBN 978-3-531-17508-9

Matthias Richter
Risk Behaviour in Adolescence
Patterns, Determinants
and Consequences
2010. 123 pp. Softc. EUR 34,95
ISBN 978-3-531-17336-8

Barbara Rinken
**Spielräume in der Konstruktion
von Geschlecht und Familie?**
Alleinerziehende Mütter und Väter
mit ost- und westdeutscher Herkunft
2010. 349 S. Br. EUR 39,95
ISBN 978-3-531-16417-5

www.vs-verlag.de

Abraham-Lincoln-Straße 46
65189 Wiesbaden
Tel. 0611.7878-722
Fax 0611.7878-400

VS Forschung | VS Research
Neu im Programm Politik

Cornelia Altenburg
Kernenergie und Politikberatung
Die Vermessung einer Kontroverse
2010. 315 S. Br. EUR 39,95
ISBN 978-3-531-17020-6

Markus Gloe / Volker Reinhardt (Hrsg.)
Politikwissenschaft und Politische Bildung
Nationale und internationale Perspektiven
2010. 269 S. Br. EUR 39,95
ISBN 978-3-531-17361-0

Farid Hafez
Islamophober Populismus
Moschee- und Minarettbauverbote österreichischer Parlamentsparteien
2010. Mit einem Geleitwort von Prof. Dr. Anton Pelinka. 212 S. Br. EUR 34,95
ISBN 978-3-531-17152-4

Annabelle Houdret
Wasserkonflikte sind Machtkonflikte
Ursachen und Lösungsansätze in Marokko
2010. 301 S. Br. EUR 34,95
ISBN 978-3-531-16982-8

Jens Maßlo
Jugendliche in der Politik
Chancen und Probleme einer institutionalisierten Jugendbeteiligung
2010. 477 S. Br. EUR 49,95
ISBN 978-3-531-17398-6

Torsten Noe
Dezentrale Arbeitsmarktpolitik
Die Implementierung der Zusammenlegung von Arbeitslosen- und Sozialhilfe
2010. 274 S. Br. EUR 39,95
ISBN 978-3-531-17588-1

Stefan Parhofer
Die funktional-orientierte Demokratie
Ein politisches Gedankenmodell zur Zukunft der Demokratie
2010. 271 S. Br. EUR 29,95
ISBN 978-3-531-17521-8

Alexander Wolf
Die U.S.-amerikanische Somaliaintervention 1992-1994
2010. 133 S. Br. EUR 29,95
ISBN 978-3-531-17298-9

Erhältlich im Buchhandel oder beim Verlag.
Änderungen vorbehalten. Stand: Juli 2010.

www.vs-verlag.de

VS VERLAG

Abraham-Lincoln-Straße 46
65189 Wiesbaden
Tel. 0611.7878-722
Fax 0611.7878-400